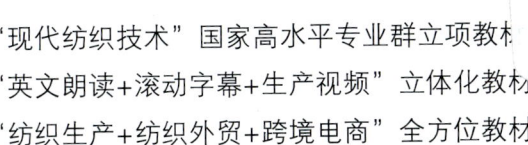

"现代纺织技术"国家高水平专业群立项教材
"英文朗读+滚动字幕+生产视频"立体化教材
"纺织生产+纺织外贸+跨境电商"全方位教材

纺织生产与贸易交流
（中英双语）

主　编　佟　昀

副主编　陈和春　尹桂波　江婉薇

参　编　吉利梅　王平平　黄　旭
　　　　隋全侠　陈桂香　洪　杰
　　　　刘　欢　徐大秀　高海荣

西南交通大学出版社
·成　都·

图书在版编目（CIP）数据

纺织生产与贸易交流：中英双语 / 佟昀主编. ——成都：西南交通大学出版社，2024.4
ISBN 978-7-5643-9774-6

Ⅰ. ①纺… Ⅱ. ①佟… Ⅲ. ①纺织工业 – 工业企业管理 – 汉、英 Ⅳ. ①F407.81

中国国家版本馆 CIP 数据核字（2024）第 054750 号

Fangzhi Shengchan yu Maoyi Jiaoliu
纺织生产与贸易交流
（中英双语）

主　编 / 佟　昀　　　　　　　　责任编辑 / 孟　媛
　　　　　　　　　　　　　　　　封面设计 / 原谋书装

西南交通大学出版社出版发行
（四川省成都市金牛区二环路北一段 111 号西南交通大学创新大厦 21 楼　610031）
营销部电话：028-87600564　　028-87600533
网址：http://www.xnjdcbs.com
印刷：成都市新都华兴印务有限公司

成品尺寸　185 mm×260 mm
印张　18
插页：6
字数　563 千
版次　2024 年 4 月第 1 版　　印次　2024 年 4 月第 1 次

书号　ISBN 978-7-5643-9774-6
定价　56.00 元

课件咨询电话：028-81435775
图书如有印装质量问题　本社负责退换
版权所有　盗版必究　举报电话：028-87600562

Chambray 青年布

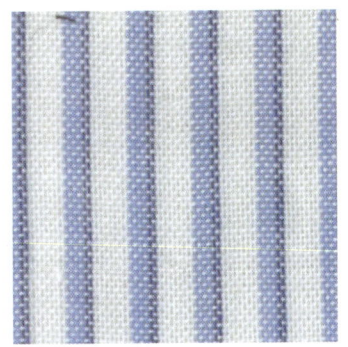
Oxford 牛津布

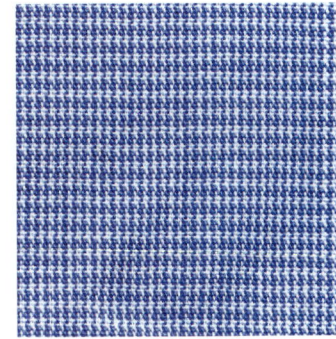
Fil-a-fil 米通布

Poplin 府绸

Extra warp weave 经起花织物

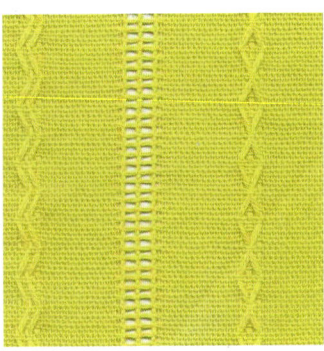
Leno fabric 绞综（纱罗）织物

Corded velveteen 灯芯绒

Seersucker 泡泡纱

Stretch crepe 弹力绉布

Bagger cloth 乞丐布

Section dyed yarn 段染纱面料

Cotton/linen 棉麻布

Polar fleece 摇粒绒（针织）

Stitching double weave 接结双层

Whipcord 马裤呢

Velvet 天鹅绒

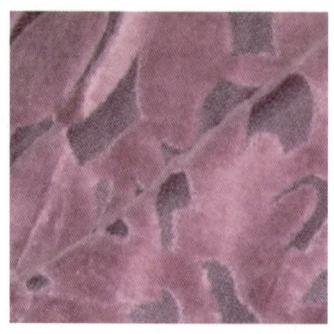
Burned out velvet 烂花天鹅绒

Embossing 轧纹织物

Brocade 织锦缎

Jacquard loom 提花织机

Embroidery machine 绣花机

Raschel blanket 拉舍尔毛毯

Water repellent finish 拒水整理

Tapestry 挂毯

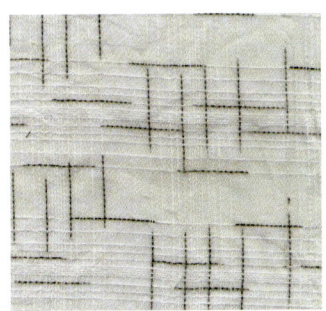
Chine fabric 印经织物

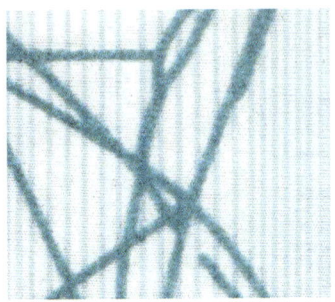
Flocking fabric 植绒织物

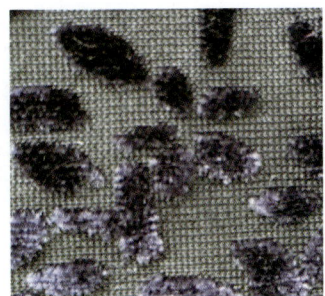
Burnt-out fabric 烂花布

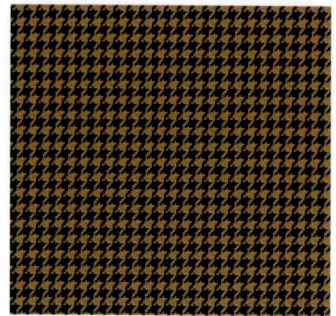
Houndstooth 千鸟格

Tartan check 苏格兰格

Glen check（威尔士亲王）格林格

Digital ink jet print 数码喷墨印花

Screen printing 筛网印花

Roller printing 圆网印花

Cheese dyeing autoclave 高温高压筒子染色机

Flat-bed transfer-printing machine 平网转移印花

Fancy yarn 花式纱

 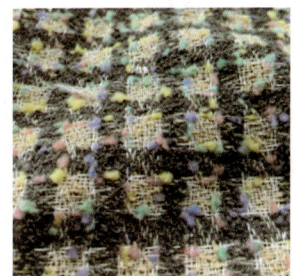

Chenille yarn & fabrics 雪尼尔纱和面料　　　　Color spot yarn & apparel 彩点纱和时装

Blending 抓棉和混棉　　　Opening 开棉　　　Carding 梳棉

 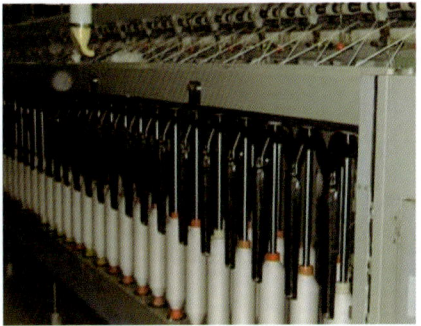

Drawing machine 并条机　　　　Roving machine 粗纱机

V

Ring spinnin 环锭纺　　　Rotor spinning 转杯纺　　　Woolen carding 梳毛

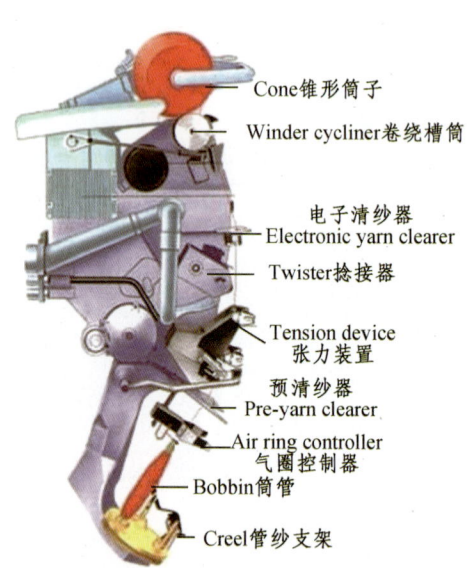 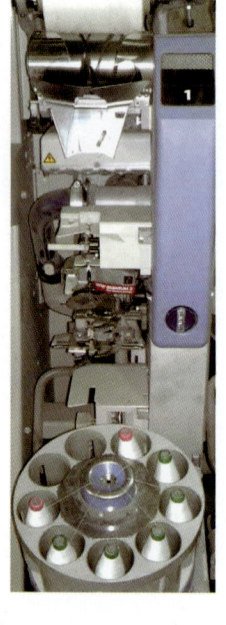

Cone 锥形筒子
Winder cycliner 卷绕槽筒
电子清纱器 Electronic yarn clearer
Twister 捻接器
Tension device 张力装置
预清纱器 Pre-yarn clearer
Air ring controller 气圈控制器
Bobbin 筒管
Creel 管纱支架

Automatic winder 自动络筒机

Beam warping 分批整经机现场

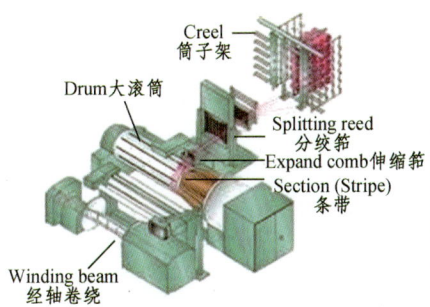  

Sectional warping 分条整经机现场

经轴退绕区　　　　　　浆槽上浆区　　　　　　烘筒烘燥

上蜡分绞区　　　　　　车头织轴卷绕区

Sizing machine 浆纱机

 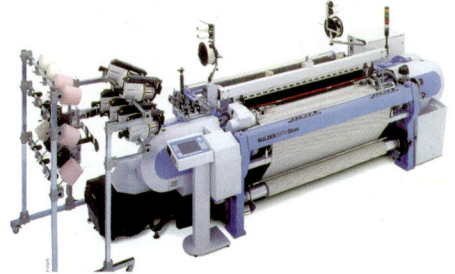

Drawing in 穿经　　　　　　Shuttleless loom 无梭织机

VII

Rapier loom 剑杆织机

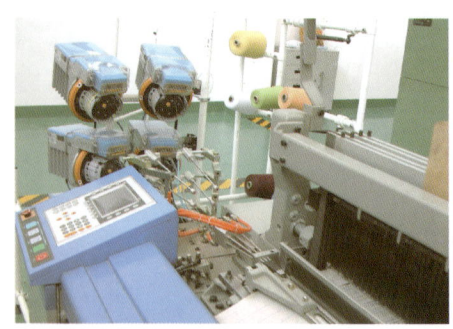
Air jet loom 喷气织机

Water jet loom 喷气织机

Let off mechanism 送经机构

Take up mechanism 卷取机构

Weft knitting machine 纬编机

Warp knitting machine 经编机

Circular knitting machine 针织大圆机

Traditional brocade 传统织锦

前言 PREFACE

本教材基于真实的工作情境，本着"源自纺织生产和外贸一线工作实践、服务现代纺织技术教学和全球化背景下纺织贸易，讲求实用、淡化学术"的宗旨，用中英文全方位、系统化讲解纺织生产、检测的流程和技术关键。在此基础上，进一步通晓纺织贸易函电、单证和跨境电商的相关知识，必要写作技能，中英文书面和口语交流技能。本教材参考了部分欧美原版教材，也汲取了国内相关教材的长处。

本书理念：

将中英文学习与纺织生产、纺织贸易与跨境电商内容相融合。

本书特色：

简明扼要、图文并茂、便于理解、易于遵循，即"纺织技术图文化以便于理解与掌握；纺织贸易函电、单证模板化、图表化、实例化以便于在未来工作中遵循"。本书是"双融合"的立体化教材：将中英文讲解、朗读视频、生产视频、面料视频相融合；纺织生产、外贸、电商的中英文教学与专业知识技能教学相融合。

本书内容：

全书内容分为纺织生产、纺织进出口贸易和跨境电商三大板块，纺织生产流程包括：纺织纤维、纺纱、面料、机织、针织、染整、检测内容；纺织进出口贸易包括公司介绍、函电、单证、合同、相关术语、口语对话与交流内容，附有企业的实际合同、单证便于提供真实的工作、学习情境，便于初始工作中遵循、模仿，提高实用性；跨境电商涉及特征、营运方式和第三方平台内容。

全书附有丰富的图片、音频和视频资源：黑白图片240余幅、彩图75幅、扫码音视频。音频朗读采用滚动字幕对照的形式，并附有生产现场和面料动态展视视频。本书中的素材、案例、图片和视频很多来自企业生产和贸易一线以及纺织展会。安排教学课时时，可根据不同的专业方向有所侧重。

本书使用：

本书分为文字和扫码音视频两部分,后者分为滚动字幕对照音频朗读和生产现场视频。文字内容图文并茂，简明扼要，为精炼篇幅，朗读字幕内容较书中原文丰富，并非完全一一对应，扫码朗读时须注意。

编写分工：

尹桂波教授编写第一章的任务一、任务二。隋全侠教授编写第四章的任务一至任务四。吉利梅副教授编写第五章。黄旭副教授编写第六章。陈和春副教授编写第九章。洪杰教授负责编写第一章的任务四、任务五。陈桂香副教授编写第七章的任务一、任务二。江婉薇博士编写第七章的任务三至任务八。刘欢博士与佟昀合编第十章。佟昀教授负责编写第一章的任务三、任务六；第二章的任务一至任务四；第三章的任务三、任务四；第四章的任务五至任务七；第八章。苏州震纶棉纺有限公司高海荣副总经理与佟昀共同编写第二章的任务五和任务六。南通中大纺织有限公司研发部王平平工程师负责编写第三章的任务一和任务二。南通迈步纺织有限公司徐大秀总经理参与了本书编写和统稿，并为本书提供了大量第一手素材。

佟昀负责书中第一至第七章、第八章任务一、任务二和任务四之第一至三单元的二维码英文朗读采集和视频制作；陈和春负责第九章和第八章任务三、任务四之第四、第五、第八和第十单元的二维码英文朗读采集和视频制作；黄旭负责第六章朗读音频采集。佟昀负责彩色封页图片内容和全书统稿。

江苏工业职业技术学院蔡永东教授、朱雪梅、周祥副教授、徐安长博士、仇明慧博士等参与了本书编写和各章统稿，并以自己丰富的专业英语教学经验对本书编写的理念和体例起到了重要影响。

北京科技大学外国语学院教授、英国语言学和中英文学比较学专家，北京市教学名师梁晓晖博士仔细审阅了本书，并提出了中肯宝贵的意见，这里一并致谢。

由于编者水平有限，错误在所难免，肯请广大读者批评指正。

目录 CONTENTS

Chapter 1　Textile Fibers 纺织纤维篇 ··· 001

- Task 1　Common Textile Fiber Classification 常见纤维分类 ··············· 001
- Task 2　Natural Cellulosic Fibers 天然纤维素纤维 ·························· 002
  - Unit 1　Cotton 棉 ··· 004
  - Unit 2　Flax 麻 ·· 007
- Task 3　Natural Protein Fibers 天然蛋白质纤维 ······························ 008
  - Unit 1　Wool 羊毛 ·· 009
  - Unit 2　Specialty Fur Fibers 特种毛 ·· 011
  - Unit 3　Silk 蚕丝 ··· 015
- Task 4　Man-made Fibers Process 人造纤维生产 ···························· 017
- Task 5　Regenerate Fibers 再生纤维 ··· 019
  - Unit 1　Viscose Fiber 黏胶纤维 ·· 019
  - Unit 2　Acetate 醋酯纤维 ··· 021
  - Unit 3　Rayon 人造丝 ·· 022
  - Unit 4　Lyocell (Tencel) 莱赛尔（天丝）··································· 023
  - Unit 5　Modal 莫代尔 ·· 024
- Task 6　Synthetic Fibers 合成纤维 ·· 024
  - Unit 1　Polyester 聚酯纤维 ··· 026
  - Unit 2　Nylon 锦纶 ··· 028
  - Unit 3　Acrylic 腈纶 ··· 029
  - Unit 4　Spandex 氨纶 ··· 031
  - Unit 5　New Fibers 新纤维 ··· 031
  - Unit 6　Specialty Fibers 特种纤维 ··· 034

Chapter 2　Spinning 纺纱篇 ·· 036

- Task 1　Cotton Ring Spinning Process 棉环锭纺纱 ·························· 036
- Task 2　Woolen & Worsted Spinning Process 毛精纺和粗纺过程 ········· 043
- Task 3　Rotor Yarn 转杯纺 ··· 048
- Task 4　Compact Yarn Spinning 紧密纺 ······································· 050
- Task 5　Fancy Yarn 花式纱 ·· 052
- Task 6　Textured Yarns 变形纱 ··· 054

Chapter 3　Weaving 机织篇 ··· 056

Task 1　To Describe the Elements of Woven Fabric Constitution 描述机织物结构要素 ······ 056
Task 2　To Describe the Woven Fabric Specification 描述机织物规格 ······························ 058
Task 3　Introduce Weaving Preparation in Brief 织造准备介绍 ························· 059
- Unit 1　Winding 络筒 ··· 061
- Unit 2　Warping 整经 ··· 063
- Unit 3　Sizing 浆纱 ·· 068
- Unit 4　Drawing in 穿经 ·· 070

Task 4　To Describe Weaving Process 描述织造过程 ······································ 070
- Unit 1　Shedding 开口 ··· 071
- Unit 2　Picking Mode—Shuttleless Looms 引纬方式——无梭织机 ·················· 074
- Unit 3　Beating-up 打纬 ··· 080
- Unit 4　Let-off & Take-up 送经和卷取 ·· 081

Chapter 4　Weaves & Fabrics 组织和面料篇 ·· 084

Task 1　Basic Weaves 基本组织 ··· 084
- Unit 1　Plain Weave 平纹 ··· 084
- Unit 2　Twill Weave 斜纹 ··· 086
- Unit 3　Satin and Sateen Weave 经面缎纹和纬面缎纹 ······································ 087

Task 2　Derivatives of Basic Weaves and Fabrics 基础组织的衍生（变化）组织 ········· 089
- Unit 1　Derivative Weaves 变化组织 ·· 089

Task 3　Combined Weaves and Fabrics 联合组织和织物 ·· 097
- Unit 1　Stripe and Check Weaves 条格组织 ·· 098
- Unit 2　Crepe Fabrics 起皱组织 ·· 099
- Unit 3　Mock Leno Weaves and Huckaback Weaves 假纱罗和透孔组织 ·············· 100
- Unit 4　Honeycomb Weaves 蜂巢组织 ·· 101
- Unit 5　Novel Appearance Fabric 新颖外观织物 ··· 102

Task 4　Compound Weaves and Fabrics 复杂组织 ······································· 104
- Unit 1　Backed Weaves 重组织 ··· 105
- Unit 2　Double Fabrics 双层织物 ··· 107
- Unit 3　Cut Pile and Terry Fabrics 割绒和毛圈织物 ··· 109

Task 5　Fabric Introduction in Brief 织物简要介绍 ·· 112
- Unit 1　Dyed Yarn Fabrics 色织物 ··· 112
- Unit 2　Filament Yarn Fabric 长丝织物 ··· 114
- Unit 3　Woolen and Worsted Fabrics 粗纺和精纺毛织物 ·································· 116
- Unit 4　Stripe & Check Fabrics 条格织物 ··· 117
- Unit 5　Finished Fabrics 后整理面料 ·· 118

Task 6　Nonwoven Fabric 非织造布 ……………………………………………………… 119

Task 7　Practical Fabric Vocabulary 实用面料词汇 …………………………………… 123

Chapter 5　Knitting 针织篇 …………………………………………………………………… 126

Task 1　To Describe the Terms & General Principles of Knitting Technology
描述针织技术的术语和一般原理 …………………………………………… 126

Task 2　To Describe the Weft Knitting Structure and Fabrics 描述纬编结构和织物 …… 131

Task 3　To Describe the Warp Knitting and Fabrics 描述经编结构和织物 …………… 138

Chapter 6　Dyeing and Finishing 染整篇 …………………………………………………… 143

Task 1　To Describe the Dyeing and Finishing Technological Process
描述染整工艺过程 …………………………………………………………… 143

　　Unit 1　Introduction of Pretreatment for Dyeing and Finishing 染整前处理介绍 … 143

　　Unit 2　Pretreatment 预处理 ……………………………………………………… 145

　　Unit 3　Dyeing 染色 ……………………………………………………………… 149

　　Unit 4　Printing 印花 ……………………………………………………………… 152

　　Unit 5　Finishing 后整理 ………………………………………………………… 154

Task 2　To Describe the Dyeing and Finishing Machines 描述染整机械 ……………… 157

　　Unit 1　Gas Singer 气体烧毛机 …………………………………………………… 157

　　Unit 2　Dyeing Machinery 染色机械 …………………………………………… 159

　　Unit 3　Transfer Printing Machines 转移印花机 ………………………………… 162

Chapter 7　Textile Testing 纺织检测篇 …………………………………………………… 165

Task 1　Fiber Identification 纤维鉴别 …………………………………………………… 165

Task 2　Fiber & Fabric Properties 纤维和织物性质 …………………………………… 169

　　Unit 1　Mechanical Properties 机械性质 ………………………………………… 169

　　Unit 2　Chemical Characteristics 化学特征 ……………………………………… 169

　　Unit 3　Fabric Tensile Properties 织物拉伸性质 ………………………………… 170

　　Unit 4　Breaking Strength and Tearing Strength 断裂和撕裂强度 ……………… 170

Task 3　Fabric Abrasion and Pilling 织物磨损性和起球性 …………………………… 172

　　Unit 1　Abrasion 摩擦 …………………………………………………………… 172

　　Unit 2　Pilling 起球 ……………………………………………………………… 174

Task 4　Flammability 阻燃性 …………………………………………………………… 174

Task 5　Fabric Hand and Drape 织物手感和悬垂性 …………………………………… 177

Task 6　Colorfastness 色牢度 …………………………………………………………… 179

Task 7　Comfort of Textiles 纺织品舒适性 …………………………………………… 182

Task 8　Practical Example & Exercise 实例与练习 …………………………………… 186

Chapter 8　Textile International Trade 纺织外贸篇······188

Task 1　Introducing Our Company 介绍我们的公司······188
- Unit 1　About Us 关于我们······188
- Unit 2　Company Profile 公司简介······189
- Unit 3　Enterprise Culture 企业文化······191
- Unit 4　Enterprise Organization Structure 企业组织架构······192

Task 2　Business Mails for International Trade 外贸函电······193
- Unit 1　Invitation for Business 约请洽谈生意······193
- Unit 2　Establishing Business Relations 建立业务关系······194
- Unit 3　Opening up New Sources of Goods 寻求新货源······194
- Unit 4　Asking for Samples 索要样品······195
- Unit 5　Inquiry 询盘······195
- Unit 6　Quotation 报价······196
- Unit 7　Offer 虚盘······197
- Unit 8　Firm Offer 实盘······198
- Unit 9　Counter Offer 还盘······198
- Unit 10　Refusal of the Offer 拒绝还盘······199
- Unit 11　Order 订货······199
- Unit 12　Request to Cancel the Order 要求撤销订货······200
- Unit 13　Refuse to Accept the Cancellation 拒绝撤销订货······201
- Unit 14　Remind 催货······201
- Unit 15　Asking for Opening a L/C 催开信用证······202
- Unit 16　Asking for Amendment of a L/C 要求修改信用证······202
- Unit 17　Shipping Advice 装船通知······203
- Unit 18　Claim 索赔······204
- Unit 19　Business Mails for Home Textile 家纺贸易往来函电（实例）······205

Task 3　Business Contract（Practical Example）商业合同（实例）······206
- Unit 1　Contract（Example）合同（案例）······206

Task 4　Certificate & Documents for International Trade 外贸单证······214
- Unit 1　Sales Confirmation 销售确认书（实例）······214
- Unit 2　Import & Export Declaration 进出口报关······219
- Unit 3　Import & Export License 进出口许可证······222
- Unit 4　Commodities Quality Inspection 商品检验······224
- Unit 5　Customs Invoice and Consular Invoice 海关和领事发票······226
- Unit 6　Commercial Invoice 商业发票······230
- Unit 7　Bill of Exchange 商业汇票······230
- Unit 8　Insurance 保险······231

  Unit 9 Shipping Order 装货单（实例） ··· 237
  Unit 10 Letter of Credit 信用证 ··· 238

Chapter 9 Cross-Border E-Commerce 跨境电子商务 ······························· 239

 Task 1 To Introduce Cross-Border E-Commerce 跨境电子商务 ················ 239
  Unit 1 Features of Cross-Border E-Commerce 跨境电子商务的特征 ········ 240
  Unit 2 Classification 跨境电商分类 ·· 242
 Task 2 Cross-Border E-Commerce Operation Mode 跨境电子商务营运方式 ········ 246
  Unit 1 Platform Trade Mode of Cross-Border E-Commerce
     跨境电子商务平台交易模式 ··· 247
  Unit 2 Advantages of Cross-Border E-Commerce Operation Mode
     跨境电子商务运营模式的优势 ·· 249
  Unit 3 Current Drawbacks and Limitations of Cross-Border
     E-Commerce Operation Mode
     当前跨境电子商务运行模式的缺陷与局限性 ························· 250
  Unit 4 Current Representative Operation Mode of Cross-Border
     E-Commerce 目前跨境电子商务具有代表性的营运模式 ············ 252
 Task 3 An Overview of Third-Party Cross-Border E-Commerce Platform
    第三方跨境电子商务平台概述 ·· 255
  Unit 1 Features of Third-Party Cross-Border E-Commerce Platform
     第三方跨境电子商务平台的特点 ······································· 255
  Unit 2 Profit Mode of Third-Party Cross-Border E-Commerce Platform
     第三方跨境电子商务平台的盈利模式 ································· 256
  Unit 3 Classification and Brief Introduction to Third-Party
     Cross-Border E-Commerce Platforms 跨境电子商务平台分类与简介 ····· 258

Chapter 10 Terminology & Oral Communication for Foreign Trade of Textiles
     外贸术语与纺织外贸口语实践 ··· 262

 Task 1 Terms of Foreign Trade 外贸术语 ·· 262
  Unit 1 Declaration 报关 ·· 262
  Unit 2 Price Terms 价格术语 ··· 262
  Unit 3 Terms of Delivery 交货条件 ·· 263
  Unit 4 Claim 索赔 ··· 264
  Unit 5 Sale 销售 ··· 264
  Unit 6 Commission 佣金 ·· 265
  Unit 7 Insurance 保险 ·· 265
  Unit 8 Quality 品质 ··· 266

Task 2　Communication and Conversation for International Trade 外贸交流与对话……266
  Unit 1　Foreign Trade Policy 外贸政策……266
  Unit 2　Establishment of Business Relation 建立贸易联系……267
  Unit 3　Inquiries 询价……268
  Unit 4　Offer 报价……268
  Unit 5　Disagreement on Price 价格争议……269
  Unit 6　Order 订货……270
  Unit 7　Discount 折扣……271
  Unit 8　Commission 佣金……272
  Unit 9　Signing a Contract 签订合同……273
  Unit 10　Terms of Payment 付款方式……274
  Unit 11　Packing 包装……274
  Unit 12　Terms of Shipping 装运条件……275
  Unit 13　Quality 品质……276
  Unit 14　Commodity Inspection 商检……277
  Unit 15　Claim 索赔……278
  Unit 16　Situational Dialogue 情景对话……279

Bibliography 参考文献……281

Chapter 1

Textile Fibers 纺织纤维篇

- To be able to classify the various types of textile materials.
  能对不同纺织材料分类。
- To describe the properties of various types of natural cellulosic fiber & natural protein fiber.
  描述各种天然纤维素纤维和天然蛋白质纤维的性质。
- To describe the properties of various types of man-made fiber as well as the new fibers.
  描述各种人造纤维和新型纤维的性质。

Task 1

Common Textile Fiber Classification 常见纤维分类

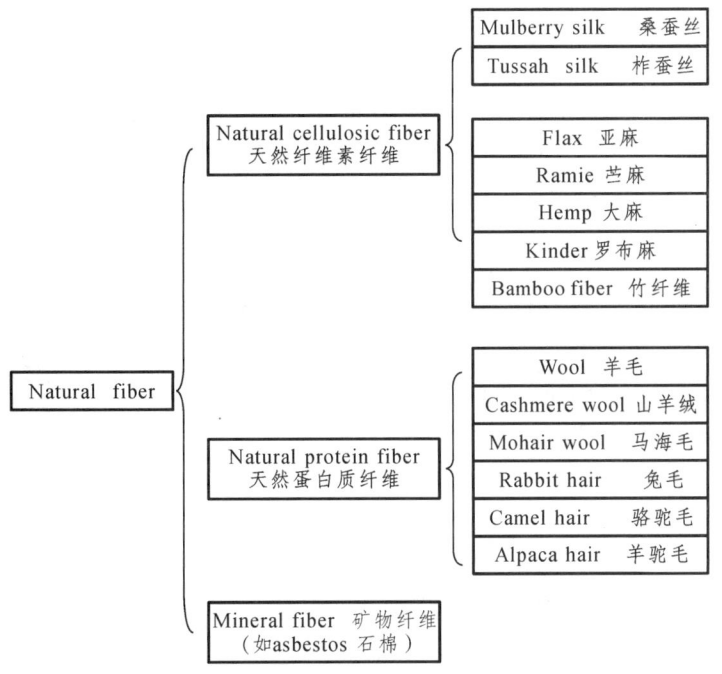

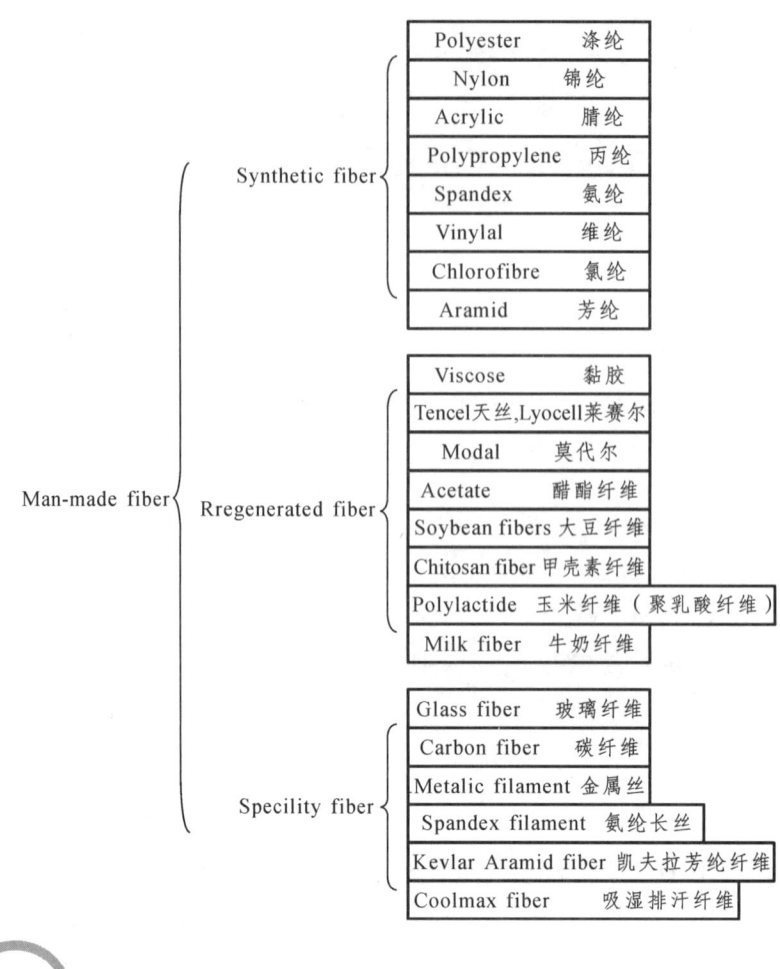

Task 2

Natural Cellulosic Fibers 天然纤维素纤维

Being derived from a wide variety of plant sources, natural cellulosic fibers are classified into various types, each possessing distinctive qualities or properties that distinguish it from others and make it especially suitable for certain end uses.

The general characteristics of natural cellulosic fibers as a class or group can be summarized as follows:

Natural cellulosic fibers
天然纤维素纤维

天然纤维素纤维来源广泛，可分为多种类型，每种纤维都具有独特的品质或性质，使其区别于其他纤维，特别适合某些最终用途。

天然纤维素纤维作为一类或一组的一般特征可概括如下：

1. Physical Properties 物理性质

The density of cellulosic fibers tends to be relatively high, which makes fabrics woven from these fibers feel comparatively heavy. As a result of their having relatively low elasticity and resilience, they wrinkle easily and do not recover from wrinkling readily. Absorbency and moisture regain are generally good. Most cellulosic fibers are, therefore, slow to dry after wetting, comfortable to wear, and easy to dye.

纤维素纤维的密度往往相对较高，这使得由这些纤维织成的织物感觉相对较重。由于它们具有相对较低的弹力和弹性，容易起皱，并且不易从起皱中恢复。吸水性和回潮性一般良好。因此，大多数纤维素纤维在湿润后干燥缓慢，穿着舒适，易于染色。

Cellulosic fibers are good conductors of heat and electricity. As good conductors of heat, they carry warmth away from the body and are favored for use in hot weather and warm climates. Since they conduct electricity, cellulosic fibers neither build up static electricity nor produce shocks when worn.

纤维素纤维是热和电的良好导体。作为良好的热导体，它们将热量从身体带走，适合在炎热的天气和温暖的气候中使用。由于纤维素纤维导电，因此穿着时既不会产生静电，也不会产生电击感。

Cellulosic fibers tend to burn easily, with a quick yellow flame, much as paper. Most cellulosic fibers can, however, withstand fairly high dry heat or ironing temperatures before they scorch.

纤维素纤维易于燃烧，具有快速燃烧的黄色火焰，就像烧纸一样。然而，大多数纤维素纤维在烧焦之前可以承受相当高的干热或熨烫温度。

2. Chemical Properties 化学性质

Chemical properties of cellulosic fibers include good resistance to alkalis. Excessive bleaching will harm cellulosic fibers, although carefully controlled bleaching is less detrimental. Such properties as the withstanding of high water temperature permit laundering of cellulosic fibers with strong detergent, controlled bleaching, and hot water temperatures.

纤维素纤维化学性质包括良好的耐碱性。过度漂白会损害纤维素纤维，尽管谨慎控制的漂白受到的损害较小。其耐高水温等性质，使之允许用强力洗涤剂进行受控漂白和高温热水洗涤。

The unique combination of properties—durability, low cost, easy washability, and comfort—has made cotton not only a material desirable for summer clothes, work clothes, towels, and sheets, but also a standard for great masses of the world's people who live in warm and subtropical climates. Even though the man-made fibers have encroached on the markets that were dominated by 100 percent cotton fibers, the cotton-look is still maintained and cotton forms up to 65 percent of the fibers in blended fabrics.

棉花具有耐久性、低成本、易洗性和舒适性的独特性质，不仅是夏装、工作服、毛巾和床单的理想材料，也是世界上生活在温暖和亚热带气候中的广大人民的纺织纤维选用标准。尽管人造纤维已经占据了曾经以 100%棉纤维为主的市场，但其仍然保持棉的外观，混纺织物中棉占纤维的 65%。

New Words and Expressions

cellulosic 纤维素的
derive 引出
summarize 概述
comparatively 比较地
resilience 弹力，回弹
readily 容易地
recover 回复
withstand 抵挡，经受住
shock 电击
alkali 碱
detrimental 损害的，有害的
launder 洗涤
washability 易洗性
encroach 侵入
unique 独特的，唯一的
dominate 统治，控制
end use 最终用途

source 来源，起源
miscellaneous 各种的
density 密度，比重
elasticity 弹性
wrinkle 折皱
absorbency 吸水性
comfortable 舒服的
ironing 熨烫
scorch 烫焦
bleach 漂白
excessive 过度的，过量的
detergent 洗涤剂，净洗剂
subtropical 亚热带的
maintain 保持，维持
blend 混合，混纺物
wrinkle recovery 折皱回复度
moisture regain 回潮率

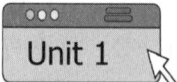 Unit 1　Cotton 棉

Cotton 棉

Cotton today is the most used textile fiber in the world. Its current consumption market share is approximately 56 percent for all fibers used for apparel and home furnishings and sold in the U.S. It is generally recognized that most consumers prefer cotton personal care items to those containing synthetic fibers. The earliest evidence of using cotton is from India and the date assigned to this fabric is 3,000 B.C. Cotton cultivation first spread from India to Egypt, China and the South Pacific. Even though cotton fiber had been known already in Southern America, the large-scale cotton cultivation in Northern America began in the 16th century with the arrival of colonists to southern parts of today's United States. With this new technology, it was possible to produce more cotton fiber, which resulted in big changes in the spinning and weaving industry, especially in England.

今天，棉花是世界上使用最多的纺织纤维。其目前在美国销售的服装和家居用纤维的消费市场份额约为56%。人们普遍认为，大多数消费者更喜欢棉质个人护理用品，而不是含有合成纤维的产品。使用棉花的最早证据来自印度，最早可追溯到公元前3000年。棉花

种植首先从印度传播到埃及、中国和南太平洋。尽管棉花在南美洲早已为人所知，但北美洲的大规模棉花种植始于 16 世纪，当时殖民者来到今天的美国南部地区。有了这项新技术，就有可能生产更多棉纤维，这引起了纺纱和机织业的巨大变化，特别是在英格兰。

Cottons are generally classified according to their length: Sea Island cotton; Upland cotton; and Egyptian cotton.

棉花一般按长度分类：海岛棉、陆地棉和埃及棉。

Cotton, as a natural cellulosic fiber, has a lot of characteristics, such as: comfortable soft hand, good absorbency, color retention, prints well, machine-washable, dry-cleanable, good strength, easy to handle and sew.

棉花，作为一种天然纤维素纤维，（面料）具有许多特点，例如：手感舒适柔软、吸水性好、保色性好、印花好、可机洗、可干洗、强度好、易于打理和缝纫。

Cotton fiber appears as a long, thin, irregular, convoluted（复杂的）and flattened（扁平的）tube. The cross section of a mature fiber shows a thin cuticle（表皮）and primary wall on the outside anda hollow collapsed（塌陷的）cavity（空腔）in the center of the fiber (See Fig. 1.1).

棉纤维呈细长、不规则、卷曲状，而且是扁平的管状，成熟纤维的横截面显示出薄的表皮。外侧的主外壳和一个凹陷坍塌空腔位于纤维中心（见图 1.1）。

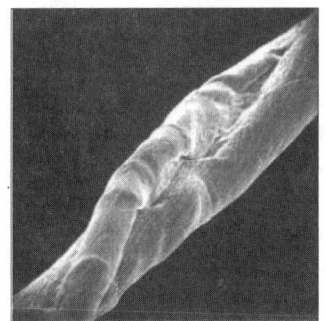
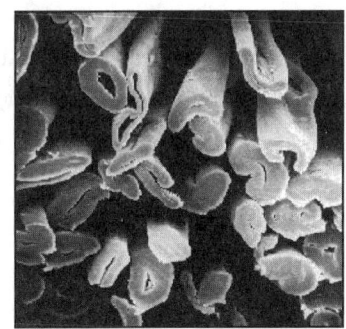

（1）Longitudinal view 纵向观察　　（2）Cross-section 横截面

Fig. 1.1　Observation under microscope 显微镜下观察

The moisture regain（回潮率）cotton is about 7.1% – 8.5% and the moisture absorption is 7% – 8%. Cotton is attacked by hot dilute or cold concentrated acid（酸）ions（离子）. Cold weak acids do not affect it. The fibers show excellent resistance to alkalis（碱）.

棉花的回潮率在 7.1%~8.5%，吸湿率为 7%~8%。棉花会受到热稀酸或冷浓酸的酸离子的侵蚀，冷弱酸不会影响它。纤维表现出优异的耐碱性。

The cotton buyer usually selects species and grades of cotton to produce specific yarns. If a fabric such as a part wool blanket is to be produced, the cotton buyer will select Peruvian, China, or Indian cottons which have a harsh, rough, wool-like handle. Where extremely fine texture, silkness and great strength are desired, the cotton buyer may choose Sea Island staple or Egyptian cotton.

棉花购买者通常选择不同品种和等级的棉花来生产特定的纱线。如果要生产羊毛毯之类的织物，棉花买家会选择秘鲁、中国或印度棉，这些棉的手感棘手、粗糙，像羊毛一样。如果需要极其精细的质地、丝滑感和强力，棉花买家可以选择海岛棉或埃及棉。

During the past 200 years, cottons have evolved hybridization to become the industrial cottons today. In the practice in United States, they are closely related to Sea Island cotton which came into prominence along the coast of South Carolina and to the Egyptian-type species which gained popularity of its high-quality fiber for use in the fine counts.

在过去的 200 年里，棉花经过杂交进化成为今天的工业用棉。在美国的使用实践中，它们与在南卡罗来纳州沿海占支配地位的海岛棉和埃及类型棉密切相关，埃及棉因其高质量的纤维，适合细支纱应用而广受欢迎。

American-grown cottons are divided into grades according to length of staple, uniformity, strength, color, cleanliness and flexibility. These are compared with a standard supplied by the United States Department of Agriculture.

美国种植的棉花根据短纤长度、均匀性、强度、颜色、清洁度和柔韧性分为不同等级。这些标准与美国农业部提供的标准相对照。

A cotton mill often average up the various grades of cotton to produce a fairly uniform yarn.

All normal cotton fibers have a soft creamy tint and some of the long staple fibers like the Egyptian cotton, are more creamy in color than the Upland and the Sea Island cotton. Cotton is never truly white and the nature of the pigment responsible for the color is really not known.

棉纺厂通常将不同等级的棉花进行均衡使用（混棉——编者注），以生产出相当均匀的纱线。

所有普通棉纤维都有柔和的奶油色，一些长纤维，如埃及棉，比高地和海岛棉的颜色更具奶油色。棉花从来都不是真正的白色，而形成这种颜色的色素的本质原因尚未清楚。

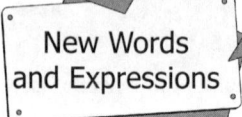
New Words and Expressions

approximately 近似
flattened 扁平的
cavity 空腔
acid 酸
Peruvian 秘鲁
rough 毛糙的，粗糙的
evolve 进化
count 支数，特数，号数
blanket 毛毯
texture 织物质地

convoluted 复杂的
collapsed 塌陷的
moisture regain 回潮率
alkalis 碱
harsh 粗糙的
desire 要求，愿望
yarn 纱线
fabric 织物
handle 手感
silkness 像丝绸一样的

Sea Island staple 海岛棉
staple 短纤维
uniformity 均匀度

hybridization 杂交
pigment 色素，颜料
flexibility 柔软度

 Flax 麻

The use of linen, or "flaxen cloth", dates back to people who lived about 10,000 years ago. Fragments of the cloth and nets have been discovered in Switzerland. Linen has served man as a textile for thousands of years, and it has been more important in the past than it is today.

Flax 麻

麻布或"亚麻布"的使用可以追溯到生活在大约 10 000 年前的人们。在瑞士发现了布和网的碎片。几千年来，亚麻布一直是人类使用的一种纺织品，麻在过去比现在更重要。

In cross section the fibers of flax are polygonal, with rounded edges, show a large cavity and a relatively thin cell wall. The flax fiber morphology is shown in Fig. 1.2.

亚麻纤维横截面是多边形的，具有圆形边缘，显示出大的空腔和相对薄的细胞壁。亚麻纤维在显微镜下观察的形态如图 1.2 所示。

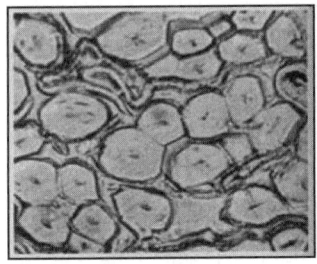 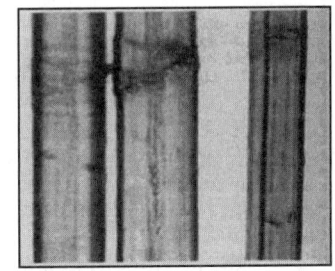

（1）Cross-section 横截面　　（2）Longitudinal view 纵向观察

Fig. 1.2　Observation under microscope 显微镜下观察

Flax fibers have silky luster much more pronounced than that of untreated cotton.

It is stronger than cotton, the normal tenacity ranges between 5.5 and 6.5 grams per denier, and its tensile strength increases when the fiber is wet.

It is less elastic than cotton.

It is better than cotton as a conductor of heat, it carries heat away from the body faster.

Its moisture regain is 6% – 12% (absorb moisture quickly).

It is composed chiefly of cellulose, but it has 15% – 30% natural impurities. It is not as durable as cotton, has poor drape, elasticity and resiliency, it is attacked by mildew and silverfish.

亚麻纤维具有比未经处理的棉花更明显的丝滑光泽。

它比棉强力高，正常强度范围在 5.5～6.5 克/旦，当纤维潮湿时，其拉伸强度增加。

它不如棉花有弹性。

作为热导体，它比棉花更好，它能更快地将热量从身体带走。

其回潮率为 6% ~ 12%（快速吸收水分）。

它主要由纤维素组成，但含有 15%~30%的天然杂质。它不像棉花那样耐用，悬垂性、弹性和回弹性差，容易发霉和被虫蛀。

New Words and Expressions

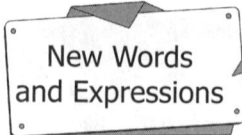

flax 亚麻
linen 亚麻布
morphology 形态，形态学
tensile strength 拉伸强力，断裂强力
natural impurity 天然杂质
resiliency 回弹，弹力
silverfish 蠹虫
pronounced 显著的
fragment 碎片，碎块
date back to 可追溯到，始于（某时期）
tenacity 强度
elastic 有弹性的
durable 耐久的，耐用的
mildew 发霉，霉变，霉菌
polygonal 多角形的，多边形的

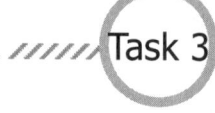

Task 3

Natural Protein Fibers 天然蛋白质纤维

Proteins are complex, high-molecular-weight compounds containing amino acids, they are essential for the growth and repair of all animal tissue. The protein fibers are naturally occurring animal products. The two major protein fibers are wool and silk. Wool is the fiber from the fleece of a sheep or lamb or the hair of a fur-bearing animal; silk is the fiber extruded by the silkworm, in the form of a cocoon, for protection in its pupal stage. Spider silk, which is extruded by the spider to form a web, sometimes is classified as a textile fiber.

Natural protein fibers
天然蛋白质纤维

蛋白质是含有氨基酸的复杂高分子量化合物，对所有动物组织的生长和修复至关重要。蛋白质纤维是天然存在的动物产品。两种主要的蛋白质纤维是羊毛和丝绸。羊毛是绵羊或羔羊的羊毛，或毛皮动物的毛发中的纤维；蚕丝是蚕蛹阶段为保护目的而由蚕茧内挤压出来的纤维。蜘蛛丝被蜘蛛挤出形成网，有时被归类为纺织纤维。

Wool fibers are the more widely used; they provide warmth, a pleasant hand, attractive appearance, good absorbency, and resiliency. Silk, noted for its lustrous appearance and unique hand feeling, has always been considered a luxury fiber.

羊毛纤维使用更为广泛；它们提供温暖和舒适的手感、迷人的外观、良好的吸水性和弹性。丝绸以其光泽的外观和独特的手感而闻名，一直被认为是一种奢侈纤维。

The oldest examples of wool fabrics in Europe come from archaeological digs in Germany and date from about 1,500 B.C. Fabrics from Danish sites have been dated about 1,300 to 1,000 B.C.; these fabrics have a rough, coarse texture.

欧洲最古老的羊毛织物源于德国的考古发掘，可追溯到公元前 1 500 年左右。丹麦遗址的织物可追溯到公元前 1 300 年到公元前 1 000 年。这些织物质地不平且粗糙。

New Words and Expressions

protein 蛋白质
high-molecular-weight 高分子重量
contain 包含
repair 修补，恢复
occur 出现，存在
fur-bearing animal 毛皮动物
silkworm 蚕
pupal 蛹的
lustrous 有光泽的，光亮的
dig 出土物

complex 复杂的
compound 化合物
amino acids 氨基酸
tissue 组织
fleece 毛被，套毛
extruded 挤压的
cocoon 蚕茧
resiliency 弹性，回弹
archaeological 考古学的
Danish 丹麦的

 Wool 羊毛

Wool was probably the first animal fiber to be made into cloth. The art of spinning wool into yarn developed about 4,000 B.C. and encouraged trade among the nations in the region of the Mediterranean Sea.

Wool 羊毛

羊毛可能是第一种制成布料的动物纤维。将羊毛纺成纱线的技艺大约在公元前 4 000 年发展起来，并激励了地中海地区各国之间的贸易。

The major wool producers in the world are Australia, Argentina, China and South Africa.

Wool is a protein fiber with 18 amino acids. Its cross section may be nearly circular, but most wool fibers tend to be slightly elliptical or oval in shape. Wool fibers have a natural crimp, a built-in waviness. The crimp increases the elasticity and elongation properties of the fiber and also aids in yarn manufacturing. The wool morphology is shown in Fig. 1.3.

世界上主要的羊毛生产国是澳大利亚、阿根廷、中国和南非。

009

羊毛是一种含有 18 种氨基酸的蛋白质纤维。它的横截面可能接近圆形，但大多数羊毛纤维的形状往往略呈椭圆形或椭圆形。羊毛纤维具有天然卷曲，内在波纹。卷曲增加了纤维的弹性和伸长率性能，也有助于纱线制造。羊毛形态如图 1.3 所示。

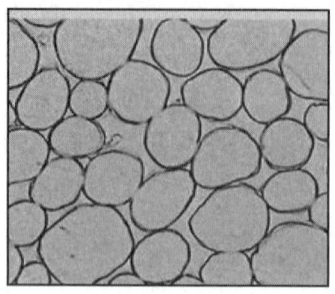
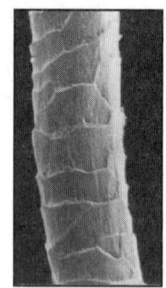

（1）Cross-section 横截面　　　（2）Longitudinal view 纵向观察

Fig. 1.3　Observation under microscope 显微镜下观察

The supply of wool available to the world every year amounts to about 5,000 million pounds. After scouring, this is reduced to about 3,000 million pounds of pure wool. The wool crop is insufficient to meet the world needs. Pure wool is often mixed with other type fibers and recovered wool to meet the demand.

全球每年可获得的羊毛供应量约为 50 亿磅重。经过洗毛后，减少到约 30 亿磅的纯羊毛。羊毛产量不足以满足世界需求。纯羊毛通常与其他类型的纤维和回用羊毛混合以满足需求。

The qualities of different wools vary greatly. The merino sheep of Australia, South America and South Africa produce very fine and soft wool. The quality of wool from these sources depends upon the conditions and heritage of the sheep. Port Philip wool is the finest in Australia and is used to produce the highest quality woolen and worsted fabrics.

不同羊毛的质量差别很大。澳大利亚、南美洲和南非的美利奴羊生产出非常细而柔软的羊毛。这些来源的羊毛质量取决于绵羊的（生长）条件和遗传基因。菲利普港羊毛是澳大利亚最好的羊毛，用于生产最高质量的羊毛粗纺和精纺面料。

Merino wool has been successfully raised in Germany, France, Spain and the United States and is of high quality.

美利奴羊毛已在德国、法国、西班牙和美国成功培育，质量上乘。

Wool is attacked by hot sulphuric acid and decomposes completely. It is generally resistant to most other mineral acids of all strengths. Wool will dissolve in caustic soda solutions that would have little effect on cotton.

羊毛被热硫酸侵蚀并完全分解。它通常能抵抗大多数其他各种强度的无机酸。羊毛会溶解在苛性钠溶液中，这（苛性钠）对棉花几乎没有影响。

Properties of the wool 羊毛的性质

Wool fiber has extremely high absorbency and high moisture regain.

It has soft hand high thermal insulation (low thermal conductivity) and low flammability.

Its elastic recovery is excellent.

It is lightweight and versatile.

It is resistant to dirt and wear and tear.

羊毛纤维具有极高的吸水性和高回潮率。

它具有柔软的手感、高隔热性（低导热性）和低可燃性。

其弹性恢复性极佳。

它重量轻，用途广泛。

它耐脏和耐磨损。

New Words and Expressions

spinning 纺纱，细纱，纺丝
amino acid 氨基酸
crimp 皱缩，卷曲
thermal insulation 热绝缘
elastic recovery 弹性恢复
morphology 形态
woolen 粗纺毛织物
caustic soda 苛性

breed 品种，血统
oval 卵形，椭圆形的
tear 撕破
flammability 可燃性
versatile 多功能的，通用的
worsted 精纺毛织物
sulfuric acid 硫酸

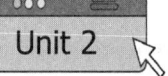

Unit 2　Specialty Fur Fibers 特种毛

Fibers from animals other than sheep frequently are referred to as specialty fibers. Most specialty fibers come from members of the goat and camel families, which are indigenous to countries other than the United States (although small numbers are being raised in this country, primarily for the use of hand-spinners and weavers). Both specialty and fur fibers are similar to sheep's wool in chemical and physical properties. They are added to wool fabrics primarily to give softness, color interest, and value.

Specialty fur fibers 特种毛

绵羊毛以外的动物纤维通常被称为特种纤维。大多数特种纤维来自山羊和骆驼家族的成员，它们原产于美国以外的国家（尽管在这个国家饲养的数量很少，主要用于手工纺纱机和织布机）。特种纤维和毛皮纤维在化学和物理性能上与羊毛相似。它们被添加到羊毛织物中，主要是为了赋予柔软性、色彩趣味性和价值。

011

1. Mohair 马海毛

Mohair is from the Angora goat and is highly resilient and strong. Mohair's luster, not softness, determines its value. They have very good abrasion resistance and are quite durable.

马海毛来自安哥拉山羊，具有很高的弹性和强力。马海毛的光泽性而不是柔软性决定了它的价值。它们具有非常好的耐磨性，非常耐用。

Mohair is used in home decorating fabrics as well as garment fabrics including tropical worsteds.

马海毛用于家庭装饰织物以及服装织物，包括热带精纺毛织品。

The United States and South Africa are the major sources of mohair fibers. Mohair fibers are circular in cross section and range 10 – 90 μm in diameter. The mohair morphology is shown in Fig. 1.4.

美国和南非是马海毛纤维的主要来源国。马海毛纤维的横截面为圆形，直径范围为 10 ~ 90 μm。马海毛形态如图 1.4 所示。

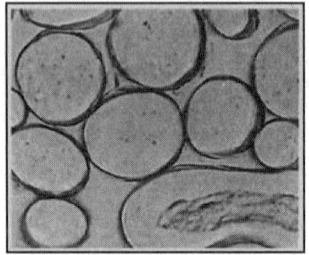 

（1）Cross-section 横截面　　（2）Longitudinal view 纵向观察

Fig. 1.4　Observation under microscope 显微镜下观察

2. Cashmere 羊绒

Cashmere is a soft, fine fiber obtained from the cashmere (Kashmir) goat of Asia. The fiber is combed, rather than sheared, from the animals. A single goat yields only 114 grams (4 oz) of good fiber. Because supply of the fiber is limited and demand for it is high, cashmere fiber is quite expensive. The fiber cross-section is regular round. The cashmere morphology is shown in Fig. 1.5.

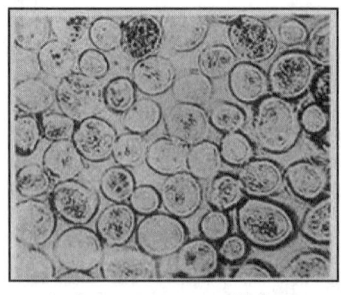 

（1）Cross-section 横截面　　（2）longitudinal view 纵向观察

Fig. 1.5　Observation under microscope 显微镜下观察

羊绒是一种柔软、精细的纤维，取自亚洲克什米尔山羊。这些纤维是从动物身上梳理出来的，而不是剪下来的。一只山羊只产 114 克（4 盎司）的优质纤维。由于羊绒纤维的供应有限，而且需求量很大，所以羊绒纤维非常昂贵。纤维横截面为规则圆形。羊绒形态如图 1.5 所示。

Cashmere is more sensitive to the action of alkalies than is wool. Cashmere fibers longer than 7.5 cm (3 in.) may be somewhat stiff and coarse. The fiber has very small, barely protruding scales. Complaints from consumers and importers about labeled cashmere fabrics are investigated via careful microscopic evaluation to determine whether cashmere fibers are present in the amount specified on the label.

羊绒比羊毛对碱的作用更敏感。长度超过 7.5 厘米（3 英寸①）的羊绒纤维可能有些僵硬和粗糙。纤维具有非常小的、几乎没有突出的鳞片。对于消费者和进口商对贴有标签的羊绒织物的投诉，可通过仔细的微观评估进行调查，以确定羊绒纤维的含量是否符合标签上的规定。

The fiber is used primarily for apparel such as scarves, sweaters, suits, and coats when a luxurious, soft fabric is desired. It is often blended with wool to reduce the cost of the products.

当需要奢华柔软的面料时，这种纤维主要用于围巾、毛衣、西装和外套等。它经常与羊毛混纺以降低产品成本。

3. Camel Hair 骆驼毛

Camel hair, animal fibre obtained from the camel and belonging to the group called specialty hair fibers. Camel-hair fiber has greater sensitivity to chemicals than wool fiber. Its strength is similar to that of wool having a similar diameter but is less than that of mohair. Fabric made of camel hair has excellent insulating properties and is warm and comfortable. Camel hair is mainly used for high-grade overcoat fabrics and is also made into knitting yarn, knitwear, blankets, and rugs. The coarse outer fiber is strong and is used in industrial fabrics such as machine beltings and press cloths employed in extracting oil from oilseeds.

The fiber cross section is circular to oval. Medulla is narrow and continuous. The fiber morphology is shown in Fig. 1.6.

骆驼毛是从骆驼中获得的动物纤维，属于特种毛纤维。骆驼毛纤维比羊毛纤维对化学物质更敏感。其强度与直径相近的羊毛相似，但小于马海毛。骆驼毛织物具有优异的隔热性能，保暖舒适。骆驼毛主要用于高档大衣面料，也可制成针织纱、针织品、毛毯和地毯。粗的外层纤维强力高，用于工业织物，例如用于从油籽中提取油的机器皮带和压榨布。

纤维横截面为圆形至椭圆形。髓质狭窄且连续。纤维形态如图 1.6 所示。

---

① 1 英寸≈2.54 厘米。

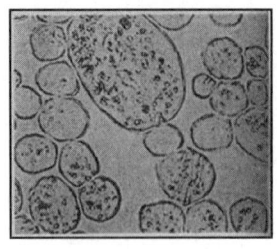 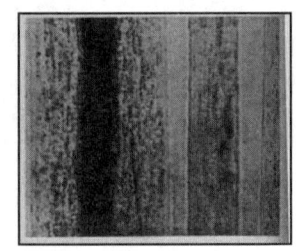

（1）Cross-section 横截面　　　（2）Longitudinal view 纵向观察

Fig. 1.6　Observation under microscope 显微镜下观察

4. Alpaca 羊驼毛

Alpacas are domestic members of the camel family from the altiplano region of South America, prized for the production of fine fleece.

羊驼是南美洲高原地区骆驼家族的本地成员，以生产细毛而闻名。

A cross section of an alpaca fiber will reveal microscopic air pockets. These pockets of air add to the insulating qualities as well as the light weight of a garment made from alpaca. The fiber morphology is shown in Fig. 1.7.

羊驼纤维的横截面显示出微小的气穴。这些空气袋赋予羊驼制成的衣服隔热性和轻量化。纤维形态如图 1.7 所示。

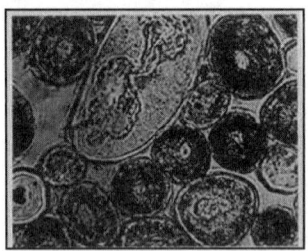 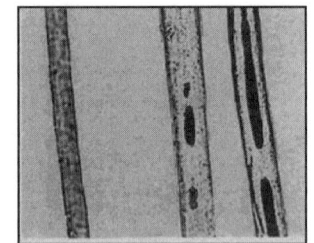

（1）Cross-section 横截面　　　（2）Longitudinal view 纵向观察

Fig. 1.7　Observation under microscope 显微镜下观察

Alpaca fiber offers the following benefits and qualities.

It's extremely fine with little guard hair.

The fiber is compatible with either the woolen or worsted systems.

It has excellent insulative or thermal qualities.

It has a rich silky sheen which has high visual appeal in the apparel industry.

It has a higher tensile strength than wool.

It can be carded and blended with other natural or synthetic fibers.

羊驼纤维具有以下优点和品质：

纤维非常细且具有很少保护性纤维质（编者注：保护性纤维质导致纤维变粗硬）；

该纤维与粗纺或精纺系统兼容；

它具有优异的绝缘或热性能；

它具有丰富的丝滑光泽，对于服装行业具有很高的视觉吸引力；

它的抗拉强度比羊毛高；

它可以经梳理并与其他天然或合成纤维混纺。

New Words and Expressions

fur fibers 毛皮纤维
primarily 最初的
Mohair 马海毛
shear 剪毛
identify 鉴定，识别
aesthetic 美观的，美感的
comb 梳理
sensitive 敏感的，灵敏的
barely 仅仅，几乎没有
evaluation 评价，估价
Camel hair 骆驼毛，驼绒毛
underhairs 下层纤维
medulla 毛髓，髓质
tan 棕褐色，棕黄色
brown 棕色，褐色
shade 色泽，色光
navy 海军蓝
altiplano 高原
rug 地毯，毯子
microscopic 极小的，微观的

indigenous 本土的，本土生长的
hand-spinner 手工纺纱
Angora goat 安哥拉山羊
label 标签
abrasion 磨蚀，磨损
cashmere 山羊绒
yield 生产
coarse 粗糙
protruding 突出的
specify 指定，详细说明
Bactrian camel 双峰驼
insulating 绝缘的
pluck 摘，拔
reddish 微红的
subsequently 随后的，后来的
gray 灰色
specialty hair fibers 特种毛发纤维
alpaca 羊驼，羊驼毛
rope 绳索
air pocket 气穴，气孔

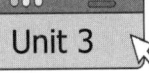 Silk 蚕丝

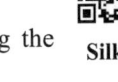

Silk 蚕丝

Silk is a continuous strand of two filaments cemented together, forming the cocoon of the silkworm.

丝由两根连续的丝黏结在一起，形成蚕茧。

For centuries silk has had a reputation as a luxurious and sensuous fabric, one associated with wealth and success. Silk is one of the oldest textile fibres known to man.

It is supposed to have been discovered in 2,640 B.C. by a Chinese princess. It is also

became a valuable commodity both in Greece and Rome. During the Roman Empire, silk was sold for its weight in gold.

几个世纪以来，丝绸一直被誉为奢华和感官愉悦的面料，与财富和成功联系在一起。丝绸是人类已知的最古老的纺织纤维之一。

它应该是在公元前 2 640 年由一位中国公主发现的。在希腊和罗马它也成为一种有价值的商品。在罗马帝国时期，丝绸以黄金（相等）重量出售。

Silk is the only natural filament fiber, triangular in cross section with rounded corners. The silk morphology is shown in Fig. 1.8.

蚕丝是唯一的天然长丝纤维，截面呈三角形，有圆角。蚕丝形态如图 1.8 所示。

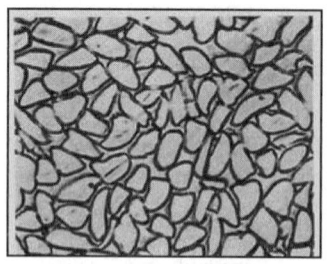 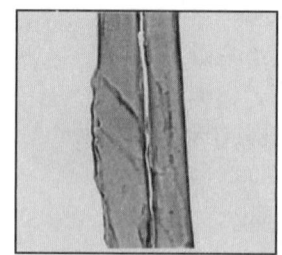

（1）Cross-section 横截面　　　（2）Longitudinal view 纵向观察

Fig. 1.8　Observation under microscope 显微镜下观察

Silk is a protein fiber with 15 amino acids. It has no cross linkages and no bulky side chains. The molecular chains are packed closely to form high molecular orientation, which contributes to its higher strength.

蚕丝是一种含有 15 种氨基酸的蛋白质纤维。分子内没有交联，也没有笨重的侧链。分子链紧密堆积形成高分子取向度，有助于其（获得）更高的强度。

It has a tenacity of 2.4 to 5.1 grams per denier when dry, wet strength is about 80 to 85 percent of the dry strength.

干强度 2.4~5.1 克/旦。湿强度为干强度的 80%~85%。

It has medium resiliency. Creases will hang out relatively well, but not so quickly or completely as for wool.

It has a relatively high standard moisture regain of 11 percent.

It has a poor resistance to sunlight exposure.

它具有中等弹性。悬挂后褶皱消失性会相对较好，但不会像羊毛织物那样会快速或完全消失。它的标准回潮率相对较高，为 11%。耐日晒性很差。

The elastic property of silk is better than those of cotton or rayon but are not as good as wool's. Like wool, silk absorbs moisture readily and can take up a third of its weight of water without feeling wet to the touch. It has a regain of 11.0%.

丝绸的弹性比棉或人造丝好，但不如羊毛。像羊毛一样，丝绸很容易吸收水分，可以吸收自身重量三分之一的水分，而不会感到潮湿。其回潮率为 11.0%。

Silk will withstand higher temperature than wool without decomposing. It will withstand a high temperature of 140 °C for prolonged periods. However, it will decompose at 175 °C.

Silk is less readily damaged by alkali than wool and like wool it is also insoluble in common solvents.

丝绸能承受比羊毛更高的温度而不会分解。它能长期承受 140 °C 的高温。然而，它会在 175 °C 分解。

丝绸相比羊毛更不易被碱损伤，而且和羊毛一样，它也不溶于普通溶剂。

New Words and Expressions

silk 丝，蚕丝，丝织品
cocoon 蚕茧
triangular 三角形的
molecular orientation 分子取向

filament 长丝
silkworm 蚕
molecular chain 分子链
crease 折印，折痕

Task 4

Man-made Fibers Process 人造纤维生产

The three major spinning, or extrusion, processes are wet spinning, dry or solvent spinning, and melt spinning. A fourth type, emulsion spinning, can be used for polymers for which the other processes are not practical. Gel spinning is a newer process that is being used for a few high-tenacity fibers.

Man-made fibers process
人造纤维生产

三种主要的纺丝或挤压（喷丝）工艺是湿法纺丝、干法或溶剂纺丝和熔融纺丝。第四种类型，乳液纺丝，可用于其他工艺不可行的聚合物。凝胶纺丝是一种新的工艺，用于一些高强度纤维。

The shape of the spinnerette and the method of spinning influence the cross-sectional shape of a fiber. Most spinnerettes are common round openings. Other shapes are available to produce fibers with special characteristics.

喷丝板的形状和纺丝方法影响纤维的横截面形状。大多数喷丝板是常见的圆形开口。其他形状可用于生产具有特殊性质的纤维。

After fibers are extruded, they are usually stretched, or drawn, to improve the orientation of the polymer chains. The amount the fiber is stretched is reported as the draw ratio: the ratio of the length of the fiber when stretched to its length when unstretched. Draw ratios of 1 or 2 are common for rayon. Ratios of 4 or 6 are not uncommon for other fibers. In some cases, drawing may occur in more than one stage. Some fibers are sold as undrawn or partially drawn yarns. Manmade fibers process is shown in Fig. 1.9.

纤维被挤压出丝后，通常会被拉伸或牵伸，以改善聚合物链的取向。纤维的牵伸量称为牵伸比：牵伸时纤维的长度与未牵伸时纤维长度的比率。人造丝的牵伸比通常为1或2，其他纤维的比率为4或6并不罕见。在某些情况下，牵伸可能在多个阶段进行。一些纤维以未牵伸或部分牵伸的纱的形式销售。人造纤维加工过程如图1.9。

Wet spinning 湿法纺丝	Dry spinning 干法纺丝	Melt spinning 熔融纺丝
Spinning from polymer solution		Spinning from polymer melt
(湿法纺丝示意图：polymer solution 聚合物乳液, metering pump 计量泵, spinneret 喷丝头, take up 卷取, drawing 牵伸, winding 卷绕, coagulation bath 凝固浴)	(干法纺丝示意图：polymer solution, warm air, metering pump, spinneret, solvent, winding, drawing)	(熔融纺丝示意图：molten polymer, metering pump, spinneret, cool air, winding, drawing)
Polymer solution is extruded into a bath containing chemicals which neutralize the solvent and coagulate (solidity) the filament. 聚合物溶液被挤入含有中和溶剂并使细丝凝结（凝固）的溶液中	Polymer solution is extruded into a stream of warm air, which evaporates the volatile solvent and solidifies the filament. 聚合物溶液被挤入热空气中，在其中蒸发挥发性溶剂并使长丝固化	The molten polymer is extruded into an air stream, which cools the melt and solidifies the filament. 熔融的聚合物被挤出到气流中，气流冷却熔体并使长丝固化
Examples: viscose, acrylics 例如黏胶，腈纶	Examples: acrylic, acetate 例如腈纶，醋酯纤维	Examples: polyester, nylon 例如涤纶，锦纶
After the filaments have been extruded and solidified, they are drawn out between rollers have different speeds. Spinneret size plus spinning and drawing conditions determine the filament diameter. 在长丝被挤出并固化后，它们在不同速度的牵伸辊之间被牵引出。纺纱机尺寸加上纺纱和牵伸条件决定了长丝直径。		

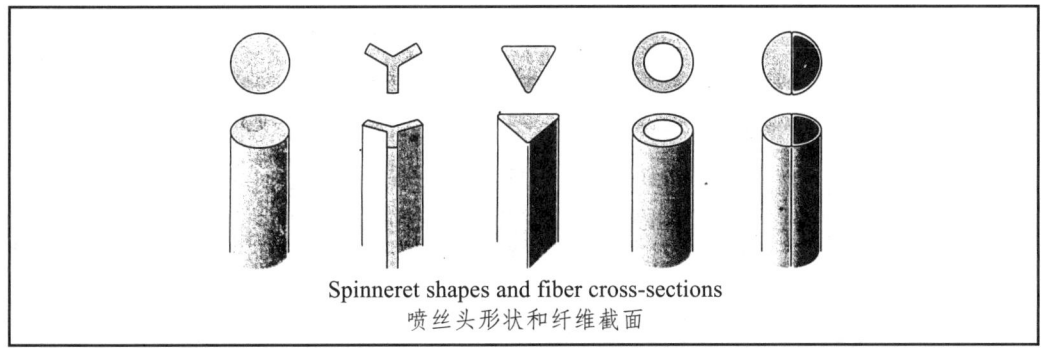

Fig. 1.9　Man-made fibers process

dissatisfaction 不满意
upheaval 动荡，动乱
competitive 竞争性的
synthesized 合成的，综合的
conversion 转变
spinnerette 喷丝板，吐丝管
stretch 拉直，拉长
emulsion spinning 乳液纺丝
cross-sectional 横截面的
orientation 定向，倾向性
texture 变形

considerable 相当多的
spur 刺激，激发
durable 耐用的，持久的
regenerated 再生的
nozzle 喷嘴，喷管
slender 细长的，苗条的
draw 牵伸
gel spinning 凝胶纺丝
round 圆的
draw ratio 拉伸比

Regenerate Fibers 再生纤维

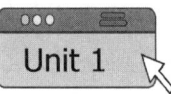 Viscose Fiber 黏胶纤维

Viscose is the first manufactured fiber. Unlike most man-made fibers, it's not a synthetic fibers, it's a man-made fiber made from purified cellulose, which usually comes from specially processed wood pulp. As a result, viscose rayon has a silky appearance and feel, and also has the ability to breathe in a

Viscose 黏胶

manner similar to cotton weaves. In addition to being an inexpensive material to use in lightweight clothing, viscose can also be used for such textiles as tablecloths, napkins, furniture slipcovers, and sheeting. One of the more popular properties of viscose rayon is that the fabric tends to drape very well, which makes it ideal for use in simple curtains, as well as the perfect fabric to line more formal draperies.

The fiber has a serrated round shape with a smooth surface. The fiber morphology is shown in Fig. 1.10.

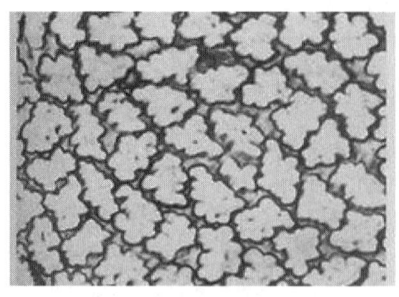　　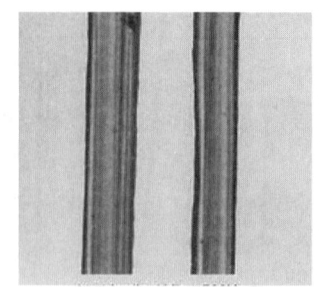

（1）Cross-section 横截面　　　　（2）Longitudinal view 纵向观察

Fig. 1.10　Observation under microscope 显微镜下观察

黏胶是第一种人造纤维。与大多数人造纤维不同，它不是一种合成纤维，而是一种由纯化的纤维素制成的人造纤维，通常来自经过特殊处理的木浆。因此，黏胶人造丝具有丝滑的外观和手感，并且具有类似于棉织物的呼吸能力。黏胶纤维除了是一种廉价的轻质服装材料外，还可用于桌布、餐巾、家具套和床单等纺织品。黏胶人造丝一个更受欢迎的性能是，这种织物往往悬垂性很好，这使得它非常适合用于简单的窗帘，也适合作为更正式的窗帘的衬里。纤维呈锯齿状，表面光滑。纤维形态如图 1.10 所示。

Viscose rayon is a medium-weight fiber with fair to good strength and abrasion resistance. It is hydrophilic (11% moisture regain).

黏胶人造丝是一种中等重量纤维，具有良好强度和耐磨性。具有亲水性（回潮率 11%）。

The fiber is washable under proper care conditions and is dry cleanable. There are no static or pilling problems.

此纤维（生产的面料）在适当打理条件下可洗涤，并且可干洗。没有静电或起球问题。

Viscose rayon loses 30% to 50% of its strength when wet, thus requiring great caution in laundering. It recovers strength when dry. It has very poor elasticity and resiliency. It also shrinks appreciably from washing.

黏胶人造丝在潮湿时会损失 30%~50% 的强度，因此在洗涤时需要格外小心。干燥后恢复强度。它的弹力和弹性非常差。它也会因洗涤而明显收缩。

Viscose fiber swell in water, this cause the fabric to shrink. Swelling and shrinkage can be reduced by treatment with synthetic resins. The treatment also improves wrinkle recovery but moisture absorbency is reduced.

黏胶纤维在水中膨胀，导致织物收缩。用合成树脂处理可以减少膨胀和收缩。该处理还改善折皱恢复性，但吸湿性降低。

New Words and Expressions

viscose 黏胶纤维
manufactured 制成的，人造的
wood pulp 木浆
abrasion resistance 耐磨牢度，抗磨损性
napkin 手帕，餐巾
sheeting 床单，被单布
pilling 起球
drape 悬垂性，褶裥

rayon 人造（纤维素）纤维，人造丝
man-made fiber 化学纤维
serrated 锯齿状的，有锯齿的
hydrophilic 亲水性的
slipcover 覆盖物，家具套
curtain 窗帘，幕布
shrink 收缩，缩水
synthetic resin 合成树脂

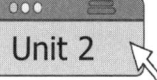

Unit 2　Acetate 醋酯纤维

Acetate
醋酯纤维

Acetate is not a strong fibre but can be extruded into fibres of different diameter and woven into fabrics that have the luxurious look of silk but do not wear like silk. Acetate does not absorb moisture readily but dries fast and resists shrinking. This is a resilient fabric that resists wrinkling in addition to being pliable and soft with a good drape. Triacetate is an improved acetate fabric which doesn't melt as easier and is easier to care for. Remember, acetate in nail polish and nail polish remover will melt acetate as alcohol so take care with perfumes and nail products including super glue.

醋酸纤维不是一种强力纤维，但可以被挤压（喷丝）成不同直径的纤维，织成具有丝绸般奢华外观但不像丝绸那样耐磨的织物。醋酯不易吸收水分，但快干，抗收缩。这是一种有弹性的织物，除柔韧、柔软的良好悬垂性外，还具抗皱性。三醋酸酯是一种改进的醋酸纤维织物，不易熔融，更易于打理。但切记，指甲油和指甲油去除剂中的醋酸酯会溶解醋酯纤维（相似相容原理——编者注），酒精也会溶解醋酯纤维，所以要留心（使之远离）香水和指甲油产品，包括超级胶水。

The spinning solution of acetate filament is made by dissolving cellulose acetate in acetone containing a small amount of water (up to 10 percent). The solution is filtered and pumped through the fine holes of a spinneret. As the jets of cellulose acetate solution emerge they meet a stream of warm air which evaporates the acetone, leaving the solid cellulose acetate in the form of fine filaments.

醋酯纤维纺丝溶液是将醋酸纤维素溶解在含有少量水（最多10%）的丙酮中制成的。溶液被过滤并通过喷丝板的细孔泵送。当醋酸纤维素溶液喷射出来时，它们遇到一股温热的空气流，使丙酮蒸发，留下细小的细丝形式的固体醋酸纤维素。

Acetate staple is now produced by cutting the continuous filaments into short lengths. The staple length is chosen to blend suitably with other fibers in making mixed yarns.

现在，通过将连续长丝切断成较短的长度来生产醋酸酯短纤维。选择短纤维以在生产混纺纱时与其他纤维混纺。

Filament yarn may be twisted to the level of consumer requirements and packaged on paper cones. One trend is the development of packages which will deliver a zero twist yarn, and the utilization of the yarn at low twist levels.

按照消费者的要求，长丝纱线可以进行不同程度的加捻，并卷装在纸筒上。一个趋势是开发无捻纱线的卷装形式和使用低捻纱线。

acetate fiber 醋酯纤维
drape 悬垂性
nail polish 指甲油
super glue 超强力胶水
cone 锥形筒子

pliable 柔韧的
triacetate 三醋酯纤维
alcohol 酒精，乙醇
acetone 丙酮
zero twist yarn 无捻纱

Unit 3　Rayon 人造丝

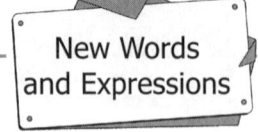

Rayon
人造丝

Rayon, from cellulose, has many of the qualities of cotton, a natural cellulose fibre. Rayon is strong, extremely absorbent, comes in a variety of qualities and weights, and can be made to resemble natural fabrics. Rayon does not melt but burns at high temperatures. Rayon drapes well, has a soft, silky hand, and has a smooth, napped, or bulky surface. Rayon will wrinkle easily and may stretch when wet and shrink when washed

人造丝由纤维素制成，具有棉的许多特性，是一种天然纤维素纤维。人造丝强力较高，吸水性极强，具有多种品质和重量（系列），可以制成类似天然织物的面料。人造丝不熔融，但在高温下会燃烧。人造丝悬垂性好，手感柔软、丝滑，表面光滑、有绒毛或蓬松感。人造丝织物很容易起皱，湿时可能拉伸，洗后会收缩。

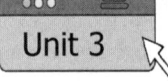

rayon 人造丝
bulky 颗粒状的

resemble 类似
napped 绒毛的

Unit 4　Lyocell（Tencel）莱赛尔（天丝）

Tencel® is the registered trade name for Lyocell. Tencel (Lyocell) is the first new fiber in 30 years, and being made of wood pulp cellulose, it is the first new natural fiber a lot longer than that. The properties and production processes were unique enough for the US Federal Trade Commission to designate Tencel as a separate fiber group. Tencel was developed by Tencel Inc., and Tencel is the registered trademark of Tencel Ltd.

Lyocell
莱赛尔

Tencel®是 Lyocell 的注册商标名。Tencel（Lyocell）是 30 年来的第一种新型纤维，由木浆纤维素制成，是比这更长时间内的第一种新天然纤维。性能和生产工艺非常独特，美国联邦贸易委员会将天丝公司指定为一个单独的纤维集团。天丝由天丝股份有限公司开发，天丝是天丝有限公司的注册商标。

The raw material for Lyocell manufacture is cellulose derived from wood, the manufacture process is short and fast, and is environmentally friendly. The solvent is almost all recovered and the waste is harmless.

生产莱赛尔的原材料是源自木材的纤维素，生产过程短而快，而且环保。溶剂几乎全部回收，废物无害。

Lyocell has good dry and wet strength—usually better than other manmade cellulosic fibers. The dry strength is better than middle grade cotton. Wet strength is lower than the dry strength. The extensibility of staple fibers, at 10 to 14%, is somewhat higher than that of cotton. Elasticity is low, as with all cellulosic fibers.

莱赛尔具有良好的干强度和湿强度，通常优于其他人造纤维素纤维。干强度优于中档棉。湿强度低于干强度。短纤维的伸长率为 10%~14%，略高于棉花。和所有纤维素纤维一样，弹性很低。

Fiber fineness can be similar to cotton or wool, ranging from 1.1—3.3dtex.

纤维细度可与棉或羊毛相似，范围为 1.1~3.3dtex。

Clothing comfort properties are comparable to other cellulosic fibers. Moisture absorption is less than viscose but greater than cotton.

服装的舒适性与其他纤维素纤维（织物的服装）相当。吸湿性低于黏胶，但高于棉。

A peach-skin finish can be obtained by emerising. Other typical process are raising and shrinking.

桃皮绒可通过喷砂处理获得。其他典型的过程是起绒和收缩（水洗起皱—编者注）。

New Words and Expressions

extensibility 延伸性
peach-skin finish 桃皮绒整理
raise 起绒

moisture absorption 吸湿性
emerise 磨毛
shrink 收缩

Unit 5　Modal 莫代尔

Modal is a trademarked fiber from an Austrian textile company, Lenzing. Modal is a fiber made from spun beechwood cellulose. Characteristics as follow.

莫代尔是一家奥地利纺织公司 Lenzing 的商标纤维。莫代尔是一种由山毛榉纤维制成的纤维。特征如下。

Modal fabrics have softness handle, good drape and comfortable wearing.

莫代尔面料手感柔软，悬垂性好，穿着舒适。

Modal fabrics have good moisture regain and air permeability which is better than cotton fabrics, it is the ideal material of body suit and health suit, which can be done favor of physiology circulation and health of body.

莫代尔面料具有良好的回潮率和透气性，优于棉质面料，是女紧身衣和健康服的理想材料，有利于身体的生理循环和健康。

Modal fabrics have level up surface, fine and smooth and velvet, which have the effect of natural silk.

莫代尔面料表面平整，细腻光滑，丝绒质地，具有天然丝绸的效果。

Modal has a high dry strength and much high wet strength than viscose.

莫代尔具有比黏胶纤维高的干强度和高得多的湿强度。

Breaking extension is 15—30%—more than double that of cotton.

断裂伸长率为 15%～30%，是棉花断裂伸长率的两倍以上。

Modal
莫代尔

New Words and Expressions

beechwood 山毛榉材
air permeability 透气性
level up 平整的
breaking extension 断裂伸长

moisture regain 回潮率
physiology 生理学，生理机能
velvet 天鹅绒（般的）

Synthetic Fibers 合成纤维

It was not until the 1920s and 1930s that man first learned how to build long chain molecules from simple substances. The war, stimulated the

Synthetic fibers
合成纤维

synthesis of additional fibers. Gradually a wide variety of synthetic fibers were introduced for public consumption.

直到20世纪20年代和30年代,人们才首次学会如何从简单物质中构建长链分子。战争刺激了更多合成纤维的产生,各种各样的合成纤维逐渐被引入公共消费。

Although each of the synthetic fibers has many individual qualities or characteristics, synthetic fibers as a class possess some common properties. One of the more widely shared characteristics of synthetics is thermoplasticity or sensitivity to heat. Many synthetic fibers are thermoplastic, so that when exposed to heat, they may shrink. To prevent this shrinkage, most synthetic fibers are treated with heat after spinning to "set" them into permanent shape. Not only can fibers be heat-set to make their dimensions permanent but many synthetic fabrics can also be heat-set into pleats, creases, or other permanent shaping.

虽然每种合成纤维都有许多独特的品质或特性,但合成纤维作为一大类,具有一些共同的性质。合成材料的一个更广泛的共同特征是热塑性或对热的敏感性。许多合成纤维是热塑性的,因此当暴露于热(环境)时,它们可能会收缩。为了防止这种收缩,大多数合成纤维在纺丝后都经过热处理,使其"定型"为永久形状。不仅纤维可以热定型,使其尺寸永久不变,许多合成纤维也可以热定型成褶皱、折痕或其他永久形状。

When viewed under the microscope longitudinally, synthetic fibers usually appear as glass rods with either a smooth or striated surface. The fibers appear sufficiently alike that solubility tests are the only means of certain identification. Synthetics tend to be hydrophobic or water resistant, and, therefore, less absorbent than the natural fibers. Lower absorbency may lead to a decrease in comfort when synthetic fibers are worn next to the skin. On the other hand, many synthetics dry quickly after laundering. Low absorbency also creates difficulties in finishing and dyeing. Static electricity buildup is common among synthetics. Fibers that are more absorbent tend to conduct electricity more readily. More conductive fibers build up electric shocks less readily.

当在显微镜下纵向观察时,合成纤维通常表现为具有光滑或条纹表面的玻璃棒状。纤维看起来非常相似,因此溶解度测试是唯一的定性鉴别方法。合成纤维往往具有疏水性或耐水性,因此比天然纤维吸水性低。当合成纤维靠近皮肤时,较低的吸湿性可能导致舒适度降低。另一方面,许多合成纤维在洗涤后会很快干燥。低吸水性也会给整理和染色带来困难。静电积聚在合成材料中很常见。吸水性更强的纤维往往更易导电。更高的导电性不易产生电击感。

Many synthetics are rather smooth and slippery to the touch. Fibers may pill, because their strength prevents the wearing away of the tangled ends. This tendency can be reduced by some of the special texturizing of yarns that is done in manufacturing. It is usually more difficult to remove oil and grease stains from synthetics, as they have an affinity for these substances. Stain removal is made more difficult by low absorbency. Once the stain has penetrated fibers, the fiber's resistance to water and other liquids prevent soil removal during laundering or cleaning as the soil is held inside the fiber while the water is kept out.

许多人造纤维摸起来相当光滑。纤维可能会起球，因为它们的强度可以防止末端缠结的纤维磨耗掉。这种趋势可以通过在生产过程中对纱线进行一些特殊的变形处理来得以减轻。一般来讲，合成纤维材料上的油渍更难去除，因为它们对这些物质有亲和力。由于吸水力低，污渍去除变得更加困难。一旦污渍渗透到纤维中，纤维对水和其他液体的抵抗力会阻碍在洗涤或清洁过程中去除污垢，因为水被阻挡在外面，而污垢被留在纤维内部。

Many of the aforementioned characteristics that present problems to the consumer can be overcome by special finishes or by blending fibers.

许多上述给消费者带来问题的特征可以通过特殊的后整理或纤维混纺来克服。

New Words and Expressions

synthetic fibers 合成纤维	nylon 尼龙
marketing 销售	stimulate 促使，激发
consumption 消费	thermoplasticity 热塑性
sensitivity 灵敏性	expose 暴露
shrink 收缩	permanent 永久的，持久的
pleat 褶裥	crease 褶裥
microscope 显微镜	longitudinally 纵向地
striate 有条纹的	identification 检验，辨认
solubility 可溶性	hydrophobic 疏水性，憎水性
dye 染色	slippery 光滑的
pill 起球	tangle 缠结
texturize 变形处理	stain 玷污
aforementioned 上述的	affinity 亲和性

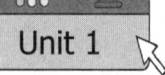 **Polyester 聚酯纤维**

Polyester 聚酯纤维

Polyester is a strong fiber that is resistant to crease and thus keeps it shape. Polyester melts at medium to high temperatures. Polyester remains a versatile and important man-made fabric. Blends of polyester give cotton a permanent press property and extend the wear of these blended garments. It became popular as a textile because of its easy care, its drape and its versatility. In fact, polyester in different forms is used widely in textile application to make polyester (PET) resin and Filament Yarn such as Partially Oriented Yarn (POY), Polyester Drawn Textured Yarn (DTY), Polyester Fully Drawn Yarn (FDY),

Polyester Staple Fiber (PSF), Polyester Spun Yarn (PSY), Technical Yarn, Tire cord and Mono filaments Yarn.

聚酯是一种强力纤维，抗褶皱，从而保持其形状。聚酯在中高温下熔融。聚酯面料仍然是一种用途广泛且重要的人造纤维织物。聚酯混纺面料赋予其中的棉成分以永久压烫性能，并延长了这些混纺服装的穿着寿命。由于其易于打理性、悬垂性和多功能性，它成为一种流行的纺织品。事实上，不同形式的聚酯在纺织应用中被广泛用于制造聚酯（PET）树脂和长丝纱，例如预取向纱（POY）、聚酯拉伸变形纱（DTY）、涤纶全拉伸纱（FDY）、涤纶短纤维（PSF）、涤丝纱（PSY）、工艺纱、轮胎帘线和单纤纱。

The most popular cross-section for polyester is round. The fiber morphology is shown in Fig. 1.11.

聚酯纤维最常见的横截面是圆形。纤维形态如图 1.11 所示。

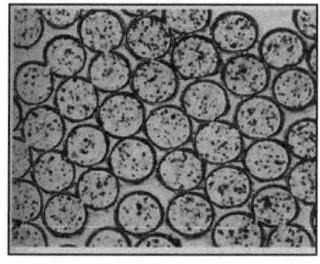 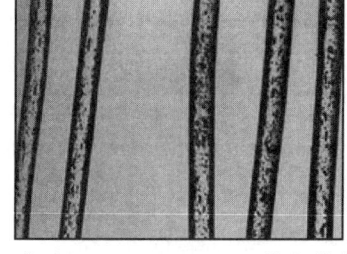

（1）Cross-section 横截面　　（2）Longitudinal view 纵向观察

Fig. 1.11　Observation under microscope 显微镜下观察

Polyester fabrics and fibers are extremely strong.

涤纶织物和纤维异常坚劳。

Polyester is very durable: resistant to most chemicals, stretching and shrinking, wrinkle resistant, mildew and abrasion resistant.

聚酯纤维非常耐用：耐大多数化学品、耐拉伸和收缩、抗皱、防霉和耐磨。

Polyester is hydrophobic in nature and quick drying. It can be used for insulation by manufacturing hollow fibers.

聚酯本质上是疏水性的，并且干燥迅速。可以通过制造中空纤维用于隔热。

Polyester retains its shape and hence is good for making outdoor clothing for harsh climates. It is easily washed and dried.

聚酯纤维保形性好，因此适合制作在恶劣气候下的户外服装。它易于清洗和干燥。

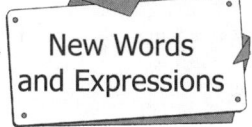

New Words and Expressions

polyester 聚酯，涤纶　　　　　　　　　　crease 起皱
polyester resin 聚酯树脂　　　　　　　　POY 预取向纱

DTY 拉伸变形丝 FDY 全拉伸丝
PSF 涤纶短纤维 PSY 涤纶短纤纱

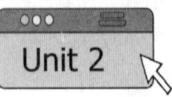 **Nylon 锦纶**

Nylon 锦纶

Nylon is stronger yet weighs less than any other commonly used fibre. It is elastic and resilient and responsive to heat setting. Nylon fibres are smooth, non-absorbent and dry quickly. Dirt doesn't cling to this smooth fibre and it is not weakened by chemicals and perspiration. Extensive washing and drying in an automatic dryer can eventually cause piling. Nylon whites should be washed separately to avoid graying.

锦纶比任何其他常用的纤维都更坚牢，但重量却更轻。它具有弹力和弹性，对热定型做出反应。锦纶纤维光滑，不吸水，干燥迅速。污垢不会附着在光滑的纤维上，纤维也不会因化学物质和汗液而变弱。在自动干燥机中过度洗涤和干燥最终会导致（面料）起球。锦纶的白色织物应单独清洗，以避免变灰。

Nylon melts at high temperatures. If ironing is necessary, always use a low temperature on the wrong side.

锦纶在高温下熔融。如果需要熨烫，请在反面使用低温熨烫。

Nylons are also called polyamides, because of the characteristic amide groups in the backbone chain. The nylon in the Fig. 1.12 is called nylon 6,6, because each repeat unit of the polymer chain has two stretches of carbon atoms, each being six carbon atoms long. Another kind of nylon is nylon 6 (see in Fig. 1.13). It's a lot like nylon 6,6 except that it only has one kind of carbon chain, which is six atoms long. Other nylons can have different numbers of carbon atoms in these stretches.

锦纶也被称为聚酰胺纤维，这是因为主链中具有特殊的酰胺基团。图 1.12 中的尼龙被称为尼龙 6,6，因为聚合物链的每个重复单元有两段碳原子，每段碳原子长六个。另一种尼龙是尼龙 6（见图 1.13）。它很像尼龙 6.6，只是只有一种碳链，有六个原子。其他尼龙在这些长链中可以有不同数量的碳原子。

nylon 6, 6

Fig. 1.12 Nylon 6,6 molecular structure

nylon 6

Fig. 1.13 Nylon 6 molecular structure

Properties of nylon 锦纶的性能

Easy to wash.

易于清洗。

Can be precolored or dyed in wide range of colors.

可预着色或染色多种颜色。
Low in moisture absorbency.
吸湿性低。
Very good physical properties.
物理性能非常好。
Very good heat resistance.
非常好的耐热性。
Excellent chemical resistance.
优异的耐化学性。
Excellent wear resistance.
优异的耐磨性。

New Words and Expressions

nylon 尼龙
polyamide 聚酰胺
melt spun 熔融纺丝
monomer 单体
draw-texturing 拉伸—变形（工艺）
heat resistance 耐热性

perspiration 汗液
backbone chain 主链
aqueous 水的，含水的，多水的
polymerization 聚合
precolored 预染色的，预着色的
chemical resistance 化学稳定性，耐化学药品性

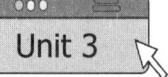 Unit 3　Acrylic 腈纶

Acrylic 腈纶

Acrylic is is a fine soft and luxurious fabric with the bulk and hand of wool. Light weight and springy, this fabric is non-allergenic, dries quickly, draws moisture away from the body and is washable. Acrylic does not take even a moderate amount of heat.

腈纶纤维织物是一种柔软而奢华的织物，具有羊毛的蓬松感和手感。面料重量轻，富有弹性，无过敏性，干燥迅速，能带走身体散发的水分，可水洗。腈纶可保持适度的热量。

In apparel the acrylic fibers are used, for instance, in jumpers, waistcoats, cardigans, jackets, socks, knee-high stockings, training and jogging suits, either pure or in blends for example with wool. The modacrylic fiber, a modified form of acrylic, is found in flame-retardant garments, children's and baby wear, and in dolls clothes and soft toys.

在服装中，腈纶纤维用于连体裤、背心、开衫、夹克、袜子、及膝长袜、训练服和慢跑服，无论是纯纤维还是羊毛混纺。改性聚丙烯腈纤维是一种改性的丙烯腈纤维，存在于阻燃服装、儿童和婴儿服装、玩偶服装和软（毛绒）玩具中。

The draw-rate and process affects the fiber diameter, birefringence, and the cross-sectional shape, from nearly round, to bean shaped, to dog-bone, to slightly crenulate. The typical shape sees in Fig1.14.

牵伸速率和牵伸工艺影响纤维直径、双折射率和横截面形状，从接近圆形到豆形，再到狗骨形，再到稍具细齿。典型形状见图1.14。

Properties of acrylic 腈纶纤维性能

Feels like wool, with high bulk.

手感像羊毛，体积蓬松。

Very good heat retention and fastness to light.

优异的保温性和耐光性。

Very good shape retention, durability, easy care and quick dry qualities.

非常好的形状保持性、耐久性、易护理性和快干性。

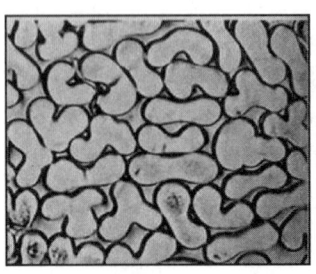 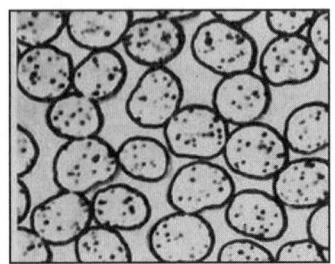

（1）Dry spinning（干纺）　　（2）Wet spinning（湿纺）

Fig. 1.14　Acrylic cross section shape（横截面形状）

New Words and Expressions

acrylic 腈纶，聚丙烯腈系纤维
jumper 工作服，短上衣，无袖套领罩衫
cardigan 羊毛衫，开襟绒线衫
knee-high stocking 中统女袜
modacrylic 改性聚丙烯腈
garment 衣服
spinning chamber 纺丝仓，（纺丝）丝室
birefringence 双折射
dog-bone 狗骨头
crenulate 细圆齿状的，小圆齿状的

springy 有弹力的
waistcoat 西装背心，马甲
sock 短袜
training and jogging suit 运动衣
flame-retardant 阻燃的
spinneret 喷丝头
coagulating bath 凝固浴，纺丝浴
bean shape 豆形的
high bulk 高蓬松
shape retention 形状保持性，定形性

Unit 4　Spandex 氨纶

Spandex 氨纶

As we know, Lycra® is a type of stretch fiber, or spandex, which is a registered trademark of Invista, formerly DuPont. It is the most recognized and popular brand of spandex throughout the world, and many designers and clothing manufacturers use Lycra® in their products.

如我们所知，Lycra®是一种弹性纤维或氨纶，是 Invista（前身为杜邦）的注册商标。它是全世界最受认可和欢迎的氨纶品牌，许多设计师和服装制造商在其产品中使用 Lycra®。

Spandex is a synthetic fibre known for its exceptional elasticity. These fibers are superior to rubber because they are stronger, lighter, and more versatile. In fact, spandex fibers can be stretched to almost 500% of their length.

氨纶是一种合成纤维，以其优异的弹性而闻名。这些纤维弹性优于橡胶，因为它们更坚劳、更轻、更通用。事实上，氨纶纤维可以拉伸到其长度的近 500%。

First produced in the early 1950s, spandex was initially developed as a replacement for rubber. Although the market for spandex remains relatively small compared to other fibers such as cotton or nylon, new applications for spandex are continually being discovered.

氨纶最初生产于 20 世纪 50 年代初，最初是作为橡胶的替代品开发的。尽管与棉或尼龙等其他纤维相比，氨纶的市场仍然相对较小，但氨纶的新应用仍在持续发现中。

New Words and Expressions

Lycra 莱卡，氨纶　　　　　　　　　　spandex 氨纶
registered trademark 注册商标　　　　Invista 英威达公司
Dupont 杜邦公司　　　　　　　　　　elastane 弹性纤维

Unit 5　New Fibers 新纤维

New fibers 新纤维

There are so many new fibers appeared in recent years, in this unit, we will introduce soybean fiber, bamboo fiber and PLA fiber.

近年来出现了许多新纤维，在本单元中，我们将介绍大豆纤维、竹纤维和聚乳酸纤维。

1. Soybean Fiber 大豆纤维

Soybean fiber was invented by Henry ford in 1937.

The main component of soybean fiber is quite similar to those of cashmere and silk, featuring fine denier, low density and good tenacity & elongation. The resulting fabric can give us cashmere-like hand touch, silk-like luster, cotton-like moisture conduction and wool-like

031

warm retentiveness. As long as we pay attention to the option of makeup of blended yarn as well as processing technology, the soybean yarn can have strong competitiveness on its novelty and functions.

1937年，亨利·福特发明了大豆纤维。

大豆纤维的主要成分与羊绒和丝绸非常相似，具有细旦、低密度和良好的韧性和伸长率。这种织物可以给我们带来羊绒般的手感、丝绸般的光泽、棉花般的导湿性和羊毛般的保暖性。只要我们注意混纺纱的组成和加工工艺的选择，大豆纤维纱就可以在其新颖性和功能上具有很强的竞争力。

2. Bamboo Fiber 竹纤维

Bamboo fiber is a cellulose fiber extracted and made from the pulp of natural bamboo plants. It is a synthetic viscose made from the bamboo cellulose. As a quick-growth plant cellulose material, the bamboo does not require irrigation, fertilization, and medicine scattering during its growth, and is resistant to drought and water logging. It can be planted in a dense manner, and regular felling is needed. The material derives the nature and can be reverted to the nature after biological degradation. This completely demonstrates that bamboo is a raw material which is easily acquired, available and environment friendly. So, bamboo gained popularity as a "green" fiber.

竹纤维是一种纤维素纤维，从天然竹子的竹浆提取并制成。这是一种由竹子纤维素制成的再生黏胶纤维。作为一种快速生长的植物纤维素材料，竹子在生长过程中不需要灌溉、施肥和药物喷洒，并且抗干旱和水涝。它可以以密集的方式种植，需要定期砍伐。材料来源于自然，在生物降解后可以恢复自然。这充分证明了竹子是一种容易获取、可利用且环境友好的原材料。因此，竹子作为一种"绿色"纤维而受到欢迎。

The cross-section of the bamboo fiber is filled with various micro-gaps and micro-holes, shown in Fig. 1.15.

竹纤维的横截面填充有各种微间隙和微孔，如图 1.15 所示。

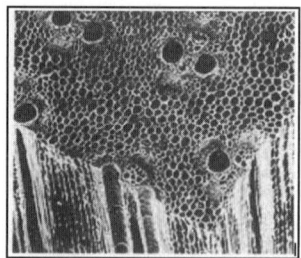

Fig. 1.15 Observation under microscope 显微镜下观察

Apart from the intrinsic characteristics of bamboo including anti-bacteria, anti-ultraviolet, excellent penetrability and coolness, bamboo fiber has also the functions of moisture absorption and desorption, thus it is called breathable fiber. As promising cellulose fiber, it is featured by biological degradation, soft handle, good drapability, easy tintage and beautiful coloration.

竹子纤维除了具有抗菌、抗紫外线、优异的渗透性和凉爽性等内在特性外，还具有吸湿和解吸的功能，因此被称为透气纤维。作为一种有前途的纤维素纤维，它具有生物降解、柔软的手感、良好的悬垂性、易着色和着色艳丽的特点。

3. PLA Fiber 聚乳酸纤维

A manufactured fiber in which the fiber-forming substance is composed of at least 85% by weight of lactic acid ester units derived from naturally occurring sugars.

这是一种人造（聚乳酸）纤维，其中纤维构成物质由至少85%的质量源自天然糖的乳酸酯单体组成。

The fundamental polymer chemistry of PLA allows control of certain fiber properties and makes the fiber suitable for a wide variety of technical textile fiber applications, especially apparel and performance apparel applications such as:

聚乳酸的基本聚合物化学构成允许某些纤维的性能可控性，并使纤维适用于各种技术纺织纤维应用，特别时装和功能性服装应用，例如：

（1）Low moisture absorption and high wicking, offering benefits for sports and performance apparel and products.

低吸湿性和高芯吸性，为运动和高性能服装和产品带来益处。

（2）High resistance to ultra violet (UV) light, a benefit for performance apparel as well as outdoor furniture and furnishings applications.

高抗紫外线（UV），适用于功能性服装以及户外家具和家居应用。

（3）Lower specific gravity, making PLA lighter in weight than other fibers.

较低的比重，使聚乳酸的重量比其他纤维轻。

（4）In addition to coming from an annually renewable resource base PLA fibers are readily melt-spun, offering manufacturing advantages that result in greater consumer choice.

除了来自每年可再生的资源基础外，聚乳酸纤维易于熔融纺丝，提供了加工优势，从而为消费者提供更多选择。

soybean fiber 大豆（蛋白）纤维
water logging 涝，水浸
anti-bacteria 抗菌
tintage 染色
lactic acid 乳酸
ester 酯

denier 旦尼尔
biological degradation 生物体退化
anti-ultraviolet 抗紫外线
PLA fiber 聚乳酸纤维
wicking 芯吸性

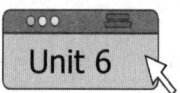

Unit 6 Specialty Fibers 特种纤维

Specialty fibers 特种纤维

Most of specialty fibers have been developed for specific end uses. The descriptive terms specialty and high-performance fibers are used for many of them. High-performance fibers are a growth market for the textile industry.

大多数特种纤维都是为特定的最终用途而开发的。其中许多纤维都使用了专用和高性能纤维这两个描述性术语。高性能纤维占有着纺织行业市场的增长份额。

1. Glass Fiber 玻璃纤维

Although, hard and rigid by nature, glass can very well be made into fine, shiny and translucent fibers which more or less look and feel like silk fibers. These glass fibers are commonly known as fiberglass.

虽然玻璃本质上是坚硬的，但它可以很容易地制成精细、有光泽和半透明的纤维，这些纤维或多或少看起来感觉像丝绸纤维。这些玻璃纤维通常也被称为纤维玻璃。

Glass fiber is a kind of excellent inorganic non-metallic materials. It is usually used as the reinforcing material in compound material, electrical insulation and heat insulation material.

玻璃纤维是一种优良无机非金属材料，常用作复合材料、电绝缘和隔热材料的增强材料。

2. Carbon Fiber 碳纤维

Carbon fibers are an important part of many products, and new applications are being developed every year. The United States, Japan, and Western Europe are the leading producers of carbon fibers.

碳纤维是许多产品的重要组成部分，每年都在开发新的应用领域。美国、日本和西欧是碳纤维的主要生产地。

Carbon fiber is very expensive, but has a fantastic weight-to-strength ratio. The material is employed in high-quality cars, boats, bicycles, and planes, including popular Formula One racecars. Depending on the orientation of the fiber, the carbon fiber composite can be stronger in a certain direction or equally strong in all directions. A small piece can withstand an impact of many tons and still deform minimally. The complex interwoven nature of the fiber makes it very difficult to break.

碳纤维非常昂贵，但重量与强度之比非常高。这种材料用于高质量的汽车、船只、自行车和飞机，包括流行的一级方程式赛车。纤维强度取决于纤维的取向度，碳纤维复合材料可以在某个方向上更强，或者在所有方向上都一样强。一个小零件可以承受许多吨的冲击，并且变形最小。纤维的复杂交织的性质使其很难断裂。

3. Aramid Fiber 芳纶纤维

A manufactured fiber in which the fiber forming substance is a long-chain synthetic polyamide in which at least 85% of the amide (-CO-NH-) linkages are attached directly between two aromatic rings.

一种人造纤维，其中形成纤维的物质是长链合成聚酰胺，其中至少 85%的酰胺（-CO-NH-）键直接连接在两个芳环之间。

The most popular aramid fiber on the world market is Kevlar. Kevlar aramid fibers has an extremely high tenacity, approximately 22 grams per denier, which is more than five times the strength of a steel wire of the same weight and more than twice the strength of high-tenacity industrial nylon, polyester, or fiberglass. It has an unusually high initial modulus of 476 grams per denier. This is about two times greater than fiberglass or steel, four times greater than industrial polyester, and nine times greater than industrial nylon. Moisture regain is about 7 percent. Elongation is low, only about 4 percent.

世界市场上最流行的芳纶纤维是凯夫拉。凯夫拉芳纶纤维具有极高的韧性，约为 22 克/旦，是同等重量钢丝强度的五倍多，是高韧性工业尼龙、聚酯或玻璃纤维强度的两倍多。它具有 476 克/旦尼尔的异常高的初始模量。这大约是玻璃纤维或钢的两倍，工业聚酯的四倍，工业尼龙的九倍。回潮率约为 7%。伸长率很低，只有 4%左右。

Thermal properties of Kevlar are superior. It has outstanding stability to heat, retaining a high percentage of strength after exposure to temperatures to 260 °C.

凯夫拉纤维的热性能优越。它具有优异的热稳定性，在暴露于 260 °C 的温度后保持高百分比的强度。

Kevlar is used in a variety of applications. One of the most interesting and important uses is in body armor or bulletproof vests. Other uses for the fibers include: bracing belts, high-pressure hoses, conveyor belts, rope and cables used as antennae supports, oceanographic cables, crane ropes, boat rigging, helicopter hoist cables, special cables for deep-sea workstations, reinforcement for concrete in various types of constructions, many parts of the space shuttles, space vehicles, body panels for race cars, boats of various types.

凯夫拉有多种应用。最有趣和重要的用途之一是护身铠甲或防弹衣。纤维的其他用途包括：支撑带、高压软管、输送带、用作天线支架的绳索和电缆、海洋电缆、起重机绳索、船索具、直升机升降电缆、深海工作站专用电缆，在各种结构中用于混凝土加固、航天飞机的许多部件、太空飞行器、赛车车身板、各种类型的船。

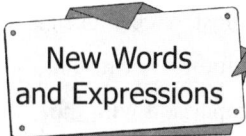

New Words and Expressions

Formula One racecar 一级方程式赛车
aramid fiber 芳纶纤维
initial modulus 初始模量
bulletproof vest 防弹背心
high-pressure hose 高压水带
oceanographic cable 海洋电缆
boat rigging 船缆
space vehicle 宇宙飞船，航天器

interwoven 交织的
aromatic ring 芳香环，芳族环
armor 盔甲，装甲
bracing belt 撑杆带
conveyor belt 传送带
crane rope 起重机吊索
helicopter hoist cable 直升机升降电缆
body panel 车身板件

Chapter 2

Spinning 纺纱篇

- To describe the cotton spinning process.
  描述棉环锭纺工序。
- To describe the woolen & worsted spinning process.
  描述毛粗纺和精纺工序。
- To describe the various new type of spinning process.
  描述各种新型纺纱工序。
- To describe the fancy yarn & textured yarns process.
  描述花式纱和变形纱加工。

Task 1

Cotton Ring Spinning Process 棉环锭纺纱

Ring spinning is a traditional common processing method. It will continue to be the most widely used form of spinning machine in the near future, because it exhibits significant advantages in comparison with the new spinning processes. Most cotton yarn is still processed in ring spinning.

Visit spinning mill
参观纺纱工厂

Cotton ring spinning
棉环锭纺纱

环锭纺纱是一种传统的常用加工方法。在不久的将来，它将继续是最广泛使用的纺纱机形式，因为它与新的纺纱工艺相比具有显著的优势。大多数棉纱仍采用环锭纺纱。

Cotton spinning is essentially a discontinuous process in which the short raw fiber goes through a series of machines that transform it into a continuous strand of yarn. The major production stages of ring spinning are opening, blending, carding, drawing, roving, and spinning, which includes twisting and winding. The spinning process can be summarized in Fig. 2.1.

棉纺本质上是一个不连续的过程，在这个过程中，短的原纤维经过一系列的机器，将其转化为连续的纱线。环锭纺纱的主要生产阶段是开松、混棉、梳棉、并条、粗纱和细纱（包括加捻和卷绕）。纺纱过程可概括为图 2.1。

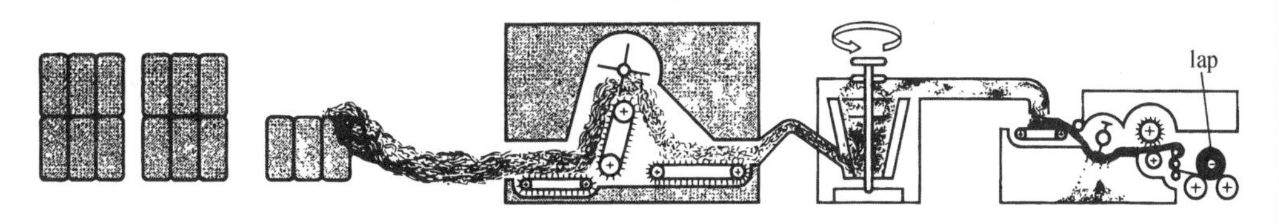

1. Bale lay down, mixing 混棉	2. Bale opening 开包	3. Opening 开棉	4. Scutcher or picker 清花机和成卷机
A spinning lot is composed by laying out a fairly large number of bales, in order to achieve a good mixing of the raw stock. 混棉是由大量的棉包组成的以实现原料的良好混合。	Preliminary opening of the bales. 将棉包初步开松。	Opening up into tufts, cleaning. 开松成束状并清洁。	Further opening and cleaning, transport of material to card of formation of a lap. 进一步开松和清洁，将材料运输至梳棉机形成棉卷。

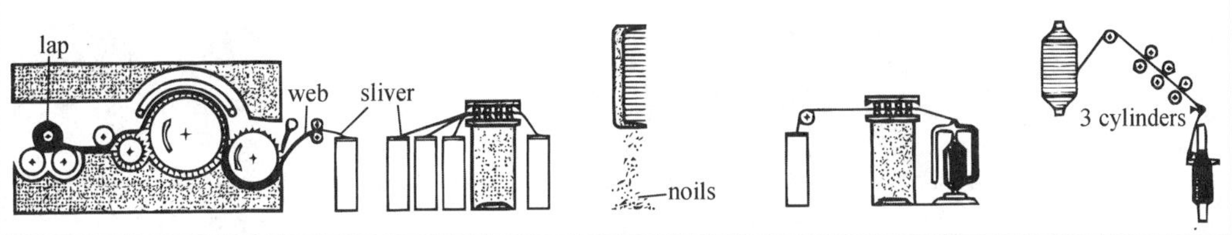

5. Carding 梳棉	6. Drawing 并条	7. Combing 精梳	8. Roving 粗纱	9. Ring spinning 细纱
Individualizing the fibers. Cleaning. Orienting. Sliver formation. 使得纤维束单纤维化，清洁纤维，增加取向度，形成棉条。	Improvement of regularity in 1 to 3 passages. Cross-mixing of slivers blending. 改善1~3阶段的纤维规律性和须条的截面混合性能。	Removal of the short fibers. Only for high quality yarn. 去除短纤维，仅适用于高品质纱线。	Drafting to a roving. Slight twist. 牵伸成粗纱，并具有微小捻度。	Drafting to the required fineness. Twisting. Winding. 牵伸至所需要的细度，加捻和卷绕。

Fig. 2.1 Ring spinning process for cotton yarn 环锭纺棉纱加工

1. Opening, Blending, and Cleaning 开棉、混棉和清棉

Blending (see Fig. 2.2) and opening (see Fig. 2.3), which separates or breaks up bales of fibers, are carried out in enclosed machinery to reduce the dust level in the plant. Fiber from the specified bales is fed into a hopper, where the process of separating the mass of fiber into tufts and removing trash is begun. Because manmade fibers are more uniform and contain less trash than natural fibers, they require less processing. Dirt and impurities that are heavier than the fibers and are not entangled in them are separated

Opening, blending, and cleaning
开、混、清棉

from the fibers by mechanical forces and air. The fibers are now in a loose, fluffy mass that may be conveyed with forced air through a chute directly to a card, or to a picker and then a card. Where pickers are used, the fibers are further opened, blended, and cleaned with a system of rollers, conveyors, and forced air. They are then transported to a collecting cylinder that forms a thin layer, or batt, of fibers. The fiber batt is rolled up, much like a very large roll of absorbent cotton, to form a picker lap. The lap is then transported to the card for further processing.

混棉（见图 2.2）和开棉（见图 2.3），是分离或分解成束的纤维的工序，在封闭的机器中进行，以降低工厂的棉尘水平。来自指定棉包的纤维被送入喂棉箱，在那里开始将大量纤维分离成簇并清除杂质。因为人造纤维比天然纤维更均匀，含有更少的杂质，所以需要更少的加工。比纤维重且未被纤维缠绕的污物和杂质通过机械力和强力空气使之与纤维分离。纤维现在呈松散蓬松的块状，可以用强力空气通过斜槽直接输送到给梳棉机，或先到清棉机上，然后输送到梳棉机。如果使用清棉机，纤维被进一步开松、混合和清洁，并用一系列的辊、输送机和强力空气系统进行清洁。然后将它们输送集棉筒中，在集棉筒形成纤维薄层或棉网。纤维棉絮被卷起，就像一个很大的吸棉卷，形成一个棉卷。然后将该棉卷传送到梳棉机上进行进一步处理。

Fig. 2.2　Blending 混棉

Fig. 2.3　Opening 开棉

2. Carding 梳棉

The fibers from blending and opening are delivered to the card in the form of a picker lap or from a chute-fed hopper. They are randomly arranged and may contain trash and short fibers that are not suitable for further processing. A card consists of a large rotating cylinder covered with wire pins or teeth and a series of flats (interlaced rectangular boards). The flats form an endless belt that rotates above the card cylinder. The cylinder and the flats rotate in the same direction but at different speeds, to tease the fibers into a thin, filmy web. In the process, short fibers and trash are removed and deposited on the flats. The fibers, which remain on the card cylinder, are partially aligned, so their longitudinal axes are somewhat parallel to each other and the length of the card web. The thin web is pulled off the cylinder and gathered into a soft mass, which is pulled through a

Carding 梳棉

cone-shaped condenser, or trumpet, to produce a ropelike strand called a sliver. A cotton card sliver has no twist and only a little strength, provided by the entangling of fibers. The strength is adequate to allow the sliver to be doffed (removed) into a can or placed on a conveyor for transfer to the next processing step, which is drawing or drafting. Carding process is shown as Fig. 2.4.

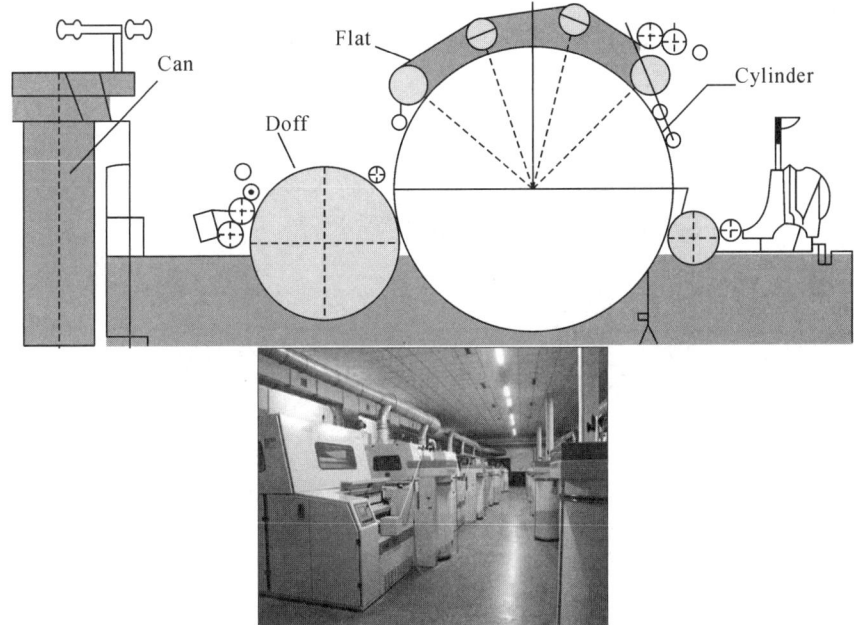

Fig. 2.4　Carding 梳棉

　　混棉和开棉后的纤维以棉卷形式，或者从斜槽喂棉箱送至梳棉机。纤维是随机排列的，可能含有不适合进一步加工的杂质和短纤维。梳棉机由一个大的旋转圆筒（锡林）和一系列平板（由矩形板编织在一起，称为盖板）组成，锡林上覆盖着金属针或金属齿。盖板形成一个环形带，在梳棉机锡林上方旋转。锡林和盖板以相同的方向旋转，但速度不同，以将纤维梳理成薄的薄膜状的网。在这个过程中，短纤维和杂质被清除并沉积在盖板上。留在梳棉机锡林上的纤维部分平齐，因此它们的纵向轴线方向和梳棉网的长度在一定程度上平行。薄纤维网被从锡林上拉出，聚集成一定质量柔软的纤维，然后通过锥形集结器或喇叭形集结器，产生一条绳状的细棉条。棉条没有捻度，只有一点强度，这是由纤维的缠结提供的。强度足以使棉条与梳棉机脱离并掉落到棉条桶中或放置在输送机上，以转移到下一个加工步骤，即拉伸或牵伸。梳理过程如图 2.4 所示。

3. Drawing 并条

　　A drawing frame (see Fig. 2.5) uses a series of rollers, arranged in pairs and rotating at different speeds, to draw out, or draft, sliver. At the first drawing frame, several card slivers (usually eight) are combined to further blend the fibers. The slivers are pulled from the back of the machine through a series of pairs of rollers. The back pair of rollers is rotating at a lower speed than the pair

Drawing 并条

at the front of the frame. Because the sliver is being taken up at a faster speed than it is being delivered, the sliver becomes thinner as it is drawn out, or drafted. Both card sliver, which has been drafted once, and comber sliver must go through finisher drawing to receive further blending and alignment. In some cases, a second finisher drawing occurs. The drafting through a series of rollers is the same in all the processes. For fine-count yarns, a higher draft producing a lighter-weight sliver is possible. After drafting, the fibers are in their most parallel alignment. The strand is not twisted, although some twisting may occur as the sliver is doffed into the sliver can.

Fig. 2.5　Drawing 并条

At this point, ring-spun yarns go through a roving process; other short-staple yarns are spun directly from drawn sliver.

并条机（见图2.5）使用一系列成对排列并以不同速度旋转的罗拉来拉出或牵伸棉条。在第一个并条机上，将几条梳棉条（通常为八条）组合在一起，以进一步混合纤维。棉条通过一系列的罗拉从机器的后部拉出。后一对罗拉的旋转速度低于机架前部的一对罗拉。由于棉条的卷绕速度比输送速度快，所以棉条在拉出或牵伸时会变薄。仅经过一次牵伸的梳棉条和精梳棉条都要经过末道并条，进一步混合和纤维定向排列。在某些情况下，会进行第二次末道并条。通过一系列罗拉的牵伸在所有过程中都是相同的。对于细支数纱线，更高的牵伸产生更轻的棉条是可能的。牵伸后，纤维处于最平行的排列状态。须条并没有捻度，尽管须条（回转状态）在落入棉条中时可能有加捻现象发生。

在这一点上，环锭纺纱经过粗纱过程，其他短纤纱是直接由并条后的棉条牵伸而成。

4. Combing 精梳

Combing 精梳

For high-quality yarns of superior evenness, smoothness, fineness, and strength, fibers are combed as well as carded. A common procedure is to combine 48 slivers from breaker drawing to form a lap for the comber (see Fig. 2.6). The 30-pound laps are moved to the comber, where fine metal wires clean out the remaining short fibers and other impurities. The combed fiber is condensed into a comber sliver.

对于具有优良的均匀度、光洁度、细度和强度的高品质纱线，纤维既要经过梳棉，也要经过精梳。一个常见的程序是将来自末道并条的48根条子组合在一起，形成纤维层供给精梳机（见图2.6），30磅重棉条被移送到精梳机，在那里细金属针可以清除残余的短纤维和其他杂质。精梳纤维被凝结成精梳棉条。

Combing is a key process that makes the difference between an ordinary yarn and a quality yarn. It enables the ultimate yarn to be smoother, finer, stronger, and more uniform than the spinning system.

精梳是一个关键过程，它决定了普通纱线和优质纱线之间的区别。它使最终的纱线比其他纺纱系统的纱更光滑、更细、更结实、更均匀。

Fig. 2.6　Comber 精梳机

Fig. 2.7　Roving frame 粗纱机

5. Roving 粗纱

Sliver cans from finisher drawing are dotted and moved to the roving frame (see Fig. 2.7), where the sliver is drafted to about one-eighth of its original diameter by three pairs of rollers rotating at different speeds. The first set moves at a relatively slow speed, the middle set at an intermediate speed, and the final set a speed about 10 times the speed of the first. This drafts the fibers out, reduces the diameter of the strand, and imparts some additional parallel alignment to the fibers. The new strand, called a roving, is wound onto a bobbin. The winding process produces a small amount of twist, which imparts some added strength to the strand. The bobbins are doffed and transferred to the spinning area.

Roving 粗纱

来自末道并条的棉条被排列组合并移动到粗纱机（见图 2.7），在粗纱机上通过三对以不同速度旋转的罗拉将棉条牵伸到其原始直径的八分之一左右。第一组以相对较慢的速度移动，中间组以中等速度移动，最后一组的速度大约是第一组速度的 10 倍。这会将纤维拉出，减小纤维束的直径，并使纤维获得一些额外的平行排列。新的须条被称为粗纱，缠绕在筒管上。缠绕过程会产生少量的扭曲，这会增加纱的强力。粗纱络筒后，并转移到细纱区。

6. Spinning 细纱

Spinning is the final process in production of single yarn. The roving is drafted to the desired diameter, and the desired amount of twist is added. The method of drafting used in spinning is the same as that used in drawing and roving. The twist is imparted by the movement of the fiber strand around the bobbin and by the speed of rotation of the spindle holding the bobbin. The fiber strand is pulled from the drafting elements; fed through a U-shaped guide called a traveler, which moves freely

Spinning 细纱

041

around the bobbin spindle on a circular track or ring; and wrapped around the bobbin. The process is called ring spinning because the twist in the yarn is produced as the traveler moves around the ring.

Spinning process is shown as Fig. 2.8.

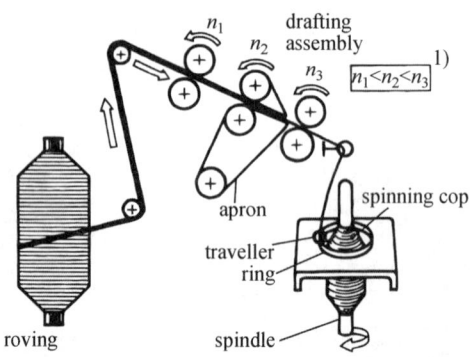

Fig. 2.8 Principle of ring spinning 环锭纺原理

细纱是生产单纱的最后一道工序。粗纱被牵伸至所需的直径，并加捻到所需的捻度。纺纱中使用的牵伸方法与粗纱中使用的牵伸方法相同。通过须条绕筒管的回转运动和支撑筒管的锭子的转速施加捻度。纤维须条从牵伸元件引出；喂入称为钢丝圈的 U 形导引器，钢丝圈（带着须条）在圆形轨道或环（钢领）上绕锭子支撑的筒管自由转动；并卷绕在筒管上。这一过程被称为环锭纺纱，因为纱线中的捻度的产生是由于钢丝圈绕着钢领的回转运动，细纱过程如图 2.8 所示。

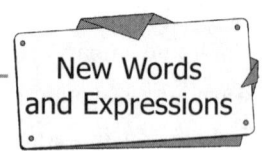

New Words and Expressions

ring spinning 环锭纺
stages 工序
blending 混合
drawing 并条，牵伸
twist 加捻，捻度
bales 棉包
hopper 棉箱
remove 除杂
manmade fiber 人造纤维，化学纤维
natural fiber 天然纤维
cylinder 锡林
batt 纤维层
picker lap 棉卷

strand 须条
opening 开清
card 梳理，梳理机
roving 粗纱
wind 卷绕
dust level 含尘量
tufts 纤维束
trash 杂质
uniform 均匀
picker 清棉机
layer 纤维层
roller 罗拉
chute-fed hopper 喂棉箱

wire pins 金属针布	flat 盖板
tease 撕扯	align 平行排列
sliver 条子	card sliver 生条
can 条筒	drafting 牵伸
drawing frame 并条机	comber sliver 精梳条
fine-count yarns 细支纱	lighter-weight 轻定量
sliver can 条筒	combing 精梳
evenness 均匀度	fineness 细度
condense 凝聚	doff 落纱
roving frame 粗纱机	bobbin 筒管
spindle 锭子	drafting elements 牵伸装置
wrap 卷绕，缠绕	traveler 钢丝圈

Task 2

Woolen & Worsted Spinning Process 毛精纺和粗纺过程

Wool spinning systems are processes that spin wool, and manmade fibers cut to the length of wool, into yarns by either the woolen or the worsted process. Woolen yarns are carded and spun; worsted yarns are carded, combed, drawn, and spun. Wool fibers are sorted and scoured as part of preliminary processing; the other fibers are not.

Woolen & worsted spinning
毛精纺和粗纺

毛纺系统是将羊毛和切断成羊毛长度的人造纤维通过粗纺或精纺工艺纺成纱线的过程。粗纺系统的毛纱线经过梳毛和细纱；精纺系统纱线经过梳毛、针梳、并条和细纱。作为初步加工的一部分，羊毛纤维被分类和洗涤；其他纤维则不是。

1. Sorting and Scouring 分级和洗毛

Each (previously graded) fleece is opened carefully at the mill, and expert graders pull it apart. The fibers are separated according to spinning qualities: fineness, length, and trash. Extremely long, coarse wools are classed as carpet wool. Fairly long fibers are classed as combing wools and are reserved for sheer wool fabrics and worsteds. Fibers shorter than 5 cm (2.5 in.) are used in woolens.

Sorting and scouring
分级和洗毛

每一团（此前分级的）羊毛都在工厂仔细地开松，由专业的评级人员将其分开。纤维根据所需纺纱品质进行分离：细度、长度和杂质。极长的粗羊毛被归为地毯羊毛。相当长的纤维被归类为针梳羊毛，用于剪毛织物和精纺毛织物。短于5厘米（2.5英寸）的纤维用于粗纺。

043

The sorted wool is scoured with water and detergent or with solvent to remove the natural grease or oil and water-soluble impurities from the fiber. The oil that is removed is recovered and sold as lanolin. The fiber is rinsed thoroughly, then dried and sprayed with a lubricant for ease in processing.

用水和清洁剂或溶剂清洗分选后的羊毛，以去除纤维中天然油脂或油以及水溶性杂质。去除的油脂被回收并作为羊毛脂出售。彻底冲洗纤维后干燥，并喷撒平滑油剂，以便加工。

Some wool is carbonized to remove the vegetable matter, such as burrs, twigs, and leaves, trapped in the fleece. The fiber is treated with a dilute sulfuric or hydrochloric acid solution or with salts that become acids when heated. Then the fiber is heated to around 95 °C (200°F) to char the vegetable matter without harming the wool. The wool is then passed through a series of rollers that crush the carbonized material and shake it out of the fiber.

一些羊毛被碳化以去除羊毛中的植物物质，如毛刺、细枝和树叶。纤维用稀硫酸或盐酸溶液或加热后变为酸的盐处理。然后将纤维加热至 95 °C 度（200 华氏度）左右，在不损害羊毛的情况下将植物物质烧焦。然后，羊毛经过一系列的罗拉，这些罗拉将碳化材料粉碎，并将其从纤维中抖出来。

2. Woolen System 粗纺系统

Fibers from several lots are combined and delivered to the wool carding machine. Although the equipment is different, the process is similar to that used for short-staple carding. Wool cards have card cloth with longer wires, and there are usually several carding cylinders operating in tandem. The fibers are pulled onto the card, where the fiber assemblage is opened up and some trash is removed. Short fibers are left in because they are needed to impart some felting qualities to wool fabrics. As the fibers are pulled from the card as roving, or roping, they are somewhat straightened out and made parallel.

Woolen system 粗纺系统

来自多个批次的纤维被合并输送到梳毛机。虽然设备不同，但其工艺与短纤维梳理所用的工艺相似。梳毛机的梳毛针布具有较长的金属针，通常有几个梳毛滚筒串联运行。纤维被送到梳毛机上，在那里纤维集合体被开松，一些杂质被清除，留下短纤维是因为需要它们来赋予羊毛织物一些毡缩的品质。当纤维以粗纱或绳状的形式从梳毛机上引出时，它们呈略微伸直并平行的状态。

The roving (roping) goes directly to the spinning frame, where it is drawn out to the desired diameter, twist is inserted, and the spun yarn is wound onto a spinning bobbin. As with cotton yarns, the yarn is then rewound on packages suitable for knitting or weaving.

粗纱直接进入细纱机，在细纱机中，粗纱被牵伸到所需的直径，并赋予捻度，成纱被卷绕到纱管上。与棉纱一样，纱线随后被重新卷绕成适合针织或机织的卷装（筒子）。

Because no separate drafting operation occurs in woolen yarn processing, the yarns have less fiber orientation than carded short-staple yarns produced on cotton-spinning systems. They are characterized by nonuniformity, bulk, and a rough, hairy surface. Woolen system can be summarized as in Fig. 2.9.

由于粗纺纱线加工过程中不进行单独的牵伸工序，因此与棉纺系统生产的短纤纱线相比，毛纺纱线的纤维取向更低。它们的特点是不均匀，体积大，表面粗糙，毛绒多。羊毛的粗纺系统可概括为图2.9。

Almost any spinnnable fiber can be processed on woolen system. The starting material is usually compressed bales of washed and sorted raw wool, or other fibers. The material is taken from the bales in layers and fed to a carding willow for opening.
几乎任何可纺纤维都可以在羊毛粗纺系统上加工。初始材料通常是经过洗涤和分拣的原羊毛或其他纤维的压缩在一起的集合体。将纤维分层从毛包中抓取出来，并将其送入开松除杂梳理机中进行开松。

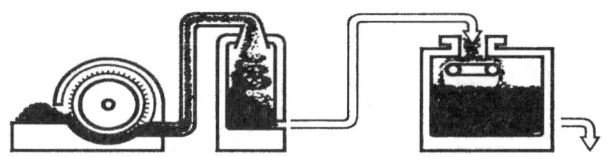

1.Willowing 开松除杂	2. Mixing and Oiling 混合加和毛油剂
Opening and cleaning of the loose stock. 松散毛的开松和除杂。	Mixing of fiber types. Oiling to improve processing characteristics. 不同类型纤维的混合，加和毛油以改善加工特性。

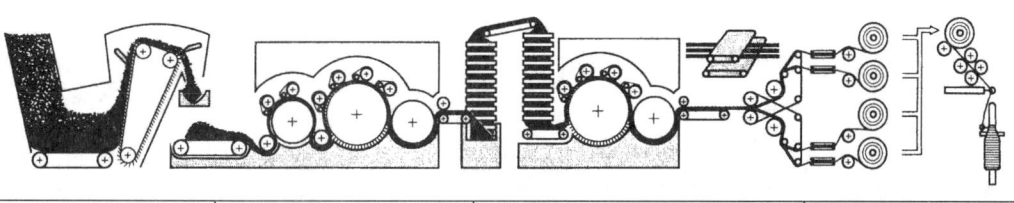

3. Weighing 称重	4. Carding 梳毛	5. Dividing the web and rubbing 分离毛网并反复摩擦	6. Spinning 纺纱
Open up the stock feeding portions of equal weights to the card. 将毛开松后按等比例的重量送入梳毛（针梳）机。	Individualising the fibers. Orientation. Removal of impurities. Formation of web. 将纤维分离成单纤维状，增加取向度，去除杂质，形成毛纤维网。	Dividing the web into ribbons. Rubbing ribbons between reciprocating. Aprons to form slubbing. 将毛网分离成带状，在往复带上摩擦形成毛粒状。	Draft to the required Fineness. Twist. Winding. 牵伸至所需细度。加捻。卷绕。

Woolen yarn have a coarse, hairy, rustic appearance.
粗纺毛纱具有粗糙、多毛和朴素的外观。

Fig. 2.9 Woolen system 毛粗纺系统

3. Worsted System 精纺系统

For worsted yarns the wool fibers are carded just as for woolen yarns. The card sliver is processed through a comber to remove short fibers and any remaining foreign matter and to produce a parallel alignment. The short fibers, which are removed to reduce felting, are called noils. The strand containing the long fibers is referred to as top. Worsted yarns have a relatively smooth,

**Worsted system
精纺系统**

even surface and compact structure. Worsted system can be summarized as in Fig. 2.10.

对于精纺纱线，纱中羊毛纤维和粗纺纱线一样经过梳理。梳毛毛条通过梳毛（针梳）机进行处理，以去除短纤维和任何残留的异物，并形成平行排列。为了减少毡化而去除的短纤维被称为精梳短毛。包含长纤维的被称为毛条。精纺纱具有相对光滑、均匀的表面和紧凑的结构。毛精纺系统可总结为图2.10。

The worsted system is used to produce smooth, uniform yarns from longer types of wool fibers. The raw wool is first prepared at the top-makers which it is washed, combed and formed into sliver.

1. Sorting 分级	2. Opening 开松	3. Washing 洗毛	4. Drying 烘干	5. Willowing 开松除杂	6. Mixing and Oiling 混合加和毛油剂
Sorting the fleece wool according to fiber quality. 根据纤维品质进行羊毛分级。	Separating the stock in tufts and removal of coarse impurities. 将块状纤维分离成束状，并去除粗纤维。	Removal of the dirt and grease with alkaline soap solution. 用碱性肥皂溶液去除污垢和油脂。	Drying with warm air. 用热空气干燥。	Opening up and cleaning the loose stock. 开松并清洁松散的毛纤维。	Mixing the fiber types and colours. Composing a spinning lot. Oiling to improve the processing characteristic. 不同纤维和颜色的毛条。组成一个纺纱批次。加油以改善加工特性。

7. Weighing 恒重送毛	8. Carding 梳毛	9. Drawing 并条	10. Combing 精梳	11. Drawing 并条
Opening up the loose stock. Feeding portions of equal weights to the cards. 将松散的毛纤维进一步开松，按等比例重量送给梳毛机。	Individualising the fibers. Orientation. Removing impurities. 将纤维分离成单纤维，增加取向度，去除杂质。	Doubling and drafting to improve regularity. Mixing the fiber types and colours. 并合和牵伸以提高规则性。混合纤维类型和颜色。	Combing out the short fibers. 通过精梳将短纤维梳理后去除。	Further regularity improvement. 进一步改善纤维规律性。

Spinning 纺纱
The bumped tops from the combing mill are fed into the worsed drawframes.
从精梳机上下来的毛条被送入毛精纺并条机。

12. Drawing 并条	13. Roving 粗纱	14. Spinning 纺纱
Further regularity improvement and mixing of different fibers. 进一步改进规律性和混合不同纤维。	Drafting and twisting into a roving. 就一步牵伸和加捻成为粗纱。	Drafting to required fineness. Twisting. Wingding. 牵伸到所需要的细度，加捻，卷绕。

Worsted yarns are particularly smooth and regular because of the repeated doubling and drafting, and the combing.
精纺纱线特别光滑、规则，因为反复的加倍和牵伸，以及梳理。

Fig. 2.10　Worsted system 毛精纺系统

4. Semi-worsted Spinning 半精纺

The designation semi-worsted means that the worsted process is followed with the exception that there is no combing stage. Instead of combed top, the drawframes are fed with card silver.

半精纺的名称是指除没有梳理阶段外，遵循精纺工艺。梳毛后毛条直接送到并条机，而非精梳毛条。

Semi-worsted spinning 半精纺

Semi-worsted are character between woolen and worsted yarns. Usually they are made from course fibers and are quite hairy but they are also quite regular due to the doubling and drafting.

半精纺是介于粗纺和精纺纱线之间的特征。通常它们是由粗纤维制成的，毛型感强，但由于并条和牵伸，它们也很规则。

New Words and Expressions

worsted 精纺
worsted yarns 精纺毛纱
scour 洗毛，皂洗
grade 分级
coarse wools 粗羊毛
sheer wool fabrics 薄型毛织物
detergent 清洁剂
grease 油脂
recover 贮存起来
rinsed 冲洗
lubricant 润滑剂
burr 草刺
trap 缠绕

woolen yarns 粗纺毛纱
sort 分级，选毛
preliminary 初加工
fleece 羊毛，套毛
fairly long 比较长的
worsteds 精纺毛织物
solvent 助剂
water-soluble 水溶性
lanolin 羊毛脂
spray 喷洒
carbonize 炭化
twig 小树枝
dilute 稀释的，淡的

047

sulfuric acid 硫酸
char 烧焦
crush 压碎
lots 批号
wool cards 梳毛机
in tandem 一前一后
orientation 取向
bulk 膨松
hairy 毛绒
parallel alignment 平行排列
noils 精短毛
willow 开松除杂机

hydrochloric acid 盐酸
harm 损伤
shake 震动，抖动
short-staple carding 梳棉机
card cloth 金属针布
assemblage 集合体
nonuniformity 不均匀
rough 粗糙
foreign matter 杂质
felting 毡缩
top 毛条

Task 3

Rotor Yarn 转杯纺

Rotor spinning is the most successful new type spinning method. In the rotor system, airborne fibers are deposited continuously upon the external or, more usually, the internal peripheral surface of a rapidly rotating drum so as to form a ring of fibers, which is then peeled off & withdrawn along the axis of rotation of the drum. Thus twist is imparted & a yarn is formed (See Fig. 2.11). One of the great advantages of rotor open-end spinning is that twist insertion & yarn take-up are completely separated from each other, which permits the twisting mechanism to operate at very high speeds, while the package need rotate at the slow speed necessary to wind on the yarn produced. And more, rotor spinning has a low cost due to its high production rate and the elimination of processing steps. So, it has a high production capability.

Rotor yarn 转杯纺

转杯纺纱是最成功的新型纺纱方法。在转杯系统中，空气传送的纤维连续沉积在快速旋转的锥形滚筒（转杯）的外表面或更通常的内周表面上，以形成纤维环，然后沿着转杯的旋转轴线将纤维剥离并取出。这样就产生了扭曲，形成了纱线，见图2.11。转杯式开放式纺纱的一大优点是，加捻和卷取完全分离，这使得加捻机构能够以非常高的速度运行，而卷装过程需要以卷绕所生产的纱线所需的低速旋转。此外，转杯纺纱由于其高生产率和减少了加工步骤而具有低成本（优势）。因此，它具有很高的生产能力。

Rotor spinning produces a weaker yarn than ring spinning, has a limited count range, and produces a yarn that is harsher in hand (See Fig. 2.12).

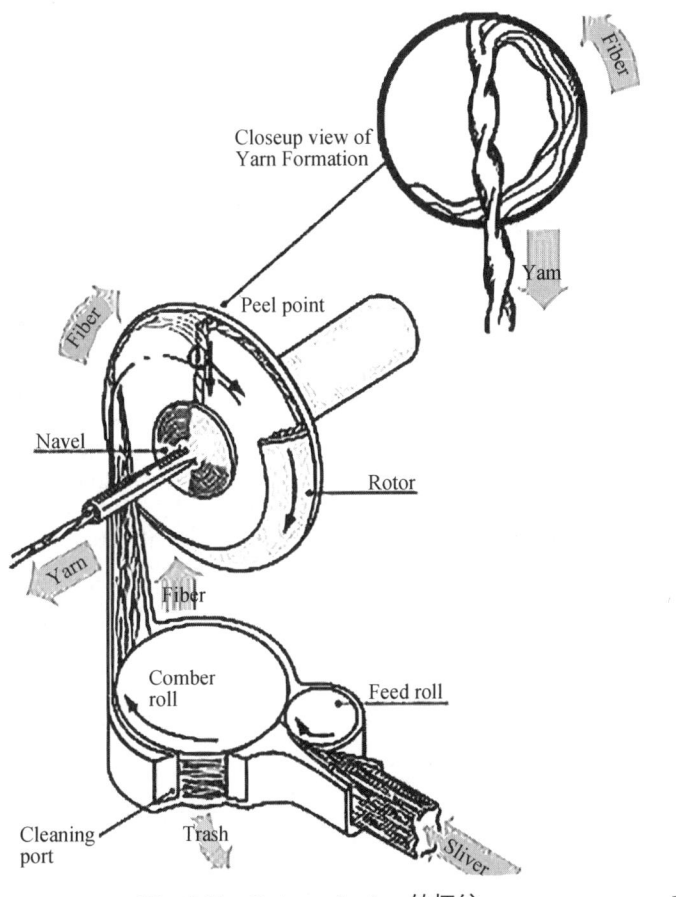
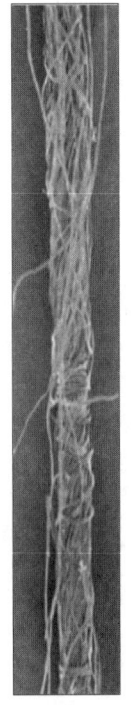

Fig. 2.11 Rotor spinning 转杯纺　　　　**Fig. 2.12 Rotor yarn 转杯纺纱**

转杯纺纱比环锭纺纱生产的纱线更弱，支数范围有限，并且生产的纱线手感更粗糙（见图 2.12）。

（编者注：转杯纺也称气流纺、开放式纺纱，用 OE 纱表示（open end），强力较环锭纺低 20%，条干均匀，手感粗糙，常用作牛仔布用纱。）

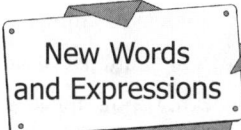

rotor spinning 转杯纺纱，气流纺纱　　rotor yarn 转杯纱，气流纱
airborne 空中传播的　　　　　　　　peripheral 外围的，外部的
rotating drum 转鼓　　　　　　　　　harsher 粗糙的
work of break 断裂功　　　　　　　　open end spun yarn 气流（纺）纱，自由端（纺）纱
elongation 伸长　　　　　　　　　　abrasion resistance 耐磨性
density 密度

049

Task 4

Compact Yarn Spinning 紧密纺

Compact spinning is basically designed to control those protruding fibers (uncontrolled fibers) which have become the part of the yarn but have no role in the yarn formation and ultimately no contribution to yarn strength, but rather an adverse effect on subsequent processes. Drafting element is shown as in Fig. 2.13.

Compact yarn spinning
紧密纺

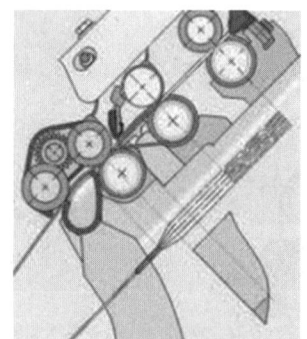

Fig. 2.13　Drafting element 牵伸单元

紧密纺纱基本上是为了控制那些突出的纤维（未控制的纤维），这些纤维已经成为纱线的一部分，但在纱线形成中没有作用，最终对纱线强度没有贡献，而是对后续工艺产生不利影响。紧密纺牵伸单元如图 2.13。

After passing through the normal drafting system, the fibers are entered in to the condensing zone, which is equipped by the suction system. In this zone, maximum free & protruding fibers becomes parallel & condensed. Immediately after this condensing zone, this fibrous bundle is twisted in normal & conventional style. The compact spinning triangle and yarn structure compared to conventional ring spinning, see in Fig. 2.14.

在通过正常的牵伸系统后，纤维进入由抽吸系统配备的凝结区。在这个区域，最大自由和突出的纤维变得平行和浓结。在这个凝结区之后，这个纤维束立即以正常和传统的方式扭曲。与传统环锭纺纱相比，紧密纺纱三角形和纱线结构见图 2.14。

The yarn achieved in this way has better & uniform yarn formation, and better strength & elongation. The advantages of compact yarn as compared with conventional ring yarn are:

以这种纺纱方式获得的纱线具有更好和更均匀的成纱性，以及更好的强度和伸长率。与传统环锭纱相比，紧密型纱的优势在于：

1. Increased Yarn Strength & Elongation 增加纱的强力和伸长

Due to better-controlled & uniform fibers in yarn the strength & elongation of yarn is increased by 20% than that of conventional ring spinning even on low twist.

由于纱线中纤维被更好地控制和更均匀，即使在低捻度下，纱线的强度和伸长率也比传统环锭纺纱提高了 20%。

2. Reduction in Yarn Hairiness 减少纱的毛羽

As the yarn enters in to front roller nip after the condensing zone for twist insertion, due to the better spinning triangle, the ends down rate is reduced significantly which ultimately reduces fluff in spinning dept & vice versa.

当纱线在凝结区后进入前罗拉进行加捻时，由于更好的纺纱三角形，末端向下的速率显著降低，这最终减少了纺纱中的绒毛，反之亦然。

As maximum number of fibers become parallel & uniform after passing through to condensing zone the hairiness value is reduced about 20% to 25% than that of normal spinning.

因最大数量纤维在通过凝结区后变得平行和均匀，毛羽值比正常纺纱降低 20%~25%。

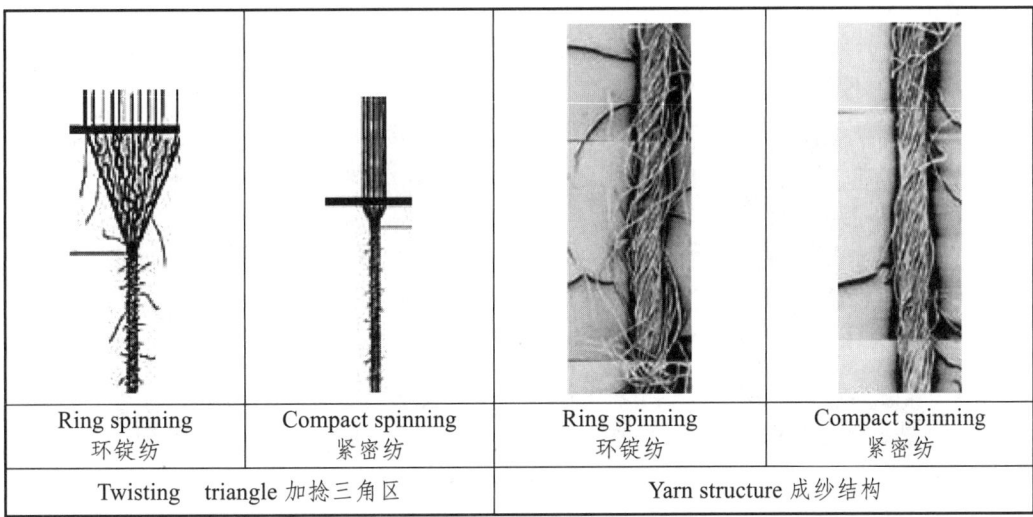

Fig. 2.14 Spinning triangle and yarn structure 纺纱三角区和成纱结构

New Words and Expressions

compact yarn 紧密纺纱线
protrude 突出，伸出
condensing zone 集聚区
condense 集聚，浓缩
nip 钳口，夹持点
hairiness value 毛羽值

compact spinning 紧密纺，集聚纺
drafting system 牵伸系统
suction system 吸入系统，吸风系统
roller 罗拉
fluff 绒毛，起毛

Task 5

Fancy Yarn 花式纱

Fancy yarn
花式纱

The basic yarns that appear very regular and uniform are known as simple yarns. A variety of other yarns that are not so regular or uniform are more complex and are referred to as fancy, novelty or complex yarns. Fancy yarns may use any number of three basic components: the base yarn, effect yarn, and binder. The base yarn provides the support for the yarn structure; the effect yarn creates the decorative appearance of the yarn; and the binder yarn helps to secure the effect yarn, providing additional support and maintaining the desired appearance. The fancy yarn structure sees in Fig. 2.15.

看起来非常规则和均匀的基本纱线被称为简单纱线。各种不那么规则或均匀的其他纱线更为复杂，被称为花式纱线、新颖纱线或复杂纱线。花式纱线可以使用任意数量的三种基本成分：基础纱线、装饰纱线和束缚纱。基础纱线为纱线结构提供支撑；装饰纱线创造了纱线的装饰外观；束缚纱线有助于固定效果纱线，提供额外的支撑并保持所需的外观。花式纱线结构见图 2.15。

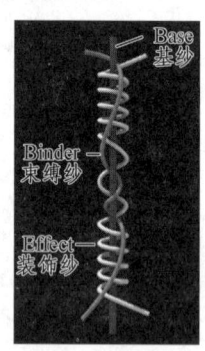 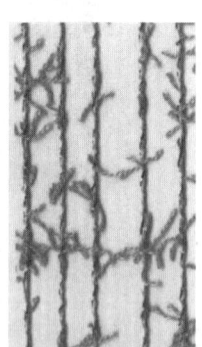 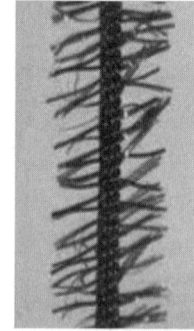 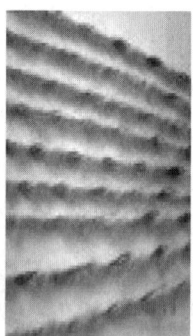

Fig. 2.15　Fancy yarn components

Fancy yarns can be produced in many ways. Different colored fibers can be blended together then spun as one yarn. Color can be applied by printing or dyeing pattern onto roving or yarn. Spots of colored fiber can be twisted in with the base yarn. Two or more threads of different, softness, thickness, weight, color or fiber content can be twisted together. Raised textures can be introduced by controlling the amount and direction of twist.

花式纱线可以通过多种方式生产。不同颜色的纤维可以混合在一起，然后纺成一根纱线。可以通过在粗纱或纱线上印花或染色的图案来应用颜色。有色斑点纤维可以与底纱一起捻入。柔软度、厚度、重量、颜色或纤维不同的两根或多根纱线能够被捻合在一起。可以通过控制扭曲的数量和方向来引入凸起的纹理。

Fancy yarns can be natural or man-made or a combination of both. By manipulating various components, yarns take on different appearances, creating a number of different types of fancy yarns. Some of the more common fancy yarns (see Fig. 2.16) are as follows:

花式纱线可以是天然的或人造的，也可以是两者的结合。通过操纵不同的部件，纱线呈现出不同的外观，形成了许多不同类型的花式纱线。一些更常见的花式纱线如图 2.16。

	Boucle yarn（毛圈纱） Boucle or looped yarns are created by loosely looping an effect yarn around a base yarn. 束线或成环纱线是通过将装饰纱线松散地绕在基础纱线上而形成的。
	Nub yarn（结子纱） A nub or knot is created by tightly twisting an effect fiber around the base fiber. The nub is most easily identified when the effect and base yarns are of different colors. 通过将装饰纤维紧紧地缠绕在基础纤维上，形成一个结节或结。当效果纱和底纱的颜色不同时，最容易识别结子。
	Slub yarn（竹节纱） A slub or thick spot in a yarn is created by varying the tightness of the twist of the yarn at various intervals. 通过以不同的间隔改变纱线的捻度，可以在纱线中产生粗节或增厚点。
	Corkscrew yarn（螺旋纱） The appearance of corkscrew or spiral yarns is achieved by using yarns of two different fibers and often twisting one under a different tension than the other. 螺旋状或螺纹形纱线的外观是通过使用两种不同纤维的纱线来实现的，并且通常在不同的张力下将其中一种纱线加捻。
	Chenille yarn（雪尼尔纱） The soft, fuzzy surface of chenille yarns can be created in several ways. Most commonly, a fabric is first produced and then cut into narrow strips resembling a yarn. Then, when the fabric is cut, the raw edges become very fuzzy and produce the chenille appearance. 雪尼尔纱线柔软、有绒毛的表面可以通过多种方式形成。最常见的是，首先生产一种织物，然后将其切成类似纱线的窄条。然后，当织物被切割时，毛边会变得非常模糊，并产生雪尼尔的外观。
	Metallic yarn（金属纱） Metallic yarns are often classified as fancy yarns but are created by merely adding a metallic fiber or yarn to the blend. 金属纱线通常被归类为花式纱线，但只需在混合物中加入金属纤维或纱线即可制成。
	Crepe yarn（皱纱） Crepe yarns may be classified as fancy yarns but are merely created by tightening the twist given to a yarn, resulting in a kinked or looped yarn. 皱纱可以被归类为花式纱线，但它只是通过收紧纱线的捻度而产生的，从而形成扭结或成圈纱线。

Fig. 2.16　Fancy yarns

New Words and Expressions

fancy yarn 花式纱（线）
effect yarn 花式线（芯纱外）的装饰线
manipulate 操纵，操作
nub yarn 结子花线，竹节纱
corkscrew yarn 螺旋花式纱线
chenille yarn 雪尼尔花线
crepe yarn 绉线

base yarn 基纱，芯线
binder 固线
boucle yarn 结子花式线，毛圈花式线
slub yarn 竹节花式纱线
spiral yarn 螺旋花线
metallic yarn 金属线，金银线

Textured Yarns 变形纱

Flat continuous filament yarns made from thermoplastic materials can be made permanently bulky by various process. This is called texturing and it results in:

- increased volume
- better thermal insulation due to the enclose air
- increased extensibility and elasticity
- high vapor permeability and moisture transport
- low luster
- soft and more comfortable fabric

Textured yarns
变形纱

Various types of textured yarns is shown in figure 2.17.

由热塑性材料制成的扁平连续长丝纱线可以通过各种工艺制成永久性的蓬松纤维。这被称为变形纱，其结果是：

- 增加了体积；
- 由于纤维内封闭的空气，隔热效果更好；
- 增加了延展性和弹性；
- 高水汽渗透性和湿气传输力；
- 低光泽（光泽柔和）；
- 面料柔软舒适。

变形纱的不同类型见图 2.17。

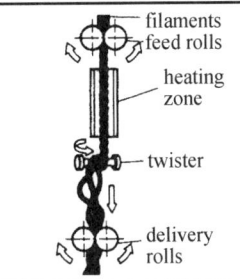	**False-twist texturing** 假捻法 The yarn is drawn through a heated zone whilst a predetermined, high lever of false twist is inserted followed by cooling and untwisting. The heat softens the filaments and deformation imparted by the twist is permanently set during cooling. This is the most economical, and therefore the most common process. 纱线被拉伸通过加热区，同时加入预定的高水平假捻，然后冷却和解捻。热量使长丝软化，再冷却。 这是最经济的，因此也是最常见的过程。
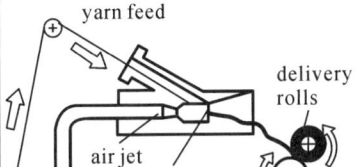	**Air jet texturized** 空气喷射法 Air jet texturized filaments are fed into a chamber at high speed and compressed air is blown through them. The filaments in the yarn are thereby forced to spread apart and form random loops, and the yarn is finally removed from the chamber more slowly. The finished yarn has bulk and stretch. 空气喷射变形丝被高速送入压缩空气室中。因此，纱线中的长丝被迫散开并形成随机的环，纱线最终以更慢的速度从腔室中移出。成品纱线具有蓬松度和伸缩性。
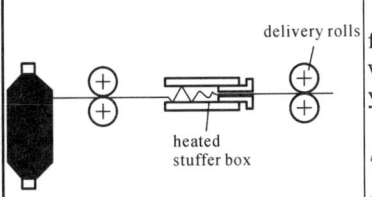	**Stuffer box texturizing** 填塞箱法 Filaments are fed into a box faster than the filament is removed from the box. While in the box, the filament is forced into a random wavy crimped pattern and heat set so it stays that way. The finished yarn has more bulk and texture. 长丝被送入加热的填塞箱内的速度比长丝从箱中取出的速度快。当在加热定型箱里时，长丝被强制形成随机的波浪形卷曲状，并加热定型，使其保持这种状态。成品纱线具有更大的体积和变化的质地。
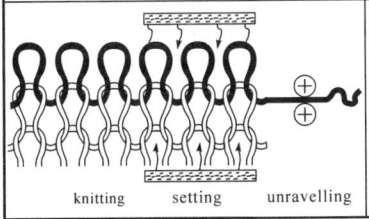	**Knit-de-knit texturing** 假编变形法 The yarn is knitted into a tube on circular knitting machine. The kintted fabric is heat set and then unravelled. The shape of the kintted loops is set into the yarn, which develops a boucle appearance. 纱线在圆形针织机上被编织成一根管状物。织物经过热定型，然后散开。毛圈的形状被设定在纱线中，从而形成束状外观。

Fig. 2.17 Texture yarns 变形纱

thermal insulation 隔热性
vapor 蒸汽
false twist texturized 假捻法变形
stuffer box texturizing 填塞箱法变形
unravell 拆散
deformation 变形

untwisting 退捻，解捻
permeability 渗透性
air jet texturized 喷气变形
knit-de-knit texturized 假编变形
boucle 毛圈
heat set 热定型

Chapter 3

Weaving 机织篇

- To describe the elements of woven fabric constitution.
  描述织物结构要素。
- To describe the woven fabric specification.
  描述机织物规格。
- To describe the preparation for weaving.
  描述织造准备工序。
- To describe weaving process.
  描述织造工序。

Task 1

To Describe the Elements of Woven Fabric Constitution
描述机织物结构要素

We shall deal here exclusively with the technology producing orthogonal fabrics by interlacing together two elements: warp and weft (see Fig. 3.1).

Elements of woven fabric
织物要素

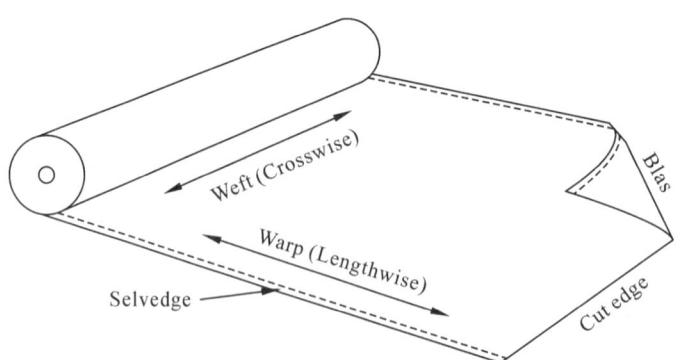

Fig. 3.1 Fabric elements 面料要素

Woven fabric consists of yarns interlaced at right angles in an established sequence, or pattern. The yarns parallel to the lengthwise direction of a woven fabric are called warp yarns or ends; those that run perpendicular to warp, across the fabric, are called weft yarns, filling yarns, or picks (see Table 3.1).

机织物由按既定顺序或图案以直角交织的纱线组成。平行于织物长度方向的纱线称为经纱；垂直于经纱穿过织物的纱线被称为纬纱（见表 3.1）（weft yarn 指已经形成织物中的纬纱统称，如 weft density 纬密；filling yarns 指织造过程的纬纱，一般用 filling 即可，如 filling cone 纬纱筒子；pick 一般指引纬运动或纬纱根数，例如 picking 引纬，weft density= 22picks/cm——编者注）。

In addition, selvedge (selvage) is the narrow reinforced edge of the fabric, it runs lengthwise and is usually made of stronger yarns in a tighter weave. The selvedge stabilises the fabric during weaving so that the cloth maintains its rectangular shape.

此外，织边（selvage）是织物的狭窄加固边缘，它纵向延伸，通常由更结实的纱线交织而成。织边使织物在织造过程中保持稳定，使织物保持矩形形状。

Table 3.1 Woven fabric constitution 机织物结构

Warp 经纱		The set of threads running lengthwise or parallel to the selvedge. 与边纱纵向平行排列的一组线。
Weft 纬纱		The set of threads that run from selvedge to selvedge, perpendicular to the warp threads. 从一个布边到另一布边的一组线，垂直于经线。
Woven 机织		Fabric or textile created by interlacing two sets of yarns on a loom. 在织机上将两组纱线交织而成的织物或纺织品。
Selvage (selvedge) 布边		The selvage is the lengthwise edge of a fabric. It is usually about 1/4 to 1/2 inch wide and exists on both sides of the cloth. 布边是织物的纵向边缘。它通常大约有 0.25~0.5 英寸宽，并且存在于布的两侧。 It is actually a self-edge, but the term selvage is now used. 它实际上是一种自我边缘，但现在使用了"布边"一词。 The main purpose of this area is to insure that the edge of the fabric will not tear when the cloth is undergoing the stresses and strains of the finishing process. 该区域的主要目的是确保织物的边缘在织物经受整理过程中的应力和应变时不会撕裂。 Various techniques are used to make the selvage area stronger than the body, including: 使用各种工艺使布边区域比布身更坚牢，包括： 1. Heavier warp yarns; 比较粗的经纱； 2. More warp yarns per inch; 每英寸更多的经纱根数； 3. Use of different weave. 使用不同的组织。 Since the selvage is usually constructed differently than the body, it is usually easy to identify. 由于布边的构造通常与布身不同，因此通常很容易识别。

New Words and Expressions

fabric 织物
lengthwise 纵向的
firmness 坚固
warp yarn，end 经纱
firmness 坚固
arrangement 排列
braid 编织物
selvedge 布边
orthogonal 正交的；直角的
stress 张力

interlace 交错，交织
perpendicular 垂直的
selvage 布边
weft yarn, filling yarn, pick 纬纱
rigidity 刚性，韧性
knit 针织物
lace 蕾丝，网眼编织物
loom 织机
exclusively 唯一地；专有地；排外地
strain 应力

 Task 2

To Describe the Woven Fabric Specification
描述机织物规格

Fabric specification see table 3.2.

Table 3.2 Fabric specification 面料规格

S/N	DESCRIPTION		CORRESPONDANT VALUE
1	Article name	品名	Bed sheet 床单
2	Grey width in cm	坯布幅宽	182
3	Finished width in cm	成品幅宽	170
4	Material	材料	Cotton 100%
5	Warp count in Ne	经纱英制支数/Ne	34
6	Weft count in Ne	纬纱英制支数/Ne	34
7	Warp density/ends/cm	经密/（根/cm）	28
8	Weft density/picks/cm	纬密/（根/cm）	21
9	Warp crimp/%	经纱织缩率/%	8.4
10	Weft crimp/%	纬纱织缩率/%	4.28
11	Number of ground ends	地经根数	5056
12	Number of selvage ends	边经根数	40×2
13	Number of total ends	总经根数	5136

续表

S/N	DESCRIPTION		CORRESPONDANT VALUE
14	Warp yarn consumption/(gm/mt)	经用纱量/（g/m）	167.673
15	Weft yarn consumption/(gm/mt)	纬用纱量/（g/m）	120.112 (Including waste allowance)
16	Total yarn consumption/(gm/mt)	总用纱量/（g/m）	287.785 (Including waste allowance)
17	Fabric weight/(gm/m^2)	织物重量/（gm/m^2）	154.27
18	Ends/dent for ground	地经每筘穿入数	2
19	Ends/dent for selvage	边经每筘穿入数	4
20	Reed count/(dents/cm)	筘号/（齿/cm）	13.4
21	Reed width for draw in/cm	穿筘幅/cm	190.14
22	Weave construction	织物组织结构	Plain 平纹
23	Type of the loom	织机类型	Rapier loom 剑杆织机
24	Treatment in finishing	后整理	Printing 印花

New Words and Expressions

article 品种　　　　　　　　　　specification 规格
grey width 坯布幅宽　　　　　　warp yarn consumption 经纱用纱量
finished width 整理后幅宽　　　ends/dent 每筘穿入数
count 英制支数　　　　　　　　reed count 筘号
density（织物）密度　　　　　　draw in 穿经
type of the loom 织机类型　　　rapier loom 剑杆织机
treatment in finishing 后整理方式　printing 印花

Task 3

Introduce Weaving Preparation in Brief
织造准备介绍

The yarn is wound on various types of packages (see Fig. 3.2), which generally depend on the technology of the spinning process from which the yarn originates.

Visit preparation mill
参观准备车间

Weaving preparation
织造准备

纱线绕在各种类型的包装上（见图3.2），这通常取决于纱线来源的纺纱工艺技术。

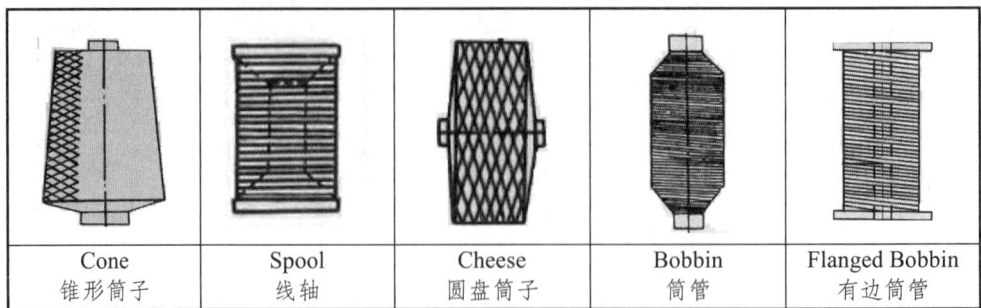

Fig. 3.2 Yarn package

It is obvious that weaving the yarns from the spinning frames have to go through the following main preparation processes:

很明显，从细纱机生产的机织用纱必须经过以下主要准备过程。

（编者注：因为细纱机的纱管卷装容量小，纱疵多，因而不适合下道织造工序对经、纬用纱大卷装，高质量需求，需要增大卷装容量，同时清除纱疵。）

1. Winding 络筒

This is to wind the yarns from the spinning frames to another form of package more suitable for the next process. Warp yarns are wound on cones for warper creels while weft yarns are wound on pirns which fit into shuttles.

将从细纱机来的细纱卷绕到另一种更适合下一道工序的卷装形式上。经纱卷绕成锥形筒子供整经机筒子架使用，而纬纱卷绕纡子上，适合装入梭子（针对有梭织机——编者注）。

（编者注：络筒目的是增大卷装长度，清除纱疵，用于后道整经或无梭织机纬纱大卷装。）

2. Warping 整经

This is the process by which a fixed number of cones of yarns in a warper creel are wound to beam.

这是将整经机筒子架上的固定数量的锥形筒子纱（退绕后）卷绕成经轴的过程。

（编者注：例如整经机筒子架上有640个筒子，则经过片状经纱退绕，将卷绕成总根数为640根的整经轴或一个经轴上的一个条带，再根据织物总经根数确定并轴数或条带数。）

3. Slashing 浆纱

This is to strengthen the warp yarns by coating them with size, so that they may not break during weaving.

这是通过在经纱上被覆浆液来增强经纱的强度，这样经纱在织造过程中不会断裂。

（编者注：浆纱工程中，除了浆液在纱线中被覆，还有浆液向纱线内部浸透的过程。）

4. Drawing-in 穿经

This is to draw-in the warp ends after slashing through the heddle eyes on the harness frames and then through the reed-splits. Whether the weave from design paper will be produced in the woven fabric depends upon this process.

这是将上浆后的经纱的头端穿入综框上的综丝眼，然后再穿过筘齿的过程。意匠纸上设计的组织是否能生产成机织物取决于这个过程。

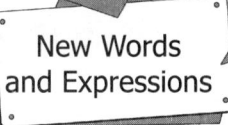

New Words and Expressions

winding 络筒
warping 整经
slashing 浆纱，也做 sizing
spun yarn 短纤纱
simultaneously 同时地
shuttle looms 有梭织机
shuttleless looms 无梭织机
quill, pirn 纡管，纬纱管
cone 圆锥筒子
cheese 筒子纱，扁圆柱筒子
weft knitting 纬编
creel 筒子架
size 浆料，上浆
heddle eye 综眼

reed-splits 筘隙
consist of 组成，构成
optimum 最佳
flanged bobbins 有边筒子
beam 经轴
warp knitting 经编
warper 整经机
draw-in 穿综筘
harness 综丝
design paper 意匠纸
at right angle 成直角
to coat with…被覆以
to fit into…装入……；适合于
go through 经过；经受

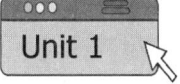 **Winding 络筒**

This first step in yarn preparation for both weaving and knitting is winding. The reasons for winding yarns are: to produce a package that is suitable for further processing, and to inspect and clear the yarns (remove thick and thin spot).

To perform the above tasks a winder is divided into three principal zones: the unwinding zone, the tension and clearing zone, and the winding zone.

As shown in Fig. 3.3.

Winding 络筒

机织和针织的纱线制备的第一步是络筒。纱线络筒的原因是：生产适合进一步加工的卷装，以及检查和清纱（去除粗节和细节）。

为了执行上述任务，络筒机被分为三个主要区域：退绕区，张力和清纱区以及卷绕区。如图 3.3 所示。

To rewind the yarns on a new package, it must first be removed the old package. This is accomplished in the unwinding zone. In the over-end withdrawal method, the packages needed not be rotated as the yarn is pulled over the end of the package. This method is the simplest and must common method of yarn withdrawal.

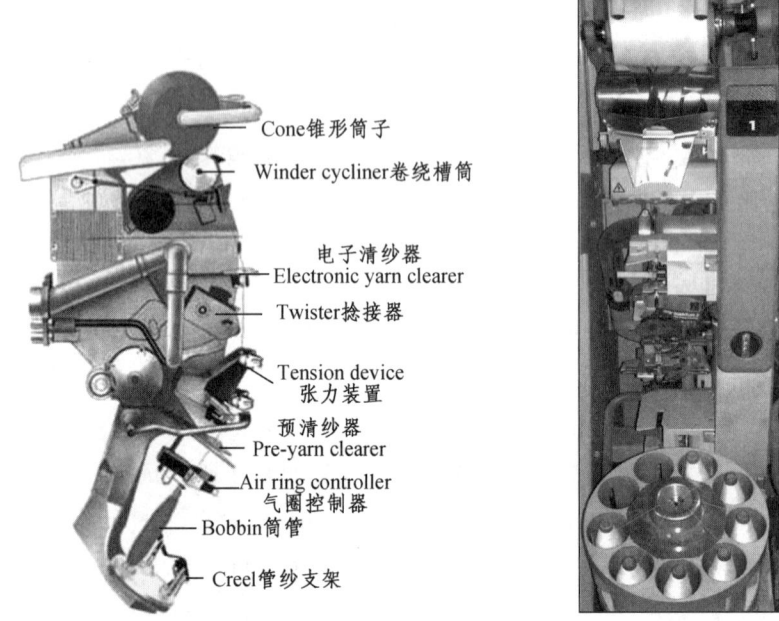

Fig. 3.3 Automatic winder 自动络筒机

要将纱线重新卷绕成新（大容量——编者注）卷装，必须首先将旧卷装（上的纱）退绕。这是在退绕区完成的。在末端退绕法（轴向）中，当纱线被拉过包装末端时，纱管卷装不需要旋转。这种方法是最简单也是最常见的退纱方法。

The next zone is the tension and clearing zone. It is in this zone that the yarn receives the proper tension to provide an acceptable package density and build for further processing. This zone consists of a tension device, a device to detect thick spots, or slubs in the yarn and a stop motion that causes the winding to stop in the case of yarn break or the depletion of a supply package. The yarn is directed into this zone by a guide.

The yarn is now ready to put on a suitable package in the winding zone. This package may be one of many types, a cone, a tube, a dye tube or a spool, depending upon the next operation the yarn must encounter. It is important that, during winding, no twist change take place.

下一个区域是张力和清纱区域。正是在这个区域中，纱线受到适当的张力，以提供可接受的卷绕密度和结构，以便进一步加工。该区域由一个张力装置、一个（清纱）装置，检验纱中的粗节或棉结，以及一个制动停止装置，使得当纱线断裂或纱线供给耗尽的情况下使卷绕运动停止。纱由一个导纱器引导进入此区。

纱线现在已经准备好在卷绕区放置在合适的卷装位置上。这种卷装可以是多种类型中的一种，锥形、管状、染色纱管或纱轴，这取决于纱线必须遇到的下一工序操作（环节）。重要的是，在络筒过程中，捻度不会有变化。

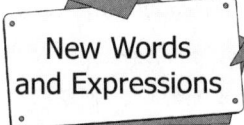

thick spot 粗节
unwinding zone 退绕区
side withdrawal 侧向退绕
tension device（纱线）张力装置
thick spot 粗节
cone 锥形筒子
electronic yarn clear 电子清纱器
tension device 张力装置
air ring controller 气圈控制器

thin spot 细节
winding zone 卷绕区
over-end withdrawal 轴向退绕
depletion 用完
slub 粗节
winding cylinder 卷绕槽筒
twister 捻接器
pre-yarn clearer 预清纱器
creel（管纱）支架

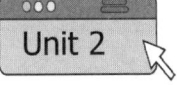 Warping 整经

Warping is aimed at preparing the weaver's beam to be set up on the weaving machine (using sectional warping) or warping beam for warp sizing or slashing process (using beam warping).

Warping 整经

Warping carries out following operations:

- Out of a limited number of creel load of warp thread, to create a warp sheet composed of any number of threads with the desired length;
- Arrangement of above-mentioned threads according to the desired sequence;
- Manufacturing of a warp beam with said characteristics.

整经的目的是准备在织机上所用的织轴（分条整经的情况）或者经轴用于经纱上浆（采用分批整经）。

整经过程执行如下操作环节：

- 在整经机有限的筒子架容量中，形成由任意根数和具有所需长度的线组成的经线片；
- 根据所需的次序排列上述经纱；
- 制备具有上述特性的经轴。

If the creeling capacity is equal or higher than the number of warp threads, the warping would simply entail the direct winding on the warp beam of the threads coming from the creel. Generally this condition does not take place and, even with creels of high capacity, the number of creeling positions never corresponds to the number of threads, which is always by far higher than the number of bobbins which the creel can contain. This problem has been solved by dividing the warping operation into two phases:

如果筒子架容量等于或高于经线的数量，则整经将简单地需要将来自筒子架的线直接卷绕在经轴上。通常情况下，这种情况不会发生，即使是高容量的筒子架，筒子架的数量也永远不会与（所需）纱线数量相对应，而纱线数量总是远远高于筒子架所能容纳的筒子数量。通过将整经操作分为两个阶段来解决此问题：

- 1st phase: Unwinding of the threads from the bobbins and their winding on intermediate carriers, till attainment of the required total number of warp threads;
- 2nd phase: Simultaneous rewinding of all these threads and subsequent winding on the weaver's beam (sectional warping system) or warping beam (beam warping system); the contemporaneity of these two operations is the prerequisite to produce a beam where all threads show same tension and length.

Depending on the kind of intermediate carrier used, the industrial warping process can be carried out according to two different technologies:

- Sectional warping
- Beam warping

第一阶段：将纱从筒管上退绕下来，并在中间载体上卷绕，直到达到所需的总经根数；

第二阶段：同时复卷所有这些纱线，并随后依次卷绕在织轴上（分条整经系统）或卷绕成经轴（分批整经系统）；这两阶段的操作是生产所有纱线都具有张力和长度相同的经轴的先决条件。

根据所使用的中间载体的类型，工业整经工序可以根据两种不同的技术进行：

- 分条整经和分批整经

（编者注：分条整经方法——筒子从分条整经机的子上退绕下来，形成一个条带，暂时卷绕在大滚筒这个中间体上，之后各条带再从大滚筒集体退绕下来，卷绕在织轴上。）

The creel (see Fig. 3.4) of warping machine is a essential part for both of sectional warping and beam warping system.

The threads are fed from bobbins placed on creels. The creels are simply metallic frames on which the feeding bobbins are fitted, they are equipped with yarn tensioning devices, which in modern machines are provided with automatic control and centralized tension variation. Moreover the creels are equipped with yarn breakage monitoring systems.

整经机的筒子架（见图 3.4）是分条整经和分批整经系统的重要组成部分。

纱线是由放置在筒子架上的筒管（筒子）喂入的。筒子架是简单的金属框架，其上安装有喂纱筒管，它们配备有纱线张力装置，在现代机械中，这些装置具有自动控制和集中张力变化功能。此外，筒子架还配备有纱线断裂监测系统。

Fig. 3.4　Creel & Head frame of warper 整经机筒子架和车头

Unit 2.1　Sectional Warping 分条整经

For sectional warping system (Fig. 3.5), several "sections" are wound in sequence and parallel to each other on a drum, the warping sections are as many as necessary to obtain, with the available creel capacity, the total number of threads composing the warp. Sectional warping is cost-effective for short and striped warps (cotton and wool fabrics).

对于分条整经系统（图 3.5），几个"部分（条带）"按顺序相互平行地卷绕在一个大滚筒上，在可用的筒子架容量下，整经条带数可根据组成织物的总经根数的需要而定。分条整经对于长度短的和经条纹（棉和羊毛织物）织物具有成本效益。

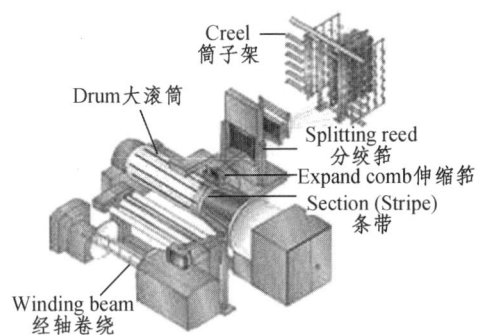 

Fig. 3.5　Sectional warping machine 分条整经机

Before carrying out warping, following calculations are necessary:

$$\text{Section number} = \frac{\text{Total Number of warp threads}}{\text{Creel loading capacity}}$$

If the calculation does not give an exact number, the last section will be produced with a number of threads lower than the other sections, or the number of threads composing each section will be reduced so as to get all sections with one and the same number of threads.

整经之前，需要进行如下计算：

条带（绞）数=总经根数/筒子架容量

如果计算没有给出确切的数字（即整数——编者注），则最后一根条带（绞）的根数少于其他条带（绞），或减少每绞根数以使各绞根数相同。

$$\text{Section width} = \frac{\text{Reed width}}{\text{Number of sections}}$$

This way the total number of warp threads will occupy on the drum a width equal to the width of the weaver's beam on which they will be finally wound.

条带（绞）宽=穿筘幅/绞数

这样，总经根数将在大滚筒所占宽度等于最终其卷绕在织轴上的宽度。

（编者注：穿筘幅是指定幅筘幅宽，定幅筘位于大滚筒和伸缩筘之间，参见图3.5。）

As soon as all the sections are wound on the drum, the weaver's beam formation is started by unwinding the threads from the drum and winding them all simultaneously on the weaver's beam, this operation is named beaming (see Fig. 3.6).

Fig. 3.6　Beaming from drum 倒轴

一旦所有条带（绞）都卷绕在滚筒上，通过纱线从滚筒上退绕，与此同时卷绕在（空）织轴上开始形成织轴，这个操作叫作倒轴（见图3.6）。

（编者注：分条整经适用于色纱排列比较复杂的织物，分为大滚筒逐条带依次卷绕和各条带集体倒成织轴两个步骤，相比于分批整经，整效率较低。）

Unit 2.2　Beam Warping 分批整经

Beam warping is used mostly when several beams of same warp length have to be prepared; also this kind of warping is carried out in following way:

- At first the proper warping takes place. The available threads (creel capacity) are wound on a large cylinder called "beam (as shown in Fig. 3.7)" and number of beams are prepared as indicated by the result of following expression:

$$\text{Number of beams} = \frac{\text{Total Number of yarns}}{\text{Creel capacity}}$$

分批（轴经）整经主要用于必须准备几个具有相同长度的经轴的情况；这种整经也是以以下方式进行的：

- 首先进行适当的整经。可用纱线（筒子架容量）卷绕在称为"经轴（如图 3.7 所示）"的大圆柱体上，经轴数如以下表达式的结果所示：

经轴数=总经根数/筒子架容量

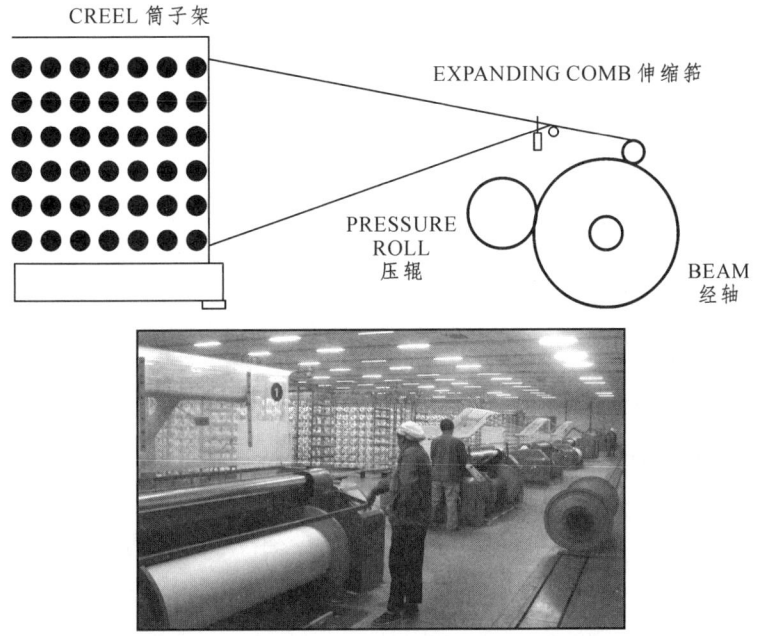

Fig. 3.7　Beam warping process 分批整经

- In a second stage, in sizing process, the threads wound on the beams are simultaneously unwound to form the weaver's beam, as shown in Fig. 3.8.

第二阶段，在上浆过程中，卷绕在经轴上的纱线同时退绕下来以形成织轴，如图 3.8 所示。

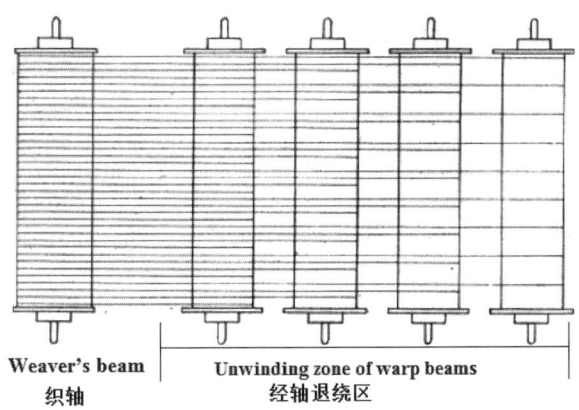

Fig. 3.8　Beam combination in sizing process 在（后道）浆纱工序的经轴组合

067

The way in which threads are assembled during this second phase shows that the number of the beams should be preferably an integer number.

在第二阶段期间纱线的排列方式表明，经轴的数量应优选为整数。

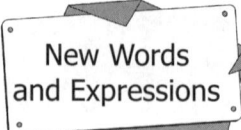

weaver's beam 织轴
intermediate carrier 媒介载体
sectional warping 分条整经
beam warping 分批整经
breakage monitoring 断头检测
drum 滚筒

splitting comb 分绞筘
expanding comb 定幅筘
section 部分
beam 经轴
creel capacity 筒子架容量
stripe 条带

编者注：

（1）splitting comb（分绞筘）的作用是将经纱片分成奇数和偶数两层，便于穿入分绞绳。

（2）分条整经（sectional warping）的步骤是经纱先逐条带（section or stripe）依次卷绕在大滚筒（drum）上，再将所有条带集体倒卷在织轴（weaver's beam）上，得到织轴的总经根数；分批整经（beam warping）是逐轴依次卷绕，浆纱工序将各个经轴集体并合，上浆后，得到织轴所需总经根数。

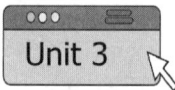 **Unit 3　　Sizing 浆纱**

Sizing 浆纱

Sizing or slashing is a complementary operation which is carried out on warps formed by spun yarns with insufficient tenacity or by continuous filament yarns with zero twist. In general, when sizing is necessary, the yarn is beam warped, therefore all beams corresponding to the beams are fed (see Fig. 3.8), as soon as warping is completed, to the sizing machine where they are assembled. Sizing consists of impregnating the yarn with particular substances which form on the yarn surface a film with the aim of improving yarn smoothness and tenacity during the subsequent weaving stage. Thanks to its improved tenacity and elasticity, the yarn can stand without problems the tensions and the rubbing caused by weaving.

浆纱是弥补环锭纺纱或者无捻度的连续长丝纱纤维间抱和力不足的加工过程。通常，当需要上浆时，纱线是分批整经方式，因此，一旦分批整经完成，所有经轴以轴对轴的形式都会被送到浆纱机（见图 3.8），在那里进行组合（组成总经根数——编者注）。上浆包括浸渍，具有特性物质的纱线在纱线表面形成薄膜，目的是在随后的织造阶段提高纱线的平滑度和韧性。由于其韧性和弹性提高，纱线可以承受织造引起的张力和摩擦而不会出现问题。

There is not just one sizing "recipe" which is valid for all processes, on the contrary the sizing methods change depending on the type of weaving machine used, on the yarn type and count, on the technician's experience and skill, but above all on the kind of material in progress. The only common denominator of the various sizing materials is that they have to be easily removable after weaving in order to allow carrying out without problems the selected finishing cycle. The traditional sizing scheme is shown in Fig. 3.9.

在整个浆纱过程中，这里不仅仅是浆液配方一个问题（需要考虑）。相反，浆纱方法会依据所用织机的类型、纱线类型和支数、技术人员的经验和技能而不同，但最重要的是取决于所用材料的种类。不同浆料的共同特性是织造后必须容易退浆，以便不给选定的染整工序带来问题，传统的浆纱流程如图 3.9 所示。

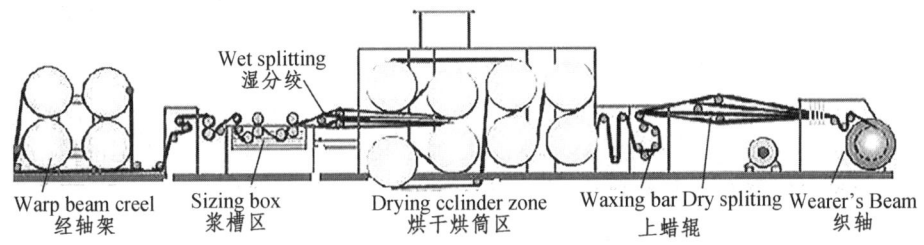

Fig. 3.9 Sizing machine 浆纱机

All beams previously are mounted on a special beam creel, the threads are taken off in sequence from all beams and introduced into a sizing box containing the proper size. The warp enters then a drying unit, where the water contained in the threads is evaporated, this result is obtained by direct contact of the threads with cylinders or by hot air circulation in a room, it is important to take care that during sizing the threads do not stick together, but remain separate to each other. The drying unit is followed by a waxing device which is aimed at increasing the threads smoothness. The process concludes with the winding by an end frame of the threads on a weaver's beam, the drying unit and the end frame there are lease rods (splitting rod): having the function of keeping the threads to be separated.

在此之前，所有经轴都安装在一个特殊的经轴架上，现在经纱从所有经轴上依次退绕下来，并将其引入内含适合浆液的浆槽中。经纱进入干燥单元，在干燥单元中，纱线中的水分被蒸发，此结果是通过纱线与烘筒的直接接触或通过烘房中的热空气循环获得的，重要的是要注意在上浆过程中，纱线不要黏附在一起，而是保持彼此分离。干燥单元之后是一个上蜡装置，旨在提高纱线的光滑度。该过程结束时，纱线通过织轴上的端部装置完成卷绕，烘干装置和车头有分经杆（分绞棒）：具有保持纱线分离的功能。

New Words and Expressions

impregnating 浸渍
film（浆）膜
sizing recipe 浆液配方
scheme 组合
beam creel 经轴
cylinders 烘筒

waxing device 上蜡装置
end frame 车头
weaver's beam 织轴
lease rods，分绞杆
splitting rod 分绞杆
beam creel 轴架

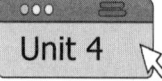

Unit 4　Drawing in 穿经

Drawing in (see Fig 3.10) consists of threading the warp yarns through the drop wires, the heald and reed. Depending on the styles of produced fabrics, this operation can be carried out manually, by female workers in drawing in process.

穿经（如图 3.10）包括将经纱穿过停经片、综框和钢筘。根据生产面料的风格，这项操作可以由女工在穿经过程中手动进行。

Drawing in 穿经

Fig. 3.10　Drawing in 穿经

Task 4

To Describe Weaving Process 描述织造过程

As shown in Fig. 3.11, the warp threads wound on a weaver's beam are bent on the back rest roller, supporting special drop wires, pass through the healds which are responsible for separating the threads at uniform spacing. The reed is responsible for beating-up the weft thread that

Visit shuttleless loom
参观无梭织机

Weaving
织造

has been left in the triangular warp shed formed by the two warp sheets and the reed, passing through the dents of the reed. The fabric produced is then drawn by a take-up roller and wound on the cloth roller.

如图 3.11 所示，卷绕在织轴上的经线在后梁上弯曲，支撑专门的停经片，穿过综框，综框负责以均匀的间距分开纱线，钢筘负责将留在三角区的纬纱打紧，这个三角区由两层经纱片形成的梭口和钢筘构成。接着穿过钢筘的筘齿。然后，生产的织物由卷取辊牵引并卷绕在卷布辊上。

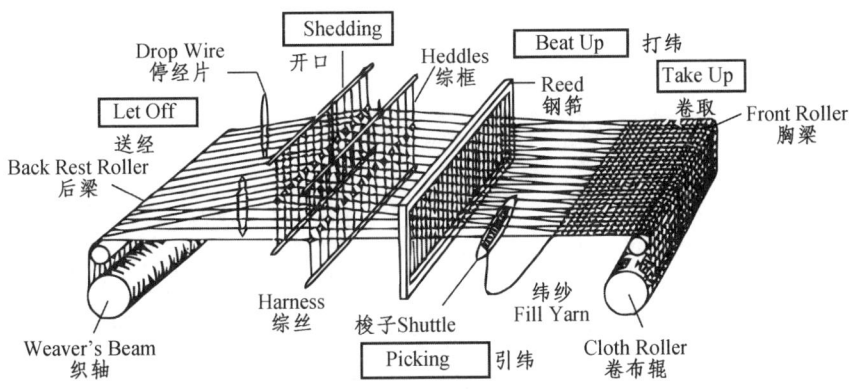

Fig. 3.11 Weaving motion 织机运动

In order to interlace warp and weft threads to produce fabric on any type of weaving machine, the following operations known as shedding, picking, beating up, let off as well as take up motion are necessary.

为了在任何类型的织机上将经纬纱交织以生产织物，需要进行以下操作：开口、引纬、打纬、送经和卷取。

 Shedding 开口

The angle which is formed by the raising threads with the threads remaining in low position is called shed, the shedding motion separates the warp ends into an upper and a lower system of threads to permit the weft carrier such as shuttle to pass through the space that has been formed, the shed must be as wide open as to permit the easy passage of the weft insertion element.

Shedding 开口

The machines used to form the shed are cam machines, dobbies and jacquard machines.

上升的纱线与保持在低位的纱线所形成的角度被称为梭口，梭口运动将经纱分为上下两层纱线，以允许纬纱载纬器例如梭子通过已经形成的空间，梭口必须敞开到允许引纬元件容易通过的程度。

用以形成梭口的机构有凸轮、多臂和和提花机。

071

1. Cam Shedding 凸轮开口

This kind of machine is employed for all fabrics produced with base weaves which have a pattern repeat of 10—12 threads and maximum 6—8 wefts (see Fig. 3.12).

These machines can operate either with positive or negative shaft motion. The principle of positive motion involves that the shafts are raised as well as lowered driven by cams.

这种机器应用于所有使用基础组织生产的织物，其图案的纱线循环为 10~12 根，最大纬纱根数循环为 6~8 根（见图 3.12）。

这些机构可积极运动，也可以消极运动。积极运动的原理涉及凸轮（曲线）的升降运动。

（编者注：综页的升降由对应的凸轮决定，例如 4 页凸轮分别控制 4 页综，凸轮由大小半径的位置高低决定综框的升降动程。）

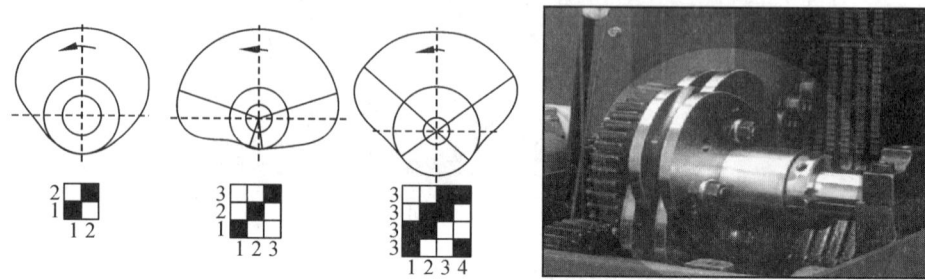

Fig. 3.12　Cams 凸轮

The cam units are as many as the working heald frames and the shaft modifies its running speed according to the weave to be produced.

凸轮装置的数量与工作综框的数量相同，凸轮轴要根据生产的织物改变其运行速度。

2. Dobby Shedding 多臂开口

Dobbies are used for the production of more complex pattern fabrics, compared with cam shedding motion, that is of fabrics characterized by maximum 16—32 threads in the weave repeat.

This loom is one on which small geometric and regular figures can be woven.

与凸轮开口运动相比，多臂用于生产更复杂的图案织物，是指织物在（经）纱线织造循环中最多有 16~32 纱（编者注：指 16~32 页综）。

多臂织机可以生产小型几何或规则纹样织物。

2.1　Mechanical Dobby 机械多臂

Fabric designs can be merely changed by inserting a series of punched cards into the pattern chain (see Fig. 3.13).

（设计者）要进行织物设计时，仅需在纹本链中植入一系列冲孔纹板（见图 3.13）。

 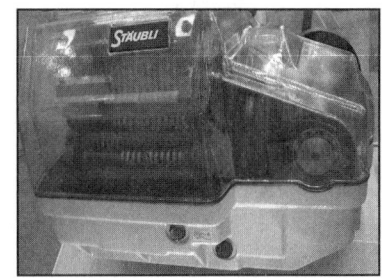

Fig. 3.13　Mechanical dobby head 机械多臂龙头　　**Fig. 3.14　Electronic dobby head 电子多臂龙头**

2.2　Electronic Dobby 电子多臂

This is a advanced mechanism in which the pattern of fabric is able to be produced by electromagnetic shedding device controlled by the instruction of software preset in computer (see Fig. 3.14).

这是一种先进的机制，通过计算机中预设的软件指令控制电磁开口装置，可以产生织物的图案（见图3.14）。

3. Jacquard Shedding 提花开口

The name Jacquard machines (as shown in Fig. 3.15) originates from the designer who improved its operation, today the name "Jacquard" is used to identify all machines with a capacity higher than 32 threads, which are therefore used to produce figured fabrics.

Jacquard（如图3.15所示）这个名字源于改进其工作的设计师，如今"Jacquard"这个名字被用来特指所有容量超过32根经纱循环的（开口）机构，因此这些织机被用来生产大花纹织物。

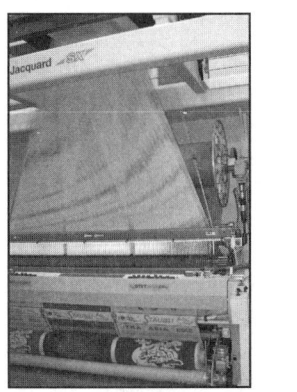 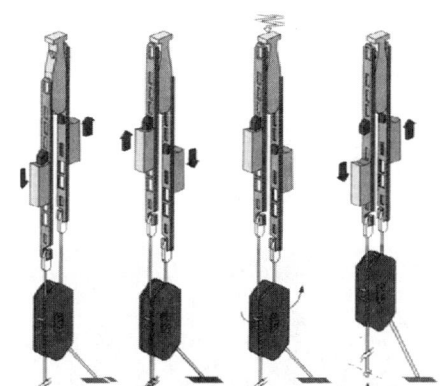

Fig. 3.15　Jacquard machine and shedding motion 大提花织机和开口机构

The indication of the capacity of the machine, which in the past was used to differentiate the various machine models, has today no significance, as the hook number is no more strictly related to the mechanical structure of the machine. The endless pattern card system is gradually disappearing in favor of the electronic system.

过去用来区分各种机器型号的纹针容量标识，如今已经没有意义了，因为纹针数不再与织机的机械结构严格相关。得益于电子系统,(大)花型所需要的很长的纹版链已经逐步(淘汰)消失了。

New Words and Expressions

shed 梭口
shedding 开口
picking 引纬
beating up 打纬
take up 卷取
let off 送经
back rest roller 后梁
front rest roller 胸梁

loom 织机
cam 凸轮
dobby 多臂
Jacquard 提花
geometric 几何
weft carrier 载纬器
card 纹版

Unit 2　Picking Mode—Shuttleless Looms 引纬方式——无梭织机

Loom designers have constantly sought to replace the shuttle as a means of filling insertion. The prime reason is the rate of production. Physical laws dictate that, to move through the shed, the shuttle must be accelerated and decelerated. This naturally takes time and energy. If less time could be spent accelerating the shuttle, and the transit time of the shuttle through the shed could be reduced, higher loom speeds could be obtained. Secondly, with the removal of the filling supply package from the filling carrier, the filling carrier could be made smaller so the yarn movement in shedding could be reduced.

Picking 引纬

Modern shuttleless looms (see Fig. 3.16) include rapier loom, projectile loom, air jet loom and water jet loom.

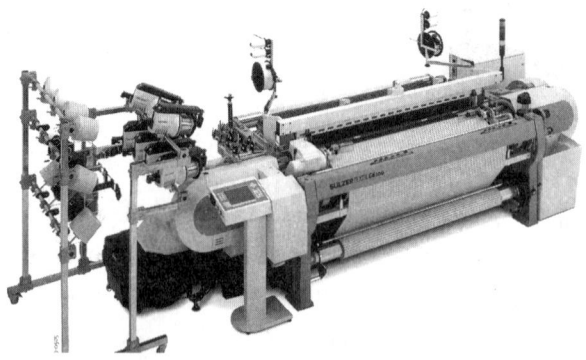

Fig. 3.16　Shuttleless loom 无梭织机

织机设计者一直在寻求取代梭子作为引纬装置的方式。主要原因是（考虑）生产率问题。从物理法则可知：要穿过梭口，梭子须加速和减速。这自然需要消耗时间和能量。如果能花费更少时间来加速梭子，并且梭子通过梭口的时间能够减少，则可以获得更高的织机速度。其次，伴随着纬纱卷装与载纬器分离，载纬器可以更小，从而可以减少（经）纱开口运动。

现代无梭织机（如图3.16）包括：剑杆织机、片梭织机、喷气织机和喷水织机。

（编者注：文中"纬纱卷装与载纬器分离，载纬器可以更小" 举例说明：纬纱卷装可以是纡子，载纬器可以是梭子，纡子不再装入质量和体积都大的梭子，引纬负担减轻，引纬所需梭口小，引纬速度快，织机速度高，这是无梭织机的优势。）

Unit 2.1　Rapier Loom 剑杆织机

Rapier loom is one type of shuttleless looms. The rapier system operates with either flexible or rigid metal arms, or rapier, attached at both sides of the weaving area. A rapier is merely a device made of metal or a composite material with an attachment on the end to carry the filling yarn through the shed.

Picking rapier loom
剑杆织机

剑杆织机是无梭织机之一，剑杆系统采用柔性或刚性金属臂或剑杆，附在织造区两侧。剑杆只是一种由金属或复合材料制成的装置，末端有一个附件，用来携带纬纱穿过梭口。

One arm carries a pick to the center of the weaving area; the arm extending from the other side grasps the pick and carries it across the remaining fabric width.

在织物一侧，送纬剑钳着纬纱到织造区中央，接纬剑从织物另一侧延伸过来接过纬纱，通过织物余下的宽度。

To overcome the potential space problem, the double flexible rapier was developed (As shown in Fig 3.17). The rapiers in this case are no longer rigid bars but flexible tapes. Since the tapes are flexible, they can be bent so as to fit under the loom, thus conserving space. The double flexible rapier consists of giver and taker similar to the double rigid rapier.

为了克服潜在的空间问题，开发了双挠性剑杆（如图3.17所示）。在这种情况下，剑杆不再是刚性杆，而是挠性带。由于剑带是挠性的，它们可以弯曲以适合织机，从而节省空间。双挠性剑杆织机由送纬剑和接纬剑器组成，类似于双刚性剑杆。

An important advantage of rapier looms is their flexibility, which permits the laying of picks of different colors. They also weave yarns of any type of fiber and can weave fabrics up to 110 inches in width without modification.

剑杆织机的一个重要优点是其灵活性，可以引入不同颜色的纬纱。它们还织造任何类型的纤维纱线，并且可不经织机改造而织造宽度高达110英寸的织物。

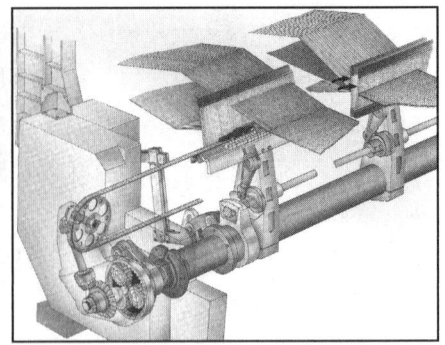

Fig. 3.17　Flexible rapier loom 挠性剑杆织机

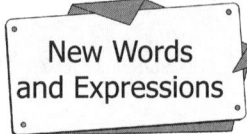

New Words and Expressions

giver 送纬剑
flexible 挠性的

taker 接纬剑
composite material 复合材料

背景知识：剑杆织机的主要优势是品种适应性广，适合棉、毛、丝麻及化纤纱织造，纬纱选色能力强（纬纱颜色可达 8 色），引纬张力小。一般用于棉、毛织物生产。

Unit 2.2　Projectile Loom 片梭织机

The projectile loom (see Fig. 3.18) uses a small projectile to carry the filling yarn through the shed. In reality, the shuttle is actually a projectile but the distinctive feature of shuttleless looms is that the filling package is exterior to the filling carrier, disqualifies the shuttle loom from consideration.

Projectile loom
片梭织机

片梭织机（见图 3.18）使用一个片梭夹持纬纱穿过梭口。事实上，梭子实际上是一种夹持器，但无梭织机的独特特征是纬纱卷装位于载纬器的外部，因此片梭织机不宜称有梭织机。

The small gripper-projectile (see Fig. 3.19) is supplied with weft yarn from a large cone and carries it through the shed, always in the same direction. The low mass of the projectile means it needs little power for its acceleration. Several projectiles are provided, together with an external return mechanism, so that the next is always ready for launching without delay. The smaller shed and the lower mass allow much wider fabrics and higher production speeds to be attained. However, the weft has to be cut and separately secured at the fabric edges. Projectile picking is as shown in Fig. 3.20.

小片梭（如图 3.19）由一个大圆锥形筒子提供的纬纱，并始终沿同一方向穿过梭口。小质量的片梭意味着它几乎不需要动力来加速。可提供几种片梭，带有一个外部片梭折返机器，以便随时准备发射下一枚片梭。较小的梭口和较低的质量允许获得更宽的织物和更高的生产速度。然而，纬纱必须被切断并单独固定在织物边缘。片梭引纬如图 3.20 所示。

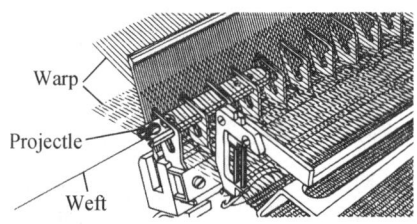

Fig. 3.18 Projectile loom 片梭织机

Fig. 3.19 Projectile 片梭

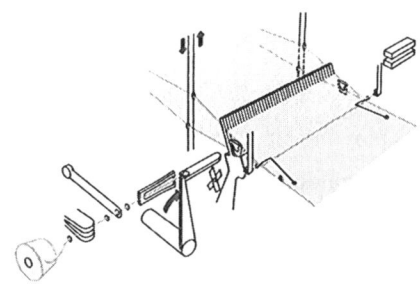

Fig. 3.20 Projectile picking 片梭引纬

Each pick is individually cut, so there is not a continuously woven selvage like that produced by a shuttle machine. A tucking device is used on both sides to interlace the fringe with the last few warp yarns along each edge.

Some modern projectile looms may be available in weaving widths up approximately 508 cm which increases productivity.

每一个纬都是单独切割的，所以没有像有梭织机那样连续交织的布边。采用折入边装置将纬纱与织物两边的最后几根经纱交织形成布边。

一些现代片梭织机的织造宽度可达约 508 厘米，提高了生产率。

背景知识：片梭织机具有低速、优质、高产、宽幅品种适应性广的特点，纬纱张力自动可调，采用折入边，布边整齐封闭，一般用于高档毛织物和棉织物。织机造价高，如瑞士苏尔寿、鲁蒂 SULZER.RUTI 生产的 P7300 片梭织机。

Unit 2.3　Air-jet Loom 喷气织机

In an air-jet loom, a high pressure air carries the filling yarn through the shed. The major drawback to this type of loom is that the air diffuses quite rapidly so the width of the fabric is limited. Modern air-jet looms use air guides or air guides with auxiliary jets to extend the distance that the yarn can be carried, as shown in Fig. 3.21.

Air-jet loom
喷气织机

喷气织机利用高压空气将纬纱牵引过梭口。这种织机的主要缺点是空气扩散得很快，因此织物的宽度有限。现代喷气织机使用空气导管（管道片筘——编者注）或带有辅助喷嘴的空气导管（异性筘——编者注）来延长纱线的牵引输送距离，如图 3.21。

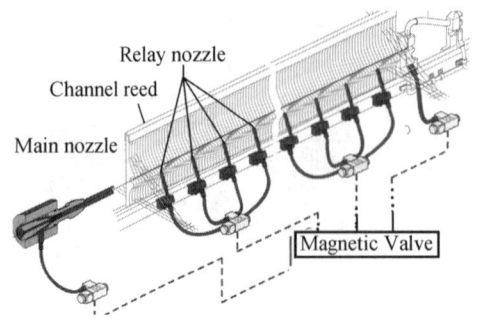

Fig. 3.21 Weft insertion by air jets & air jet loom 气流引纬和片梭织机

The measuring disk removes a length of yarn appropriate to the width of the fabric being woven. The main nozzle begins blowing air so that the yarn is set in motion as soon as the clamp opens. The yarn is blown into the guiding channel of the reed with the shed open. The yarn is carried through the shed by the air currents emitted by the relay nozzles along the channel. The maximum effective width for air-jet looms is about 355 cm. At the end of each insertion cycle, the yarn closed by the clamp is beaten in, then cut, after the shed is closed. Again, some selvage-forming device is required to provide stability to the edges of the fabric.

测长鼓引出的纬纱长度和进行织造的织物宽度相适应。主喷嘴开始吹送空气，使纱线在挡纱针打开时立即进入运动状态。纱线在梭口打开的情况下被吹入异型筘的引导通道。纱线由接力喷嘴（即辅助喷嘴——编者注）喷射的气流携带，沿（异型筘）通道通过梭口。喷气织机的最大有效宽度约为355厘米。在每个引纬周期结束时，由挡纱针夹持的纱线在梭口闭合后被关紧，然后被切割。同样，需要一些布边形成装置来为织物的布边提供稳定性。

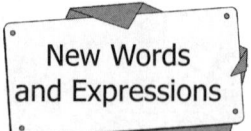

New Words and Expressions

diffuse 扩散
air guide 空气导引装置
auxiliary jet 辅助喷嘴
relay nozzle 接力喷嘴

main nozzle 主喷嘴
measuring disk 测长盘
clamp 挡纱针（用于控制引纬长度）
air current 气流

背景知识：现代喷气织机采用主喷嘴+辅助喷嘴+异型筘的引纬方式，其中异型筘由于克服气流的扩散问题，辅助（接力）喷嘴用于解决气流能量的衰减问题。

喷气织机具有车速高、入纬率高的特点，但要和异型筘和空压机配套使用，纬纱选色能力有限（4~6色），一般用作量大面广的棉织物生产，也可用于化纤长丝织物生产。

Unit 2.4 Water-jet Loom 喷水织机

Water-jet looms are preferred for some type of fabrics. The water-jet loom is unsuitable for yarns of hydrophilic fibers because the fabric picks up too much moisture.

Water-jet loom 喷水织机

The filling yarn is carried by a high pressure jet of water. Since water diffuses much more slowly than air, wider fabric can be made with water-jet looms without using guides. However, because water is the carrier, there are restrictions as to yarn types and pre-weaving processing, such as slashing.

喷水织机是某些（疏水性合成长丝——编者注）类型织物的首选。喷水织机不适用于亲水性纤维的纱线，因为织物吸湿性太强。

纬丝由高压水射流牵引。由于水的扩散速度比空气慢得多，因此可以在不使用导纱器（增加流体集束性的异型筘或管道片——编者注）的情况下，使用喷水织机织造更宽的织物。然而，由于水是载体，因此对纱线类型和织前准备工序（如浆丝）有限制。

The water-jet loom uses a high pressure jet of water to carry the filling yarns across the warp. It works on the principle of continuous feed and minimum tension of the filling yarns, the filling yarn comes from a stationary package at the side of the loom, goes to a measuring drum that controls the length of each filling, and continuous by going through a guide to the water nozzle, where a jet of water carries it across through the warp shed. After the filling is carried back, it is cut off. If the fibers are thermoplastic, a hot wire is used to cut the yarn, fusing the ends so they serve as a selvage. Water-jet loom is shown as in Fig. 3.22.

喷水织机使用高压水射流牵引纬纱越过经纱。它的工作原理是连续喂入和最小的纬纱张力，纬纱来自织机侧面的固定卷装，进入控制每根纬纱长度的测长鼓，并通过一个导向器接连不断地到达水喷嘴，在那里，一股水流携带纬纱经过经纱梭口。当纬纱折回时（在布边处——编者注）被切断。如果纤维是热塑性的，就用热融丝切断纬纱，将末端融化，使其成为布边，喷水织机如图3.22。

Fig. 3.22　Water-jet loom 喷水织机

The water is removed from the loom by a suction device. Water from the jet will dissolve regular warp sizing so one of the problems has been that of developing water-resistant sizing that can be removed easily in cloth finishing processes. The fabric is wet when it comes from the loom and must be dried.

从织机带来的（织物中的）水通过吸水装置被去除。喷嘴中（喷射的）水会溶解常规的经纱上浆剂，因此问题之一是开发（织造时）拒水上浆剂，这种上浆剂在织物整理过程中很容易去除。织物从织机上下来时是湿的，必须烘干。

Both air- and water-jet looms weave rapidly, provide for laying different colors in the filling direction, and produce uniform, high-quality fabrics. They are less noisy and require less space than most other types of looms. They cause minimal damage to warp yarns during the weaving operation, because the air or water jets are less abrasive than moving metal parts.

喷气织机和喷水织机都能快速织造，在纬向上提供不同颜色的纬纱，并生产出均匀、高质量的织物。与大多数其他类型的织机相比，它们噪音更小，所需空间也更小。在织造过程中，它们对经纱的损伤最小，因为空气或水的喷射比移动的金属部件对纱线磨损更小。

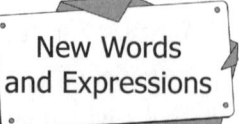

New Words and Expressions

hydrophilic 亲水性
moisture 湿度
measuring drum 测长鼓
pre-weaving processing 织前准备

thermoplastic 热塑性
fuse 熔融
suction device 吸水装置
minimal 最低的

背景知识：喷水织机适合疏水性化纤长丝织物织造，由于水流的集束性好，因而不需要采用异型筘和辅助喷嘴，但是幅宽受到限制，常见幅宽不超过 2.3 米，织物织造后需脱水烘干。

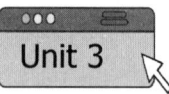 **Unit 3** Beating-up 打纬

Beating-up follows the picking motion. After the filling is inserted, by whatever means of insertion, it must be incorporated into the body of the fabric. This is the purpose of beat-up.

Beating-up 打纬

引纬运动之后是打纬。纬纱引入后，无论采用何种引纬方式，都必须将其合并到织物的主体中。这就是打纬的目的。

Beating-up is accomplished by use of a reed. At the beginning of weaving cycle, the reed is moved backward to allow for filling insertion. After the filling is inserted, the reed moved forward to beat the weft to fell with each consecutive turn of the crank shaft. The loose pick that has just been placed in the shed of the loom is actually beaten into place. Beating-up makes each and every deposited yarn a component part of the woven cloth. The usual mechanism that gives the reed its motion is known as the sley. Beating-up mechanism is shown as in Fig. 3.23 and Fig. 3.24.

打纬是用钢筘完成的。在织造循环开始时，钢筘向后移动，以便引入纬纱。纬纱引入后，纬纱向前移动，伴随着曲柄轴每连续转动一圈，将纬纱打向织口，刚刚放置在织机梭口里的松弛的纬纱实际上已经达到了相应位置。打纬使每根引入（存入梭口）的纱线成为织物的组成部分。通常驱动钢筘运动的机构称为筘座。打纬机器如图 3.23 和图 3.24 所示。

The operations known as shedding, picking and beating are often called the primary motions of weaving and must occur in a given sequence, but their precise timing in relation to one anther is also of extreme importance and will be considered in detail.

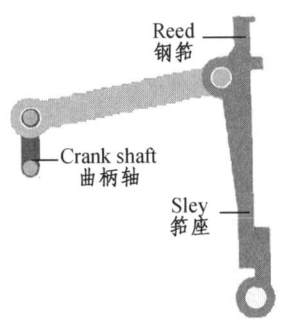 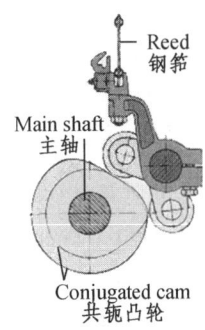

Fig. 3.23 Four bar beating mechanism 四连杆打纬机器　　Fig. 3.24 Conjugated cam beating mechanism 共轭凸轮打纬机器

所谓开口、引纬和打纬的动作，通常被称为织造的主要运动，必须按照给定的顺序进行，但它们相对于另一个动作的精确配合时间也非常重要，将被详细考虑。

fell 织口　　　　　　　　　　　　conjugated cam 共轭凸轮
crank shaft 曲柄轴　　　　　　　　deposite 存储
sley 筘座　　　　　　　　　　　　precise timing 精确的时间配合
four bar 四连杆　　　　　　　　　mechanism 机构

背景知识：相比于连杆打纬机构，共轭凸轮打纬机构具有筘座静止时期长，从而有利于宽幅，有利于降低车速，有利于减少开车横档次布的特点。

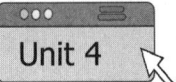 Unit 4　Let-off & Take-up 送经和卷取

Let-off: This motion delivers warp to the weaving area at the required rate and at a suitable constant tension by unwinding it from a flanged tube known as the weaver's beam (See Fig. 3.25).

这个运动以所需的速率和适当的恒定张力将经纱从有盘片的织轴上退绕下来（如图 3.25）。

Let-off & Take-up
送经和卷取

Take-up: This motion withdraws fabric the weaving area at the constant rate that will give the required picking-spacing and then winds it onto a roller. The yarn from the weaver's beam passes round the back rest and comes forward to the heald, and the reed. Temples（边撑）hold the cloth firm at the fell to assist in the formation of a uniform fabric, which then passes over the front rest, round the take-up roller, and onto the cloth roller (see Fig. 3.26).

这种运动以恒定的速度将织物从织造区引出，从而提供所需的纬纱间距，然后将其卷绕到卷布辊上。从织轴上来的纱线绕过后梁，向前穿过综片和钢筘。边撑在织口处牢牢地握持织物，有助于形成匀整的织物，然后织物经过胸梁，绕过卷取辊，然后到达卷布辊上（如图 3.26）。

By now all modern weaving machines use integrated electronic systems which are operated by the drive and control unit of the machine. The weaver's beam and the take-up motions are driven by high precision servomotors（伺服电机）equipped with speed reducer（减速器），connected with the machine's PLC through an encoder（编码器）and controlled through a closed adjustment ring. This ensures the synchronization（同步性）of the weaving machine with the let-of and take-up motions (operating in series): practically the controller can know at any moment the exact position of the various devices (see Fig. 3.27).

Fig. 3.25　Let-off mechanism
送经机构

Fig. 3.26　Take-up mechanism
卷取机构

到目前为止，所有现代织机都是使用由机器驱动和控制单元操作的一体化的电子系统。织轴和卷取运动由和减速器配套的高精度伺服电机驱动，PLC 借助于编码器对其实现闭环形式的调整控制。这样可以确保织机的送经和卷取运动（串联运行）同步：实际上，控制器可以随时获悉各种装置的确切位置（如图 3.27）。

A position sensor（传感器）or a load cell（测力传感器）signals at any moment the tension operating on the back rest roller and permits to adjust the let-off speed so that the tension remains absolutely constant from the start to the end of the weaving cycle. In order to avoid stripes on the fabric. Also the weft density can be varied without limitations during weaving and it is also possible to modify the warp tension by means of a simple keying in.

位置传感器和测力传感器随时在后梁导辊处发出信号以调整送经速度，使得整个织造过程张力始终恒定。为了避免织物上出现条影（疵点）。纬纱密度在织造过程中也可以不受限制地变化，也可以通过简单的键入来改变经纱张力。

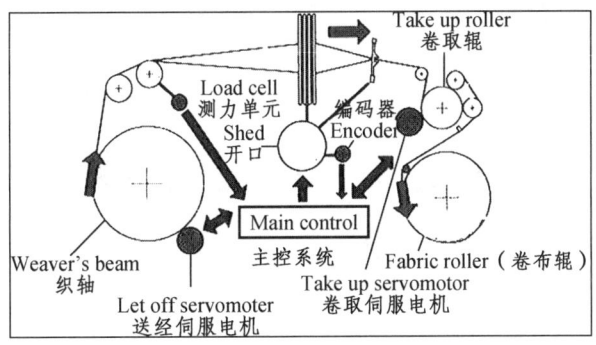

Fig. 3.27　Electronic adjusting system 电子调节系统

temple 边撑
integrated 整体的、综合的
sensor 传感器
load cell 测力传感器
key in 键入
PLC Programmable Logic Controller 可编程逻辑控制器

encoder 编码器
synchronization 同步性
servomotors 伺服电机
speed reducer 减速器

背景知识：

1. 本文涉及纺织机电一体化知识，如传感器、伺服电机、PLC 等应用。

2. closed adjustment ring：闭环调整模式，指检测—修正—再检测—再修正，直至目标值在规定范围之内的封闭调整模式，较之"检测—修正"开环模式更为先进。

Chapter 4

Weaves & Fabrics 组织和面料篇

- To describe basic weaves and fabrics made from basic weaves.
  描述基本组织和织物。
- To describe derivatives of basic weaves and fabrics made from them.
  描述衍生组织和织物。
- To describe combined weaves and fabrics made from them.
  描述联合组织和织物。
- To describe compound weaves and made from compound weaves.
  描述复杂组织和织物。
- To describe nonwoven fabric.
  描述非织造布。

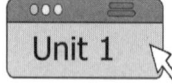 Task 1

Basic Weaves 基本组织

There are three basic weaves. They are plain weave, twill weave and satin weave. All other weaves are a variation or a combination of these weaves.

（织物）有三种基本组织。它们是平纹组织、斜纹组织和缎面组织。所有其他组织都是由这些组织变化或联合构成的。

Unit 1　Plain Weave 平纹

Plain Weave (see Fig. 4.1) is the simplest and the tightest method of interlacing warp and weft. Each warp yarn passes alternately over and under each weft. The interlacing is opposite in all neighboring cells. The

Plain weave 平纹

repeat is over two ends and two picks. Opposite sides of the fabric are the same.

平纹组织（见图 4.1）是最简单、最紧密的经纬交织方法。每根经纱在每根纬纱上下交替通过。在所有相邻的组织点中，交错是相反的。一个组织循环需要两根经纱和两根纬纱，织物的正反面相同。

Plain weave allows the highest possible number of interlacing which, depending on the fiber and yarn type, the thread density and the finishing, can yield fabrics with high abrasion resistance and resistance to yarn slippage. Some fabric made from the plain weave are listed below (see Table 4.1).

平纹组织的可织密度较大，根据纤维和纱线类型、线密度和后整理，可以生产出具有高耐磨性和抗纱线打滑性能的织物。下面列出了一些平纹组织织物（见表 4.1）。

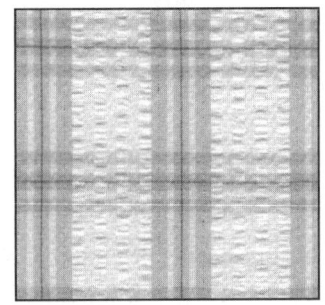

Fig. 4.1　Plain & seersucker 平纹和泡泡纱

Table. 4.1　Fabrics made from plain weave 平纹组织织物

1. Cotton & linen fabric 棉麻织物		2. Woolen fabric 羊毛织物		3. Silk fabric 丝织物	
fine fabric	细布	afgalaine	平纹毛呢	chiffon	雪纺
seersucker	泡泡纱	delaine	薄花呢	grosgrain	罗缎
crepe	绉布	flannel	法兰绒	organza	透明纱
poplin	府绸	panama	巴拿马薄呢	poult	波纹绸
voile	巴厘纱	tropical suiting	薄型精纺呢	taffeta	塔夫绸

The fabrics in Group 1 were commonly produced from cotton or linen, those in Group 2 from wool, and those in Group 3 from silk. Nowadays some of those fabric may also be made from manufactured fibers.

第一组织物通常由棉或亚麻制成，第二组织物由羊毛制成，第三组织物则由蚕丝制成。如今，这些织物中的一些也可以由人造纤维制成。

New Words and Expressions

basic weaves 原组织，基本组织　　　　plain weave 平纹组织
twill weave 斜纹组织　　　　　　　　　satin weave 缎纹组织
variation 变化，改变　　　　　　　　　combination 结合，联合
repeat 完全组织，组织循环　　　　　　thread density 线密度
finishing 后整理　　　　　　　　　　　yield 生产
abrasion resistance 耐磨性　　　　　　manufactured fibers 人造纤维

 Unit 2　Twill Weave 斜纹

Twill weave 斜纹

Twill weave (see Fig. 4.2) is characterized by a diagonal line on the face, and often on the back, of the fabric. The face diagonal can vary from reclining twill, with a low 14-degree angle, to steep twill, with a 75-degree angle. A twill angle of 45-degree is considered to be a medium diagonal or a regular twill; it is the most common. The angle of the diagonal is determined by the closeness of the warp ends, the number of yarns per inch, the diameter of the yarns used, and the actual progression forming the repeat.

斜纹组织（见图 4.2）的特点是在织物的正面和反面有一条斜纹线。正面的斜纹线可以从 14 度角的缓斜纹到 75 度角的急斜纹不等。45 度的斜纹角被认为是中等斜纹线或规则斜纹；它是最常见的。斜纹线的倾角由经密即每英寸纱线的数量、所用纱线的直径以及形成一个组织循环的飞数决定的。

Fig. 4.2　Twill & gabardine 斜纹与华达呢

Twill weave fabrics have a distinctive and attractive appearance. In general, fabric made by the twill weave interlacing are strong and durable. The simplest twill contains three ends and three picks. Twill fabrics can be made soft and loose or smooth, dense, and durable depending on the fabric construction and thread density.

斜纹织物具有独特而吸引人的外观。一般来说，斜纹组织织物结实耐用。最简单的斜纹组织由三根经纱和三根纬纱构成。根据织物结构和线密度的不同，斜纹组织可以制成柔软、宽松或光滑、致密、耐用的织物。

Some fabrics made from twill weaves are listed below (see Table 4.2).

下面列出了一些斜纹组织织物（表4.2）。

Table 4.2　Fabrics made from twill weave 斜纹组织织物

Cotton fabric		Woolen fabric		Silk fabric	
denim	牛仔布	whipcord	马裤呢	foulard	薄软绸
drill	卡其	glen check	格林格	surah	斜纹软绸

New Words and Expressions

diagonal line 斜纹线
back 反面
reclining twill 缓斜纹
regular twill 正则斜纹
inch 英寸
progression 飞数
loose 松的

face 正面
vary 改变
steep twill 急斜纹
closeness 密度，严密
diameter 直径
durable 耐久性
dense 密集的

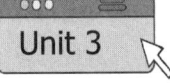

Unit 3　Satin and Sateen Weave 经面缎纹和纬面缎纹

The feature of the satin (see Fig. 4.3) and sateen (see Fig. 4.4) weaves is a uniform distribution of the interlacing, which are never adjacent to one another. Satin and sateen repeat over at least 5 ends and 5 picks but the warp ends interlace only once per repeat. This results in the long floats which determine the appearance and the properties of these fabrics. The face and back of the fabric look quite different.

Satin and sateen weave 缎纹

经面缎纹（见图4.3）和纬面缎纹（见图4.4）的特点是交织点均匀分布，每个单独的组织点相距较远。缎纹组织一个循环至少需要5根经纱和5根纬纱，但在一个循环中，因为每根经纱与纬纱只交织一次，所以就产生了较长的浮长线，使得织物的外观和性能有所不同。缎纹织物的正面和反面看起来有很大差别。

Warp satins have a predominance of warp on the face side.

经面缎纹的正面，经纱占主导地位。

The less popular weft sateen have the weft on the face.

087

不太常见的纬面缎纹，在正面，纬纱占主导地位（编者注：经面缎纹在白坯织造后染色织物中应用较为普遍，纬面缎纹在纬线显花的大提花面料中很普遍）。

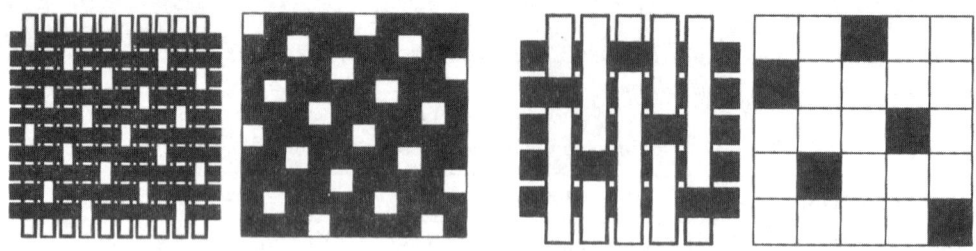

Fig. 4.3　Satin 经面缎纹　　　　　Fig. 4.4　Sateen 纬面缎纹

Satins and sateen fabric (see Fig. 4.5) are smooth, uniform, and lustrous due to the scarcity of interlacing and the density of threads. A soft and supple handle and drape can be obtained with relatively loose constructions.

经面和纬面缎纹织物（见图 4.5）光滑、匀整、有光泽，这是由于经纬纱交织稀疏。相对疏松的组织结构可以使织物获得柔软的手感和悬垂性。

Fig. 4.5　Satins & sateen fabric 经纬面缎纹织物

Some fabrics made from satin and sateen weaves are listed below (see Table 4.3)
下面列出了一些经面缎纹和纬面缎纹织物（表 4.3）。

Table 4.3　Fabrics made from satin and sateen weaves 经面和纬面缎纹组织织物

Cotton fabric		Woolen fabric		Silk fabric	
Italian	意大利缎	doeskin cloth	驼丝锦	duchesse satin	丝硬缎
satin drill	直贡	satin-back gabardine	缎背华达呢	satin-back crepe	缎背绉

New Words and Expressions

satin weaves 经面缎纹　　　　　　　　sateen weaves 纬面缎纹
uniform 均匀的　　　　　　　　　　　distribution 分布，分配

adjacent 邻近的
lustrous 有光泽的
handle 手感
obtained 得到，获得
supple 柔软的，灵活的

floats 浮长
scarcity 不足，缺乏
drape 悬垂性
relatively 相对地
predominance 优势，卓越

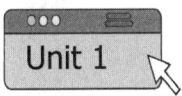

Derivatives of Basic Weaves and Fabrics
基础组织的衍生（变化）组织

 Derivative Weaves 变化组织

The weaves are constructed by means of developing basic weaves. They are derived by changing the floats, number of shift, direction of diagonal lines, from plain, twill, satin/sateen weaves, and retaining their structural features.

变化组织是以原组织（平纹组织、斜纹组织、缎纹组织）为基础再加以变化而得到的各种不同的组织。变化的方法有改变组织的组织点浮长、飞数、斜纹线的方向，并保留了其结构特征。

Derivative weaves
变化组织

The derivatives of basic weaves include:

1. Plain weave derivatives: rib weaves, hopsack weaves, etc.

2. Twill weave derivatives: reinforced twill, compound twill, angled twill, curved twill, waved twill, broken twill, diamond twill, zigzag twill, entwined twill, etc.

3. Satin/sateen derivatives: reinforced satin/sateen, rearranged satin/sateen.

变化组织包括：

1. 平纹变化组织：重平组织、方平组织等。

2. 斜纹变化组织：加强斜纹、复合斜纹、角度斜纹、曲线斜纹、山形斜纹、破斜纹、菱形斜纹、锯齿斜纹、芦席斜纹等。

3. 缎纹变化组织：加强缎纹、重设缎纹。

This group of structures comprises various simple weaves which are varieties of the plain weave and can be produced on two harness（综页）. Extension of the plain weave can proceed either vertically, grouping together several picks in the same shed, which results in warp rib, with groups of neighboring ends working in tandem and producing weft rib, or in both directions simultaneously, resulting in hopsack weave. Plain weave and its derivatives are often used for producing fabric selvedges.

089

平纹变化组织是由平纹变化而来的各种简单的组织，可以用两页综进行生产。平纹组织可以沿着经向延长组织点，在同一梭口中将几根纬纱组合在一起，形成经重平；沿着纬向延长组织点，几根相邻的经纱交织规律相同，形成纬重平；或者在两个方向同时延长组织点，形成方平组织。平纹组织及其变化组织常用于织物的布边组织。

Unit 1.1　Rib Weaves 重平组织

Rib weaves are obtained by extending the plain weave in either warp or weft direction. A rib fabric is one whose surface shows raised lines and ridges.

重平组织是以平纹组织为基础，沿着经向或纬向延长组织点而得到的组织。重平组织织物表面有凸起的条纹。

Rib weave
重平

Rib gives a more flexible cloth than plain weave and has many applications. Fabrics are woven in silk, cotton, wool and man-made fibers. Their end uses range from dress fabrics, coats, suits, and wedding to upholstery.

重平组织织物比平纹织物更具弹性，应用也很广泛。织物可由丝、棉、毛和人造纤维织造而成。它们的最终用途从服装面料、外套、西装、婚纱到室内装饰织物等。

1. Warp Rib Weaves 经重平组织

Warp ribs (see Fig. 4.6) are constructed by inserting several picks in succession into the same shed of an ordinary plain weave. This forms a rib effect across the fabric. They are woven with a substantially higher number of ends than picks. The warp should cover the weft on both sides of the fabric. The weft yarn has usually less twist and is of thicker count.

经重平组织（见图 4.6）是将几根纬纱连续引入平纹组织的同一梭口中而形成的。在织物上可形成凸条效果。经重平织物经密比纬密大。在织物的正反两面，经纱应覆盖纬纱。纬纱通常捻度较小，支数较粗。

 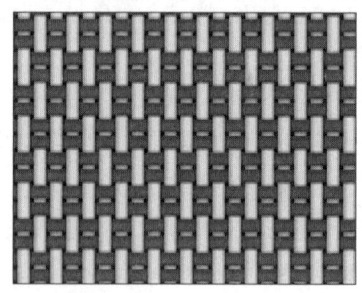

Fig. 4.6　Warp rib 经重平

A ribbed appearance can also be obtained in plain weave by using coarse weft and fine warp yarns. The properties and the appearance are determined by the fiber and yarn qualities used in the warp, since this predominates on both sides of the fabric.

在平纹组织中，通过使用粗纬纱和细经纱也可以获得凸条外观效果。织物的性能和外观由经纱中使用的纤维和纱线质量决定，因为经纱在织物的两面都占主导地位。

2. Weft Rib Weaves 纬重平组织

Weft ribs (see Fig. 4.7) are constructed with several warp threads used as one when interlacing with each pick in succession. They form a vertical rib in the fabric. They have a considerably higher number of picks than ends. The weft should cover the warp on either side of the fabric. Finer weft yarns will give better coverage and make it easier to achieve the required pick density. Weft rib, due to its high number of picks, increases the production costs. The high density of weft results in a lower weaving production rate, so these fabrics are not very common. The properties and appearance depend primarily on the nature of the weft yarns.

纬重平组织（见图 4.7）由多根经线与纬线交织构成，当与每根纬纱连续交织时，这些经线被当作一组经线。它们在织物上可形成纵向的凸条。它们的纬密比经密大。在织物的两面，纬纱应覆盖经线。较细的纬纱可获得更好的覆盖率，并使其更容易达到所需的纬密。纬重平组织由于纬密较大，增加了生产成本。纬密高导致织造生产率较低，因此这些织物并不常见。纬重平织物的性能和外观主要取决于纬纱的性质。

Fig. 4.7　Weft rib & oxford fabric 纬重平组织和牛津布

The most popular fabric based on weft rib is oxford which is shown as in Fig. 4.7.

最流行的纬重平面料是牛津布，如图 4.7 所示。

3. Basket Weaves 方平组织

Basket weaves are obtained by prolonging interlace points along both warp and weft direction of plain weave, as shown in Fig. 4.8.

方平组织是在平纹组织的基础上，沿着经向和纬向同时延长组织点而形成，如 4.8 所示。

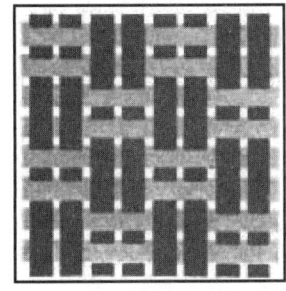 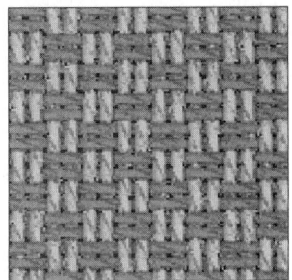

Fig. 4.8　Basket weave 方平组织

New Words and Expressions

derivative 派生物
millinery 女帽
ribbons 丝带
reinforced twill 加强斜纹
derivatives of basic weaves 变化组织
plain weave derivatives 平纹变化组织
harness 综页
vertically 垂直的
in succession 接连的
upholstery 家居饰品
proceed 开始，继续进行

rib weaves 重平组织
warp rib 经重平
weft rib 纬重平
hopsack weaves 方平组织
rearrange 重新排列
ridge 脊，山脊
proceed 开始，进行
in tandem 一前一后的
oxford 牛津布
predominate 支配
in tandem 一前一后地

Unit 1.2　Twill Weave Derivatives 斜纹变化组织

Variations of twill weaves are many. Twill weaves can be modified by extending the floats, changing the shift or both. It has a great potential for introducing ornamentation into fabrics.

斜纹变化组织有很多。通过延长组织点、改变组织点飞数或同时采用这两种方法，改变斜纹组织。将花型植入面料具有很大的潜力。

Twill weave derivatives
斜纹变化组织

1. Reinforced Twills 加强斜纹

Reinforced twill weaves are the simplest twill weave derivatives, which can be constructed by adding warp or weft marks beside the original ones. In reinforced twill weaves, the warp and weft floats are of equal sizes and face and back of the cloth look the same, apart from the direction of the twill line.

加强斜纹是最简单的斜纹变化组织，是在原组织斜纹的单个组织点旁延长经或纬组织点而成的。在加强斜纹组织中，织物正反面的经浮长和纬浮长相等，除了斜纹线方向外，织物的正反面看起来相同。

Reinforced twill（see Fig. 4.9）weaves are widely used in varies fabrics, such as serge, gabardine, drill, cheviot, and are also used in selvedges of other fabrics.

加强斜纹（见图4.9）广泛用于各种织物中，如哔叽、华达呢、斜纹布、啥味呢，并且也用于其他织物的布边。

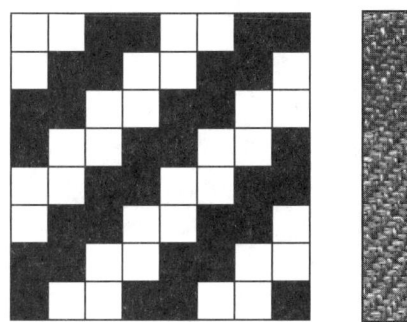

Fig. 4.9　Reinforced twill & serge 加强斜纹和哔叽

2. Angled Twills 角度斜纹

Twill constructed with an increased shift is called angled twill. There are two angled twill, steep twill and reclining twill.

通过增加飞数形成的斜纹称为角度斜纹。有两种角度斜纹，即急斜纹和缓斜纹。

Steep twill line can be obtained either by increasing the relative density of the warp or by using a move number of two in the pattern, or by special constructions. The Angle of diagonal line is much greater than 45 degrees. The fabrics based on steep twill is Keluodine, whipcord, as shown in Fig. 4.10.

急斜纹可以通过增加经纱的相对密度，或者在组织循环中使飞数大于 1，或者通过特殊的结构来获得。斜纹线的倾角远大于 45 度。急斜纹典型面料是克罗丁和马裤呢，如图 4.10 所示。

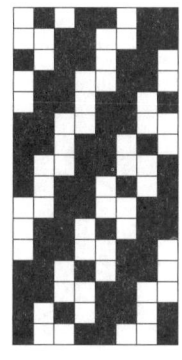

Steep twill 急斜纹　　　Keluodine 克罗丁　　　Whipcord 马裤呢

Fig. 4.10　Steep twill and fabrics

Reclining twill (see Fig. 4.11) line is formed by the weft yarn and the warp yarn is mainly on the back of the fabric. Some fabrics made from the diagonal weave are lady's cloth. The angle of diagonal line is much less than 45 degrees.

缓斜纹（见图 4.11）由纬纱形成，经纱主要在织物的反面。一些缓斜纹织物用于女士服装。斜纹线线的倾角远小于 45 度。

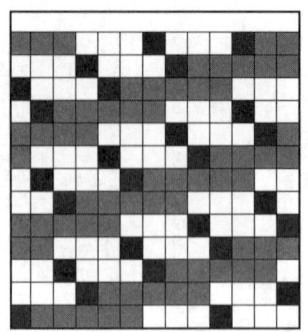

Fig. 4.11　Reclining twill 缓斜纹

3. Curved Twills 曲线斜纹

Curved twills (see Fig. 4.12) produce a curvilinear appearance when the angle of diagonal increases gradually. As we know, the angle of the diagonal may be changed by changing the shift. The curved twill can be constructed by using varying shifts of the basic twill. An increase of the shift makes the angle of the twill diagonal bigger and a decrease of the shift makes the angle smaller. Curved twill weaves are widely used for decorative fabrics and apparel fabrics.

当斜纹线角度逐渐增加时，曲线斜纹（见图4.12）会产生曲线外观。正如我们所知，通过改变组织点飞数来改变斜纹线的倾角。曲线斜纹就是通过改变原组织斜纹的组织点飞数而形成的。飞数增加使得斜纹线倾角变大，飞数降低使得斜纹线倾角变小。曲线斜纹织物广泛用于装饰织物和服装织物。

Fig. 4.12　Curved twill 曲线融合

4. Waved Twills 山形斜纹

Waved twill (see Fig. 4.13) is constructed by changing the sign of shift from plus to minus, after a given number of threads. With the change of sign, the direction of the twill line is changed. Waved twill can be divided into vertical angled twill and horizontal angled twill.

山形斜纹（见图 4.13）是通过将组织点飞数由正改变为负形成的。随着飞数正负的变化，斜纹线的方向也发生了变化。山形斜纹可以分为经山形斜纹和纬山形斜纹。

Fig. 4.13　Waved twill & skirt cloth 曲线斜纹和裙料

5. Broken Twill 破斜纹

Broken twill (see Fig. 4.14) is formed by reversing the pattern part way through the repeat. Usually the break will be at the center of the repeat, with only one reversal, but more complicated breaks can be made. The pattern can be broken either in the warp or in the weft direction, and no twill line will be generated.

破斜纹（见图 4.14）是通过在组织循环中进行底片翻转而形成的。通常，断界在组织循环的中心，只有一次翻转，但也可以进行更复杂的翻转。断界可以在经纱方向或纬纱方向上，不会产生斜纹线。

Fig. 4.14　Broken twill & overcoating 破斜纹和大衣面料

6. Zigzag Twill 锯齿形斜纹

This is a variation of the waved twill. In an waved twill, all weave are on the same level, whereas in a zigzag weave (see Fig. 4.15), the position of the weave are arranged in a ascending or descending diagonal line. Each top point moves a number of threads which is called the zigzag move。

这是山形斜纹变化得来的。在山形斜纹中，所有山顶都在同一水平面上，而在锯齿形斜纹中（见图 4.15），每一个齿顶的位置在一条上升或下降的斜线上。每个齿顶移动的纱线根数，称为锯齿飞数。

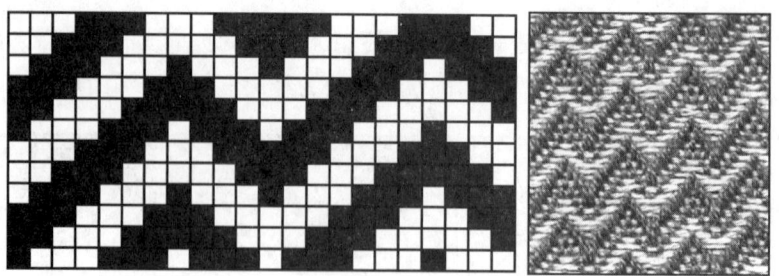

Fig. 4.15　Zigzag twill & curtain 锯齿斜纹和窗帘

7. Diamond Twill 菱形（钻石）斜纹

Diamond designs are based on waved twill and can be considered as a combination of a vertical angled twill and a horizontal angled twill. Diamond twill is as shown in Fig. 4.16 as following.

菱形斜纹的设计基于山形斜纹，可以认为是经山形斜纹和纬山形斜纹的组合。菱形斜纹如下图 4.16 所示。

Fig. 4.16　Diamond twill & table cover 菱形斜纹和桌布

8. Entwined Twill 芦席斜纹

This is a variation of the broken twill. It is generally developed from a combination of even sided Z and S twills and gives the fabric a simulated lattice appearance. Entwined twill is as shown in Fig. 4.17 as following.

Fig. 4.17　Entwined twill & lady cloth 芦席斜纹和女装面料

这是破斜纹变化得来的。它通常由 Z 向和 S 向双面斜纹的组合而成，织物外观好像编织的芦席，芦席斜纹如图 4.17 所示。

New Words and Expressions

twill weave derivatives 斜纹变化组织
reinforced twill 加强斜纹
compound twill 复合斜纹
angled twill 角度斜纹
curved twill 曲线斜纹
zigzag twill 锯齿斜纹
serge 哔叽
gabardine 华达呢
whipcord 马裤呢
cheviot 啥味呢
drill 卡其
lady's cloth 女衣呢
lattice appearance 窗格外观
simulated 模仿

thicker count 低支
diamond twill 菱形斜纹
entwined twill 芦席斜纹
waved twill 山形斜纹
broken twill 破斜纹
vertical angled twill 经山形斜纹
horizontal angled twill 纬山形斜纹
shift 飞数
reversal 反转
ascending 上升的
descending 下降的
decorative fabrics 装饰织物
minus 减号
plus 加号

Task 3

Combined Weaves and Fabrics 联合组织和织物

Fabric woven with basic weaves usually has a smooth surface. The plain weave has an even and regular surface. On the face of twill fabrics there are distinct diagonal lines. The face of sateen weave fabric is smooth and lustrous due to uniform arrangement of single warp floats.

原组织织物通常具有光滑的表面。平纹织物具有均匀而规则的表面。斜纹织物的表面有明显的斜纹线。经面缎纹的表面由于经浮长的均匀排列，织物光滑且光泽好。

Contrary to basic weaves the combined weaves produce irregular or uneven fabric surface or small woven figures on the fabric. These weaves are constructed on the basis of two or more basic weaves and their derivatives.

与原组织相反，联合组织在织物上产生不规则或不平整的织物表面或小的织造花纹。这些组织是由两种或两种以上原组织和变化组织联合而成的。

Combined weaves may be divided into the following groups:

Stripe and check weaves, crepe weaves, mock leno weaves, huckaback, honeycomb weaves, bedford cord weaves, and distorted weaves.

联合组织分为以下各类：

条格组织，绉组织，假纱罗组织，浮松组织，蜂巢组织，凸条组织和网目组织。

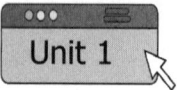 **Unit 1　Stripe and Check Weaves 条格组织**

Some fabrics are made with longitudinal and cross stripes of different widths and different weaves on the surface.

有些织物是由纵向的或横向的条纹以不同的宽度形成于织物的表面。

Combination of longitudinal and cross stripes on the fabrics forms checks in places of their intersection. These weaves are constructed on the basis of two or more basic weaves or their derivatives. The stripe and check weaves are as shown in Fig. 4.18 and Fig. 4.19.

织物上的纵向和横向条纹的组合在交叉处形成格子。这些组织是由两种或两种以上原组织和变化组织联合构成的。条纹组织和格子组织如图 4.18 和图 4.19 所示。

Stripe and check weaves 条格组织

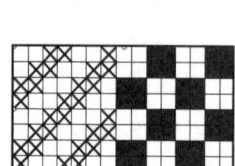  

Fig. 4.18　Longitudinal stripes 经条纹

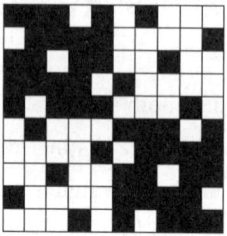 

Fig. 4.19　Check weaves 格子织物

New Words and Expressions

combined weaves 联合组织　　　　　　longitudinal 纵向的
crepe weaves 绉组织　　　　　　　　longitudinal stripes 纵条纹
even 均匀的　　　　　　　　　　　　huckaback weaves 浮松组织
lustrous 光泽的　　　　　　　　　　honeycomb weaves 蜂巢组织
uneven 不均匀　　　　　　　　　　　leno weaves 纱罗组织（透孔组织）

stripes 条子
checks 方格
tripe and check weaves 条格组织

mock leno weaves 假纱罗组织
distorted weaves 网目组织
bedford cord weaves 凸条组织

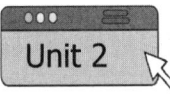 ## Unit 2　Crepe Fabrics 起皱组织

Crepe fabrics (see Fig. 4.20) are characterized by a pebbly（卵石）or crinkled（皱纹）surface. The size of pebbles and their arrangement on the fabric surface determine the type of crepe fabric such as crepe-de-chine（双皱）, crepe-Georgette（乔其皱）, and so on.

Crepe fabrics
起皱组织

起皱织物（见图 4.20）的特点是织物表面具有像小卵石纹一样的绉效应。织物表面褶皱的程度和安排取决于绉织物的类型，如双绉、乔其皱等等。

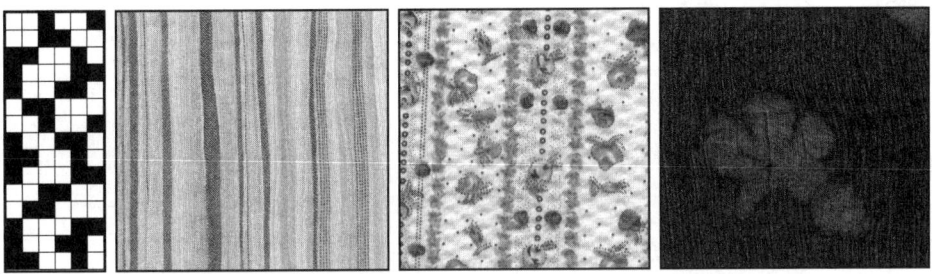

Fig. 4.20　Crepe weaves and fabric 皱组织和织物

The crepe effect can be achieved either by the use of crepe yarns or a crepe weave, or sometimes by special process of finishing, i.e. embossing（压纹）. The fabric is embossed with a metal roll, which has a raised relief engraving（雕刻）, under the conditions of high temperature and pressure. The surface of fabric changes from smooth into uneven or irregular.

起皱效果可以通过使用起皱纱线或绉组织来实现，有时也可以通过特殊的整理过程来实现，即压花。织物采用金属压花辊进行压花，在高温高压的条件下，能增强起绉的效果，使织物表面由光滑变得不均匀。

Using the crepe yarns either in warp or weft gives a crepe fabric. Crepe yarns are tightly twisted. These yarns are composed each of two pairs of untwisted singles, where one pair is tightly twisted in the S direction and the other in the Z direction, and then both pairs are twisted around each other with a low twist. Crepe twist yarns of the fabric snarl（缠结）and shrink during the wet finishing treatment throwing up pebbles wherever there is the least resistance. This method of crepe producing was widely used with natural silk.

在经纱或纬纱中使用起皱纱可以得到起皱织物。起皱纱线捻度很大。这些纱线由两根未加捻的单纱组成，其中一根在 S 方向加强捻，另一根在 Z 方向加强捻，然后两根纱以低捻度相互合股加捻。织物的绉捻纱在湿整理过程中缠结收缩，阻力最小的地方产生鹅卵石状外观。这种织物起皱方法广泛用于真丝起皱（编者注：例如雪纺、顺纡皱）。

Crepe weaves can be constructed on the basis of basic weaves through removing the monotony（单调）of the fabric surfaces of these weaves by means of changing the arrangement of warp overlaps. There are no-general rules for the construction of crepe weaves, but many different methods are known.

绉组织是以原组织为基础，通过改变经纬浮长，使其在纵横方向错综排列，进而改变了原组织织物表面单一的特点。绉织物的形成没有统一的规则，但已知有许多不同的方法。

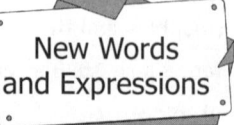

New Words and Expressions

crinkle 卷曲
crepe-Georgette 乔其纱
crepe weave 绉组织
relief engraving 浮雕滚筒
snarl 扭结
wet finishing 湿整理
pebbles 鹅卵石
engraving 雕刻

crepe-de-chine 双绉
crepe yarns 绉纱
embossing 浮雕印花，压纹
tightly twisted 高捻度
shrink 收缩
overlaps 重叠
monotony 单调，千篇一律

Unit 3　Mock Leno Weaves and Huckaback Weaves 假纱罗和透孔组织

1. Mock Leno Weaves 假纱罗组织

These fabrics form an open structure with small holes or gaps similar to leno weave fabrics. These fabrics produce an imitation of leno effects and, due to this, the weaves of these fabrics are called the mock leno weaves. Mock leno weaves is shown in Fig. 4.21.

Mock leno & huckaback
假纱和透孔组织

这类织物由于具有一些小孔而结构疏松，类似于纱罗组织织物。因为模仿了纱罗组织的效果，所以这类组织又称为假纱罗组织，如图 4.21。

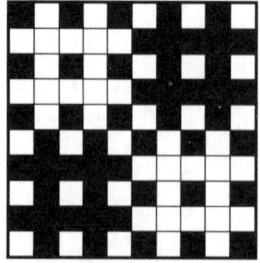 

Fig. 4.21　Mock leno weaves 假纱罗组织

These light and open fabrics are used for many articles, such as curtains, dress, underclothing, and so on.

这些轻薄带孔的织物被用于许多纺织品，如窗帘、连衣裙、内衣等。

2. Huckaback Weaves 花式透孔组织

This weave contains, on one hand, a number of warp and weft threads with long floats which make the fabric soft and moisture absorbent, and, on the other hand, the plain weave threads which ensure the firmness of the structure.

在这种组织中，一方面，因为具有经纬浮长线，使得织物柔软、吸水性好；另一方面，平纹组织的部分使得织物坚实稳固。

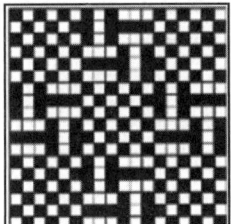 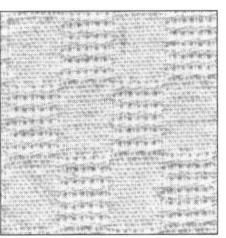

Fig. 4.22　Huckaback weaves 花式透孔组织

Huckaback weaves (see Fig. 4.22) are used for bathroom towels, glass cloths and for counterpanes.

花式透孔组织（见图 4.22）用于浴室毛巾、眼镜布和床单。

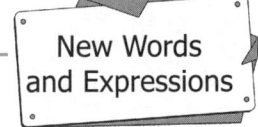

gap 裂口
imitation 模仿
huckaback weaves 浮松组织（花式透孔）

underclothing 内衣
moisture absorbent 吸湿性
counterpanes 床罩

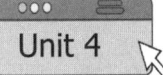 **Honeycomb Weaves 蜂巢组织**

A group of weaves forms an embossed cell-like appearance of fabric. These so-called "cellular（多孔的）" fabrics are characterized by orderly distribution of hollows（中空）and ridges（凹陷）. The honeycomb weave (see Fig. 4.23) is one of the most interesting weaves of this group. The surface of the weave looks like the honeycomb cells made of wax by the bees. The rough and loose structure of these fabrics makes them good absorbents of moisture. Due to this, these fabrics are widely used for bathroom towels and also for bedcovers, quilts, winter garments, and so on.

Honeycomb
蜂巢组织

这类织物的表面具有像细胞一样的凹凸花纹。这些所谓的"多孔"织物具有小孔均匀分布的特点。蜂巢组织（见图 4.23）是这类组织中最有趣的一种组织。它的表面看起来像蜜蜂用蜡做成的蜂窝。这些织物粗糙和疏松的结构使它们具有很好的吸湿性。正因为如此，这些织物被广泛用于浴巾、床上用品、被子、冬装等。

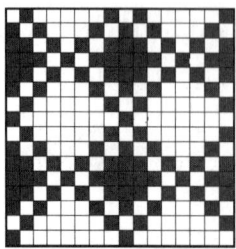  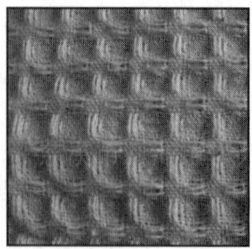

Fig. 4.23　Honeycomb 蜂巢组织

embossed 凹凸的　　　　　　　　　　hollow 中空的
cellular 多孔的　　　　　　　　　　　ridges 凹的

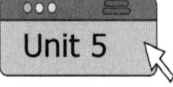 **Novel Appearance Fabric 新颖外观织物**

1. Bedford Cord Weaves 纵凸条组织

Both of these weaves are characterized by rounded cords with fine sunken lines between. The distinction between a bedford cord and pique（凹凸组织）is that the former the cord runs along the length of the cloth, see Fig. 4.24.

Novel fabric
新颖织物

这类组织的特点是织物正面有圆形凸条而反面是纬浮长线。纵凸条和横凸条之间的区别是前者的凸条是沿着织物的长度方向，如图 4.24。

 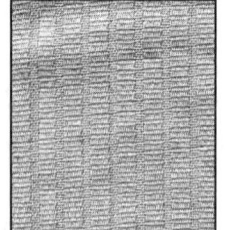

Fig. 4.24　Bedford cord weaves & fabric 凸条组织和织物

2. Distorted Weaves 网目组织

In distorted warp weaves, the ends are creating the distorted effect. A number of weft floats are surrounded by plain weave ground. The weft floats allow the end to move into the area of least resistance causing a vertical zigzag（之字形）line，see Fig. 4.25.

在经网目组织中，由经纱产生网目效应。纬浮长线周围是大面积的平纹，纬浮长线允许经纱移动到阻力最小的区域，这样就产生了纵向曲折的线，如图4.25。

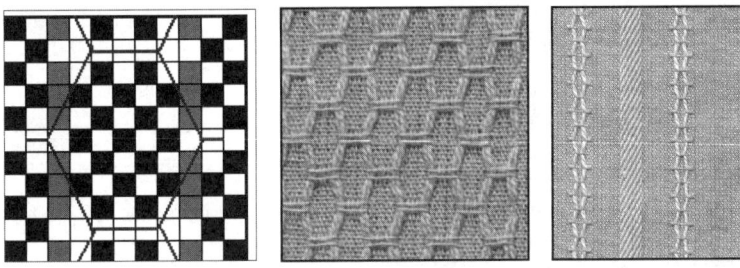

Fig. 4.25　Distorted weave & fabric 网目组织和织物

These ends are placed on a separate beam or roller, woven with less tension and drawn in additionally to the ground ends into the reed.

这些经纱被放置在一个单独的织轴上，织造时张力较小，并和地经同时穿入钢筘中。

Generally, thicker yarns of contrasting colors are employed to highlight the effect. The weave is arranged on a pointed draft and the shafts for the distorted ends are located at the front. To avoid long warp floats on the back of the fabric, ground ends are lifted at certain intervals to shorten these floats.

一般情况下，利用粗的纱线或者颜色对比比较明显的纱线做网目经纱可以增强网目的效果。组织中的网目经纱被卷绕在专门的轴上，放置在前面。为了避免织物背面出现长的经浮长线，地经按一定间隔提起（与纬纱交织）以缩短浮长线。

3. Color and Weave Effects 配色模纹

Various colored patterns can be obtained in fabric by combining colored yarns and weaves. That means, the patterns are not only depended on weaves, but also color sequence，see Fig. 4.26.

通过色纱和组织相配合，可以在织物中获得各种彩色花纹。也就是说，花纹不仅取决于组织，还取决于色纱排列，如图4.26。

Fig. 4.26　Color and weave effects 配色模纹

New Words and Expressions

pique 凹凸组织
bedford cord 纵凸条
distorted warp weaves 经网目
ground ends 地经
color and weave effects 色纱与组织的配合（配色模纹）
colored patterns 花型花纹
sunken 沉没的，凹陷的
vertical 垂直的

fine sunken lines 细沟槽
shafts 轴，杆
least resistance 阻力小
distorted ends 网目经
color sequence 色纱排列
zigzag 曲折的，锯齿形的
highlight 突出，强调

Task 4

Compound Weaves and Fabrics 复杂组织

Fundamental and combined weaves are considered to be simple, through there is a great variety of types and constructions. In these weaves, only one system of warp threads is interlaced with one system of weft threads at right angles. Due to this, the methods of construction of these weaves and production of fabrics of such weaves at textile mills are rather simple.

Compound weaves 复杂组织

基本组织和联合组织被认为是简单的组织，可以有各种各样的类型和结构。在这类组织中，只有一个系统的经纱和一个系统的纬纱成直角交织。因此，这些组织的构成方法和纺织厂生产这种织物的方法相对简单。

Compound weave fabrics are of a specific structure, therefore special methods and mechanisms should be used in their production.

复杂组织织物具有特殊的结构，因此在生产中应采用特殊的方法和机构。

More than one system of warp and weft threads are used in these weaves. Very often the threads of different systems are arranged in different planes, forming two or more layers. If the tension in weaving or crimp of the warp of additional system differs from those of the systems of the ground thread, a separate weaver's beam is necessary. If the system of weft threads differs in yarn count, type of fibers or color, the loom should be equipped with a multi-shuttle mechanism.

在这些组织中采用了不止一种经纱和纬纱系统。经常把不同系统的纱线安排在不同的位面上，这样就能形成两层或更多层织物。如果在织造或卷取过程中地经和另一个系统的经纱张力不一致，则必须增加一个织轴。如果几个系统的纬纱在纱支、原料或颜色上不同，则织机需配备多梭箱机构。

 **Unit 1**　　Backed Weaves 重组织

The principle of backing a cloth with a second series of either weft or warp threads is to add extra weight and warmth without interfering with the smooth surface of the fabric. The end uses of backed cloths range from apparel to furnishing.

Backed weaves
重组织

用两个系统的经纱或两个系统的纬纱形成的二重组织织物可以增加织物的重量及厚度，而不会影响织物表面的细腻感。

1. Warp Backed Weaves 经二重组织

These are weaves, which have two systems of warp and one system of weft. The face weave is formed by interlacing face warp and weft. The back weave is formed by interlacing back warp and weft. The system of weft plays an important role due to interlacing with both systems of warp. The weft threads are raised above the face warp and lowered the back warp. The warp backed weave is shown in Fig. 4.27.

这些组织由两个系统经纱和一个系统纬纱构成。表面组织是由表经和纬纱交织而成。里面组织是由里经和纬线交织而成。一个系统的纬纱由于和两个系统的经纱相交织，所以显得很重要。纬纱位于表经的上方，里经的下方。经二重组织如图 4.27 所示。

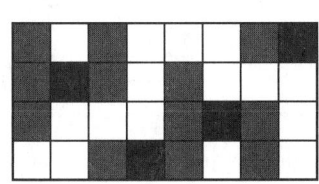 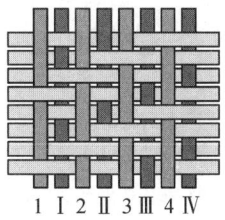

Fig. 4.27　　Warp backed weave 经二重组织

2. Weft Backed Weaves 纬二重组织

These are weaves which have two systems of weft and one system of warp. The face weave is formed by interlacing warp and face weft. The back weave is formed by interlacing warp and back weft. The backed weft weaves are widely used for blankets, thick woolens and some industrial fabrics. The weft backed weave is shown in Fig. 4.28.

这类组织是由两个系统的纬纱和一个系统的经纱构成的。经纱和表纬交织形成表面组织。经纱和里纬交织形成反面组织。纬二重组织被广泛用于毛毯、厚毛织物和一些工业织物（编者注：纬二重也经常用于色织纬剪花、大提花丝绸织物）。纬二重组织如图 4.28 所示。

105

 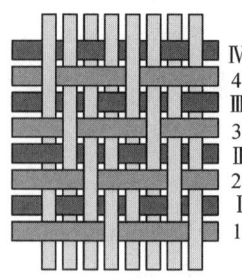

Fig. 4.28 Weft backed weave 纬重平

3. Extra Warp and Extra Weft Weaves 经起花组织和纬起花组织

Extra warp or extra weft yarns can be used on a plain, twill, or satin ground to produce small figured designs, somewhat like embroidery. The extra yarn stands out from the ground due to its figured pattern of interlacing and it usually has a distinctive color, fiber type, or luster. Extra warp weave and fabric is as shown in Fig. 4.29.

Extra warp and extra weft weaves 经纬起花

起花经纱或起花纬纱可以在平纹、斜纹或缎面上使用，以产生小的花纹图案，有点像刺绣。由于花经与地经可以选择不同颜色、不同原料或不同光泽的纱线，所以花经与纬纱交织形成的花型在地布上很突出。经起花组织及其织物如图 4.29 所示。

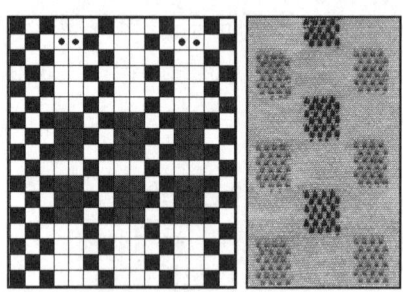 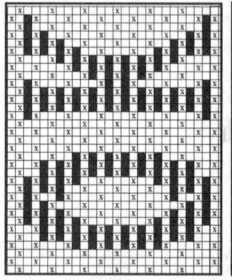 

Fig. 4.29 Extra warp weaves & fabrics 经起花组织和织物

Extra weft yields figures across the width. Extra warp gives figures along the length. Both effects can be combined. Extra weft weave and fabric is as shown in Fig. 4.30.

起花纬纱在宽度上产生花纹图案。起花经纱在长度上产生花纹图案。这两种效果可以结合在一起。起花纬组织和织物如图 4.30 所示。

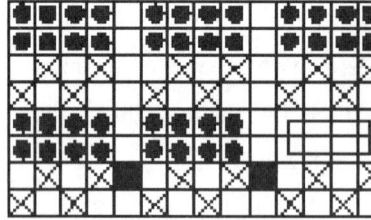 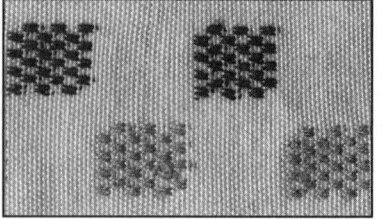

Fig. 4.30 Extra weft weave &fabric 纬起花组织和织物

The extra yarn produces the figure on the face side but it may float unbound on the back, depending on the yarn and fabric properties and the end-use requirements. If there are large spaces between the figures, then the extra yarn can be bound in at intervals, if the long extra yarn floats would show through, they can be cut away from the back.

起花纱线会在织物正面产生花形，但（不起花时）它可能会浮在织物反面，这取决于纱线和织物的性能以及最终使用要求。如果起花部分间隔距离较长，则需间隔一定距离与纬纱交织一次；如果花经在织物反面的浮长线很长，可以将浮长线剪断。

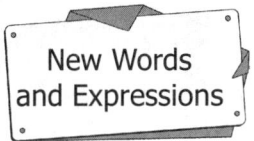

New Words and Expressions

compound weaves 复杂组织
planes 位面
layers 层
tension 张力
separate 使分离，使分开
backed weaves 二重组织
smooth surface 平整表面
warp backed weaves 经二重组织
thick woolens 粗厚呢
extra warp 花经
figure 花型
unbound 自由的，不受束缚的

at right angles 成直角
specific 特殊的，详细的
crimp 卷发，束缚
additional 附加的，额外的
yarn count 纱支
interfering 干涉的
furnishing 装饰织物
blankets 毛毯
industrial fabrics 产业用布
extra weft 花纬
embroidery 刺绣

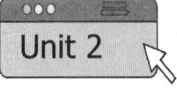 **Unit 2**　Double Fabrics 双层织物

Double fabric consists of two layers which are woven one above the other. This fabric contains as a minimum two system of warps, face and back, and two systems of weft. This fabric can also be called double fabric. The upper layer is formed by interlacing the face warp threads with the face weft threads, and the lower layer by interlacing the back warp threads with the back weft threads.

Double fabrics
双层织物

双层织物由两层组成，一层在另一层之上。这种织物至少包含两个经纱系统，正面和反面，以及两个纬纱系统。这种织物也可以称为双层织物。表经与表纬交织形成织物上层，里经与里纬交织形成织物下层。

1. Stitching Double Weave and Fabrics 接结双层组织及其织物

In this case, the two fabrics are stitched together by a stitching system. They are softer and fuller but are less firmly united and can be pulled apart. The fabrics are suitable for making reversible garments. Stitching double weave & fabric is as shown in Fig. 4.31.

在这种情况下,两层织物通过接结系统接结在一起,使得织物更加柔软、丰满,但质地不够坚牢,容易撕开。这类织物适合制作双面服装。接结双层组织及其织物如图 4.31 所示。

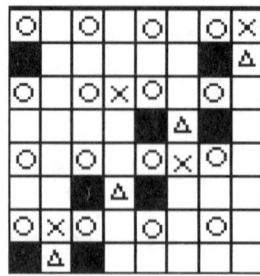 

Fig. 4.31　**Stitching double weave &fabric** 接结双层组织和织物

2. Interchanging Double Cloths 表里换层双层布

These are double cloths in which the face and back fabrics interchange according to a specified design. The fabrics may be unstitched between the interchanges, leaving holes between the two. The pattern is the same on both sides, through they may be oppositely colored. The fabrics may be used reversibly. They can be used for cloaks, shawls, and tablecloths, see Fig. 4.32.

这是一种双面布,根据特定的设计,正面和反面的织物可以互换。在表里换层期间织物并没有接结在一起,两层之间留有一些空间。织物正反面的花型是一样的,但颜色可能相反。这种织物可以正反使用。它们可用做斗篷、披肩和桌布(编者注:也可用作夏季服饰面料),如图 4.32。

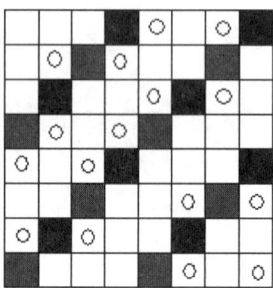 

Fig. 4.32　**Interchanging double cloth** 表里换层组织

New Words and Expressions

double fabrics 双层组织织物　　　　　　　fuller 丰满
two-ply 两层的　　　　　　　　　　　　　stitched 缝纫
stitching double fabrics 接结双层织物　　　layer 层

reversible 可逆的，双面布料　　　　　interchange 交换
cloaks 斗篷，宽大外衣　　　　　　　　shawls 围巾

Unit 3　Cut Pile and Terry Fabrics 割绒和毛圈织物

Cut pile fabrics are made by using the third yarn system to form a cut fiber pile on the face of the fabric. Fabrics with a short pile are called velvet or velveteen, long-pile fabrics are called plush.

割绒织物是通过使用第三纱线系统在织物表面形成割绒纤维而制成的。短绒毛的织物被称为天鹅绒或平绒，长绒毛的织品被称为毛绒。

Cut pile and terry fabrics
割绒和毛圈织物

Cut pile fabrics can be made either with an additional warp or with an additional weft. The former are velvets, the latter are velveteen.

剪绒织物可以用额外的经纱或额外的纬纱制成。前者是经绒（天鹅绒），后者是纬绒。

The quality is determined by the density of the ground weave and by the height and density of the pile. There are different ways of binding the pile into the ground fabric, according to end-use requirements.

质量由地组织的密度以及绒头的高度和密度决定。根据最终用途的要求，有不同的方法将绒毛固结在底布上。

Velveteen are constructed so that the pile weft floats largely on the surface of the fabric. After cutting, the tufts are held by the warp yarns. The density of the fabric and the pile height are determined by the interlacing pattern of ground and pile. The pile is cut in a special separate operation. It is then brushed open and cropped to a uniform height.

平绒组织的结构使得绒头纬纱大部分浮在织物的表面上。在割绒之后，纬纱簇被经纱固结。织物的密度和绒头高度由地面和绒头的交织图案决定。割绒是一个特殊的独立操作，之后刷毛并通过割绒而达到一致的高度。

1. Plain Velveteen 平绒

If the binding points for the pile yarn are uniformly distributed, then a plain velveteen（see Fig. 4.33）results.

如果绒头纱的结合点分布均匀，则会形成平绒（见图 4.33）。

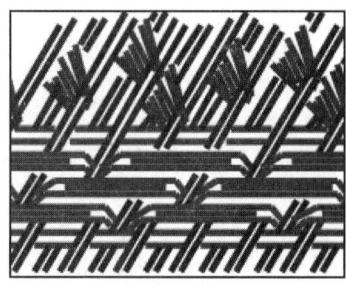

Fig. 4.33　Plain velveteen 平绒

2. Corded Velveteen 灯芯绒

If the pile yarns always float between the same warp yarns, then corded velveteen (see Fig. 4.34) are produced after cutting. The cords may be fine, medium or broad. Cord width can be mixed in the same fabric.

如果绒头纱总是浮在相同的经纱之间，那么在切割后就会形成灯芯绒（见图 4.34）。灯芯绒条可以是细的、中等的或宽的。不同宽度的灯芯绒条可以在同一织物中混合。

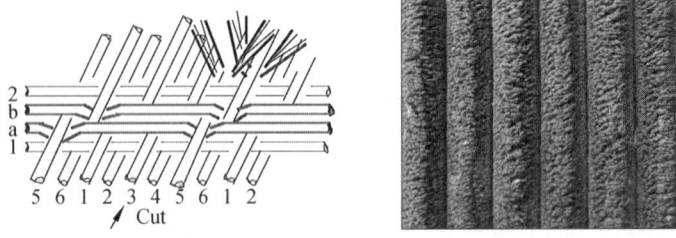

Fig. 4.34　Corded velveteen 灯芯绒

3. Velvet 天鹅绒

Velvets are made with an additional warp and the cut fiber tufts are bound into the ground fabric by the weft.

天鹅绒是用额外经线制成的，切割后形成的纤维簇通过纬线固结到底布中。

The two main production techniques are wire weaving and double plush weaving. The latter is more economical but less uniform. Two fabrics are woven together on a special loom. The ground fabrics are independent but they share a single pile warp. The pile yarns are subsequently cut through the middle by a reciprocating knife. Thus five sets of yarns make two fabrics, each with three yarn sets.

两种主要的生产工艺是金属钢丝杆起绒法和双层毛绒编织。后者更经济，但起绒布不很均匀。两种织物在特殊的织机上织在一起。底布是独立的，但它们共用一个绒经纱。绒经纱随后被往复式刀具从中间切割。因此，五组纱线构成两种织物，每种织物有三组纱线。

In wire weaving, see Fig. 4.35, the pile warp is led over either looping wires or cutting wires. When the wires are withdrawn the pile either forms loops or is cut. The pile may be cropped, to make it level then brushed and steamed.

在金属丝杆起绒法中，如图4.35，绒头经纱被引导到成圈的金属起绒杆或割绒的金属杆上。当金属起绒杆抽出时，绒经要么形成环，要么被切断。可以修剪绒毛，使其平整，然后刷毛蒸制。

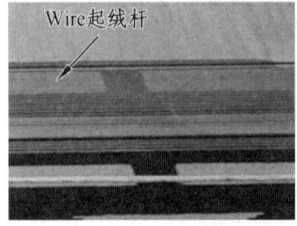 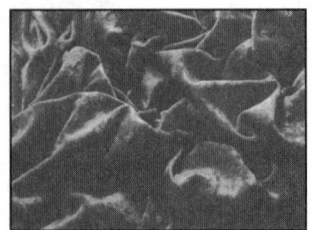

Fig. 4.35　Velvet 天鹅绒

4. Burned out Velvets 烂花天鹅绒

Burned out velvets (see Fig. 4.36) are made by printing a pattern onto the pile using a chemical which dissolves or destroys it.

烂花天鹅绒（见图 4.36）是通过溶解或破坏它的化学物质在绒毛上印制图案而制成的（编者注：烂花天鹅绒一般采用涤纶或尼龙包锦纶纱织造，芯丝是聚酯或锦纶长丝，外包棉或黏胶短纤维，织造成坯布后，在表面局部用硫酸印花，外层棉或黏胶被酸溶解，仅留下耐酸的聚酯或锦纶长丝，呈现局部半透明状，不印酸的部分保持天鹅绒状）。

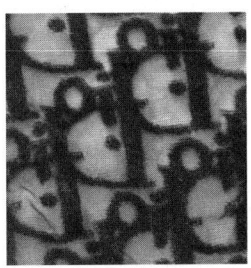

Fig. 4.36　Burned out velvet 烂花天鹅绒

5. Terry Fabrics 毛巾织物

Terry, or loop-pile fabrics are made from two warps. The ground warp is normally or tightly tensioned, the pile warp is looser. Two or three weft yarns are introduced but are not fully beaten up into the cloth. With the next weft yarn all three or four threads are beaten up together. They slide over the tensioned ground warp but the pile warp is simultaneously slackened off so that it is bent up into a loop whose size corresponds to the final beating-up distance. Loops can be formed on one or both sides of the fabric. Pattern effects are achieved by introducing color into the pile warp, and by having loops of different sizes.

毛圈织物是由两组经纱织造的。地经张力正常或张紧，毛经较松。引入两根或三根纬纱，但纬纱没有完全打入织口。伴随下一根纬纱织入，将三根或四根纬纱一起打入织口，它们在张紧的地经上滑动，但毛经同时松弛，使其弯曲成一个环（毛圈），其大小与最终的打纬距离相对应。可以在织物的一面或两面形成毛圈。图案效果是通过将颜色引入毛经中，并通过具有不同尺寸的毛圈来实现的。

The pile yarns can be singles or two-fold. The fabrics can be made more dense and durable by a full process.

毛经纱可以是单纱或股线。通过一个完整生产过程，织物可以变得更加致密和耐用。

Terry velour is produced by cropping and brushing the loops to give a velvet-like appearance.

Loop yarn fabric has the appearance of terry but is made from only two sets of yarns, with a loop yarn in the weft.

毛圈绒是通过修剪和刷毛圈来产生天鹅绒般的外观。

毛圈纱织物外观像毛圈布，但只由两组纱线制成，纬纱中有一根毛圈纱。

New Words and Expressions

pile 毛圈
velveteen 平绒
tufts 一簇，一丛
cropped 切割的
corded velveteen 灯芯绒
double plush weaving 双层织造
reciprocating 往复的，交互的
burned out velvets 烂花丝绒
terry fabrics 起圈织物
slackened off 放松

velvet 天鹅绒，丝绒
cut pile fabrics 起绒织物
brushed 刷绒，拉过绒的
plain velveteen 纬平绒
terry velour 起圈丝绒
pile warp 绒经
steamed 汽蒸的
dissolves 溶解
loop yarn fabric 起圈花线织物
two-fold 双重的，双折的

Task 5

Fabric Introduction in Brief 织物简要介绍

Unit 1 Dyed Yarn Fabrics 色织物

1. Poplin 府绸

A fabric is made of a plain weave with high density and fine yarn. Poplin used to be associated with casual（休闲）clothing, this fabric has developed into a staple of men's wardrobes（衣柜）.

织物是由高密和细纱以平纹组织制成。府绸曾经与休闲服饰相联系，这种面料已发展成为男士衣橱的主要面料。

Dyed yarn fabrics show
色织物展示

Dyed yarn fabrics
色织物

2. Chambray 青年布

A plain woven fabric that can be made from cotton or manufactured fibers, but is most commonly cotton. It incorporates a colored warp (often blue) and white filling yarns.

一种平纹织物，可以由棉或人造纤维制成，但最常见的是棉。它融合了彩色经纱（通常是蓝色的）和白色纬纱（即色经白纬——编者注）。

3. Oxford 牛津布

A fine, soft, lightweight woven cotton or blended with manufactured fibers in a 2 × 1 basket weave variation of the plain weave construction. The fabric is used primarily in shirtings.

一种精细、柔软、轻便的编织棉，或与人造纤维混纺，采用平纹织物结构的 2×1 变化重平组织。这种面料主要用于衬衫。

4. Fil-a-fil (end-on-end) 米通条

Dark and light yarns alternate in warp is woven with a weft yarn of single colour, or the opposite.

深色和浅色经纱交替和单色纬纱交织，抑或相反。

5. Double Cloth 双层布

A fabric construction, in which two fabrics are woven on the loom at the same time, one on top of the other. In the weaving process, the two layers of woven fabric are held together using binder threads. The woven patterns in each layer of fabric can be similar or completely different.

一种织物结构，其中两种织物同时在织机上织造，一种在另一种之上。在编织过程中，两层织物用接结线固定在一起。每层织物中的编织图案可以相似，也可以完全不同。

6. Seersucker 泡泡纱

A woven fabric which incorporates modification of tension control. In the production of seersucker, some of the warp yarns are held under controlled tension at all times during the weaving, while other warp yarns are in a relaxed state and tend to pucker（折叠）when the filling yarns are placed. The result produces a puckered stripe effect in the fabric. Seersucker is traditionally made into summer sportswear such as shirts, trousers, and informal（非正式的）suits.

一种结合了张力控制变化装置的机织物。在泡泡纱的生产中，一些经纱在织造过程中始终处于受控的张力下，而其他经纱则处于松弛状态，容易起皱（折叠）。当织入纬纱时，其结果是在织物中产生褶皱条纹效果。泡泡纱传统上被制成夏季运动服，如衬衫、裤子和非正式服装套装。

7. Leno Weave Fabric 绞综（纱罗）布

A construction of woven fabrics in which the resulting fabric is very sheer（透明），yet durable. In this weave, two or more warp yarns are twisted（扭转）around each other as they are interlaced with the filling yarns; thus securing a firm hold on the filling yarn and preventing them from slipping out of position. Also called the gauze weave. Leno weave fabrics are frequently used for fashion in summer, because their structure gives good durability with almost no yarn slippage, and permits the passage of light and air.

机织物的一种结构，其织物非常透明，但耐用。在这种织造工艺中，两根或多根经纱被扭转，当它们与纬纱交织时彼此围绕，从而确保了对纬纱的牢固夹持并防止它们滑出位置。也称为薄纱组织。纱罗织物常用于夏季时装，因为它们的结构具有良好的耐用性，几乎没有纱线打滑，并且透光透气。

8. Denim 牛仔布

True denim is a twill weave cotton-like fabric made with different colored yarns in the warp and the weft. Due to the twill construction, one color predominates（支配）on the fabric surface.

纯正的牛仔布是一种似棉的斜纹织物，由不同颜色的经纱和纬纱制成。由于采用了斜纹结构，所以以一种颜色为主在织物表面（编者注：牛仔布是色经白纬的厚重色织物，以3/1斜纹组织织造。正面一般靛蓝经纱颜色为主，白色纬纱为辅助，反面则相反）。

9. Voile 巴厘纱

A crisp, lightweight, plain weave cotton-like fabric, made with high twist yarns in a high yarn count construction. Similar in appearance to organdy（蝉翼纱）. Used in blouses dresses（女装恤衫）and curtains.

一种挺括、轻盈、平纹仿棉织物，由高捻纱线制成，具有高支数结构。外表与蝉翼纱相似。用于女装恤衫和窗帘（编者注：巴厘纱风格特征是挺爽、透气、不贴身，技术特征是高支、低密、经纬强捻）。

10. Corduroy 灯芯绒

A fabric, usually made of cotton, utilizing a cut-pile weave construction. Extra sets of filling yarns are woven into the fabric to form ridges of yarn on the surface. The ridges are built so that clear lines can be seen when the pile is cut.

灯芯绒通常为棉织物，采用割绒组织结构。织物中织入额外的纬纱，在表面形成纱线脊。线脊的构造是为了在割绒后可以看到清晰的线条（编者注：灯芯绒是一种纬起毛织物，经割绒割断纬浮长线形成灯芯条，纬密大于经密）。

11. Pile Weave 起毛织物

A type of decorative weave in which a pile is formed by additional warp or filling yarns interlaced in such a way that loops are formed on the surface or face of the fabric. The loops may be left uncut, or they may be cut to expose yarn ends and produce cut pile fabric.

一种具有装饰感织物，由额外的经纱或纬纱交织而成，在织物的表面或外表形成环。线圈可以不切割，也可以切割以露出纱线末端并生产割绒织物。

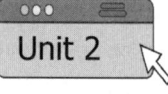

Unit 2　Filament Yarn Fabric 长丝织物

1. Chiffon 雪纺

A plain woven lightweight, extremely sheer, airy, and soft silk fabric, containing highly twisted filament yarns. The fabric, used mainly in evening dresses and scarves, can also be made from rayon and other manufactured fibers.

Filament fabric show
长丝面料展示

Filament yarn fabric
长丝织物

一种平纹织物，重量轻，非常透明、透气、柔软，含有高度扭曲的长丝。这种面料主要用于晚礼服和围巾，也可以由人造丝和其他人造纤维制成。

2. Pongee 春亚纺

The most common form is a naturally colored lightweight, plain weave, silk-like fabric with a slubbed effect. End-uses include blouses, dresses, etc.

最常见的形式是一种颜色自然、质地轻盈、类似丝绸的平纹织物，具有粗节效果。最终用途包括衬衫、连衣裙等。

3. Taffeta 塔夫绸

A lustrous, medium weight, plain weave fabric with a slight ribbed appearance in the filling (crosswise) direction. For formal wear, taffeta is a favorite choice. Silk taffeta gives the ultimate rustle, but other fibers are also good choices.

一种有光泽的中等重量平纹织物，在纬纱（横向）方向上有轻微的罗纹外观。对于正式服装，塔夫绸是最受欢迎的选择。蚕丝的塔夫绸能发出极致的沙沙声，但其他纤维也是不错的选择。

4. Georgette 乔其纱

A sheer lightweight fabric, often made of silk or from such manufactured fibers as polyester, with a crepe surface. End-uses include dresses and blouses.

一种轻薄的纱织物，通常由蚕丝或聚酯等人造纤维制成，表面有褶皱。最终用途有连衣裙和衬衫等。

5. Shantung 山东绸

A medium-weight, plain weave fabric, characterized by a ribbed effect, resulting from slubbed yarns used in the warp or filling direction. End-uses include dresses and suits.

一种中等重量的平纹织物，其特征是有罗纹效果，由在经纱或纬纱方向上使用粗纱产生。最终用途包括连衣裙和西装。

6. Surah 斜纹软绸

A light weight, lustrous twill weave constructed fabric with a silk-like hand. Surah is the fabric of ties, dresses, and furnishings. It is available in silk, polyester, and rayon.

一种质地轻盈、有光泽的斜纹织物，有丝绸般的手感，用于领带、连衣裙和家居织物。它有蚕丝、聚酯纤维和人造丝三种。

7. Embroidery 绣花

An embellishment of a fabric or garment in which colored threads are sewn on to the fabric to create a design. Embroidery may be done either by hand or machine.

一种织物或服装的装饰，将彩色线缝在织物上以形成图案。刺绣可以手工完成，也可以用机器完成。

8. Brocade 织锦缎

A heavy, exquisite jacquard type fabric with an all-over raised pattern or floral design（花卉图案）. Common end-uses include such formal applications as upholstery（家居装饰织物）, draperies（装饰织物）, and eveningwear.

一种厚重、精致的提花织物，具有全凸起图案或花卉设计。常见的最终用途包括室内装饰等正式的家居织物，装饰织物以及晚装（编者注：织锦缎一般采用重组织，多重色纬或色经织造的大提花丝织物，如我国云锦、宋锦、蜀锦、壮锦、土家锦、黎锦，日本的西阵织等）。

Unit 3　Woolen and Worsted Fabrics 粗纺和精纺毛织物

1. Gabardine 华达呢

A tightly woven, twilled, worsted fabric with a slight diagonal line on the right side. Wool gabardine is known as a year-round fabric for business suiting. Polyester, cotton, rayon, and various blends are also used in making gabardine.

Woolen and worsted fabrics show
毛织物展示

Woolen and worsted fabrics
毛织物

一种紧密织造的、斜纹的精纺毛织物，有一条轻微的右斜线。羊毛华达呢是众所周知的全年商务西装面料。涤纶、棉、人造丝和各种混纺面料也被用于制作华达呢。

2. Doeskin 驼丝锦

Generally applied to a type of fabric finish in which a low nap is brushed in one direction to create a soft suede-like（麂皮样的，绒面的）hand on the fabric surface. End-uses include billiard table surfaces and men's sportswear.

通常用于一种织物表面处理，在这种表面处理中，向一个方向刷低高度绒毛，在织物表面形成柔软的仿麂皮绒手感，最终用途包括台球桌表面布和男士运动服。

3. Serge 哔叽

A fabric with a smooth hand that is created by a two-up, two-down twill weave.

一种手感光滑的织物，由 2/2 的斜纹交织而成。

4. Flannel 法兰绒

A medium-weight, plain or twill weave fabric that is typically made from cotton, a cotton blend, or wool. The fabric has a very soft hand, brushed on both sides to lift the fiber ends out of the base fabric and create a soft, fuzzy surface. End-uses include shirts and pajamas.

一种中等重量的平纹或斜纹织物，通常由纯棉、棉混纺或羊毛制成。这种织物手感非常柔软，双面刷毛，可以将纤维末端从底布拉起，形成柔软、模糊的表面。最终用途包括衬衫和睡衣（编者注：法兰绒的要素是低捻度、斜纹组织、坯布织造后经起绒机起绒）。

5. Melton 麦尔登

A heavyweight, dense, compacted, and tightly woven wool or wool blend fabric used mainly for coats.

一种主要用于外套的厚重、密实、紧密的羊毛或羊毛混纺织物。

6. Tweed 花呢

A medium to heavy weight, fluffy（毛绒）woolen, twill weave fabric containing colored slubbed yarns. Common end-uses include coats and suits.

中等至重磅，蓬松且含有彩色粗节纱线的羊毛、斜纹织物。常见的最终用途包括外套和西装。

7. Tapestry 挂毯

A heavy, often hand-woven, ribbed fabric, featuring an elaborate design depicting a historical or current pictorial display. The weft-faced fabric design is made by using colored filling yarns, only in areas where needed, that are worked back and forth over spun warp yarns, which are visible on the back. End-uses include wall hangings and upholstery.

一种厚重的、通常是手工编织的重经织物，其特点是精心设计，描绘了历史或当前的图片展示。通过采用彩色纬纱进行纬面织物设计，只有在需要时，（纬纱才浮在织物正面）纬纱在经纱上反复交织，在织物背面可见。最终用途包括壁挂和室内装潢。

Unit 4　Stripe & Check Fabrics 条格织物

A medium weight, plain weave fabric with a stripe or check pattern. End-uses include dresses, shirts, and curtains.

条纹或格子图案的中等重量平纹织物。最终用途为连衣裙、衬衫和窗帘。

Stripe & check fabrics
条格面料

1. Tartan 苏格兰格

Large squares of colour over laid by warp and weft stripes, from coloured warp and weft. The patterns and colours derive from traditional Scottish（苏格兰人）dress.

由彩色经条和纬条覆盖形成大方形纹样，这些条纹来自彩色经纬纱，图案和色彩源自苏格兰传统连衣裙。

2. Glen Check 格林格

Glen check is made on a 2/2 twill base by having dark and white threads and a colouring order of n sets of 4:4 followed by 2n sets of 2:2 in both directions.

以 2/2 斜纹为基础组织织造，由深色和白色的线组成，颜色顺序为 n 组 4:4，然后是 2n 组 2:2。

3. Houndstooth 千鸟格，犬牙格

Houndstooth is particular types based on 2/2 twill. Small check in contrasting colours, usually on a 2/2 twill base with 4:4, 6:6 or 8:8 colouring. Also made in 4/4 twill and 4/4 basket weave.

基于 2/2 斜纹的特殊类型。对比色小格子，通常以 2/2 斜纹基础，颜色为 4:4、6:6 或 8:8。同样采用 4/4 斜纹和 4/4 方平组织交织而成。

Unit 5　Finished Fabrics 后整理面料

Finished fabrics
后整理面料

1. Flocking 植绒

A type of raised decoration applied to the surface of a fabric in which an adhesive is printed on the fabric in a specific pattern, and then finely chopped fibers are applied by means of dusting, air-brushing, or electrostatic charges. The fibers adhere only to the areas where the adhesive has been applied, and the excess fibers are removed by mechanical means.

一种应用于织物表面的凸起装饰（方法），其中黏合剂以特定的图案印刷在织物上，然后通过除尘、空气刷或静电荷作用，施加细小的被切短纤维上，纤维只黏附在已经施加黏合剂的区域，多余的纤维通过机械方式去除。

2. Burn-out 烂花

A brocade-like pattern effect is created on the fabric through the application of a chemical, instead of color, during the burn-out printing process. Sulfuric acid, mixed into a colorless print paste, is the most common chemical used. Many simulated eyelet（孔眼）effects can be created using this method. In these instances, the chemical destroys the fiber and creates a hole in the fabric in a specific design, where the chemical comes in contact with the fabric. The fabric is then over-printed with a simulated embroidery stitch to create the eyelet effect. However, burn-out effects can also be created on velvets made of blended fibers, in which the ground fabric is of one fiber like a polyester, and the pile may be of a cellulosic fiber like rayon or acetate. In this case, when the chemical is printed in a certain pattern, it destroys the pile in those areas where the chemical comes in contact with the fabric, but leave the ground fabric unharmed.

在烂花印花过程中，通过使用化学物质而不是色彩，在织物上产生类似织锦的图案效果。有硫酸混入的无色的印花糊，是最常用的化学物质。使用这种方法可以让织物产生许多模拟孔眼效果。在这些条件下，化学物质会破坏纤维，并以特定设计在织物上产生一个孔洞（实际上是利用包芯纱形成局部半透明的效果，参见烂花天鹅绒——编者注），化学物质在那里与织物接触。然后用模拟刺绣针脚对织物进行过度印花，以产生孔眼效果。然而，在由混纺纤维制成的天鹅绒上也会产生烂花效应，其中，织物底布由聚酯等一种纤维制成，绒毛可以由人造丝或醋酸纤维等纤维素纤维制成。在这种情况下，当化学物质以某种图案印刷时，它会破坏化学物质与织物接触的区域的绒毛，但织物底布不受损伤。

3. Calendering 轧光

A process for finishing fabrics in which such special effects as high luster, embossing, and moiré（波纹）are produced.

一种整理织物的工艺，会产生高光、压花和莫尔条纹等特殊效果（波纹）。

dyed yarn fabric 色织布
casual 休闲
chambray 青年布
fil-a`-fil (end-on-end) 米通条
pucker 折叠
informal 非正式的
predominates 支配
corduroy 灯芯绒
chiffon 雪纺
tartan 苏格兰格
houndstooth 千鸟格，犬牙格
simulate 模拟
calendering 轧光
moiré 波纹

pongee 春亚纺
georgette 乔其纱
surah 斜纹软绸
embroidery 绣花
tapestry 挂毯
brocade 织锦缎
flannel 法兰绒
melton 麦尔登
tweed 花呢
fluffy 毛绒
glen check 格林格
flocking 植绒
eyelet 孔眼

 Task 6

Nonwoven Fabric 非织造布

Nonwoven fabrics are made directly from individual fibers that are matted together by forming an interlocking web of fibers either mechanically (tangling together) or chemically (gluing, bonding, or melting together).

非织造织物是由单纤维直接制成的，这些纤维通过机械（缠结在一起）或化学（黏合、黏合或融熔在一起）形成互锁的纤维网而缠结在一起。

Nonwoven fabric
非织造布

The name nonwoven fabric is unfortunate because it initially suggests that these fabrics are made by any processes other than weaving. Actually, nonwoven are defined as textile materials made directly from fibers and held together as a fabric by adhesives, heat fusion (if thermoplastic fibers) or through entanglement of the fibers. These materials are generally flat, flexible, porous sheet structures with high surface areas-to-weight characteristics.

非织造布这个名字很不恰当，因为它最初表明这些织物是通过织造以外的任何工艺制成的。实际上，非织造布被定义为直接由纤维制成的纺织材料，并通过黏合剂、热熔（如果是热塑性纤维）或通过纤维的缠结将其作为织物固定在一起。这些材料通常是平坦的、柔性的、多孔的片材结构，具有高表面积重量比特性。

1. Needle Punched Nonwovens 针刺法非织造布

Needle punched nonwovens (see Fig. 4.37) are sometimes called mechanical felt or needle punched felt, which they somewhat resemble. Unlike felt (which is made primarily from wool), needle punched nonwovens can be made from any staple fibers.

针刺非织造布（见图 4.37）有时被称为机械毡或针刺毡，它们有点相似。与毛毡（主要由羊毛制成）不同，针刺非织造布可以由任何短纤维制成。

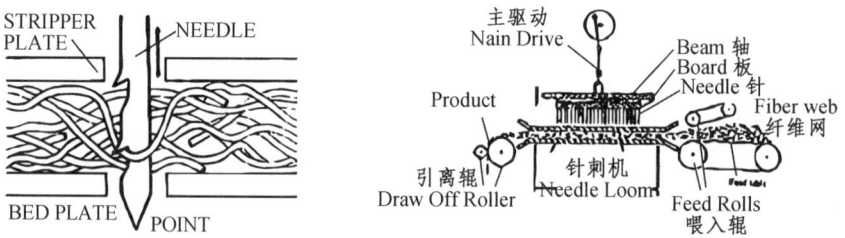

Fig. 4.37　Needle Punched Nonwovens Process 针刺非织造布

Needle-punched nonwovens (dry laid) are made by a method which involves the entanglement of fibers to hold them together. The process for making this material consists of passing a continuous web of fibers through a needle machine. The essential parts of the machine are a multitude of barbed needle punch hooks (the barb somewhat resembles a fish hook barb) mounted on a grid which vibrates up and down. As the web of fibers passes the vibrating grid, the needles pierce through the web and entangle the fibers as they withdraw. When this occurs continuously, the fibers form an entangled mass of material.

针刺非织造布（干铺）是通过一种将纤维缠绕在一起的方法制成的。制造这种材料的过程包括使连续的纤维网通过针刺机。机器的主要部件是安装在上下振动的格栅上的多个带倒钩的针刺钩（倒钩有点像鱼钩倒钩）。当纤维网通过振动格栅时，针头刺穿纤维网，并在纤维退出时缠绕纤维。当这种情况持续发生时，纤维会形成一团纠缠在一起的物质。

2. Bonded Web Nonwovens 黏合网非织造布

Bonded web nonwovens（see Fig. 4.38）were the first nonwovens, produced in the early 1940s. They can be made from any staple fibers and are produced by forming a web of fibers, then bonding the fibers. The web is formed by using mechanical means (e.g., carding machine), air blowing of fibers (dry laid) or using liquid to manipulate the fibers (wet laid). Bonding of fibers may be accomplished with an adhesive or through heat fusion if the fibers from which the nonwoven is being made are of the thermoplastic fiber type.

黏合网非织造布（见图4.38）是第一种非织造布，生产于20世纪40年代初。它们可以由任何短纤维制成，通过形成纤维网，然后将纤维黏合而成。纤维网是通过使用机械手段（如梳理机）、纤维的空气吹扫（干铺）或使用液体操纵纤维（湿铺）形成的。可以用黏合剂黏合法，如果制造非织造布的纤维是热塑性纤维类型，也可以用热融法获得非织造布。

Bonded web nonwovens may be unidirectional, cross laid or random web, indicating the orientation of the fibers in a specific fabric. The largest volume of nonwovens is made using this method.

黏合网的非织造布可以是单向的、交叉铺设的或随机的网，表明纤维在特定织物中的方向。最大体积（蓬松）的非织造布是用这种方法制成的。

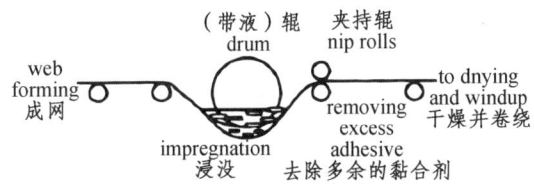

Fig. 4.38　Bonded web nonwovens 黏合成网非织造布

3. Spunlaced Nonwovens 水刺非织造布

The oldest technique for consolidating fibers in a web is mechanical bonding, which entangles the fibers to give strength to the web. Under mechanical bonding, the two most widely used methods are needle punching and spun lacing (hydroen tanglement). Spunlacing uses high-speed jets of water to strike a web so that the fibers knot about one another. As a result, nonwoven fabrics made by this method have specific properties, as soft handle and drapability.

将纤维固结在纤维网中最古老的技术是机械黏合，它将纤维缠绕在一起，使纤维网具有强度。在机械黏合的情况下，两种最广泛使用的方法是针刺和旋转编织（水刺缠结）。水刺使用高速水流击打纤维网，使纤维相互打结。因此，用这种方法制成的非织造布具有特殊的性质，如柔软的手感和悬垂性。

4. Spunbonded Nonwovens 纺粘非织造布

Spunbonded nonwovens are made from the continuous extrusion of filaments into a web (polymer laid). They consist of randomly oriented filament fibers subsequently consolidated by thermal bonding, mechanical entanglement, adhesive bonding, or etched filament surfaces to interlock the fibers. This method produces the second largest amount of nonwovens.

纺粘非织造布是由长丝连续挤出成网（铺设聚合物）制成的。它们由随机取向的长丝纤维组成，随后通过热黏合、机械缠绕、黏合剂黏合或蚀刻的长丝表面将纤维黏合在一起。这种方法生产的非织造布数量位居第二。

5. Melt-blown Nonwovens 熔喷非织造布

Melt-blow nonwovens are produced in a similar process to spunbonded nonwovens in that fiber extrusion is used (polymer laid). However, upon passage through the extrusion orifice, the molten polymer is accelerated by high velocity hot air jets which reduce the filaments to microdenier size. The individual fibers are propelled to a collection surface. As the fibers are in a tacky state upon collection, cohesive web structures result. Some of the potential shortcomings include low fiber strength and low abrasion resistance. This method is the most popular technique for producing microdenier fibers. Melt-blown Nonwovens is shown in Fig. 4.39.

熔喷非织造布的生产工艺与纺粘非织造布相似，即使纤维挤出（聚合物铺设）铺设。然而，在通过挤出口时，熔融的聚合物被高速热空气射流加速，这将细丝减小到更微小的尺寸。单纤维被推进到收集表面。由于纤维在收集时处于黏性状态，因此产生了内聚的网状结构。一些潜在的缺点包括纤维强度低和耐磨性低。这种方法是生产超细纤维最常用的技术。熔喷法生产非织造布如图4.39。

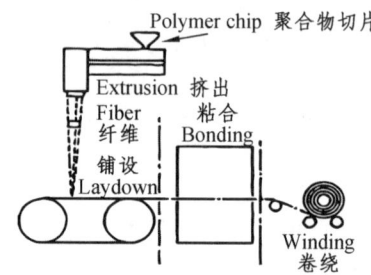

Fig. 4.39 Melt-blown nonwovens 熔喷法非织造布

thermoplastic 热塑性的	adhesive 黏着剂
porous 多空透气的	heat fusion 热熔
punched 穿孔	extrusion 挤出；推出；赶出；喷出
felt 毡子，毡化	etched filament 蚀刻丝
barb 倒钩，倒刺	spunbonded nonwovens 纺粘型非织造布
grid 网格	orifice 孔口
vibrate 摆动，振动	tacky state 发黏的状态
withdraw 拉开，撤回	microdenier 细旦的

Practical Fabric Vocabulary 实用面料词汇

府绸 poplin
细纺 cambric
细平布 fine plain
哔叽 serge
纱府绸 poplinette
绉布 crepe
线府绸 thready poplin
绒布 flannelette
滤布 filtration fabric
牛津布 oxford
靛蓝青年布 indigo chambray
直贡 twilled satin
粗斜纹 coarse drill
横贡 sateen
提花布 figured cloth
提格布 checks
纱罗组织 leno and gauze
华夫格 walf checks
竹节布 slubbed fabric
羽绸 satinet
麻棉混纺布 linen/cotton blended fabric
麻棉交织布 linen/cotton mixed fabric
结子布 knop fabric
双经布 double ends fabric
双纬布 double weft fabric
双层布 double-layer
细斜纹布 jeanette
单面卡其 one-sided drill
双面卡其 reversible drill
纱直贡 single twilled satin
线直贡 thready twilled satin
氨纶弹力织物 spandex stretch fabric

羊毛双面呢 double-faced woolen goods
立绒呢 cut velvet
麦尔登 melton
法兰绒 flannel
华达呢 gabardine
哔叽 serge
花瑶 faille
乔其 georgette
雪纺 chiffon
春亚纺 polyester pongee
涤塔夫 polyester taffeta
塔丝隆 nylon taslon
桃皮绒 peach skin
卡丹绒 peach twill
纬长丝织物 weft filament mixed fabric
蚂蚁布 fleece in one side
全消光春亚纺 full dull polyester pongee
春亚纺格 polyester pongee rip-stop
塔丝隆格 taslon ripstop
尼龙格 nylon rip-stop
涤纶格 polyester taffeta rip-stop
全消光塔丝隆 full dull nylon taslon
涤纶蜂巢塔丝隆 polyester honey taslon
尼丝纺 nylon taffeta
全消光尼丝纺 full dull nylon taffeta
半消光尼丝纺 semi-dull nylon taffeta
亮光尼龙 trilobal nylon
尼龙塔夫泡泡纱 nylon seersucker taffeta
全消光涤纶桃皮绒 full dull polyester peach
宽斜纹桃皮绒 big twill polyester peach
涤锦复合桃皮绒 poly/nylon peach
超细麦克布 micro fiber

中长化纤织物 midfibre fabric
粗条灯芯绒 spacious waled corduroy
医药用纱布 medical gauze
尿布 diaper
中条灯芯绒 mid-wale corduroy
白坯布 grey fabric
漂白织物 bleached fabric
纯纺织物 pure yarn fabric
混纺织物 blended fabric
防绒布 down-proof fabric
染色织物 dyed fabric
印花织物 printed fabric
黏纤织物 spun rayon fabric
富纤织物 polynosic fabric
混纺纱烂花布 blended yarn etched-out fabric
家具布 upholstery fabric
帆布 canvas
双色 two-tone
服装衬布 pading cloth
树脂衬布 resin padding cloth
热熔黏合衬布 hot melt adhesive lining cloth
黑炭衬 hair interlining
马尾衬 hair cloth
产业用织物 technical fabric
素色毛巾布 solid terry
素色天鹅绒 solid velvet
抽条磨毛天鹅绒 rib fleece velvet
雪花天鹅绒 melange velvet
粒粒绒布 pellet fleece velvet
平绒 velveteen (velvet-plain)
倒毛 down pile making
粗花呢 costume tweed
顺毛呢 over coating
巴拿马 panama
珠粒绒 claimond veins
斜纹锦棉纺 nylon-cotton fabric (twill)
纬长丝大提花仿绸织物 silk-like fabric jacquard

锦棉绸 nylon-cotton fabric
蜡光缎 cire satine
全消光牛津布 full dull nylon oxford
仿麂皮织物 suede fabric
仿麻布 linen type cloth
雪尼尔织物 chenille fabric
人棉布植绒 rayon cloth flocking
凉爽呢 wool-like fabric
针织布植绒 knitting cloth flocking
雕印植绒 embossing flocking
素面植绒 plain flocking
印花植绒 flocking (flower)
仿麂皮 micro suede
弹力仿麂皮 micro suede with spandex
减量整理织物 deweighting finish fabric
增重整理织物 weighted finish fabric
液氨整理织物 liquid ammonia finish fabric
电光整理织物 schreiner finish fabric
轧光整理织物 calendar finish fabric
涂层整理织物 coated finish fabric
轧纹整理织物 gauffered finish fabric
磨绒整理织物 sanded finish fabric
防蛀整理织物 moth proof finish fabric
拒水整理织物 water repellent finish fabric
拒油整理织物 oil-repellent finish fabric
阻燃整理织物 flame retardant finish fabric
预缩整理织物 shrunk finish fabric
防皱整理织物 crease resistant finish fabric
柔软电整理织物 antistatic finish fabric
易去污整理织物 soil release finish fabric
烂花布 etched-out fabric
弹力呢 lycra woolen goods
羊绒大衣呢 cachmere overcoat
彩条汗布 color-stripes single jersey
摇粒绒 polar fleece

合纤长丝仿麻布 polyester linen type filament fabric
全消光涤纶低弹牛津布 full dull poly textured oxford
包芯纱烂花布 composite yarn etched-out fabric
涤锦交织桃皮绒 nylon/polyester inter-woven peach
重平锦棉绸 nylon-cotton-cotton fabric (double weft)
低弹涤纶丝仿毛织物 wool-like fabrics with trueran low- elastic fabric
仿麂皮羊羔绒复合布 100% polyester micro suede bounding with lamb fur
仿麂皮瑶粒绒复合布 100% polyester micro suede bounding with polar fleece
仿麂皮针织布复合 100% polyester bounding with knitting micro suede fabric

Chapter 5

Knitting 针织篇

- To describe general and principles of knitting technology.
  描述针织技术的一般术语和原理。
- To describe the weft knitting structures and fabrics.
  描述纬编结构和织物。
- To describe the warp knitting structures and fabrics.
  描述经编结构和织物。

 Task 1

To Describe the Terms & General Principles of Knitting Technology 描述针织技术的术语和一般原理

Knitting is defined to be the formation of fabric by the intermeshing of loops of yarn. Unlike weaving, which requires two yarn sets, knitting is possible using only a single set of yarns. Knitting may be divided into two types according to the formation method: warp knitting and weft knitting. In weft knitting, the loops of yarn are formed by a single weft thread. The loops are formed, more or less, across the width of the fabric usually with horizontal rows of loops, or courses, being built one loop at a time. In warp knitting, all of the loops making up a single course are formed simultaneously. Thus the lengths of each vertical column of loops, the wales, increase at the time.

Term & principle
术语和原理

针织是将线圈相互串套形成织物。不同于机织物，需要两个系统纱线进行织造，针织物只需要一组纱线完成编织。针织根据生产方式的不同可分为两种：经编和纬编。在纬编中，一组纱线沿着纬向顺序地垫放在织针上形成线圈，并在纵向相互串套形成纬编针织物。在经编中，一组纱线沿着经向同时垫放在织针上形成线圈，并在纵向相互串套形成经编针织物。

1. Loop 线圈

The knit loop (see Fig. 5.1 & Fig. 5.2) is the simplest unit of the knitted structure. It consists of needle loop and sinker loop. The needle loop include a head and two side limbs. When tension in the fabric is balanced and there is sufficient take-away tension during knitting, it is an upright noose formed in the needle hook. The sinker loop is the piece of yarn that joins one weft knitted needle loop to the next.

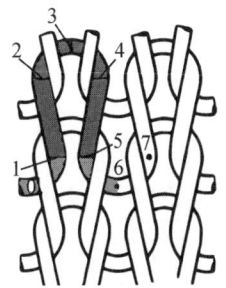 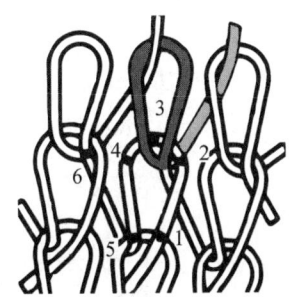

Fig. 5.1　Weft knitting loop 纬编线圈　　**Fig. 5.2　Warp knitting loop 经编线圈**

线圈（见图 5.1 和 5.2）是构成针织物的基本结构单元。线圈包括圈干和沉降弧，其中圈干包括针编弧和两个圈柱。当织物的张力平衡，并且在编织过程中有足够的牵拉张力时，它是在针钩中形成的一个纵向串套。沉降弧是将一个纬编针织线圈连接到下一个纬纱针织线圈的纱线部分。

2. Face loop stitch 正面线圈

The side of the stitch shows the new loop coming towards the viewer as it passes over and covers the head of the old loop. It is referred to as the right side in Europe. Face loop stitches tend to show the side limbs of the needle loops or overlaps as a series of interfitting "V" s. The face loop-side is the underside of the stitch on the needle (see Fig. 5.3).

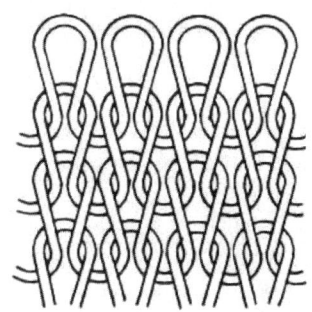 

Fig. 5.3　Face loop stitch 正面线圈

织物面向观察者的那一面，新线圈从旧线圈的反面穿向正面。在欧洲，一般指织物正面。正面线圈圈柱覆盖于圈弧之上，圈干部分呈现"V"型。正面线圈的针编弧隐藏在织物反面（见图 5.3）。

127

3. Reverse loop stitch 反面线圈

This is the opposite side of the stitch to the face loop-side and shows the new loop meshing away from the viewer as it passes under the head of the old loop. It is referred to as the left side in Europe. Reverse stitches show the sinker loops in weft knitting and the underlaps in warp knitting most prominently on the surface. The reverse loop side is the nearest to the head of the needle because the needle draws the new loop downwards through the old loop (see Fig. 5.4).

反面线圈是正面线圈相对应的反面，显示了新线圈在穿过旧线圈针编弧远离观察者。在欧洲，一般指织物反面。反面线圈在纬编针织物中显露沉降弧，而在经编针织物中显露延展线。反面线圈离针头最近，因为针头通过旧线圈向下拉动新线圈（见图5.4）。

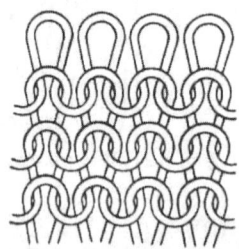 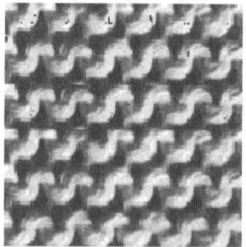

Fig. 5.4　Reverse loop stitch 反面线圈

4. A course 线圈横列

A course (see Fig. 5.5 & Fig. 5.6) is a predominantly horizontal row of needle loops produced by adjacent needles during the same knitting cycle. In weft knitted fabrics a course is composed of yarn from a single supply.

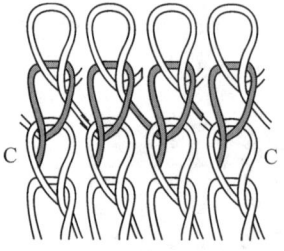 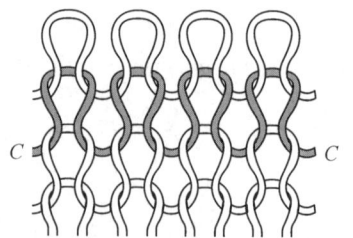

Fig. 5.5　Course (warp knitting) 横列（经编针织）　　**Fig. 5.6　Course (weft knitting) 横列（纬编针织）**

线圈横列（见图 5.5、5.6）是在同一编织周期内纱线沿织物横向组成的一排线圈。在纬编针织物中一个横列由一个系统纱线组成。

5. A wale 线圈纵行

A wale (Fig. 5.7 & Fig. 5.8) is a predominantly vertical column of needle loops produced by the same needle knitting at successive knitting cycles and thus intermeshing each new loop through the previous loop. Wales are joined to each other by the sinker loops. In warp knitting a wale can be produced from the same yarn.

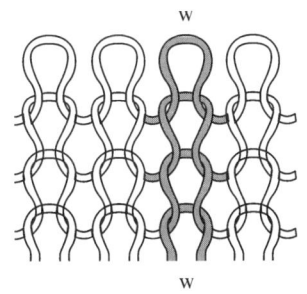
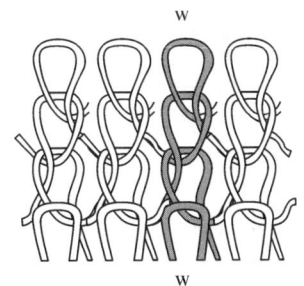

Fig. 5.7 Wale (weft knitting) 纵行（纬编针织）　　**Fig. 5.8** Wale (warp knitting) 纵行（经编针织）

线圈纵行（图 5.7 和图 5.8）是由相同的针织物在连续的编织循环中产生的一列主要垂直的线圈，因此每个新的线圈通过前一个线圈相互串套。纵行是通过沉降弧连接。在经编针织物中，可以用同一根纱线来生产纵行。

6. Single-faced structures 单面织物

Single-faced structures are produced in weft knitting by the needles (arranged either in a straight line or in a circle) operating as a single set. Adjacent needles will thus have their hooks facing towards the same direction and the heads of the needles will always draw the new loops downwards through the old loops in the same direction.

单面织物是由纬编针织中一个针床（横机或圆机中）编织而成。相邻的针将使它们的钩面向相同的方向，并且针的头部将总是在相同的方向上通过旧的线圈向下拉动新的线圈。

The under surface of the fabric on the needles (termed the "technical face" or "right side") will thus only show the face stitches in the form of the side limbs of the loops as a series of interfitting "V" s. The upper surface of the fabric on the needles (termed the "technical back" or "left side") will only show reverse stitched in the form of sinker loops and the heads of the loops.

因此，针织物的下表面（称为"工艺面"或"正面"）仅显示出圈柱，呈"V"字型。针织物的上表面（称为"工艺反面"或"反面"）仅显示由沉降弧和针编弧构成的圈弧。

7. Double-faced structures 双面织物

Double-faced structures are produced in weft knitting when two sets of independently controlled needles are employed with the hooks of one set knitting or facing in the opposite direction to the other set. The two sets of needles thus draw their loops from the same yarn in opposite directions, so that the fabric, formed in the gap between the two sets, shows the face loops of one set on one side and the face loops of the other set on the opposite side. The two faces of the fabric are held together by the sinker loops which are inside the fabric so that the reverse stitches tend to be hidden. Sometimes the two faces are cohesively produced and are far enough apart for the connecting sinker loops to be severed in order to produce two single-faced fabrics.

当使用两组独立控制的针时，纬编中会产生双面结构，其中一组针的钩与另一组针相反。因此，两组针从同一根纱线沿相反的方向拉出线圈，使得在两组针之间的间隙中形成的织物在一侧显示出一组针的面线圈，而在相对侧显示出另一组的面线圈。织物的两面由织物内部的沉降环固定在一起，因此反向缝线往往被隐藏起来。有时，这两个面是黏合产生的，并且相距足够远，以便切断连接的沉降环，从而产生两个单面织物。

8. Stitch density 线圈密度

Stitch density refers to the total number of loops in a measured area of fabric and not to the length of yarn in a loop. It can be divided into two types: wale density and course density.

线圈密度是指织物测量区域内的线圈总数，而不是线圈中纱线的长度。它可以分为两种类型：横密和纵密。

Wale density refers to the wales in a centimeter or 5 centimeters or in an inch along the course. Course density refers to the course in a centimeters or 5 centimeters or in an inch along the course.

横密是指沿着横列方向每 5 厘米或 1 英寸所有的纵行数；纵密是指沿着纵行方向每 5 厘米或 1 英寸所有的横列数。

9. Stitch length 线圈长度

Stitch length is theoretically a single length of yarn which includes one needle loop and half the length of yarn (half a sinker loop) between that needle loop and the adjacent needle loops on either side of it. Generally, the larger the stitch length the more elastic and lighter the fabric, and the poorer its cover opacity and bursting strength.

从理论上讲，线圈长度是指单个线圈的纱线长度，它包括一个圈干和该圈干与相邻两个圈干之间的沉降弧长的一半。通常，线圈长度越大，织物的弹性越大，重量越轻，其覆盖物的不透明度和断裂强度就越差。

New Words and Expressions

knitting 针织；针织品
warp knitting 经编针织
weft knitting 纬编针织
loop 线圈
wale 线圈纵行；凸条纹
course 线圈横列；组织循环
face loop 正面线圈
reverse loop 反面线圈
single-faced structures 单面织物
technical face 工艺正面

double-faced structures 双面织物
technical back 工艺反面
intermesh（针织线圈）相互串套.
stitch density 线圈密度
take-away from 牵拉张力
head 针编弧
sinker loop 沉降弧
needle loop 圈干
stitch length 线圈长度
hook 针钩

130

Task 2

To Describe the Weft Knitting Structure and Fabrics
描述纬编结构和织物

Four primary structures—plain, rib, purl and interlock—are the base structures from which all weft knitted fabrics are derived. Each is composed of a different combination of face and reverse meshed stitches knitted on a particular arrangement of needle beds. Each primary structure may exist alone, or in combination with another primary structure in a garment-length sequence.

Visit weft knitting
参观纬编机

Weft knitting
纬编

纬编针织物有四种基本组织：平针、罗纹、双反面和双罗纹组织，是所有纬编针织物的基础结构。每一种组织都是由不同的正面线圈和反面线圈组合而成，编织在特定的针床上。每个主要结构可以单独存在，或者沿着服装长度方向不同的基本组织组合存在。

Plain is produced by the needles knitting as a single set, drawing the loops away from the technical back and towards the technical face side of the fabric.

平针组织由一个针床编织而成，把线圈从织物的背面引向织物的正面。

Rib requires two sets of needles operating in between each other so that wales of face stitches and wales of reverse stitches are knitted on each side of the fabric.

罗纹组织需要两组织针编织而成，以便在织物的每一面编织有正面线圈纵行和反面线圈纵行。

Purl is the only structure having certain wales containing both face and reverse meshed loops. Although normally knitted on machines employing double-ended latch needles, some V-bed flat machines with rib loop transfer and racking facilities can knit structures of this type.

双反面组织每一个纵行既有正面线又有反面线圈。尽管通常在双头舌针的机器上编织，但一些带有罗纹环转移设施的横机可以编织这种类型的结构。

Interlock was originally derived from rib but requires a special arrangement of needles knitting back-to-back in an alternate sequence of two sets so that the two courses of loops show wales of face loops on each side of the fabric exactly in line with each other thus hiding the appearance of the reverse loops.

双罗纹组织最初是由罗纹组织变化而来的，但需要两组织针背对背交替排列，因此，两个线圈横列显示出织物每一面的正面线圈，一个罗纹组织的反面线圈纵行为另一个罗纹组织的正面线圈纵行所遮盖。

Single-jersey machines can only produce one type of base structure. Rib machines, particularly of the garment producing type, can often produce sequences of plain knitting. Interlock machines can sometimes be changed to rib knitting, while purl machines are capable of producing rib or plain knitting sequence during the production of a garment or other knitted article.

单面针织机只能生产一种类型的基本组织。罗纹机，特别是服装生产类型的罗纹机，通常可以生产普通纬平针组织。双罗纹机有时可以改为罗纹编织，而双反面机上可以编织罗纹组织和平针组织。

1. Plain 平针组织

Plain (the stocking stitch of hand knitting) is the base structure of ladies' hosiery, fully fashioned knitwear and single-jersey fabrics. Other names for plain include stockinette whilst in the U.S.A. The term "shaker stitch" is applied to it when knitted in a coarse gauge of about 3.5 needles per inch (25.4 mm). Its technical face (see Fig. 5.9) is smooth, with the side limbs of the needle loops having the appearance of columns of Vs in the wales, these are useful as design units when knitting with different colored yarns. On the technical back, the heads of the needle loops and the bases of the sinker loops form columns of interlocking semi-circles whose appearance is sometimes emphasized by knitting alternate courses in different colored yarns.

平针组织（手工编织的袜子组织）是女式袜子、全成型针织品和单面针织面料的基本结构。纬平针的其他名称还包括短袜，而在美国，当以大约每英寸 3.5 针（25.4 毫米）的粗规格针织时，术语"粗平针织物"适用于它。它的工艺正面（见图 5.9）是光滑的，线圈的圈柱在纵行中有"V"型外观，当用不同颜色的纱线编织时，这些是有用的设计单元。当织物被剪开时，织物在横列方向卷向织物正面，在纵行方向卷向织物反面。在工艺反面有时在用不同色纱交替编织不同横列时，圈干中的针编弧部分和沉降弧的底部构成了相互连接的半圆形纵行这一外观特征得以凸现。

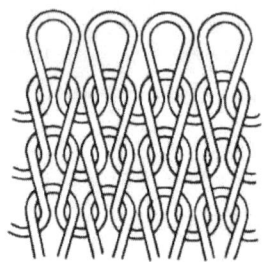

Fig. 5.9 plain 平针组织

Plain can be unroved from the course knitted last by pulling the needle loops through from the technical back or from the course knitted first, by pulling the sinker loops through from the technical face side. Similarly, if the yarn breaks, needle loops successively unmesh down a wale and sinker loops unmesh up a wale, this structural breakdown is termed laddering. It is particularly prevalent in ladies' hosiery where loops of fine smooth filaments are in a tensioned state, to reduce this tendency certain ladder-resist structures have been devised. The tendency of the cut edges of plain fabric to unrove and fray when not in tubular or flat selvedged form can be overcome by securing them during seaming.

平针组织可以沿着逆编织方向脱散，将针编弧从工艺反面或前一个编织横列脱散；或者将沉降弧从工艺正面脱散。类似地，如果纱线断裂，针编弧相继沿纵行向下脱套，沉降弧沿纵行向上脱套，这种结构上的破坏称为线圈纵向脱散。这种情况在女士袜中尤其普遍，因为细而光滑的细丝环处于拉紧状态，为了减少这种情况，已经设计了防脱散组织。不管是横机织物或圆机织物边缘会脱散和磨损，可以在缝制时有效克服卷边和脱散。

Knitted structure have a three-dimensional structure. When the fabric is cut the fabric curls towards the face at the top and bottom and towards the back at the sides. The same configuration causes face meshed wales of loops to be prominent in rib fabrics and the heads of loops and the sinker loops to be prominent in wales of purl stitches.

针织物组织是三维空间结构。当织物被剪开后在织物上下边缘卷向织物正面。相同配置的罗纹组织中的正面线圈纵行，或者双反面组织中的针编弧和沉降弧也会出现类似情况。

Plain is the simplest and most economical weft knitted structure to produce and has the maximum covering power. It normally has a potential recovery of 40 per cent in width after stretching.

平针是最简单、最经济的纬编结构，具有最大的覆盖力。拉伸后，其宽度通常有40%的潜在恢复率。

2. Rib 罗纹组织

The simplest rib fabric is 1×1 rib (see Fig. 5.10). Rib has a vertical cord appearance because the face loop wales tend to move over and in front of the reverse loop wales. As the face loops show a reverse loop intermeshing on the other side, 1×1 rib has the appearance of the technical face of plain fabric on both sides until stretched to reveal the reverse loop wales in between.

最简单的罗纹组织是1×1罗纹（如图5.10）。罗纹组织具有纵向条纹外观，因为正面线圈纵行倾向于在反向线圈纵行的上方和前方移动。由于正面线圈在另一侧显示出反向圈相互串套，1×1的罗纹在两面具有与纬平针组织正面相同的外观，直到拉伸以露出中间的反向线圈纵行。

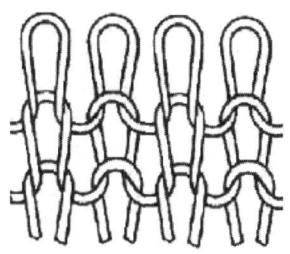 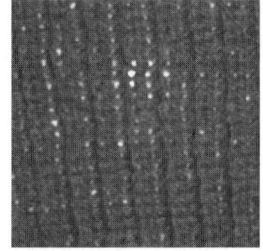

Fig. 5.10　1×1 rib 罗纹组织

1 × 1 rib is, produced by two sets of needles being alternately set or gated between each other. Relaxed 1 × 1 rib is theoretically twice as thick and half the width of an equivalent plain fabric, but it has twice as much width-wise recoverable stretch. In practice 1 × 1 rib normally relaxes by approximately 30 per cent compared with its knitting width. 1 × 1 rib is balanced by alternate wales of face loops in each side, it therefore lies fiat without curl when cut. It is a more expensive fabric to produce than plain and is a heavier structure, the rib machine also requires a finer yarn than a similar gauge plain machine. Like all weft-knitted fabrics it can be unroved from the end knitted last by drawing the free loop heads through to the back of each stitch and it can be distinguished from plain by the fact that the loops of certain wales are withdrawn in one direction and those of others in the opposite direction, whereas the loops of plain are always withdrawn in the same direction from the technical face to the technical back.

1 × 1 罗纹是由两组针交替配置而成。自然状态下的 1 × 1 罗纹组织理论上是同样纬平针织物的两倍厚和一半宽，但它在宽度上的可恢复拉伸度是其两倍。在实践中，1 × 1 罗纹通常比其编织宽度松弛约 30%。1 × 1 罗纹组织由相互交替的纵行保持平衡，因此，剪切后罗纹组织不会产生卷边。与平针组织相比，罗纹组织生产成本更高，织物更厚实，同样机号的罗纹机比单面机所需的纱线更细。像所有纬编织物一样，罗纹组织可以从最后编织的织物一端，通过拽动自由线圈穿到每个线圈的反面进行脱散，它可以通过将自由线圈头拉到每一针的背面而从最后编织的末端展开，而平针组织总是以相同方向从工艺正面撤回到工艺反面。

Rib can not be unroved from the end knitted because the sinker loops are securely anchored by the cross-meshing between face and reverse loop wales, this characteristic, together with its elasticity, makes rib particularly suitable for the extremities of articles such as tops of socks, the cuffs of sleeves, rib borders for garments, and stolling and strapping for cardigans. Rib structures are elastic, form-fitting, and retain warmth better than plain structures.

罗纹组织顺着编织方向不能脱散，因为沉降弧通过正面线圈和反向线圈之间的交叉啮合牢固地固定着，这一特性及其弹性使罗纹特别适用于织物的末端，如袜子的顶部、袖子的袖口、衣服的罗纹边，以及羊毛衫的下摆和袖口。罗纹结构具有弹性，贴合身体，比普通结构更能保暖。

There are a range of rib set-outs apart from 1 × 1 rib, the first figure in the designation indicates the number of adjacent plain wales and the second figure, the number of adjacent rib wales. Single or simple ribs have more than one plain wale but only one rib wale such as 2/1, 3/1, etc. Broad ribs have a number of adjacent rib as well as plain wales, for example 6/3 Derby rib. Adjacent wales of the same type are produced by adjacent needles in the same bed without needles from the other bed knitting in between them at that point.

除了 1 × 1 罗纹外，还有一系列罗纹配置，名称中的第一个数字表示正面线圈纵行数量，第二个数字表示反面线圈纵行数量。窄罗纹，正面线圈纵行与反面线圈纵行配置时，总有一个正面线圈纵行或反面线圈纵行，如 2 × 1，3 × 1 等。宽罗纹具有多个正面线圈纵行，比如德比式罗纹（6/3 罗纹组织）。相同类型的相邻纵行是由同一床中的相邻织针产生的，没有来自另一床的针在它们之间编织。

3. Purl 双反面组织

Purl (see Fig. 5.11) was originally spelt "pearl" and was so named because of the similar appearance to pearl droplets.

双反面组织（见图 5.11）最初拼写为"珍珠"，之所以如此命名，是因为它的外观与珍珠液滴相似。

Purl structures have one or more wales which contain both face and reverse loops which can only be achieved with double-ended latch needles or by rib loop transfer. The semi-circles of the needle and sinker loops produced by the reverse loop intermeshing tend to be prominent on both sides of the structure and this has led to the term "links-links" being generally applied to purl fabrics and machines. Links is the German word for left and it indicates that there are left or reverse loops visible on both sides.

双反面组织具有一个或多个包含正面线圈和反向线圈的纵行，这只能通过双头舌针或带有移圈装置的罗纹机实现。由相反的线圈相互串套而形成的半圆状的针编弧和沉降弧趋向于凸出在织物的两面。这导致术语"双反面组织"通常适用于双反面织物和机器。Links 是德语中 left 的意思，它表示两边都有左循环或反向循环。

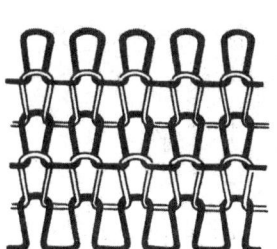 

Fig. 5.11　Purl 双反面组织

The simplest purl is 1×1 purl which is the garter stitch of hand knitters and consists of alternate courses of all face and all reverse loops and is produced by the needles knitting in one bed and then transferring over to the other bed to knit the next course. Its lateral stretch is equal to plain, but its length-wise elasticity is almost double. When relaxed the face loop courses cover the reverse loop courses making it twice as thick as plain. It can be unroved from both ends because the free sinker loops can be pulled through at the bottom of the fabric. In America 1×1 purl is sometimes made up at right angles to the knitting sequence and is then termed Alpaca stitch.

最简单的双反面组织是 1×1 双反面组织，它是手工编织袜口下端常用的组织，由所有正面和反面线圈交替组成，由在一个床上编织的织针，然后转移到另一个针床来编织下一个线圈。它的横向拉伸相当于纬平针组织，但其长度方向的弹性几乎是纬平针组织的两倍。自由状态下，正面线圈横列覆盖反面线圈横列，使其厚度为纬平针织物的两倍。

它顺逆编织方向均可以脱散，可以从两端展开，因为沉降弧可以在织物底部穿过。在美国，1×1双反面组织有时与编织顺序成直角，被称为阿尔帕卡组织。

The reverse stitches of purl give it the appearance of hand knitting and this is enhanced by using softly spun yarns. It is particularly suitable for baby wear, where width and length stretch is required, and also for adult knitwear. The double-cylinder half-hose machine is actually a small diameter purl machine which produces ribs by retaining needles in the same set out for a large number of successive courses.

双反面组织的反面线圈外观使其看起来像手工编织，并通过使用柔软纱线来增强这一点。它特别适合需要宽度和长度拉伸的婴儿服装，也适用于成人针织衫，双针筒短袜机实际上是一台小筒径的双反面机，通过把织针保持相同的配置，编织大量连续横列的罗纹组织。

4. Interlock 双罗纹组织

Interlock (see Fig. 5.12) has the technical face of plain fabric on both sides but its smooth surface can not be stretched out to reveal the reverse meshed loop wales because the wales on each side are exactly opposite to each other and are locked together. Each interlock pattern row (often termed an "interlock course") requires two feeder course each with a separate yarn which knits on separate alternate needles producing two half-gauge 1×1 rib courses whose sinker loops cross over each other, thus odd feeders will produce alternate wales of loops on each side and even feeders will produce the other wales.

双罗纹组织（见图5.12）的两面与平针组织的工艺正面一样的外观，表面光滑但延展性一般，即使在拉伸时，也不会露出反面线圈纵行，因为两面的纵行正好相反，并且相互串套在一起。双罗纹组织的每个线圈横列需要两个导纱系统来形成，每个导纱系统在交替编织的织针上单独喂入一根纱线，织出沉降弧相互交错的两个1×1罗纹横列。因此奇数导纱器将在每侧产生相互交替的线圈纵行，偶数导纱器将产生另一线圈纵行。

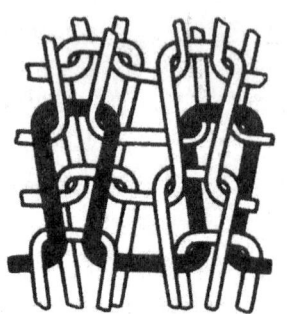

Fig. 5.12　Interlock 双罗纹组织

Interlock relaxes by about 30—40 per cent or more compared with its knitted width so that a 76.2 cm (30 inches) diameter machine will produce a tube at 238.3 cm (94 inches) open width which finishes at 152.4—167.6 cm (60-66 inches) wide. It is a balanced, smooth stable structure, which lies flat without curl. Like 1×1 rib, it will not unrove from the end knitted first but it is thicker, heavier and narrower than rib of equivalent gauge, and requires a finer, better, more expensive yarn.

自由状态下，双罗纹组织的宽度比编织宽度减少30%～40%或更多，因此直径76.2厘米（30英寸）的机器将生产出开口宽度为238.3厘米（94英寸）的筒状织物，开口宽度为152.4～167.6厘米（60～66英寸）。它是一个平衡、光滑、稳定的结构，平整无卷曲。与1×1罗纹一样，它不会沿顺编织方向脱散，但它比同等规格的罗纹更厚、更重、更窄，并且需要更细、更好、更昂贵的纱线。

As only alternate needles knit at a feeder, interlock machines can be produced in finer gauges, with less danger of press-offs than rib. Interlock knitting is, however, more of a problem than rib knitting because productivity is half, less feeders can be accommodated, and there are finer tolerances. When two different-colored yarns are used, horizontal stripes are produced if the same color is knitted at two consecutive number of interlock pattern rows. Per inch is often double the machine gauge in needles per inch.

因为在一个成圈系统中，只有一种针编织。双罗纹机可以用更细的机号生产，比罗纹机脱套的风险更小。然而，双罗纹组织编织比罗纹编织更成问题，因为生产率只有一半，可以容纳的导纱器更少，而且公差更细。当使用两种不同颜色的纱线编织时，如果一双罗纹组织的完全组织使用相同颜色的纱线，则会产生横条纹。每英寸双罗纹组织的花纹数通常是（每英寸）针数的两倍。

New Words and Expressions

primary structure 基本组织
plain 平针线圈，平针组织
rib 罗纹线圈，罗纹组织
purl 双反面线圈，双反面组织
interlock 双罗纹组织，棉毛布
loop transfer 移圈
loop racking 线圈移位
stockinette 平针织物，弹力织物（内衣用）
shaker stitch 粗平针织物
curl 卷边
ladder-resist 防脱散
rib set-outs 罗纹配置
relax 松弛，回缩
cuff 袖口，罗口

cardigan 羊毛衫，开襟绒线衫
border （女装的）滚边，下摆
strap 布带，吊带
form-fitting 贴身的
covering power 覆盖能力
recovery 弹性回复率
stretching 拉伸
double-ended latch needle 双头舌针
pearl fabric 双反面针织物
links-links 双反面组织
interlock gating 双罗纹织针的配置
garter 袜口下段
alpaca stitch 阿尔帕卡组织（1×1双反面组织）
latch needle 舌针

right angle 直角
press-off 脱套

tolerance 公差，容限
double-cylinder half-hose machine 双针筒短袜机

Task 3

To Describe the Warp Knitting and Fabrics
描述经编结构和织物

The term warp knitting is also adapted from weaving technology. Warp knitting differs from weft or filling knitting in that the loops are formed in a vertical or warpwise direction and yarns lying side by side are interlooped.

Visit warp knitting machine
参观经编机

Warp knitting
经编

Machines used for warp knitting tend to look somewhat like weaving machines. All of the yarns are placed on the beams and are located behind and above the actual knitting area. All yarns feed into the knitting area at the same time. Each yarn is manipulated by one specific needle as the interlooping proceeds; however, guide bars control the placement of the yarn, and the particular needle forming the loop may vary from one interlooping action to the next. Jacquard attachments can be used to provide for special needle controls and the making of highly patterned warp knits. Because of the knitting process used in warp knitting, the location of the yarn supply, and the interlooping of the parallel yarns, the machine used sometime called knitting looms.

经编一词也源自机织技术。经编与纬编的不同之处在于，线圈沿垂直或经向形成，并排放置的纱线相互套结。经编机看起来与机织设备很相像。所有纱线都放置在经轴上，并位于实际编织区域的后方和上方。所有纱线同时进入编织区域。随着交织的进行，每根纱线都由一个导纱针控制；然而，导纱梳栉控制纱线，特殊的织针形成的线圈可以从一个相互套结的动作变化到另一个。提花装置可用于提供特殊的织针控制，制作复杂图案经编织物的编织。由于经编中使用的编织工艺、喂纱位置以及平行纱线的交织，该机器有时称为针织布机。

Essentially, warp knitting is a system for producing fabric that is flat, has straight side edges, and is manufactured rapidly and in large quantities. Warp knits are classified according to the type of equipment used and to special characteristics of the resulting fabrics. The types are tricot, raschel, milanese, and simplex. The most common types are tricot and raschel.

从本质上讲，经编是一种生产平型、侧边平直，生产速度快、产量高织物系统。经编针织物根据使用的设备类型和织物的特殊特性进行分类。可以分为特里科、拉舍尔、米兰尼斯经编、辛普勒克斯经编织物。最常见的类型是特里科和拉舍尔。

In a warp knitted structure, all ends supplied from the same warp sheet normally have identical lapping movements because each is lapped by a guide attached to the same guide bar. Beams supply the warp sheets in parallel form to the guide bars, whose pattern control determines the timing and configuration of the lapping movements in the form of overlaps and underlaps. The needles intermesh the new overlaps through the old overlaps to form the intermeshed loop structure.

在经编结构中，由同一经轴提供的通常具有相同的垫纱运动，因为每个导纱针都是受控于导纱梳栉。经轴以平行的形式将经纱片提供给导纱梳栉，花型要求决定导纱梳栉的运动时间和针前垫纱和针背垫纱规律。织针通过旧的针前垫纱将新的针前垫纱相互串套以形成线圈。

When using either open or closed laps there are three possible arrangements of lapping at successive courses, which may be used alone or in combination.

当使用开口或闭口线圈，有三种可能的排序方式，可以单独使用，也可以组合使用。

1. The Pillar Stitch 经编编链组织

In the pillar or chain stitch (see Fig. 5.13), the same guide always overlaps the same needle. This lapping movement will produce chains of loops in unconnected wales, which must be connected together by the underlaps of a second guide bar. Generally, pillar stitches are made by front guide bars, either to produce vertical stripe effects or to hold the inlays of other guide bars into the structure. Open-lap pillar stitches are commonly used in warp knitting. They can be unroved from the end knitted last. Closed-lap pillar stitches are employed on crochet machines because the lapping movement is simple to achieve and is necessary when using self-closing carbine needles, which must always be fed with yarn from the same side.

The pillar stitch
经编编链组织

在编链组织（见图 5.13）中，同一个导针器始终在同一枚织针上作针前垫纱。这种垫纱运动的方式将会形成相互没有联系的纵行条，这些纵行必须与下一个导纱梳栉配合运动产生关联。通常，编链组织由前导纱梳栉形成，要么产生垂直条纹效果，要么将其他导纱梳栉的镶嵌物固定在结构中。开口编链通常用于经编针织物。它们可以沿着逆变编织方向脱散。钩编机常用于编织闭口编链，因为利用自闭针钩，垫纱很容易实现，因为必须始终在同一枚织针上喂入纱线。

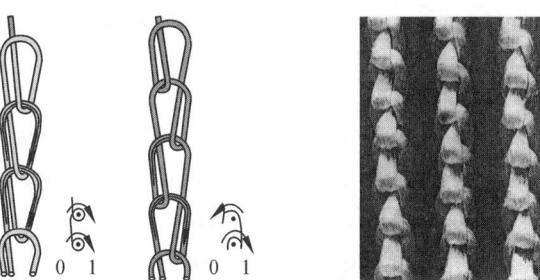

Fig. 5.13　Pillar stitch 编链组织

2. The tricot stitch 经平组织

Balanced advance and return lapping in two courses. Many tricot structures (see Fig. 5.14) are based on this type of lapping movement. Its extent may be described by indicating the number of needles underlapped, followed by the number of needles overlapped (usually one). With a fully-threaded guide bar every one needle space increase in the underlap movement will cause an extra warp thread from that bar to cross between each wale. Tricot lapping (1 × 1) is the simplest of these movements, producing overlaps in alternate wales at alternate courses with only one thread crossing between adjacent wales. Two threads will cross between wales with a 2 × 1 or cord lap, three threads with a 3 × 1 or satin lap, four threads with a 4 × 1 or velvet lap, and so on. Each increase in the extent of the underlap tends to make the structure stronger, more opaque and heavier. The increasing float of the underlap has a more horizontal appearance, whilst overlaps produced by the same thread will be separated from each other at successive courses by an extra wale in width.

The tricot stitch
经平组织

两个横列对称轮流垫纱成圈。许多特里科经编组织结构（见图 5.14）都是基于这种类型的垫纱运动。它可以通过针前垫纱针距数和针背横移的针距数（通常是一个）来描述。在导纱梳栉满穿情况下，每增加一根针的空间，就会在两个纵行间产生针背垫纱。1×1 经平组织是最简单的经平组织，每根纱线的相邻两枚针上轮流垫纱；两根纱线以两针经平轮流垫纱、三根纱线以三针经平轮流垫纱、四根纱线以四针经平轮流垫纱，依此类推。延展线增加会使织物结构更坚固、更不透明、更厚重。延展线增加使得织物具有更水平的外观，而由同一根线产生的针前垫纱部分将在连续的横列中通过额外的纵行宽度相互分离。

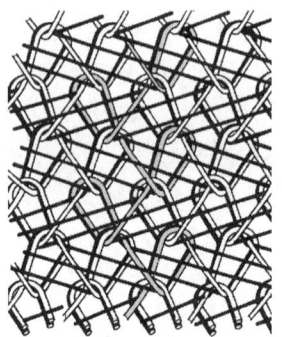 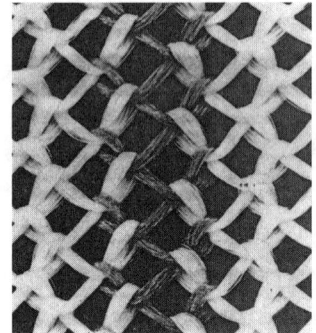

Fig. 5.14　Tricot stitch 经平组织

3. The Atlas Stitch 经缎组织

Atlas lapping (see Fig. 5.15) is a movement where the guide bar laps progressively in the same direction for a minimum of two consecutive courses, normally followed by an identical lapping movement in the opposite direction. Usually, the progressive lapping is in the form of open laps and the change of direction course is in the form of a closed lap, but these roles may

The atlas stitch
经缎组织

140

be reversed. From the change of direction course, tension tends to cause the heads of the loops to incline in the opposite direction to that of the previous lapping progression. The change of direction course is normally tighter and the return progression course cause reflected light to produce a faint, transverse shadow, stripe effect.

经缎组织（见图 5.15）是指导纱梳栉在相同方向上垫纱成圈至少两个连续的过程，随后在相反方向上进行相同的垫纱运动。一般，在垫纱转向时采用闭口线圈，而在中间的则为开口线圈，但有时可能会颠倒过来。从横列方向的变化来看，张力往往会导致针编弧朝着与之前垫纱过程相反的方向倾斜。横列方向变化通常更紧密，不同方向倾斜的线圈横列对光线反射不同，针织物表面形成横向条纹。

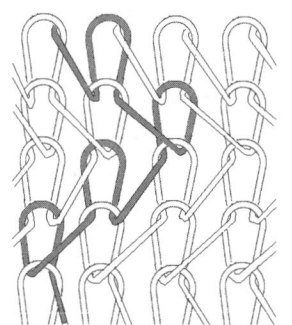 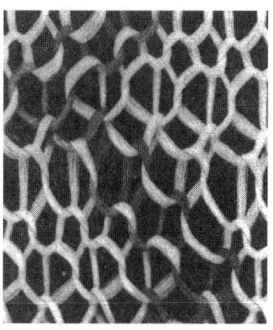

Fig. 5.15   Atlas stitch 经缎组织

Warp knit fabrics have some elongation or stretchability, although it may be less than that of filling knits. The amount of extension is influenced by the type of construction (such as single bar tricot, double-bar tricot, raschel); the tightness of the knitting (the tighter the knit, he lower the amount of stretch); finishing techniques, which can impart good dimensional stability; gage (number of needles per unit of width); and type of yarn (for example, core-spun stretch yarns, complex yarns with little or no stretch, single or ply yarns of high dimensional stability).

经编织物具有一定的伸长率或拉伸性，尽管它可能低于纬编针织物。延伸量受结构类型（如单针床特里科、双针床特里科、拉舍尔经编织物）、编织的紧密性（编织得越紧，拉伸量就越低）；可以赋予良好的尺寸稳定性的精加工技术；规格（每单位宽度的针数）和纱线类型（例如，包芯弹力纱线、弹力很少或没有弹力的复杂纱线、具有高尺寸稳定性的单层或多层纱线）的影响。

The strength of warp knitting fabrics may be increased by using yarns of strong fibers, yarns of balanced construction, and a high gauge with strong fine yarns. A combination of yarns of different fibers, or different types of yarns (simple, ply, complex), and space between loops affects the strength of the fabric.

经编织物的强度可以通过使用强力纤维纱线、结构平衡的纱线和具有强而细纱线的高规格纱线来提高。不同纤维的纱线或不同类型的纱线（简单纱线、帘布层纱线、复杂纱线）的组合以及线圈之间的空间会影响织物的强度。

New Words and Expressions

interloop 相互套结
tricot 特里科经编
raschel 拉舍尔经编
milanese 米兰尼斯经编织物
gauge 机号
guide bar 导纱梳栉
single bar tricot 单梳栉经编机
double bar tricot 双梳栉经编机
filling knit 纬编
pillar stitch 经编编链组织
chains of loop 线圈链
front guide bar 前梳栉
balanced advance and return lapping 前后横列平衡垫纱

vertical stripe effect 纵条纹效应
underlap 针背垫纱
open-lap pillar stitch 开口编链线圈
closed-lap pillar stitch 闭口编链线圈
tricot stitch 经平组织
cord lap 两针经平垫纱
satin lap 三针经平垫纱
velvet lap 四针经平垫纱
horizontal appearance 横条外观
atlas stitch 经缎组织
elongation 伸长性
stretchability 拉伸性

Chapter 6

Dyeing and Finishing 染整篇

- To describe the dyeing and finishing technological process.
  描述染整工艺过程
- To describe the dyeing and finishing machines.
  描述染整机械。

Task 1

To Describe the Dyeing and Finishing Technological Process
描述染整工艺过程

Unit 1 Introduction of Pretreatment for Dyeing and Finishing
染整前处理介绍

Before a cloth can be dyed, printed, or conditioned with special finishing, it must go through a series of preliminary treatments. The reason such treatments are necessary is to ensure that the dyeing, printing and/or finishing are acceptable, predictable and reproducible. The impurities present, either natural or man-introduced, must be removed and the material rendered absorbent and receptive in a uniform way. The preparatory treatments needed depend on the type of fiber in the material and particular dyeing and finishing treatments that are to be done. Fabrics which have been prepared for dying and finishing must have sufficient absorbency and whiteness.

Visit dyeing and finishing mill
参观染整工厂

Introduction of pretreatment
预处理介绍

织物必须经历一系列预处理才可以染色、印花，或经特种处理而改善状态。这些预处理之所以成为必须，是为了要保证染色、印花和/或整理达到可接受、可预期、可再现的目的。(织物中)存在杂质,天然的或是人为的,必须予以去除,从而使织物能有均匀的吸水性和吸收(如染料——编者注)性能。预处理加工工艺取决于材料中纤维的种类,特别是进行染整加工工艺的种类。准备进行染整加工的织物必须具有良好的吸收性能和白度。

The preparation processes of fabric include examining of gray goods, cloth turning (in batches, in boxes), stamping or marking, sewing, singeing, desizing, scouring, bleaching, mercerizing and heat setting.

织物加工的准备过程包括检验坯件、翻布(批量、装箱形式)、压印记或做标记、缝纫、烧毛、退浆、煮练、漂白、丝光和热定型。

Textile's colour is normally obtained by applying a colorant to the textile substrate. There are two ways of adding colour to a textile substrate: i.e. dyeing and printing. Colorants used for dyeing can be classified as dyes or pigments. Dyes are water soluble and have substantivity (affinity) for fibres and can be absorbed into the fibres. Pigments are not water soluble and possess no specific attraction for any particular fibre type. Pigments usually adhere to the surface of the fibre. Dyes are used far more widely and frequently than pigments in the textile dyeing process.

纺织品色彩通常是通过在纺织品基底上涂上着色剂来获得的。有两种方法可以为纺织品底布添加颜色:染色和印花。用于染色的着色剂可分为染料或颜料。染料是水溶性的,对纤维具有实质性(亲和力),可以被吸收到纤维中。颜料不溶于水,对任何特定的纤维类型都没有特定的吸引力。颜料通常黏附在纤维表面。在纺织品染色过程中,染料的使用范围和频率远远超过颜料。

Finishing is a general term which usually refers to treatments on textile fabrics after dyeing or printing but before the fabrics is cut and sewn into garments, household textiles, or other products. However, many of the finishing principles can apply to treatment of yarns and garments as well.

整理是一个通用术语,通常指在染色或印花后,但在织物被裁剪并缝制成服装、家用纺织品或其他产品之前对织物进行的处理。然而,许多整理原理也可以应用于纱线和服装加工。

Finishes have a wide variety of functions all of which are intended to make the fabric more suitable for its intended use. Functions of finishes include the following.

整理具有多种功能,所有这些功能都旨在使织物更适合其预期用途。整理功能包括以下内容。

(1) Accentuate or inhibit some natural characteristic of the fabric. Examples are softening, stiffening (firming), delustering, brightening, and changing surface characteristics.

增强或抑制织物某些自然特征。例如软化、硬化(紧致)、消光、增亮和改变表面特性。

(2) Impart new characteristics or properties to the fabric. Durable press finishes, flame retardant finishes, and soil release finish.

赋予织物新的特性或性质。耐用的压烫(如轧光、压纹——编者注)效果、阻燃整理和去污整理。

(3) Increase life and durability of the fabric.

增加织物寿命期和耐久性。

(4) Set the fabric so it maintains its shape and structure.

保持织物形态和结构。

New Words and Expressions

dye 染料
predictable 可预见的
absorbency 吸收性，吸光度，吸收能力
cloth turning 翻布
sewing 缝头
desize 退浆
mercerize 丝光
colorant 着色剂
pigment 颜料
affinity 亲和力
intend 想要，打算
stiffening 硬挺整理
flame retardant finish 阻燃整理
durability 耐久性

finish 整理
impurity 杂质
whiteness 白度
in batches 分批
singeing 烧毛
scour 煮练
heat setting 热定型
substrate 基质，基材
substantivity 直接性
garment 衣服，服装
accentuate 强调，重读
delustering 消光法
soil release finish 易去污整理

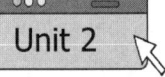 **Unit 2　Pretreatment 预处理**

1. Examining for Gray Goods 坯布检验

Each piece of gray goods on entering the finishing works is examined in the gray room for fault weaving, dirt, damages and other defects. If something wrong is found, some measures will be taken on time so as to guarantee the quality of the end product and avoid the loss. Due to a large quantity of gray goods, generally only about 10% is examined. Examining

Pretreatment
预处理

Examining for gray goods
坯布检验

contents consist of two respects: specification and quality. The examining of specification for gray goods includes length, width, weight, number of warp and weft and density, strength etc. index points. The examining of quality for gray goods mainly refer to formed faulty work during spinning and weaving, such as broken end, cut weft, skips, nep, oil-stained yarn, reed mark.

Examining process is shown in Fig. 6.1。

在进行加工之前，每件坯布都会在坯布间检查是否有错织、污垢、损坏和其他疵点。如果发现问题，将及时采取措施，以保证最终产品的质量，避免损失。由于坯布量大，通常只有10%左右的货物被抽检。检验内容包括规格和质量两个方面。坯布的规格检查包括长度、宽度、重量、经纬度、密度、强度等指标。坯布的质量检验主要是指纺纱和织造过程中形成的疵点，如断头、断纬、漏纱、棉结、油纱、筘路等。检查过程如图6.1。

Fig. 6.1 Examining 验布

2. Cloth Turning 翻布

To manage conveniently and avoid confusion, the same specification's gray goods that is often processed in the same techniques is classified as one kind, and in batches and in boxes. Each box of the gray goods is enclosed a card, known as box card, with batch number, box number and variety so as to manage and examine conveniently.

为方便管理和避免混淆，通常将相同加工工艺的同一规格原布放在一起处理、分批和分箱。每箱坯布都附有一张卡片，称为箱卡，上面有批号、箱号和品种，便于管理和检查。

3. Marking/Stamping 打印

After examining being passed, two ends of each box of gray goods must be stamped or marked with distinctive letter and number so that one can distinguish and manage them and not confuse the technique with different kinds of gray goods. The mark indicated variety, processing techniques, batch number, box number, date of delivery goods, code of cloth turning worker, etc., should be stamped in area of 10—20 cm from the end of gray goods.

坯布检验后，每箱中织物的头尾两端必须打印记，或标记独特的字母和数字，以便区分和管理，从而不会将不同工艺与品种的坯布混淆。应在距坯布末端10~20厘米的区域内加盖标明品种、加工工艺、批号、箱号、交货日期、翻布工代码等标记。

4. Sewing 缝头

Most of processing in dyeing and finishing plant is continuous. The length of the gray cloth from the loom is commonly 30—120 m or so, therefore a suitable number of pieces are then sewn end to end so as to make a continuous length, but the sewing is done by means of a chain-stitch so that after the processing the thread can be easily withdrawn and the fabrics separated. When sewing, the edge of the cloth must be level and straight and justified without confusing with both the front and back of the cloth so as to prevent from producing crease and missing stitches. After being sewn, the pieces are run into the singeing room.

染整厂加工大部分是连续的。织机上织造的坯布长度通常为 30 ~ 120 米，因此，可以将适量的坯布头尾缝合，以形成连续的长度。缝头是通过链式缝合完成的，这样在处理后，缝线可以很容易地抽出，织物可以分离。缝纫时，布边必须平整、笔直，且不要将织物的正反面混淆，以防止产生折痕和漏针。缝好后，这些织物将被送入烧毛室。

5. Singeing 烧毛

In singeing (see Fig. 6.2), the fibers which protrude from the fabric are burned away to give the fabric a smooth surface (see Fig. 6.3). Singeing is usually done by passing the fabric through a burning gas flame at high speed followed by quenching in water or the desizing bath to extinguish the smoldering fibers. Alternatively, the fabric may be passed close to a very hot plate to ignite the protruding fiber. Singeing is sometimes done after scouring since heating of the fabric in the singer can increase the difficulty of removing size and soil from the fabric.

在烧毛过程（如图 6.2）中，织物表面突出的绒毛被烧去，使布面光洁（如图 6.3）。通常，织物高速通过燃烧的煤气火焰，之后进入含水的或含有退浆剂的灭火槽，来熄灭阴燃的纤维。或者，织物可以通过靠近炙热的铜板点燃突出的纤维。烧毛工序有时安排在煮练之后，因为织物在烧毛过程中受热会增加去除浆料和污物的难度。

Fig. 6.2　Singeing 烧毛

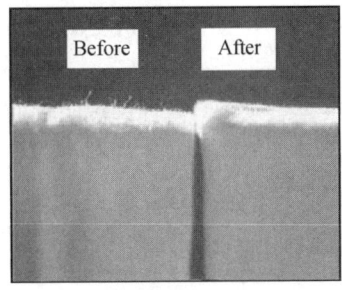

Fig. 6.3　Result of singeing 丝光效果

6. Desizing 退浆

Sizing materials are applied to yarns, particularly warp yarns, before they are woven into cloth. These form a protective coating over the yarns and keep them from chafing or breaking during weaving. Desizing is the process of removing the size material from the warp yarn in fabrics. Typical synthetic sizes are polyvinyl alcohol, acrylic copolymers, and carboxymethyl cellulose.

在织造前，必须给纱线（特别是经纱）上浆。通过上浆给纱线施加了保护层，在织造时减少了对纱线的摩擦和纱线的断头。退浆是从织物的纱线上去除浆料的过程。典型的合成浆料是聚乙烯醇、丙烯酸共聚体和羧甲基纤维素。

7. Scouring 煮练

Scouring of textile materials refers to removal of impurities by wet treatments so that the impurities do not interfere with dyeing and finish applications. The amounts and types of impurities present depend on the type of fiber in the material.

纺织品的煮练是指去除杂质的加工过程，因此减少杂质对染整应用的影响。杂质的量和类型取决于织物内纤维的类型。

8. Bleaching 漂白

The goal of bleaching is to decolorize the impurities which mask the natural whiteness of fibers. Oxidizing agents are used to bleach fibers. Bleaching processes must be closely controlled so that the color in the fibers is destroyed while damage due to oxidation of the fibrous material is minimized.

漂白的目的是脱掉遮掩纤维本白的杂质。采用氧化剂漂白纤维。漂白过程必须严格控制，以便既能使纤维中的色素遭到破坏，又能使由于纤维素纤维的氧化作用造成的损伤降到最低程度。

9. Mercerization 丝光

The process of treating cotton with a concentrated solution of sodium hydroxide is called mercerization. Mercerizing is a chemical finish applied to cellulosic fiber, especially cotton. Treatment of cotton with alkali has many beneficial effects including: added luster to fabrics (if done under tension) and softness, increased strength, improved affinity for dyes and dyeability of immature fibers and got high water sorption.

用浓氢氧化钠溶液处理棉织物的过程称为丝光。丝光是一种应用于纤维素纤维，尤其是棉的化学整理。用碱处理棉织物有许多优良效果，包括增加织物光泽（如果在张力下进行）和柔软度，增加强度，提高对染料的亲和力，提高未成熟纤维的可染性，并获得高吸水性。

10. Heat Setting 热定型

It is necessary to subject the majority of fabrics woven or knitted with man-made fibers to a setting treatment at some stage in the preparatory, dyeing or finishing processes. The main object of heat setting is to release strains imposed during the weaving or knitting processes, minimize creasing during wet processing and impart the high degree of dimensional and configurational stability which will be required in subsequent processing and ultimate use, and improve the dyeability of fabrics. Stenter heat setting machine is as shown in Fig. 6.4.

大多数化纤制成的机织物或针织物均需在前处理、染色或整理过程中的某一阶段进行热定型处理。热定形的主要目的在于消除机织或针织时所产生的应力；减少湿处理时产生的折皱，使织物获得高度的尺寸及形态稳定性，以满足后续加工和成品的需要，并且改善织物的可染性。拉幅热定型机如图6.4。

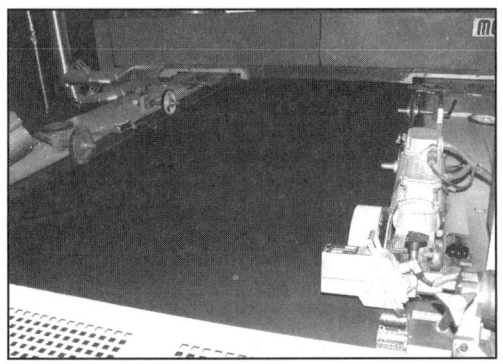

Fig. 6.4　Stenter heat setting machine 拉幅热定型机

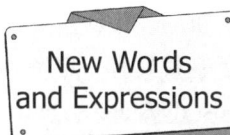

New Words and Expressions

grey goods 坯布
index point 指标
cut weft 断纬
nep 棉结
in boxes 分箱
chain-stitch 链式针迹
protruding fiber 突出的纤维
polyvinyl alcohol 聚乙烯醇
carboxymethyl cellulose 羧甲基纤维素
oxidize 氧化
strain 张力
configurational 结构的，外形的

end product 成品
broken end 缺经，断头
skips 跳纱，跳花
reed mark 筘路，筘痕，筘柳（织疵）
variety 品种
quench 熄灭
size 浆料
acrylic copolymer 丙烯酸共聚物
decolorize 脱色
alkali 碱
dimensional 尺寸的，空间的
stenter 拉幅

Unit 3　Dyeing 染色

Dyeing 染色

　　The objective of dyeing is the uniform coloration of the fibres constituting the material, usually to match a pre-specified colour. Synthetic fibres can be manufactured ready coloured. Dye is added to the liquid even before it is forced through tiny holes to come out as filaments. Other synthetic and natural fibres can be dyed in a solution in large drums. Mixing the colours of woollen fibres gives very pleasantly shaded yarns.

　　染色的目的是使纤维所有构成材料均匀着色，并往往要配出预先规定的颜色。合成纤维可以在纺丝的过程中着色。在纺丝液被压力通过细小的孔洞形成长丝之前，将染料加入纺丝液中。其他合成纤维和天然纤维可以在大染缸内的染液中着色。将不同颜色的羊毛纤维混拼，制得的纱线颜色令人愉悦。

Unit 3.1　Classification of Dyes 染料分类

In the book of *Textile Terms and Definitions* edited by British Textile Institute, dye is defined as "a colorant, usually organic, soluble or dispersed in its medium of application and which is designed to be absorbed or adsorbed by, made to react with, or deposited within a substrate in order to impart colour to that substrate with some degree of permanence".

在英国纺织学会编写的《纺织术语及其定义》中，染料的定义为"一种可溶解或分散于其应用介质中的着色剂，通常是有机的。染料研发目的是能被基材吸收或吸附，与基材发生反应或沉积在基材内，从而赋予基材具有一定持久性的颜色"。

Based on their application methods, dyes are essentially divided into acid, direct, disperse, reactive, cationic, sulphur and vat dyes. Certain dyes are substantive for certain fibre types.

根据它们的应用方法，染料主要被分为酸性、直接、分散、活性、阳离子、硫化和还原染料。特定的纤维能吸引某些特定类型的染料。

Reactive dyes：This class has appeared more recently. The dyes have high fastness due to dyes/fiber covalent bonds.

活性染料：这种染料最常用，染料和纤维以共价键连接，因此具有高色牢度。

Direct dyes：They have a direct affinity for cellulosic fibers. They do not require the use of mordants and the dyeing procedure is quite simple.

直接染料：对纤维素纤维具有直接的亲和力，染色过程不需要使用媒染剂，染色过程十分简单。

Acid dyes：The name "acid dye" derives from the use of an acidic dyebath. The colour fastness properties of various acid dyes are range from good to excellent.

酸性染料："酸性染料"名字来源于其在酸性染浴中的使用。各种酸性染料的色牢度从一般到好不等。

Disperse dyes：Disperse dyes are almost insoluble in water, are slightly soluble in water. They can be applied to nylon, cellulose acetate, acrylics and occasionally other fibers, but the major consumption is for dyeing of polyester. Wash fastness and light fastness of disperse dyes is generally goods.

分散染料：散染料几乎不溶于水，微溶于水。可以用于锦纶、醋酸纤维、丙烯酸和等其他纤维，但主要用于聚酯纤维的染色。分散染料耐洗色牢度和耐光色牢度比较好。

Unit 3.2　Dyeing Method 染色方法

Dyeing of textile is achieved by transferring dye molecules from a medium (usually water) in which the dye is dissolved or dispersed onto the textile fibers. The dyeing can be undertaken either as a batch process or a continuous technique.

纺织品的染色是通过溶解或分散在介质（通常是水）的染料分子转移到纺织纤维上实现的。染色可以采用间歇工艺或连续工艺。

Batch processes are the most common method to dye textile materials. Batch dyeing is sometimes called exhaust dyeing because the dye moves from the dyebath liquor on to the fibre in a set time. During that time, it diffuses or migrates into the interior of the fibre, and is fixed. The dye liquor, with initial high dye content, becomes gradually exhausted while the dye accumulates in the fibre.

间歇式工艺是纺织材料染色最常用的方法。因为染料在一定时间内从染浴向纤维转移，所以间歇式染色有时被称为竭染。在染色时间内，染料扩散或迁移进入纤维内部并固着。随着染料在纤维内的聚集，染浴内初始浓度较高的染料逐步耗尽。

Continuous dyeing is most economic for production of very large lots of a single colour. Most continuous dyeing processes can be divided into four stages:

对于大批量单色染色，连续染色最为经济。大多数连续染色过程可以分为如下四个阶段：

（1）Dye application by padding;

（1）通过浸轧施加染料；

（2）Dye fixation, usually in hot air or steam;

（2）通过热风或蒸汽固色；

（3）Washing-off of unfixed dye and auxiliary chemicals;

（3）洗去未固着染料和助剂；

（4）Drying, usually on infrared dryer or steam-heated cylinders.

（4）烘干，通常采用红外线烘干机或蒸汽加热的烘筒。

New Words and Expressions

constitute 组成，构成
filament 长丝
colorant 着色剂
direct dyes 直接染料
disperse dyes 分散染料
vat dyes 还原染料
mordant 媒染剂
migrate 移动，迁移
padding 浸轧
steam-heated cylinder 蒸汽烘筒

match 相配，匹配
drum 染缸
reactive dyes 活性染料
acid dyes 酸性染料
cationic 阳离子的
covalent bond 共价键
diffuse 扩散
accumulate 聚集
infrared dryer 红外烘干机

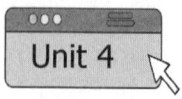 **Unit 4　　Printing 印花**

Unit 4.1　Printing Method 印花方法

Printing involves localised coloration. This is usually achieved by applying thickened pastes containing dyes or pigments onto a fabric surface according to a given colour design.

Visit printing process
参观印花工序

Printing method
印花方法

印花就是定位染色。这通常是根据给定的颜色设计，在织物表面印染含有染料或颜料的增稠浆料来实现的。

The most important printing method today is pigment printing. This involves printing the coloured pattern onto the fabric surface and curing the printed areas by heating in air. The print paste contains coloured pigments and a binding agent. On baking in hot air, the binder forms a solid film of transparent polymer that holds the pigments in place on the yarn surfaces. The great advantage of pigment printing is that the fabric does not require washing after the fixation process.

目前，最重要的印花方法是颜料印花，工艺步骤是将有色图案印到织物表面，并将已印花的区域在空气中加热焙烘。印花浆料中含有色颜料和黏合剂。在热空气中焙烘时，黏合剂形成紧密的聚合物透明膜，它将颜料按图案要求固定在纱线表面。颜料印花的最大优点是固色加工以后织物无需洗涤处理。

The dyes used in printing are the same as that in dyeing. The basic operations of printing include: dye is first dissolved and pasted with a small quantity of water and a suitable thickening agent; then applied to fabric and dried immediately; and then fixed on the fabric by steaming or heating, finally soaped and washed with water.

印花使用的染料和染色是相同的。印花的基本操作包括：首先用少量水和适当的增稠剂将染料溶解并调成糊状，然后应用到织物上并立即烘干，再通过汽蒸或加热将染料固定在织物上，最后皂洗和水洗。

Pigment and dye printing are both direct printing methods. Two other important indirect printing methods called discharge and resist printing also give coloured designs.

颜料和染料印花都是直接印花方法。另外两种非直接印花方法叫作拔染和防染印花，也能产生有色花纹。

Over many centuries, a variety of techniques for printing designs have evolved, such as block printing, mordant printing, resist printing, screen printing (see Fig. 6.5), roller printing (see Fig. 6.6), transfer printing, photographic printing, etc. Printing can be applied to warp yarns, to fabrics, or to apparel pieces. Most textiles are printed in the fabric form.

几个世纪以来，各种印花技术不断发展，如雕版印花、媒染印花、防染印花、筛网印花（见图 6.5）、圆网印花（见图 6.6）、转移印花、照片印花等。印花可以应用于经纱、织物或服装。大多数纺织品都是以织物的形式印花的。

Fig. 6.5 Screen printing 筛网印花

Fig. 6.6 Roller printing 圆网印花

Unit 4.2 Special Printing 特种印花

Flocking consists of attacking very short fibres to the surface of the fabric by means of an adhesive. The result is a textured surface and is usually in a pattern that involves areas of flocked and areas of smooth fabric. The adhesive is printed onto fabric in the desired pattern, and then the flock is applied onto the surface of fabric.

Special printing show 特种印花展示   Special printing 特种印花

植绒是通过黏合剂将非常短的纤维黏结到织物表面。植绒效果是产生有纹理表面，通常图案中包括绒面和光滑布面。需要有花型的区域印上黏合剂，将短绒施加于织物表面。

Photographic printing is done in manner similar to the photochemical preparation of screens for screen printing. A photosensitive dye is coated on the fabric, a negative is placed over the fabric, light is applied, and a photographic type of printing takes place.

照片印花是一种类似于筛网印花网框的光化学制备的方法。将光敏染料涂在织物上，放上底片，进行光照，即产生了照片印花。

Electrostatic printing, a plate with an electrostatic charge is placed behind the fabric. A stencil in the form of the pattern is placed over the fabric. Special powdered inks that can be attracted by the electrostatic charge are passed over the surface fabric, and colour the fabric in the open areas of the stencil.

静电印花，将带有电荷的平板放在织物后面。有花型的模板放在织物上。特殊粉末装油墨被静电荷吸引而穿过织物表面，使织物在模板空白处着色。

Ombre printing is the printing of a rainbow or various tone effects. The tone may change from light to dark shades of one colour, or the effect may be of shading from one colour into another.

彩虹印花是一种印制彩虹或多彩色泽效果方法。色泽的变化可以是一种颜色从淡到浓的变化，或不同颜色间转变。

Foam printing, a variant of the foam dyeing process, can be used to apply dye to selected areas of fabric to create a multi-coloured effect. Foam printing offers the same energy saving advantages as foam dyeing.

泡沫印花，不同于泡沫染色过程，可以将染料应用于织物上选择的区域产生多种色彩的效果。泡沫印花与泡沫染色同样具有节能的优点。

New Words and Expressions

pattern 图案
binding agent 黏合剂
discharge printing 拔染印花
block printing 雕版印刷
roller printing 滚筒印花
adhesive 黏合剂
stencil 模板
tone 色调

curing 固化，焙烘
thickening agent 增稠剂
resist printing 防染印花
screen printing 筛网印花
flocking 植绒
photosensitive 光敏的，感光的
ombre printing 虹彩印花
flock 植绒毛

Unit 5　Finishing 后整理

Finishing is a general term which usually refers to treatments on textile fabrics after dyeing or printing but before the fabrics is cut and sewn into garments, household textiles, or other products. However, many of the finishing principles can apply to treatment of yarns and garments as well.

Visit finishing
参观后整理工序

Finishing（mechanical）
后整理（机械整理）

整理是统称，通常指对染色或印花后但还没有裁剪成服装、家用纺织品或其他产品的纺织品的处理。然而许多整理的原理也可以应用到对于纱线和服装的处理。

On the basis of their technical features the finishing processes can be divided into two main groups: i.e. mechanical and chemical finishes.

根据整理工艺的技术特点，可分为两大类，即机械整理和化学整理。

Unit 5.1　Mechanical Finishing 机械整理

Most mechanical finishing processes modify the appearance and handle of a fabric. These processes are used on a variety of fabrics containing different types of fibres. Their major effect is to modify the fabric surface, usually either to make it smoother, or to raise a pile. Both effects can cause a change in the perceived colour of the material because they modify the reflection of light from the fabric surface. The mechanical finishes used frequently may be listed as:

多数机械整理加工可改良织物的外观和手感。这些加工被用于含不同种类纤维的各种织物。它们的主要效果是修饰织物的表面，一般或是使它平滑，或是起绒。两种效果都能引起材料可察觉的颜色变化，因为它们改变了织物表面的光反射。常见机械整理罗列如下：

1. Calendering 轧光

Compression of the fabric between two heavy rollers to give a flattened, smooth appearance to the surface of a fabric.

织物通过两个重压罗拉的压缩，使织物外表平整、光滑。

2. Raising 起绒

Plucking the fibres from a woven or knitted fabric to give a nap effect on the surface.

从机织或针织物上挑出纤维，赋予织物绒面效果。

3. Cropping 剪绒

Cutting the surface hairs from the fabric to give a smooth appearance, often used on woolen goods where the removal of surface hair by a singeing process is not possible.

将织物表面绒毛剪掉，赋予织物平滑表面。这种方法常用于羊毛织物，因为羊毛织物不能用烧毛工艺来去除其表面绒毛。

Unit 5.2　Chemical Finishing 化学整理

1. Anti-Pilling Finish 抗起球整理

Pilling is the formation of small balls of fiber and other contaminants, called pills, which are held to the surface of cloth by linking fibers. They are caused by abrasion as different parts of a garment rub against each other, or as cloth is rubbed against another surface.

Anti-pilling finish
抗起球整理

由纤维和其他污染物形成的小绒球依靠纤维的联接黏附在织物表面的现象称为起球现象。起球的原因是服装不同部位之间的摩擦，或是织物与其他物体表面的摩擦。

Resins used for easy care finishes usually reduce pilling by improving the adhesion of fibers in yarns. Shrink resistant treatments for wool or wool/synthetic blends usually reduce pilling by preventing fiber migration.

在免烫整理中使用的树脂改变了纱线中纤维的黏附力，通常可以减少起球。对毛织物或毛与化纤混纺织物的防缩整理可以防止纤维的迁移，从而减少起球。

Fiber producers have reduced pilling by lowering the tenacity of their fibers so that pills may be more easily abraded from the surface of cloth. Fabric softeners may sometimes be effective in reducing pilling, since they lubricate the surface of the cloth and reduce the abrasive forces.

纤维生产厂通过降低纤维强度来减少起球，这样，摩擦生成的纤维球就可能更易从织物表面脱落。织物柔软剂有时对减少起球也起作用，因为柔软剂润滑织物表面，降低摩擦力。

2. Antistatic Finish 抗静电整理

Cotton has very good antistatic properties and few problems are encountered with this material. The basic reason for this is that the moisture regain of cotton is high which provides the fibre with sufficient conductivity

Antistatic finish
抗静电整理

to dissipate any charge that might accumulate. In synthetic fibres, which have low water content and are sufficiently non-conductive to hold a static charge on the surface, severe static problems can arise.

棉有非常好的抗静电性，很少遇到这个问题。根本原因是棉的回潮率很高，纤维有足够的导电性使可能积累的静电消散。合成纤维含水率低且不易导电，表面带静电，导致严重的静电问题。

Since it is impossible to prevent the generation of electrostatic charges on the surface of fibers, it is necessary to improve the charge dissipation process so that the charge is conducted away from the fiber. This is done by using chemical finishes called antistatic agents or antistats, or by copolymerizing hydrophilic monomers with the fibers.

要防止在纤维表面产生静电荷是不可能的事，因此有必要改变电荷的扩散过程，将其从纤维上导走。可以使用抗静电剂进行化学整理或使亲水单体与纤维共聚以达此目的。

3. Water Repellent Finish 拒水整理

Water repellent finish
拒水整理

The term water repellent should not be confused with the term waterproof. A water-repellent fabric allows air but prevent water to pass through itself, it only resists penetration by water but are not completely waterproof. The passage of air is imperative if one is to have a garment that is comfortable to wear. Water proofing finish makes the wearer feel uneasy and uncomfortable, as the air circulation is not here. Water repellent finish has no the problem.

Fig. 6.7　Water repellent finish

"拒水"和"防水"的概念不能混淆。拒水织物允许气体而非水透过，它仅阻止水的穿过而不是完全防水。任何穿着舒适的衣服必须透气。由于没有气体流动，防水整理使穿着者感到不自在和不舒服，而拒水整理就没有此问题。

Water repellent finishes (see Fig. 6.7) are important in the sportswear and leisurewear fields because they impart an ability to withstand wetting or penetration by water in outdoor conditions. A water repellent finish on a fabric repels liquid water but the fabric remains permeable to air, an important comfort factor where garments are worn in conditions where the wearer needs to transpire water vapor. In condition of high metabolic activity the perspiration may thus be evaporated through the fabric without the inside of the garment becoming damp, clammy and uncomfortable.

拒水整理（见 6.7）在运动服和休闲服领域十分重要，因为拒水整理使这些服装具有在户外抗润湿和抗水渗透的能力。织物经拒水整理后，能驱开液态水，但保留了空气的可渗透性，这是一个重要的舒适性因素，在穿衣者需要散发水蒸气时，这些服装均做到了这点。在高新陈代谢活动进行时，可通过织物蒸发，使成衣内部不会变得潮湿、不舒服，而这些都与热损失有关。

New Words and Expressions

raise a pile 起毛	calendaring 压光
raising 起绒	nap 绒毛
cropping 剪毛	pilling 起球
abrasion 磨损	resin 树脂
shrink resistant 防缩	tenacity 韧性
softener 柔软剂	antistatic finish 抗静电整理
electron 电子	conductivity 导电性
dissipate 消散，驱散	static charge 静电荷
antistat 抗静电剂	copolymerize 异分子聚合
hydrophilic 亲水的	monomer 单体
water repellent 拒水	waterproof 防水
uneasy 不舒服	repel 排斥
permeable 能透过的，可渗透的	metabolic activity 新陈代谢
damp 潮湿的	clammy 湿冷的

Task 2

To Describe the Dyeing and Finishing Machines 描述染整机械

 Gas Singer 气体烧毛机

For gas singeing (see Fig. 6.8), the cloth is passing over and in direct contract with an open gas flame. Before this cloth surfaces may be brushed lightly to raise unwanted fiber ends so that they will singe more easily, and at the same time some impurities in the cloth, as dust, hanging ends, etc., are also removed. The modern gas singer is fitted with a single or double row of gas

Gas singer
气体烧毛机

burners at the number of 4—6, and 8—12 respectively. The burners are so arranged that one or both sides of the cloth may be singed during a single passage of the cloth over the flames. Singeing speeds may vary with the different kinds of fabrics, as well as the number of gas burners and the intensity of the heat. Generally, gas singer runs about 80—140 meters per minute.

气体烧毛机（见图6.8），织物是在煤气明火上通过并与之直接接触。在此之前，织物表面可加以轻微擦刷，使要去掉的茸毛端隆起而更易于进行烧毛；同时织物里有些杂质，如灰尘、悬浮的纱头等也得到去除。现代的气体烧毛机装有单或双排的煤气火口，数目分别为4～6只和8～12只。火口这样安排为织物在火焰上通过一次，即可得到一面或双面烧毛。烧毛速度可随织物的不同种类，以及煤气火口的数目和热量强度而有所不同。一般说来，气体烧毛机每分钟烧毛约80～140米。

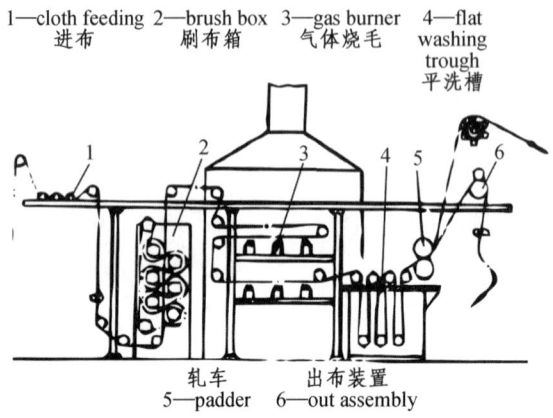

Fig. 6.8 Structure of gas singeing 气体烧毛机构造

Extreme care must be taken when singeing fabrics containing thermoplastic fibers in order to avoid dyeing problems. Thermoplastic fibers such as polyester melt when singed, and the fiber ends form beads on the fabric surface. These beads have greater dye affinity than the polyester fibers so the dyeability of singed fabrics by batch processes is usually not satisfactory. Yarns, sewing threads, felt, and carpet backing can also be singed.

当织物中含有热塑性纤维时,烧毛必须相当严格控制来避免之后的染色过程发生问题。热塑性纤维，例如涤纶织物在烧毛过程中会熔化，且熔化的纤维末端在织物表面形成球珠。这些球珠对染料比涤纶纤维有更高的亲和力，导致烧毛后织物在间歇式染色时通常会产生问题。纱线，缝纫线，毛毯和地毯背面也能够进行烧毛。

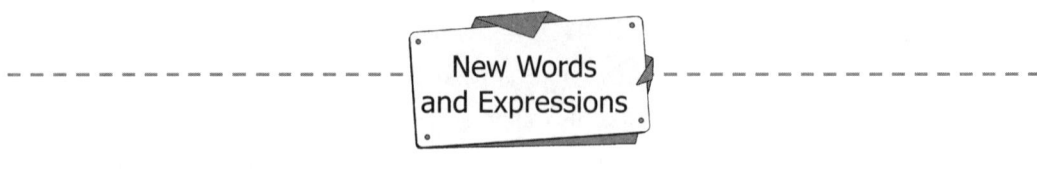

hanging ends 悬浮的纱头　　　　　　　　　burner 火口
run 运行　　　　　　　　　　　　　　　　cloth feeding 进布

flat washing trough 平洗槽
out assembly 出布装置
thermoplastic 热塑性的

padder 轧车
felt 毡

Unit 2　Dyeing Machinery 染色机械

Stainless steel used for dyeing machinery is high resistance to wear and corrosion. Modern machines have automatic controls for regulation of the dyeing temperature. These allow controlled heating at a given rate and maintenance of a set maximum dyeing temperature. Programmable microprocessors were also used widely.

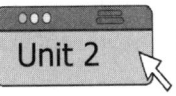

Dyeing machinery
染色机械

不锈钢用于染色机可以高度耐磨损及腐蚀。现代机器有调节染色温度的自动控制系统，它们允许在给定速率下受控加热，并维持设定的最高染色温度。可编程微处理器同样得到广泛应用。

Dyes can be applied to fibres, yarns, fabrics or garments, so dyeing machines may be divided into four types: i.e. dyeing machines for fibre, for yarn, for fabric or for garment.

染料可用于纤维、纱、织物或服装，因此染色机器可以分为四种类型，即纤维染色机、纱线染色机、织物染色机和服装染色机。

1. Dyeing Machines for Textile Fibres 纤维染色机

Fibres are dyed in the form of staple or sliver. Both of them can be dyed in dyeing autoclaves, which can be classified into two categories: machines that work at a temperature of up to 100 °C and machines that work at temperature of over 100 °C. A dyeing autoclave essentially

Fibres dyeing machines
纤维染色机

consists of a metallic container containing the dyebath in which a cage containing the fibres to be dyed. The dyeing comes about by means of the passage of the dyebath through the fibres, which are arranged to ensure the uniform impregnation of the fibres' entire mass; generally, the fibres are stationary while the liquor circulates through them. This type of circulation can prevent the fibres from entanglement.

纤维是以短纤或纤维条的形式在染色釜中染色。染色釜可分为两类：工作温度达到100 °C和超过100 °C。染色釜基本由装染液的金属容器和装纤维笼子构成。染色通过染液流过纤维进行，纤维排列确保其整体浸渍均匀，通常，纤维固定而染液循环。这种循环可防止纤维纠缠。

2. Dyeing Machines for Yarns 纱线染色机

The machines used frequently for the dyeing of yarn include cheese dyeing autoclave (see Fig. 6.9) and hank dyeing machines. In cheese

Yarns dyeing machines
纱线染色机

159

dyeing autoclave, yarn is wound and dyed on bobbins that are perforated tubes, through the holes of which the liquor comes into contact with the yarn. Hank dyeing is a traditionally method used in yarn dyeing. According to how the solution comes into contact with the hanks the hank dyeing machines can be divided into two types: i.e. the machine in which hanks and bath is in movement and the machines in which hanks is static while liquor is in movement. In the first type of machine the hanks are held by a horizontal support with a rotary motion, and which at the same time functions as a feed pipe for the dye bath, which, driven by a pump, is distributed through the yarn held by the supports. The second type of machine such as compartment machine or cupboard machine is frequently used for the dyeing of wool and cotton. This type of machine essentially consists of a metallic container containing the dyebath in which cages in which there are many supports used to hold the hanks to be dyed. The liquor is pumped and circulates through the hanks.

Fig. 6.9　Cheese dyeing autoclave 高温高压筒子染色机

常用于纱线染色的机器有染色釜（见图 6.9）和绞纱染色机。在染色釜中，将纱线绕在带孔的筒管上染色，染液通过小孔与纱线接触。绞纱染色是用于纱线染色的传统方法。绞纱染色机按染液与绞纱的接触方式可分为两类，即染色机中绞纱、染液都运动和绞纱静止而染液运动。在第一种机器中，绞纱挂在一个能够旋转的水平支撑管上，支撑管同时还起到染液喂液管的作用，染液在泵的驱动下传递到绞纱中。第二种机器有厢式或柜式染色机，常用于羊毛和棉的染色。此类机器基本上由装染液的金属容器和内有许多用于挂绞纱的支撑管的笼子构成。染液在泵作用下循环流过绞纱。

3. Dyeing Machines for Fabrics 织物染色机

Fabrics may be dyed either in batches or semi-continuously or continuously. Many different kinds of machines are used for fabric dyeing. These machines used more frequently include winch dyeing machine, jig dyeing machine, and pad dyeing machine. Jig dyeing machine (see Fig. 6.10)

Fabrics dyeing machinery 织物染色机

is frequently used for the dyeing of the fabrics with a fairly close weave that will not lose their shape even though under the relatively high tension created by the machine. The jigger works with an exceedingly low liquor ratio and can produce a relatively high tension, so it is very suitable for the dyeing of cotton woven fabric with the dyes whose affinity is not high. Pad dyeing machine (see Fig. 6.11) provides a continuous dyeing process. It is used in producing large quantities of fabrics that can withstand tension and pressure. The operations of pad dyeing include that fabrics first pass through a dyebath, then through pad rollers that squeeze out the excess dye, and then into a steam or heated chamber in which the dye is fixed.

Fig. 6.10　Jig dyeing machine 卷染机

Fig. 6.11　Pad dyeing machine 浸轧机

织物可以采用间歇式、半连续式或连续式工艺进行染色。许多不同类型的机器可用于织物染色。常用的机器有绞盘喷射染色机、卷染机和浸轧染色机。卷染机（见图 6.10）常用于结构紧密的织物染色，尽管机器产生的张力相对较大但织物不会变形。卷染机工作时浴比非常低，产生的张力相对较高，因此非常适合于亲和力不高的染料染棉机织物。浸轧染色机（见图 6.11）采用连续染色工艺，常用于加工大量的能承受张力和压力的织物。浸轧染色的过程包括：先将织物通过染浴，然后经轧辊将多余的染料榨出，再进入蒸汽或加热箱内固色。

4. Dyeing Machines for Garments 服装染色机

Drum-type dyeing machine (see Fig. 6.12) is used most frequently for the dyeing of cotton garment, which consists of a stationary container containing dye liquor in which there is a perforated drums, and is very similar to those of the domestic washing machine. The garments to be dyed are put in the drum and then the drum is rotated in the dye liquor to form a circulation through them. Paddle dyeing machine is suitable for the dyeing of knitted wool garments. It consists of a large stationary container and a paddle that is placed above the container. To dye garments, the dye liquor and the garments to be dyed are first put in the container, and then the paddle starts to rotate and agitate in the dye liquor slowly. The dyeing of the textiles with small size, such as short fabric lengths, hosiery and towel, can also be carried out in the garment dyeing machines.

Garments dyeing machinery 服装染色机

转鼓式染色机（见图 6.12）最常用于棉布服装染色，它由一个固定的装有染液的容器和一个浸在染液中的多孔的转鼓组成，与家用洗衣机十分相似。将要染色的衣服放入转鼓，转鼓在染液中旋转形成循环。桨叶式染色机适用于针织羊毛衫的染色，它由一个大的固定容器和安在容器上方的桨叶组成。染色时首先将染液和要染的衣服放入容器中，然后开始转动桨叶，缓慢搅动液。当所染的纺织品尺寸较小，如长度较短的织物，如袜子和手巾，也能在服装染色机进行染色。

Fig. 6.12　Garment dyeing machine 服装染色机

New Words and Expressions

base 碱
wear 磨损
automatic 自动的
sliver 纱条，棉条，条子
cage 笼
wind 绕,缠
bobbin 筒管，筒子
rotary motion 转动
compartment machine 厢式染色机
winch 绞盘，绞车
pad dyeing machine 浸轧染色机
chamber 室
container 容器
paddle dyeing machine 桨叶式染色机
hosiery 袜类，针织品

stainless steel 不锈钢
corrosion 腐蚀
microprocessor 微处理器
dyeing autoclave 染色釜
entanglement 纠缠
hank dyeing machine 绞纱染色机
static 静态的
feed pipe 喂液管
cupboard machine 柜式染色机
jig dyeing machine 卷染机
exceedingly 非常地，极度地
drum-type 转鼓式
paddle 桨，踏板，桨状搅拌器
agitate 搅动
towel 手巾，毛巾

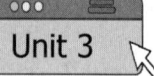 **Unit 3　Transfer Printing Machines 转移印花机**

Transfer printing machines (see Fig. 6.13) can be divided into two types: i.e. flat-bed and continuous calender types.

转移印花机（见图6.13）分为两种类型，即平板式和连续轧光式。

The flat-bed transfer-printing machines are mainly used for garment. In a typical flat-bed machine, the actual printing station consists of a top and a bottom board, both provided with direct electrical heating with temperature control within ±5 °C over the entire working surface. The pressure is applied pneumatically by two cylinders.

Transfer printing machines 转移印花机

The printing process is carried out in three phases: feeding, printing and stacking. The material is prepared at the loading station and carried to a position (printing station) under the electrically heating head, when the conveyor stops and the head is lowered down for the time set on a dial, during the period the next garment is prepared at the loading station. After the predetermined time, the head rises and the conveyor is made to travel to take the material to the unloading station and a new one to the printing station.

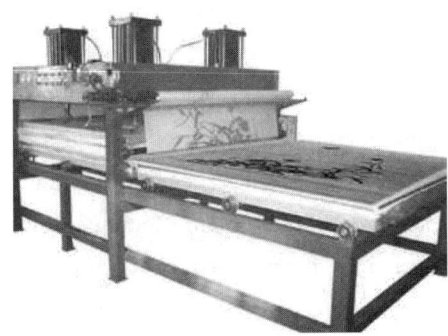

Fig. 6.13   Flat-bed transfer-printing machine 平板转移印花

平板转移印花机主要用于服装。在典型的平板转移印花机中，实际的印花区由一块顶板和一块底板组成，这两块板用电直接加热，整个工作面的温度控制在±5 ℃内。通过两个气动加压辊筒。印花工艺分为三个阶段步：进布、印花和堆置。在装料位置准备好原料，然后送到电加热头下的位置（印花区）。当传送带停止时，电热头压下并保持到表盘所设定的时间，与此同时另一件服装在装料位置已准备好。预定时间之后，加热头抬起，传送带启动并将所印服装送到卸载区，同时新的一件抵达印花位置。

Continuous transfer printing machine is used for the printing of fabric. A continuous transfer printing machine consists mainly of a hot metal cylinder and an endless belt. The printed paper, the fabric to be printed and the back paper are mounted respectively on the rollers at the entry of the machine. They move downwards to a pair of nip rollers at where they join to form a sandwich and enter the machine. The fabric-paper sandwich is held by the pressure exerted by the endless belt against the hot metal cylinder as it passes through the machine. This cylinder is usually heated internally by hot oil, reaching temperatures approaching 180 ℃. Under these conditions of controlled temperature, pressure and time, the dye becomes gaseous by a process of sublimation, transfers to the fabric and then diffuses into the fibres. After leaving this calender, the dye is usually adequately fixed for most end-use, requiring no further fixation or wash-off processes.

连续式转移印花机常用于织物印花，主要由一个热金属辊筒和一个循环带组成。印花纸、要印的织物以及衬纸分别装在机器入口的滚筒上。它们向下输送到一对压轧辊筒处，结合形成夹心结构然后喂入机器。当其通过机器时，受到传送带对热的金属辊筒施加的压力，保持织物与纸的夹心结构。辊筒由其内部的热油加热，温度接近180 ℃。根据染料经升华过程变成气体、转移到织物然后扩散到纤维内部等条件，设定温度、压力和时间。离开辊筒后，对大多数最终用途而言，通常染料已充分固着在织物上，不需要进一步的固色或水洗加工。

The transfer printing achieves the designs with clear and sharp definition that other types of printing cannot match. All colors are printed at the same time, thereby simplifying the operation and requiring lower processing costs. Production can change rapidly from one design to another simply by changing the design paper. Short runs are feasible, fast deliveries are possible. Transfer printing has proved especially successful in printing knitted fabrics. Knitted goods are less dimensionally stable than woven fabrics. Manufacturers using conventional screen and roller printing techniques on knitted fabrics experienced difficulties in making multicolour prints in which segments of the print must fit together accurately. In transfer printing, all parts of the design are applied at once, eliminating the problem of stretching of fabrics as they move from one roller to another. The capital cost of the equipment is low and so also are the space requirements. A skilled printer is not required though careful control of temperature and throughput is necessary. The proportion of sub-standard quality is low. Since the printed fabric does not need any wet treatment, it does not contribute to water pollution problem.

转移印花生产的图案准确清晰，是其他印花法所不能比拟的。所有颜色同时印制，因此操作简化、加工成本低。仅需改变印花纸，就能迅速地将产品从一种图案变为另一种图案。可生产批量少，交货迅速。实践证明，转移印花对针织物印花尤其成功。针织物较机织物尺寸稳定性差。当生产商用传统的筛网印花或滚筒印花技术进行多色印花时，由于印花部位必须对花准确，使其遇到许多困难。在转移印花中，所有图案一次完成，避免了织物从一个辊筒到另一个辊筒时对织物的拉伸问题。设备投资低，生产场地小。虽然要准确控制温度和进布速度，但并不需要相当熟练的印花工。不合格产品率低。由于所印织物不需任何湿处理，因此不会产生水污染。

New Words and Expressions

flat-bed 平板
pneumatically 气动的
conveyor 传送带
endless belt 环形带
nip roller 轧辊
check 格子布
sub-standard 标准以下的

calendar 轧光
stacking 堆置
dial 表盘
mount 安装
sublimation 升华
capital cost 资本费用

Chapter 7

Textile Testing 纺织检测篇

- Task 1: To know the basic items of textile and garment testing.
  了解纺织品和服装检测基本项目。
- Task 2: To know the detailed examples of various testing standards.
  了解不同的检测标准的详尽案例。

Task 1

Fiber Identification 纤维鉴别

The number of different fibers used in the textile industry is quite large. Identification of these fibers is frequently difficult since it is usually not possible to distinguish one fiber from another merely by touch or sight. Other tests must be performed. There are advantages and disadvantages to each. Some are easy, quick and relatively inexpensive, but do not allow clear distinctions to be made between fibers with the same characteristics.

Fiber identification
纤维鉴别

For example, a burning test (see Fig. 7.1) will not differentiate between flax and cotton since both have the same burning properties. Others enable positive identification, but require much more time and more sophisticated testing apparatus (e.g., chemical analysis).

纺织工业中使用的不同纤维数量相当多。识别这些纤维通常是困难的，因为仅仅通过触摸或视觉（观察）通常不可能区分一种纤维和另一种纤维。必须进行其他测试。每一种都有其优点和缺点。有些是简单、快速且相对便宜的，但不允许在具有相同特性的纤维之间进行明确的区分。例如，燃烧试验（见图 7.1）无法区分亚麻和棉花，因为两者具有相同的燃烧性质。其他方法可以进行阳性鉴定，但需要更多的时间和更复杂的检测设备（例如化学分析）。

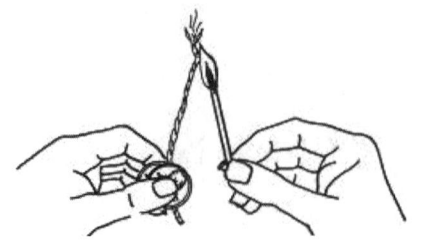

Fig. 7.1　Burning test 燃烧试验

1. Burning Test 燃烧

The burning test is a good preliminary test. It provides valuable data regarding appropriate care and will help place a fiber into a specific category. It is not, however, a test that can be used alone to provide exact identification of specific fibers. In the case of yarns composed of two or more fibers, the test will usually give the reaction of the fiber that burns most easily; if a fiber is heat-sensitive, it will tend to melt or withdraw from the flame, leaving the flammable fiber to burn. Burning characteristics of textiles is shown in table 7.1.

Fiber identify methods
纤维鉴别各种方法

燃烧测试是一个很好的初步测试。它提供了有关适当观察的宝贵数据，并将有助于将纤维归入特定类别。然而，这不是一种可以单独用于提供特定纤维的精确识别的测试。对于由两种或两种以上纤维组成的纱线，测试通常会给出最容易燃烧的纤维的反应；如果纤维是热敏的，它将倾向于熔化或从火焰中退出，留下易燃的纤维燃烧。纺织品燃烧性质见表 7.1。

Table 7.1　Burning characteristics of textiles 纺织品燃烧性质

Fiber 纤维	Burn or melt 燃烧或熔融	Shrinks from flame 近火焰收缩	Odor 气味	Residue 残留	Other properties 其他性质
Cotton 棉	Burns only 仅燃烧	No	Burning paper, leaves or wood 似烧纸、树叶和木头	Fine, feathery, gray ash 细腻轻软灰烬	/
Flax, hemp, jute, ramie, etc. 亚麻、大麻、黄麻、苎麻等			All burning characteristics are the same as cotton. 所有燃烧性质与棉花相同。		
Rayon 人造丝			All burning characteristics are the same as cotton. 所有燃烧性质与棉花相同。		
Wool, mohair, cashmere, alpaca, etc. 羊毛、马海毛、羊绒、羊驼毛等	Burns only	Yes	Very strong odor of burning hair 非常强的烧毛发的味道	Black, hollow irregular bead which crushes easily to a gritty, black power 黑色、中空、不规则的珠子，很容易压碎成粗糙的黑色粉末	Self-extinguishing 自熄

续表

Silk 蚕丝		Same as for wool, except odor is not as strong and may smell like charred or burning meat (no sulphur content like wool). 与羊毛相同，只是气味没有那么强烈，可能闻起来像烧焦或燃烧的肉（没有羊毛那样含硫）。
Acetate 醋酯纤维	Burn and melt	yes	Combination of burning paper and vinegar 烧纸和醋的混合物	Dark, hard, solid bead 深色、坚硬、实心珠子	/
Acrylic 腈纶	Burn and melt	yes	Broiled fish 烤鱼味	Hard, irregularly shaped bead 坚硬、形状不规则的珠子	Flame gives off black smoke 火焰冒出黑烟
Aramid 芳纶	Burn and melt	yes	Sweet 甜味	Hard, black bead 坚硬的黑色珠子	Self-extinguishing
Glass 玻璃纤维	Melt only	Very slowly	No odor 无味	Hard, whitish bead 坚硬的白色珠子	Flame resistant fiber; heat from match will not cause fiber to melt 阻燃纤维点燃的热量不会引起纤维熔融
Modacrylic 腈氯纶	Burns and melt	Yes	Chemical 化学品味	Hard, black irregular bead	Self-extinguishing
Nylon 锦纶	Burns and melt	Yes	Celery 芹菜味	Hard, cream-colored bead. If fibers are overheat, bead will become dark 坚硬的奶油色珠子。如果纤维过热，珠就会变黑	drops of melted fiber may fall from heated portion of sample 熔化的纤维可能从样品的受热部分掉滴落
Olefin 烯烃	Burns and melt	Yes	Chemical	Hard, tan bead	Flame gives off black smoke
Polyester 聚酯纤维	Burns and melt	Yes	Sweet chemical 甜味化学品	Hard, cream-colored bead. If fibers are overheat, bead will become dark	Drops of melted fiber may fall from heated portion of sample; flame gives off black smoke 样品被加热的部分会有融滴滴落；火焰会产生黑
Spandex 氨纶	Burns and melt	Yes	Chemical	Soft, black ash	/
Vinal 聚乙烯醇纤维	Burns and melt	Yes	Paraffin-like or Chemical 类石蜡或化学品	Hard, tan bead	/

Remember that the burning test is a preliminary test indicates general grouping or categories only. The test is relatively simple but must be used with care to avoid injury and guard against fire.

请记住，燃烧测试是一个初步测试，仅指示一般分组或类别。该测试相对简单，但必须小心使用，以避免受伤和防火。

2. Microscopic Evaluation 显微镜评估

Most fibers provide different view of both their lengthwise and crosswise, natural fibers have their specific shape in their cross-section, man-made fibers are similar in their microscopic appearance.

大多数纤维提供了不同的纵向和横向视图，天然纤维在横截面上有其特定的形状，人造纤维在微观外观上相似。

3. Chlorine Bleach Test 氯漂白试验

For silk or wool fibers, they will be wet with liquid chlorine bleach, these fibers turn yellow and after a while disintegrate from the action of the chemical.

对于丝绸或羊毛纤维，它们会被液氯漂白剂弄湿，这些纤维会变黄，过一段时间就会因化学物质的作用而分解。

4. Dry and Wet Strength Test 干湿强力测试

The strength of many fibers is affected by the amount of water they contain, a few fibers get a little stronger when wet, such as cotton fibers; some retain about the same in strength; and others get weaker.

许多纤维的强度受其含水量的影响，少数纤维在潮湿时会变得更强，如棉纤维；有些在强度上保持大致相同；而其他则变得更弱。

5. Stain Test 染色试验

The stains are a mixture of several different classes and colors of dyes so that each fiber will be dyed a specific color.

污渍是几种不同种类和颜色的染料的混合物，因此每种纤维都会被染成特定的颜色。

New Words and Expressions

general test methods 常规测试方法
shrink 收缩
melt 熔融
odor 气味
residue 余烬
gray ash 灰色的灰烬
feathery 柔软如羽毛的；生有羽毛的
hollow irregular bead 中空且不规则的珠状物
celery 芹菜
self-extinguishing 自动熄灭
lengthwise and crosswise 长度和断面方向

gritty 碎末，粉末
sulphur 硫
broiled 烧烤；炙烤
araffin 石蜡
burning test 燃烧实验
microscopic evaluation 显微镜法
chlorine bleach test 氯漂法
stain test 着色法
tan 棕褐色，黄褐色，黝黑色

Fiber & Fabric Properties 纤维和织物性质

 Mechanical Properties 机械性质

There are standard test methods for measuring breaking strength, elongation, elasticity, resilience and related mechanical properties of either single fibers or bundles of fibers. These fiber characteristics are very much related to the mechanical characteristics of yarns and fabrics, although yarn and fabric structures also have a powerful influence.

Mechanical properties
机械性质

有测量单纤维或纤维束的断裂强度、伸长率、弹性、回弹和相关机械性质的标准试验方法。这些纤维特性与纱线和织物的机械特性密切相关，尽管纱线和织物结构也有很大的影响。

In staple fiber yarns, the yarn strength can never be more than a fraction of the strengths of the fibers in the yarn, because even tightly twisted yarns fail only partly because of fiber breakage. After some fibers break, any staple yarn structure becomes loosened and the remaining unbroken fibers slip apart as the clamped ends of the yarn are pulled farther apart.

在短纤维纱线中，纱线强度永远不会超过纱线中纤维强度的一小部分，因为即使是紧捻的纱线也只能部分由于纤维断裂而失效。一些纤维断裂后，任何短纤维纱线结构都会变松，剩余的未断裂纤维会随着纱线被夹持住的末端被拉开而滑开。

A special test of fiber loop strength or knot strength, as compared to the tensile strength of straight fibers, provides a measure of the brittleness of staple fibers or filaments.

与直纤维的拉伸强度相比，纤维环强度或结强度特殊测试提供了短纤维或长丝脆性测量。

 Chemical Characteristics 化学特征

In general, the chemical characteristics of a fiber material are the same as those of the bulk polymer from which the fibers are made. However, the physical arrangement of molecular chains in a fiber, their orientation, and their degree of crystallinity strongly affect rates of chemical reactions. Such techniques as flammability tests, solubility tests, and dye staining tests are

Chemical characteristic
化学特征

windows into fiber chemistry. Numerous chemical tests are used to detect or identify different kinds of fiber damage or contamination. Infrared spectral analysis and more recent spectral methods as well as chromatography have proved to be increasingly powerful tools in the hands of textile chemists.

通常，纤维材料的化学特性与制造纤维的本体聚合物的化学特性相同。然而，纤维中分子链的物理排列、取向和结晶度强烈影响化学反应的速率。可燃性测试、溶解性测试和染料染色测试等技术是了解纤维化学的窗口。许多化学测试用于检测或识别不同种类的纤维损伤或污染。红外光谱分析和最近的光谱方法以及色谱法已被证明是纺织品化学家手中越来越强大的工具。

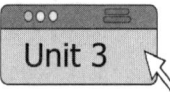

Unit 3　　Fabric Tensile Properties 织物拉伸性质

Acceptable levels of tensile properties depend on the end use for which the textile was produced. The level of tensile force that a seat belt or parachute fabric is expected to withstand is higher than that expected for apparel fabrics. American Society for Testing Material (ASTM) specifications list minimum levels of fabric strength for a wide range of textile products. These minimum strength levels can be used in selecting fabrics in product development or in evaluating retail products. The recommended breaking strength of fabrics for men's heavy-weight work clothing is more than twice that required for men's dress shirt fabrics, and should be considered in product selection.

Tensile properties
拉伸性质

可接受的拉伸性能水平取决于生产纺织品的最终用途。安全带或降落伞织物预计能承受的拉力水平高于服装织物的预期水平。美国试验材料学会标准列出了各种纺织品的织物强度的最低水平。这些最低强度水平可用于在产品开发中选择织物或评估零售产品。男士重型工作服面料的推荐断裂强度是男士衬衫面料所需断裂强度的两倍以上，在产品选择时应予以考虑。

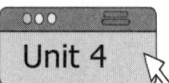

Unit 4　　Breaking Strength and Tearing Strength 断裂和撕裂强度

For fabrics, breaking strength is tested by stretching many warp or filling yarns in a specimen at once (see Fig. 7.2). Another type of action that is applicable for performance testing is tearing strength (see Fig. 7.3). This is the ability of a fabric to withstand a tearing force where yarns are broken one or a few yarns at a time. Fabrics that have a high tearing strength usually have a lower breaking strength. Under a breaking force many yarns in the test direction are gripped at once and subjected to the tensile

Breaking & tearing strength
断裂和撕裂强度

force; therefore, they are all contributing to the resistance to the force.

对于织物，断裂强度是通过在一个样品中同时拉伸许多经纱或纬纱来测试的（如图 7.2）。适用于性能测试的另一种作用类型是撕裂强度（如图 7.3）。指织物在纱线一次断裂一根或几根纱线的情况下承受撕裂力能力。具有高撕裂强度的织物通常具有较低的断裂强度。在断裂力的作用下，测试方向上许多纱线同时被夹住并受到拉力；因此，它们都有助于增加抵抗力。

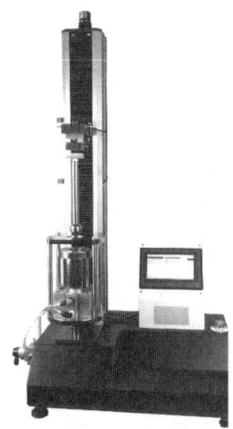
Fig. 7.2　Tensile strength tester 拉伸强力机

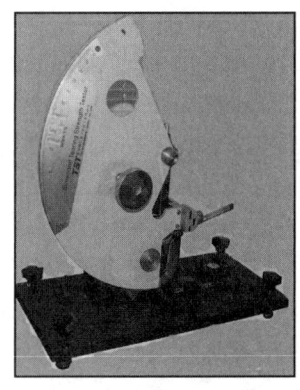
Fig. 7.3　Tearing strength tester 撕破强力机

For tearing, yarns are subjected to an applied tensile force one or two at a time. In loosely woven constructions and those with fewer interlacings, where the yarns can easily move and bunch together, there is a higher resistance to the applied force because several yarns must be broken simultaneously. Consequently, these fabrics have a higher tearing strength.

对于撕裂，纱线一次经受一种或者两种拉伸力。在松散编织的结构和交织较少的结构中，纱线可以很容易地移动和聚集在一起，对所施加的力有更高的阻力，因为必须同时断开几根纱线。因此，这些织物具有更高的撕裂强度。

New Words and Expressions

mechanical properties 机械性能
fabric tensile properties 织物拉伸性能
breaking strength 断裂强力
tearing strength 撕破强力
bundles of fibers 纤维束
fraction 小部分

clamped ends 被束缚的纱线
brittleness 脆性
infrared spectral 红外线
chromatography 色谱分析
specimen 样本
subjected to 承受

Task 3

Fabric Abrasion and Pilling 织物磨损性和起球性

Abrasion is the mechanical deterioration of fabric components by rubbing against another surface. Abrasion ultimately results in the loss of performance characteristics, such as strength, but it also affects the appearance of the fabric. Although maintenance of strength and other properties that enter into performance is crucial in the life of a fabric, often apparel and other textile items are discarded because the fabric appears worn, sometimes long before fabric strength is significantly compromised.

Abrasion and pilling
磨损和起球性

磨损是指织物部件通过与另一个表面摩擦而发生的机械退化。磨损最终会导致性能特征（如强度）的损失，但也会影响织物的外观。虽然保持织物的强度和其他性质对织物的使用寿命至关重要，但服装和其他纺织品往往会因为织物出现磨损而被丢弃，有时甚至早在织物强度严重受损之前。

 Abrasion 摩擦

Abrasion 摩擦

1. Types of Abrasion 磨损类型

There are several ways in which a fabric can be abraded.
有几种方法可以磨损织物。

（1）As a fabric rubs on another fabric.
当一块织物在另一块织品上摩擦时。

（2）As a fabric rubs against another object.
当一块织物与另一个物体摩擦时。

（3）As fibers or yarns within the fabric rub against each other when the fabric bends, flexes, or stretches.
当织物弯折、弯曲或拉伸时，织物内的纤维或纱线相互摩擦；

（4）As dust, grit, or other particles held within the fabric rub against fibers inside the fabric.
In many end uses, two or more of these types of abrasion occur simultaneously.
由于保持在织物内的灰尘、砂砾或其他颗粒与织物内纤维摩擦。
在许多最终用途中，这些类型的磨损中的两种或多种同时发生。

2. Properties Affecting Abrasion Resistance 影响耐磨性的因素

Fabric properties：One of the most important influences on the abrasion resistance of a textile fabric is the fiber content. Some fibers are inherently more resistant to abrasion than others. For example, nylon and polyester have a high ability to absorb energy (i.e., toughness), which contributes to the abrasion resistance of fabrics made from these fibers. Nylon's high resiliency and low coefficient of friction also contribute to good abrasion resistance, making nylon an appropriate choice for end uses such as jacket shells, rope, carpet, or luggage. See Fig. 7.4.

织物性能：纤维含量是影响织物耐磨性的最重要因素之一。有些纤维天生就比其他纤维更耐磨。例如，尼龙和聚酯具有很高的吸收能量的能力（即韧性），这有助于由这些纤维制成的织物的耐磨性。尼龙的高弹性和低摩擦系数也有助于良好的耐磨性，使尼龙成为夹克外壳、绳索、地毯或行李等最终用途的合适选择。

Other factors in abrasion resistance: In addition to fiber, yarn, and fabric properties, and fabric configuration during abrasion, abrasion is also influenced by moisture and by the direction of the abrasive force. Just as it affects the strength of textiles, moisture also affects abrasion resistance. The effect of moisture is complicated, in that it can either improve abrasion resistance or cause fibers to abrade more quickly. Moisture can serve as a lubricant, reducing the friction between a fabric and another surface, and slowing the abrasion process. However, in general, fabrics made of fibers that are stronger when wet have better resistance to wet abrasion than to dry abrasion.

耐磨性的其他因素：除了纤维、纱线和织物的性质以及磨损过程中的织物配置外，磨损还受水分和磨料施力方向的影响。正如它会影响纺织品的强度一样，湿度也会影响耐磨性。水分的作用很复杂，因为它可以提高耐磨性，也可以使纤维更快地磨损。水分可以作为润滑剂，减少织物和另一个表面之间的摩擦，减缓磨损过程。然而，一般来说，由湿态更强的纤维制成的织物对湿态磨损的抵抗力比干态磨损的更好。

3. Abrasion Testing 摩擦试验

Because of the difficulty of reproducing "in use" abrasion in the laboratory, there are probably more instrumental methods and instruments for testing abrasion than for any other textile property. One reason for the difficulty in reproducing abrasion in the laboratory is that laboratory abrasion tests are usually conducted on new fabrics while, in actual use, abrasion occurs both before and after laundering or dry cleaning. In actual use, many different abradant forces also act on a fabric at one time, while most laboratory tests simulate only one type of abrasion.

由于在实验室中很难再现"使用中"的磨损，因此测试磨损的仪器方法和仪器可能比测试任何其他纺织品性能的仪器方法都多。实验室难以再现磨损的一个原因是，实验室磨损测试通常在新织物上进行，而在实际使用中，磨损发生在洗涤或干洗前后。在实际使用中，许多不同的研磨力也同时作用在织物上，而大多数实验室测试只模拟一种类型的磨损。

Unit 2　Pilling 起球

Pilling is a fabric surface fault characterized by little balls or "pills" of entangled fibers clinging to the fabric surface. The unsightly pills are formed during use and laundering of the textile product, and most often are seen in areas of a garment that undergo the most rubbing, such as under the arms or inside the collar of a shirt. Pilling is due to yarn structure, both yarn type as well as degree of twist, and inherent fiber strength.

Pilling 起球

起球是一种织物表面疵点，其特征是缠结纤维的小球或"球粒"黏附在织物表面。难看的球粒是在纺织品的使用和洗涤过程中形成的，最常见于衣服摩擦最严重的部位，如腋下或衬衫领子内侧。起球是由于纱线结构、纱线类型和捻度以及固有的纤维强度造成的。

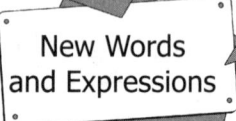

New Words and Expressions

abrasion 磨损
apparel 服装
friction 摩擦，冲突，不和
laundering 洗涤
entangled 纠缠的，扭结的
collar 衣领，领子
clinging to 坚持，黏附

crucial 关键性的，决定性的
discard 丢弃，抛弃
configuration 组合，布置，结构
pilling 起球
deterioration 机械损伤
fabric properties 织物性能

Task 4

Flammability 阻燃性

Flammability of textile products refers to their burning behavior, specifically to ease of ignition and continued burning after ignition. Some fabrics are highly flammable, while others are less so; all textiles currently produced, except asbestos, will burn under some conditions. Two terms that are often confused are flame resistant and flame retardant.

Flammability 阻燃性

纺织品的阻燃性是指其燃烧行为，特别是指其易于点燃和点燃后继续燃烧。有些织物具有高度易燃性，而另一些则不那么易燃；除石棉外，目前生产的所有纺织品在某些条件下都会燃烧。两个经常混淆的术语是拒燃和阻燃。

174

A textile is flame resistant when it extinguishes the flame after ignition, regardless of whether the source of ignition is removed. A flame-resistant (FR) treated fabric is one that has been treated with a finish to give it flame-resistant properties. ASTM standard provides standard definitions of these terms as well as others related to burning behaviors of textiles.

当纺织品在点燃后火焰熄灭时,无论火源是否被清除,它都是阻燃的。阻燃(FR)处理过的织物经过表面处理,具有阻燃性质。ASTM 标准提供了这些术语以及与纺织品燃烧行为相关的其他术语的标准定义。

1. Flammability Standards 阻燃标准

Interest in the flammability of fabrics began in U.S in the late 1940s when several people received serious burn injuries due to ignition of apparel. The most highly publicized burns were caused by several fabrics of brushed rayon. Notable examples were the rayon "torch sweaters," so-called because of their high flammability. In reaction to several cases of severe burns, American congress passed the *Flammable Fabrics Act* (FFA) in 1953. This law was designed to keep dangerously flammable apparel fabrics, such as brushed rayon, off the market in the United States.

20 世纪 40 年代末,美国开始对织物的易燃性产生兴趣,当时有几人因服装着火而严重烧伤。最广为人知的烧伤是由几种拉毛人造丝织物引起的。著名的例子是人造丝"火炬毛衣",因为其易燃性高而被称为"火炬毛衣"。1953 年,美国国会通过了《易燃织物法》,以应对几起严重烧伤。这项法律旨在阻止危险易燃的服装面料,如拉毛人造丝,进入美国市场。

2. Properties Affecting Flammability 影响阻燃性的因素

Fiber content is probably the most important general fabric property flammability. Some textiles are inherently flame resistant by virtue of the fibers which they are composed. Modacrylic is a flame-resistant fiber and specialty fibers, such as aramids and polybenzimidazole (PBI) were engineered for flame resistance. They are used in applications such as protective clothing for firefighters and military pilots. Wool fabrics, especially in heavier weights, often self-extinguish. Cotton and other cellulosic fabrics without an FR finish burn easily.

纤维含量可能是最重要的一般织物阻燃性因素。一些纺织品由于其所组成的纤维而具有固有的阻燃性。腈氯纶是一种阻燃纤维和特种纤维,如芳族聚酰胺和聚苯并咪唑被设计用于阻燃。它们被用于消防员和军事飞行员的防护服等。羊毛织物,尤其是重量较重的织物,通常会自行熄灭。没有 FR 涂层的棉花和其他纤维素织物很容易燃烧。

3. Forty-five Degree Angle Test 45°角试验

The 45° angle test developed for the first flammability legislation in the 1950s. It is intended to classify the flammability of apparel fabrics, except for children's sleepwear that is covered by other tests, and accessories, such as hats, gloves, and shoes. The specimen, mounted in a holder, is positioned in a metal cabinet at a 45° angle, and ignited with a butane gas flame for one second. The ignition flame is removed and the time for the specimen to burn its entire length (150 mm) is recorded. A cotton stop cord at the top of the specimen signals the flame time when it burns through. The stop cord is attached to a weight that drops onto a stopwatch, giving a fairly sensitive measure of burning time.

45°角测试是为 20 世纪 50 年代的第一部阻燃性立法而开发的。它旨在对服装面料的易燃性进行分类，但其他测试涵盖的儿童睡衣以及帽子、手套和鞋子等配件除外。样品安装在支架中，以 45°角放置在金属柜中，并用丁烷气体火焰点燃一秒钟。移除点火火焰，并记录试样燃烧其整个长度（150 毫米）的时间。试样顶部的一根棉质止动绳表示燃烧通过时的火焰时间。停止线连接在一个落在秒表上的重物上，可以相当灵敏地测量燃烧时间。

4. Vertical Flame Tests 垂直燃烧试验

The tests developed by the National Bureau of Standards (NBS) and now specified in detail standard, for the children's sleepwear standards dictate vertical placement of specimen holders in the test chamber. The free end of the 3.5 in. × 10 in. specimen is ignited with a methane gas flame for three seconds. Char length, that is the length from the lower edge of the specimen to the end of the charred area, is measured. To aid in measuring the char length, a weight is hooked to one corner of the charred end and the specimen is held by the other corner, forming a rip similar to the tongue tearing procedure for strength. The length of the tear is the char length.

由国家标准局开发的测试，现在在儿童睡衣标准的详细标准中规定了样品支架在测试室内的垂直放置。3.5 英寸 × 10 英寸试样的自由端用甲烷气体火焰点燃 3 秒钟。测量炭化长度，即从试样下边缘到炭化区域末端的长度。为了帮助测量烧焦的长度，将重物钩在烧焦端的一个角上，并用另一个角夹住试样，形成一个类似于嵌接式撕裂程序，撕裂的长度就是烧焦的长度。

New Words and Expressions

flammability 可燃性
ignition 点燃
extinguish 熄灭
publicized 公众的
notable 显著的
torch 火炬
sweaters 毛衣
modacrylic 变性腈纶
flame resistant 阻燃
forty-five degree angle test 45 度角燃烧测试法

aramids aramid 芳族聚酰胺
polybenzimidazole 聚苯并咪唑（耐高温材料）
legislation 立法
butane 丁烷
methane gas 沼气
char length 碳化长度
tongue tear 切口撕裂
procedure 程序
asbesto 石棉
vertical flame tests 垂直燃烧测试法

Task 5

Fabric Hand and Drape 织物手感和悬垂性

1. Fabric Hand 织物手感

Fabric hand, called handle in many countries, is an individual's response to touch when fabrics are held in the hand. A great number of adjectives, or hand descriptors, have been used to describe this response—smooth, rough, stiff, soft, and others. Some fabrics, such as those made from silk and wool, have a distinctive hand. Wool is often described as scratchy or rough. The hand of silk has been characterized as "dry" and raw silk has a scroop or rustle when it moves or is compressed. Sheets made from smooth filament yarns have a very different feel than those made from cotton or cotton-blend fabrics.

Fabric hand and drape
织物手感和悬垂性

织物手感，在许多国家被称为手感，是当织物握在手中时，个人对触摸的反应。大量的形容词或手感描述词被用来描述这种反应：光滑、粗糙、僵硬、柔软等。有些织物，如丝绸和羊毛织物，具有独特的手感。羊毛通常被描述为棘手或粗糙。丝绸的手感被描述为"干"，生丝在移动或压缩时会发出吱吱声或沙沙声。由光滑长丝制成的床单与由棉或棉混纺织物制成的床单有着截然不同的感觉。

2. Drape 悬垂性

Drape is a fabric's ability to form pleasing folds when bent under its own weight. We call many window coverings "drapes" because of the soft folds they exhibit when hung. Drape has been shown to be related to bending and shearing behavior and also to fabric weight, which takes into account the gravity force on the draping specimen. In order to form folds easily, a fabric should have low resistance to bending. For curtains, drapes, and gathered skirts, this bending is usually in only one direction. More complex draping configurations, however, such as occur in many garments and draped window valances, exhibit a double curvature that requires bending in more than one direction. Under these conditions, the fabric must undergo shearing as well.

悬垂性是一种织物在自重作用下弯曲时能够形成令人愉悦的褶皱。我们将许多窗帘称为"垂帘"，因为它们在悬挂时会呈现出柔软的褶皱。悬垂性已被证明与弯曲和剪切行为有关，也与织物重量有关，考虑到悬垂试样上的重力。为了容易形成褶皱，织物应该具有低的抗弯曲性。对于窗帘、悬垂感织物和褶裥裙来说，这种弯曲通常只有一个方向。然而，更复杂的悬垂配置，如许多服装和悬垂窗帘，表现出需要在多个方向上弯曲的双曲度。在这些条件下，织物也必须经过剪裁。

3. Measurement of Hand and Drape 手感和悬垂性的度量

Assessment of fabric hand and drape has generally followed one of approaches:

(1) Subjective evaluation;

(2) Direct quantitative measurement, primarily of stiffness (a component hand) and drape;

(3) Quantitative measurement of individual mechanical properties thought to influence hand and drape.

织物手感和悬垂性的评估通常采用以下方法之一：

（1）主观评价；

（2）直接定量测量，主要是硬挺度（手感的组成部分）和悬垂性；

（3）单独机械性定量测量（指标）被认为是影响手感和悬垂性的影响因素。

4. Kawabata Evaluation System 川端评估系统

The KES-FB was developed by Dr. Sueo Kawabata of Japan to relate objective measurement of the important properties in fabric hand to subjective evaluation. The subjective component of the system was supplied by a team of textile experts in Japan who evaluated a large number of apparel fabrics. The fabrics were classified into specific categories: men's winter suiting fabrics, men's summer suiting fabrics, women's medium-thick dress fabrics, and women's thin dress fabrics. Hand descriptors were developed for each category. For example, relative values of stiffness, smoothness, and fullness and softness were considered important descriptors of women's medium-thick dress fabrics. These separate hand properties were termed primary hand values.

KES-FB 由日本川端康夫博士开发，用于将织物手感重要性质的客观测量与主观评估联系起来。该系统的主观成分由日本的一个纺织专家团队提供，他们对大量服装面料进行了评估。面料分为特定类别：男士冬装面料、男士夏装面料、女式中厚连衣裙面料以及女式薄连衣裙面料。为每个类别开发了手感描述符。例如，硬度、光滑度、丰满度和柔软度的相对值被认为是女性中厚连衣裙面料的重要指标。这些单独的手感性质被称为主要手感值。

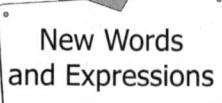

New Words and Expressions

scratchy 粗糙的
rough 粗糙的
scroop 嘎嘎的响声
rustle 沙沙声；急忙；飒飒声
stiff 僵硬的，坚硬的
quantitative 定量的
assessment 评估

bending 弯曲
shearing behavior 抗剪性能
takes into account 考虑
gravity force 重力
draping configuration 悬垂情形
curvature 双曲率
fullness 丰满

Task 6

Colorfastness 色牢度

Retention of color is equally important to consumers and is often a determining factor in the serviceability of a textile item. Consumers may discard an otherwise satisfactory item because it has faded or has changed color in some other way. A textile that resists loss of color is said to be colorfast. The word "fast" in this case means firmly fixed; in other words, the dye or colorant holds "fast" to the fiber. The test method is shown in Fig. 7.4.

Colorfastness
色牢度

色牢度对消费者来说同样重要，并且通常是纺织品适用性的决定因素。消费者可能会丢弃一件原本令人满意的商品，因为它已经褪色或以其他方式改变了颜色。一种能抵抗颜色损失的纺织品被认为是不褪色的。在这种情况下，"fast"一词的意思是牢度；换句话说，染料或着色剂对纤维保持"牢固"。试验方法如图7.4。

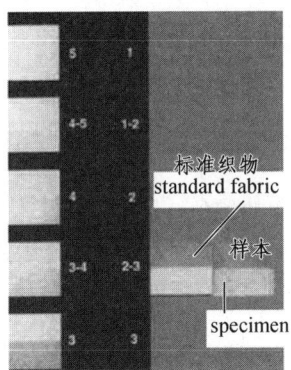

Fig. 7.4 Colorfastness test 色牢度试验

AATCC definition of colorfastness: The resistance of a material to any change in any of its color characteristics, to transfer of its colorant (s) to adjacent materials, or both, as a result of exposure of the material to any environment that might be encountered during the processing, testing, storage, or use of the material.

Colorfastness test
色牢度试验

AATCC对色牢度的定义：由于材料在加工、测试、储存或使用过程中暴露在任何环境中，材料对其任何颜色特性的任何变化的抵抗力，对其着色剂转移到相邻材料或两者的抵抗力。

1. Colorfastness to Crocking 耐摩擦色牢度

Clocking is the transfer of color from a colored textile to another fabric surface through the process of rubbing. The extent of crocking may be influenced by moisture, as many textiles transfer more color when wet AATCC Test Method outlines the procedure that can be used on most textile fabrics.

摩擦是指通过摩擦过程将颜色从一种有色纺织品转移到另一种织物表面。摩擦程度可能会受到水分的影响，因为当潮湿时，许多纺织品会转移更多的颜色。AATCC 测试方法概述了可用于大多数纺织品的程序。

2. Colorfastness to Laundering and Bleaching 耐洗涤和漂白色牢度

As most consumers know, fabric can change color in home laundering using washing machines, or even in hand laundering. This can be a result of the effects of water, detergent, bleach, or other laundry additives, and is also related to temperature and agitation, as well as the stability of the dye. AATCC Method is the primary test method for colorfastness to laundering.

正如大多数消费者所知，使用洗衣机对织物进行洗涤时，甚至在手洗时都会变色。这可能是水、洗涤剂、漂白剂或其他洗衣添加剂作用的结果，也与温度和搅拌以及染料的稳定性有关。AATCC 法是耐洗涤色牢度的主要测试方法。

3. Colorfastness to Drycleaning 耐干洗色牢度

Cleaning products and solvents can change the color of fabrics. Consumers sometimes encounter this problem when using spot-cleaning products at home. Such problems can often be avoided by following product label instructions and precautions and by testing the product on an inner seam allowance prior to use.

清洁产品和溶剂可以改变织物的颜色。消费者在家使用污渍清洁产品时有时会遇到这个问题。通过遵循产品标签说明和注意事项，以及在使用前对产品的内接缝余量进行测试，通常可以避免此类问题。

4. Colorfastness to Perspiration 耐汗渍色牢度

AATCC Method is used to test colorfastness to perspiration. This test requires a device called a perspirometer, which applies pressure to tile specimen as it is healed to body temperature after being wetted in a simulated perspiration solution.

AATCC 法用于测试耐汗渍色牢度。这个试验需要耐汗牢度测试仪,在模拟汗液浸湿的片状样本上施加压力，使其达到体温的温度。

5. Colorfastness to Water 耐水色牢度

Several colorfastness tests involve the effects of water on the color of fabric. AATCC Method is the standard colorfastness to water test. It is conducted in a manner similar to the colorfastness to perspiration test. Distilled water or de-ionized water is used instead of the artificial perspiration solution.

一些色牢度测试涉及水对织物颜色的影响。AATCC 法是标准的耐水色牢度试验。它是以类似于耐汗色牢度测试的方式进行的。使用蒸馏水或去离子水而不是人造汗液。

6. Colorfastness to Light 耐光色牢度

Light, particularly in the UV region of the spectrum, can cause fading by changing the structure of tile dye molecules in a fabric. AATCC Method provides guidelines for testing the colorfastness of textiles. Fabrics are exposed either outdoors in a standard test flame or in a machine that simulates sunlight. The test method includes one option for outdoor exposure and seven options for instrumental exposure that vary according to the type of instrument used, the temperature and humidity during testing, whether or not light exposure is continuous, and the type of light that is simulated through the use of lamp filters.

光线，特定波长范围的紫外光，会通过改变织物中染料分子的结构而导致褪色。AATCC 方法为纺织品的色牢度测试提供了指南。织物暴露在室外的标准测试火焰中或模拟阳光的机器中。测试方法包括一个户外暴露选项和七个仪器暴露选项，这些选项根据所使用的仪器类型、测试期间的温度和湿度、光暴露是否连续以及通过使用滤光器模拟的光类型而变化。

7. Colorfastness to Atmospheric Contaminants 耐大气污染物的色牢度

AATCC Methods were developed to evaluate colorfastness of textiles to ozone in the atmosphere. Method 109 is a low humidity test; method 129 addresses the effect of ozone under high humidity. In both tests, specimens are placed in an ozone exposure chamber under ambient temperature with a control fabric specimen and a standard fading fabric.

开发了 AATCC 方法来评估纺织品在大气中对臭氧的色牢度。方法 109 是一种低湿度测试；方法 129 解决了臭氧在高湿度下的影响。在这两项测试中，将样品与对照织物样品和标准褪色织物一起放置在环境温度下的臭氧暴露室中。

New Words and Expressions

colorfastness to crocking 摩擦色牢度
colorfastness to drycleaning 干洗色牢度
colorfastness to perspiration 汗渍色牢度
perspirometer 耐汗牢度测试仪
colorfastness to water 耐水浸色牢度
colorfastness to Light 光照色牢度
laundry additives 洗涤添加剂
agitation 搅动
spot 斑点
inner seam allowance 内接缝余量

tile specimen 片状样品
simulate 模拟
solution 溶液
distilled water 蒸馏水
de-ionized water 去离子水
artificial 人造的
lamp filters 滤光片
ozone 臭氧
exposure chamber 接触室
ambient 周围环境

colorfastness to laundering and bleaching 洗涤和漂白色牢度

colorfastness to atmospheric contaminants 耐空气污染色牢度

Note

AATCC (American Association of Textile Chemists and Colorists)：美国纺织品染化师协会，职责是采用标准化办法普及纺织品染料和化学物质的深层知识，其适用范围为纺织产品化学性能和纺织品研究测试方法。

Task 7

Comfort of Textiles 纺织品舒适性

Is your clothing comfortable? What are some of the factors that influence your answer with regard to the clothes that you are presently wearing?

It is likely that some of the textile characteristics of fabrics will influence your answer. It may also depend on how the garments fit or even on psychological factors, such as how you feel or whether you like the garments that you are wearing. Other factors that may influence your answer are whether you feel hot, cold, dry, or damp wearing these particular garments.

Comfort of textiles
纺织品舒适性

你的衣服舒服吗？关于你目前穿的衣服，哪些因素会影响你的回答？

织物的一些纺织特性很可能会影响你的答案。这也可能取决于衣服的合身程度，甚至取决于心理因素，比如你的感觉或你是否喜欢你穿的衣服。其他可能影响你答案的因素是，你穿着这些特定的衣服是否感到热、冷、干或潮湿。

1. Physical Phenomena Affecting Thermal Comfort 影响热舒适性的物理现象

Textiles serve as both a barrier and a transporter of heat, air, and moisture from one environment to another. In the case of clothing, apparel fabrics provide a boundary between the micro-environment immediately surrounding the body and the larger indoor or outdoor environment. In the case of interior furnishings fabrics, such as draperies, blankets, or carpets, textiles form the boundary between two larger environments. In either case, whether the fabric takes on the role of barrier or transporter depends on the physical characteristics of the textile and the differences in conditions such as temperature or moisture between the two environments.

Physical phenomena
物理现象

纺织品既是一种屏障，也是热量、空气和水分从一个环境到另一个环境的运输工具。在作为服装的情况下，服装织物提供了身体周围的微环境与较大的室内或室外环境之间的边界。对于室内装饰织物，如窗帘、毯子或地毯，纺织品形成了两个较大环境之间的边界。在任何一种情况下，不管织物是承担热的边界阻隔还是输送者的角色，其性能都取决于纺织品的物理性质和两者环境条件诸如温度和湿度的差异。

2. Heat Transfer 热传导

Heat transfer refers to the transfer of heat energy from one environment to another. Heat transfer occurs whenever a temperature difference exists between the two environments; heat moves from the warmer surface or area to the cooler surface or area. Heat transfer will continue until the two areas are the same temperature (at equilibrium). The rate at which heat is transferred depends on temperature variation as well as any resistance imposed between the two environments. For people, this means that if the ambient temperature is lower than the body temperature (37 ℃), heat will flow from the body to the surrounding area. If the ambient temperature is higher than the body, heat will flow to the body and the body will become warmer. Clothing can provide resistance to heat transfer in either direction by serving as insulation between the two environments.

Heat transfer
热传导

热传导是指热能从一个环境传递到另一个环境。只要两种环境之间存在温差，就会发生热传导；热量从较温暖的表面或区域移动到较凉爽的表面或地区。热传导将持续到两个区域的温度相同（处于平衡状态）。热量传递的速率取决于温度变化以及在两种环境之间施加的任何阻力。对人（体）来说，这意味着如果环境温度低于体温（37 ℃），热量就会从身体流向周围区域。如果环境温度高于身体温度，热量会流向身体，身体会变得更暖和。衣服可以在两种环境之间起到隔热作用，从而在任何一个方向上提供对热传导的阻力。

3. Moisture Transfer 湿转移

Moisture transfer is another physical phenomenon that affects thermal comfort. Water is a much better heat conductor than air, and its presence lowers the effectiveness of a structure in preventing heat loss. Whether in liquid or vapor form, and whether produced by perspiration in a clothing assembly, high humidity in a room, or condensation in a commercial insulation application, moisture enhances heat transfer and reduces the effective r-value of a textile or a non-textile material.

Moisture transfer
湿转移

湿度转移是影响热舒适性的另一种物理现象。水是比空气更好的导热体，它的存在使得结构防止热损失的有效性降低。无论是液体还是蒸汽形式，无论是由服装组合部分的汗水、房间中的高湿度还是商业隔热应用中的冷凝产生，湿气都会增强传热，降低纺织品或非纺织品材料的有效 r 值。

4. Water Repellency 防水性

The restriction of moisture transport can significantly affect comfort. Water-repellent apparel fabrics, such as rainwear, provide the desired comfort of protecting the wearer from the penetration of water through the fabric. However, in many fabrics, properties that provide water repellency may also restrict transfer of moisture vapor, resulting in the buildup of moisture near the skin due to perspiration. Microporous fabrics provide an effective solution to this problem. The pores in these fabrics are small enough to prevent the penetration of liquid water, which is several water molecules bonded together, but are larger than a molecule of water vapor. Thus, they provide both water repellency and a means of moisture vapor transport, keeping the wearer dry and comfortable.

Water repellency
防水性

湿气传输的限制会显著影响舒适度。防水服装织物，例如雨衣，提供了保护穿着者免受水通过织物渗透的期望舒适性。然而，在许多织物中，提供拒水性的性能也可能限制水分蒸汽的传递，从而导致汗水在皮肤附近积聚水分。微孔织物为这个问题提供了一个有效的解决方案。这些织物中的孔隙足够小，可以防止液态水渗透，液态水是几个水分子结合在一起，但比一个水蒸气分子大。因此，它们既提供了防水性，又提供了湿气传输的手段，使穿着者保持干燥舒适。

5. Evaluations of Textile properties Related to Comfort 与舒适性相关的纺织品性能评估

Because comfort testing is so subjective, it is difficult to devise a test method to simulate this property. It is also usually easier to determine the different physical characteristics that contribute to comfort separately, rather than simultaneously. Several textile tests of properties that may contribute to the potential comfort of the wearer or user are described in this section.

Evaluations of comfort
舒适度评估

Test methods for comfort related properties of textile fabrics is shown in table 7.2.

由于舒适性测试过于主观，因此很难设计出一种测试方法来模拟这种特性。通常来说，测定影响舒适性的单一的物理性质比测定多重因素同时作用的影响要相对容易。本节介绍了几种可能有助于穿戴者或使用者潜在舒适性的纺织品测试。

纺织品舒适性相关性质的测试方法如表 7.2 所示。

Table 7.2　Test methods for comfort related properties 与舒适性相关的测试方法

Subject 项目	Method 方法
Air permeability 透气	Air permeability of textile fabrics 纺织品的透气性
Thermal transmittance 热传导	Thermal transmittance of textile materials 纺织品的热传导
Moisture transmission 湿转移	Water vapor transmission of materials 材料水蒸气转移

续表

Subject 项目	Method 方法
Absorbency 吸水性	Absorbency of bleached textiles 漂白材料的吸水性
Electrical resistivity 电阻率	Electrical resistivity of fabrics 织物电阻率
Electrical resistivity 电阻率	Electrical resistivity of yarns 纱线电阻率
Electrostatic 静电性	Electrostatic propensity of carpets 地毯的静电倾向
Electrostatic 静电性	Electrostatic clinging of fabrics: fabric to metal test 织物的静电黏附：织物与金属的试验

6. Air Permeability 透气性

ASTM is a widely used standard test method for air permeability. Using this method, a fabric specimen is placed on an air permometer instrument and clamped so that the edges of the specimen are secured tightly against the machine. Compressed air is then forced through a known area of the fabric specimen. The rate of air flow is adjusted so that a prescribed pressure differential is achieved between the two sides of the fabric. The prescribed pressure differential is 12.7 mm of water, which is equivalent to 124 Pa.

Air permeability 透气性

ASTM 是一种广泛使用的透气性标准测试方法。使用这种方法，将织物样品放置在空气渗透计仪器上并夹紧，使样品的边缘紧紧固定在机器上。然后，压缩空气被强制通过织物样本的已知区域。调节空气流速，使织物两侧之间达到规定的压差。规定的压差为12.7毫米水柱，相当于124帕斯卡。

New Words and Expressions

psychological factor 心理因素
barrier 屏障
transporter 输送者
boundary 边界
interior furnishing 室内家具
heat transfer
equilibrium 平衡，均衡
water repellency 拒水性
air permeability 透气性

r-value 热阻
air permeability（透气性）
microporous 多微孔的
pore 气孔
subjective 主观的
devise 设计
simultaneously 同时的
electrostatic 静电
permeometer 透过性试验机

Task 8

Practical Example & Exercise 实例与练习

1. Translate the Practical Test Report into Chinese 将下列测试报告翻译成中文

SGS

Test Report   No. QD1017343/TX   Date: Oct. 18, 2010   Page 5 of 6

	(A)	(B)	Requirement

Dimensional Stability to Washing (Ref. ISO 5077-2007/ISO 6330-2000+A1:2008; Wash Program No.5A, Using front load, horizontal drum type machine, machine wash at 30 degree C with 2kg total dry mass(knitted polyester ballast + specimen), and 77% 'ECE' detergent A+20% sodium perborate+3%TAED, line dry)

After 1 wash
	(A)	(B)	Requirement
Lengthwise (%)	-1.2	-1.0	+/-3%
Widthwise (%)	-3.9	-2.8	

Remarks: (+) Means Extension   (-) Means Shrinkage

Color Fastness to Washing (Ref.ISO 105 C06-2010; Test No.A2S; mechanical wash at 30 degree C; with 4g/l 'ECE (B)' detergent and 1g/l sodium perborate solution with 10 steel balls)

	(A)	(B)	Requirement
Change in shade	4-5	4-5	4
Staining on multi-fiber stripe			
Acetate	4-5	4-5	4
Cotton	4-5	4-5	
Nylon	4-5	4-5	
Polyester	4-5	4-5	
Acrylic	4-5	4-5	
Wool	4-5	4-5	

Color Fastness to Rubbing (ISO 105 X12-2001)

	(A)	(B)	Requirement
Dry staining	4-5	4-5	3-4
Wet staining	4-5	4-5	3-4

Remarks: Grey Scale Rating is based on the 5-step scale of 1 to 5, where 1 is bad and 5 is good.

Fibre Content (NF G06-006:2006)

	(A)	(B)	Requirement
Cotton (%)	100	100	-

pH Value of Aqueous Extract (ISO 3071-2005: 0.1 mol/L KCL extraction)

(A)	(B)	Requirement
5.9	6.1	5-7.5

Free Formaldehyde Content (ISO 14184-1-1998)

	(A)+(B)	Requirement
(mg/kg)	n.d.	Max. 16

Note: (1) n.d.=not detectable
   (2) Detection Limit<20 mg/kg

背景知识:

SGS: Societe Generale de Surveillance S. A. 的简称,译为"通用公证行",它创建于1887年,是目前世界上最大、资格最深的民间第三方从事产品质量控制和技术鉴定的跨国公司。总部设在日内瓦,在世界各地设有251家分支机构、256个专业实验室和27 000名专业技术人员,在142个国家开展产品质检、监控和保证活动,具有权威性和公正性。

Chapter 8

Textile International Trade 纺织外贸篇

- To be able to introduce your company and your business to foreigners.
  能介绍你的公司和业务给外国人。
- To be acquaint with the procedures for international trade.
  熟悉外贸流程。
- To be familiar with drafting the commercial contract.
  熟悉商业合同的起草。
- To be able to interpret & fill in the documents and certificates as sales confirmation, inspection certificate, import & export licence, etc.
  能解释和填写销售确认书、检验证书、进出口许可证等文件和证书。

Task 1

Introducing Our Company 介绍我们的公司

 About Us 关于我们

About us
关于我们

ASIA & PACIFIC TEXTILES CO., LTD is a professional company engaged in the clothing and textiles' export. Our company specializes in linen, ramie, tencell and other colored weaving textile interweaved or blended with them and other fiber. We have an annual exporting capacity of well over 12million yards and our fabric exported to North American, Europe, Japan and other regions and countries. More than 400—500 new patterns are created by us each year. We are a fast growing company of broad prospect, having been established for more than 10 years. We mainly deal with the exports of linen which is considered as our great advantage in this field. Equipped with the sense of making progress and sophisticated techniques, we are somewhat leading company dealing with linen textiles and our products are relatively competitive.

We keep a market-oriented policy, continually improving our management and enterprise structure, as well as workers' training and abilities.

亚太纺织品有限公司是一家从事服装和纺织品出口的专业公司。本公司专业生产亚麻、苎麻、天丝等与其他纤维交织或混纺的色织纺织品。我们的年出口能力远远超过1200万码，我们的面料出口到北美、欧洲、日本和其他地区和国家。我们每年开发超过400~500种新花色。我们是一家发展迅速、前景广阔的公司，已经成立十多年了。我们主要经营亚麻布的出口，这被认为是我们在这一领域的巨大优势。我们有进取意识和先进的技术，在亚麻纺织品方面处于领先地位，我们的产品也比较有竞争力。

我们秉承以市场为导向的政策，不断改善我们的管理和企业结构及工人能力培训。

Customers worldwide are welcome to start mutual cooperation with us.

We intend to work in close partnership with our clients, to achieve sustainable profitable growth through our quality and cost efficiency.

欢迎世界各地的客户与我们开始相互合作。

我们期待与客户密切合作，通过我们的质量和成本效益实现可持续的盈利增长。

MISSION: We provide special products that other suppliers lack. We have superior quality of goods with same level.

使命：我们提供其他供应商所缺乏的特殊产品。我们有同等水平的优质商品。

ADVANTAGES: Our products are more professional. We have more professional skills and advanced techs in creating new products.

优势：我们的产品更专业。我们在开发新产品方面拥有更多的专业技能和先进技术。

New Words and Expressions

professional 专业的
broad prospect 广阔的前景
engaged in 致力于，投身于，受雇于
specialize in 专业做
mission 使命

annual 年度的
deal with 经营
region 地区的
mutual cooperation 双边合作
advantage 优势

 **Unit 2** Company Profile 公司简介

Weihai Dishang Huaqi Woolen Fabric Co, Ltd. was reorganized from Shandong Weihai No.2 Woolen Fabric Factory (Weihai Caiyuan Woolen Fabric Co, Ltd) and has won the title of Provincial Advanced Enterprise of Shandong Province. In March 2002, it was approved by Qingdao Municipal Government to reorganized into a corporate enterprise invested and held by Shandong Group.

Company profile
公司简介

威海迪尚华旗毛织物有限公司有限公司。由山东威海第二毛纺厂（威海才远毛纺有限公司）改制而成，荣获山东省省级先进企业称号。2002年3月，经青岛市政府批准，改组为由山东集团投资控股的企业法人。

The company has over 500 employees, 4 departments, 5 workshops, 1central laboratory and complete office automation system. It has strong technical force, precise process flow and advanced equipments and facilities. Its key finishing equipments are imported from Germany and Italy. Its product quality meets national industrial standards and European quality standard and it has passed the certifications of ISO-9000 Quality Management System and Oeko-Tex Standard 100. It keeps regular cooperation with international brand companies and produces and sells Calyuan Brand top-grade wool fabrics made of pure or blended goat cashmere, sheep cashmere, cony hair, wool, mohair and alpaca, etc. The fabrics are of complete categories, novel styles, unique pattern and superior quality and enjoy high reputation on domestic market and international market. The products are sold to Beijing, Shanghai, Guangzhou, Hangzhou, Nanjing, Shenzhen, Dalian, and other cities in China and exported direct or indirect to Europe, America, Janpan, South Korea, Russia, Bengal, Turkey, and other countries and regions.

公司现有员工500余人，下设4个部门、5个车间、1个中心实验室和完善的办公自动化系统。技术力量雄厚，工艺流程精确，设备设施先进，主要精加工设备从德国和意大利进口。产品质量符合国家行业标准和欧洲质量标准，并通过了ISO-9000质量管理体系和Oeko-Tex标准100的认证。与国际品牌公司保持定期合作，生产和销售由纯纺或混纺山羊绒、绵羊绒、兔毛、羊毛、马海毛和羊驼毛制成的凯元牌高档羊毛面料，面料种类齐全、款式新颖、图案独特、质量上乘，在国内外市场享有盛誉。产品销往北京、上海、广州、杭州、南京、深圳、大连等中国城市，并直接或间接出口到欧洲、美国、日本、韩国、俄罗斯、孟加拉、土耳其等国家和地区。

Since its reorganization, the company's business performance and market share increase stably for the sake of 10-year effort of all employees. To speed up development and expand business scale, the company moves to Weihai New industrial Zone in April 2010 according to Overall Urban Planning of Weihai City. The total investment in factory construction and equipments is RMB 150,000,000 Yuan. The factory covers 122 mu land and planning construction area is over 6,000 m^2. It upgrades roving machines at key process and also purchases advanced roving machines and semi-worsted machines to grow into the leading and high-standard roved wool fabric and semi-worsted wool fabric production base to make mass production. It produces 4,000,000 m carded wool fabric and 600,000 m semi-worsed wool fabric, sales revenue of RMB 220,000,000 Yuan, makes profit and tax of RMB 23,000,000 Yuan and earns foreign exchange of U.S, 8,000,000 Dollars a year.

重组以来，历经全体员工10年的努力，公司的经营业绩和市场份额稳步增长。为了加快发展，扩大业务规模，根据《威海市城市总体规划》，公司于2010年4月迁至威海新工业区。工厂建设和设备总投资为人民币 1500 万元。工厂占地 122 亩，规划建筑面积 6000 多平方米。对关键工序的粗纱机进行升级改造，并采购先进的粗纱机和半精纺纱机，发展成为领先、高标准的精纺毛纺和半精毛织物生产基地，实现批量生产。生产精梳毛织物 400 万吨，半精纺毛织物 60 万吨，销售收入 22 亿元，利税 230 万元，年创汇 800 万美元。

New Words and Expressions

process flow 工艺流程
brand 商标，品牌
cony hair 兔毛
complete category 种类齐全
unique pattern 花型别致
reorganization 改制
to speed up development 加快发展
semi-worst 半精纺
carded wool fabric 粗纺呢绒织物
profit and tax 利税

facility 设施
top-grade 顶级
novel styles 款式新颖
superior quality 品质上乘
enjoy high reputation 享有盛誉
market share 市场份额
expand business scale 扩大经营规模
mass production 批量生产，规模化生产
sales revenue 销售收入
earns foreign exchang 创汇

Unit 3　Enterprise Culture 企业文化

Enterprise culture
企业文化

Enterprise Sprit: Enthusiastic leader, exuberant employees, energetic enterprise and famous products.

企业精神：领导有志气、员工有朝气、企业有生气、产品有名气。

Enterprise Mission: To create life space, serve and feedback the society.

创造生活空间，服务社会，回馈社会。

Business Philosophy: International strategy, professional business and value-added products.

经营理念：战略国际化、经营专业化、产品增值化。

Service Philosophy: Client's satisfaction is our permanent pursuit, and market's recognition is our reputation.

服务理念：客户满意是我们永恒的追求，市场认可是我们的荣誉。

Talent Philosophy: Enterprise is the boat, and talent is the sea.

人才哲学：企业是船，人才是海。

Work Philosophy: Not to find excuse, just to find ways.

工作理念：不找借口，只想办法。

Enterprise Value: To collet more information, to think over before making decision and to do more practice.

收集更多的信息，在做出决定之前进行更多思考，更多的实践。

New Words and Expressions

enthusiastic 热情的；热心的；狂热的
exuberant 繁茂的；生气勃勃的
energetic energetic 精力充沛的
feedback 回馈，反馈
talent 人才，天才，天资，才华

permanent 持久的，永恒的
pursuit 追求
recognition 承认，认可
reputation 荣誉
excuse 借口

 **Enterprise Organization Structure 企业组织架构**

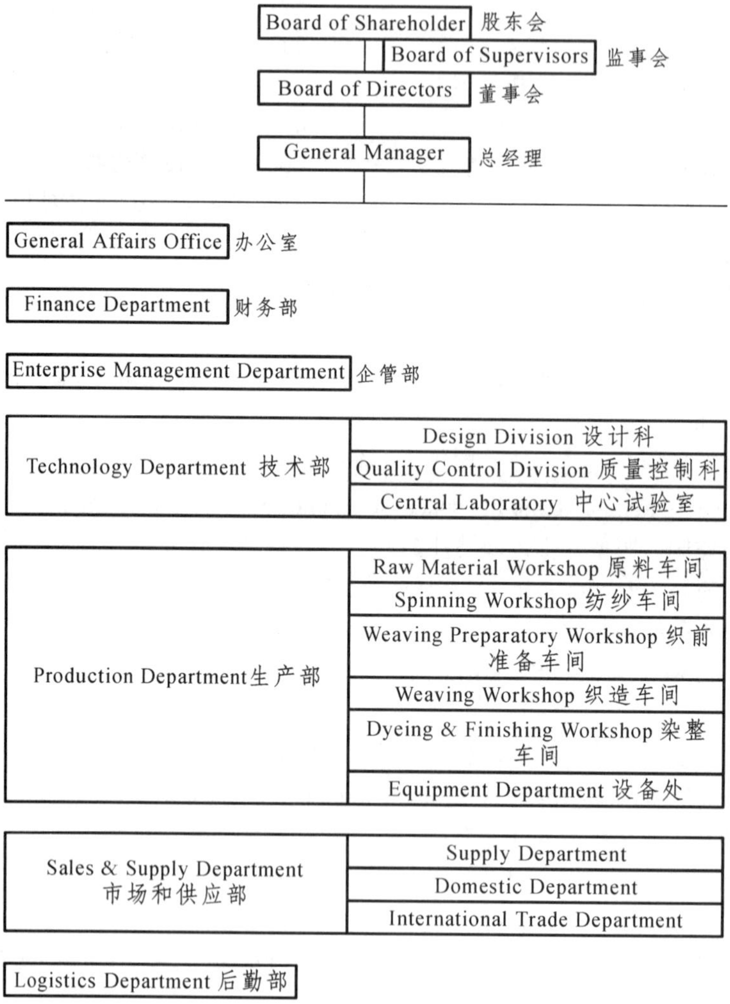

| General Affairs Office | 办公室 |

| Finance Department | 财务部 |

| Enterprise Management Department | 企管部 |

Technology Department 技术部	Design Division 设计科
	Quality Control Division 质量控制科
	Central Laboratory 中心试验室

Production Department 生产部	Raw Material Workshop 原料车间
	Spinning Workshop 纺纱车间
	Weaving Preparatory Workshop 织前准备车间
	Weaving Workshop 织造车间
	Dyeing & Finishing Workshop 染整车间
	Equipment Department 设备处

Sales & Supply Department 市场和供应部	Supply Department
	Domestic Department
	International Trade Department

| Logistics Department 后勤部 |

New Words and Expressions

Board of Shareholder 股东会
Board of Supervisors 监事会
Board of Director 董事会
General Manager 总经理
General Affairs Office 办公室
Finance Department 财务部
Division 科室，部门
Domestic Trade Department 国内贸易部
International Trade Department 国际贸易部
Logistics Department 后勤部

Task 2

Business Mails for International Trade 外贸函电

 Invitation for Business 约请洽谈生意

Dear Sir,

　　Your name and address have been given to us by the China Bank in Hong Kong. We are now writing to you for the establishment of business relations. We have no contact with your corporation before. In view of the development of friendly relations between our two countries, and between our two corporations, we wish to invite your Director General Mr. … to visit China in the fall this year. Upon his arrival we would like to talk with him and his colleagues about the possibilities of exporting textile machinery to your country. On the other hand, if you have any kind of textile products in which we are interested, we are equally pleased to discuss with you. In that case, please favor us with a list of your export goods and we shall gladly study the sale possibilities in our market.

　　We are looking forward to our early reply.

　　Yours faithfully,

　　（Signature）

Invitation for business
约请洽谈生意

尊敬的先生：

　　香港的中国银行已将你公司的名称及地址告诉了我们，现特写信与你们建立业务联系。我们与贵公司以前没有过交往。为了发展我们两国及两公司之间的友谊，我们热忱邀请贵公司总经理×××先生今秋访华。届时，我将乐意与他和他的同事们洽谈向贵国

193

出口纺织机械的可能性。另一方面，贵国有任何我们感兴趣的纺织品，我们同样也乐意洽谈，请贵方随行带来希望向我国出口的货单，我们将乐意研究该产品在我方市场上销售的可能性。

盼早复！

至诚问候

 **Establishing Business Relations 建立业务关系**

Gentlemen,

We are Textile Material Import & Export Branch of the China National Textiles Import & Export Corp. We can handle import and export of all kinds of textile materials, such as wool, cotton, silk, ramie, polyester, acrylic, nylon, vinylon, cashmere, etc. Our end-users are all over the world.

Our materials have long been accepted by domestic and overseas end-users.

We hope to hear your specific inquiry.

Truly yours,

（Signature）

先生：

我们是中国纺织品进出口公司所属纺织原料进出口公司，我们可以直接经营各种纺织原料的进出口，如棉、毛、丝、麻、涤纶、尼龙、维尼纶、羊绒等。我们的用户遍布全球，我们的原料畅销国内外。希望能收到您的具体询盘。

至诚问候

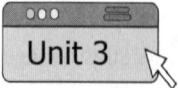 **Opening up New Sources of Goods 寻求新货源**

Gentlemen,

The CCPIT has advised us to get into touch with you concerning import of garment from your country. We are interested in importing all kinds of ladies garments, such as skirts, underskirts, pleatedskirts, miniskirts, microskirts, housecoats, blouse, brassieres, tights, morning, gowns, shirtwaists, divided skirts, etc.

Opening up new sources of goods 寻求新货源

We will be thankful if you could give us your best possible quotation with detailed specifications, packing and quantity available.

We await your information.

Truly yours.

先生：

中国贸促会建议我们就从贵国进口服装事宜同贵公司联系。我们有意进口各种女装，如裙子、衬裙、百褶裙、超短裙、露臀裙、便服、罩衫、乳罩、紧身衣裤、晨衣、衬衫、裙裤。

如您能给我们报最低价和详细规格、包装、可供数量，将不胜感激。

等待着您的消息。

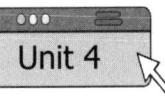 **Asking for Samples 索要样品**

Dear Sirs,

We have received your letter Dec. 15, 2013 with a price list of garments enclosed therein.

As we have much interest in boxers and sun suits and often receive inquiries about them from our friends in various countries, we shall be obliged if you will kindly send us some samples for inspection.

We look forward to your early reply.

Yours truly.

Asking for samples 索要样品

先生：

贵方 2013 年 12 月 15 日附有服装价格单的信已收到。

由于我们对拳击裤和日光服很感兴趣，而且我们经常接到各国朋友关于它们的询盘，如蒙您能给我们寄样品检验将非常感谢。

我们等待着您尽早回音。

 **Inquiry 询盘**

Dear Sirs,

Our company is one of the largest textile import and export companies in Iraq. We are very much interested in your product "the watered poplin 4040" because there is a high demand in our market. Please let us have your latest CIF Basra price together with your terms of payment and state whether you would be able to effect delivery within one month after receiving our order. We should like to place an order in large quantities if your quoted price is reasonable and competitive.

Inquiry 询盘

195

We should also like to know if you allow a quantity rebate for regular purchases of large quantities.

We look forward to your early reply.

Yours faithfully.

尊敬的先生：

我们公司是伊拉克最大的纺织品进出口公司之一。我们对贵方产品"4040波纹府绸"甚感兴趣。该产品在我方市场上需求量很大。请告知贵方最近的巴士拉到岸价以及付款条件，并请说明能否在一个月内交货。如果贵方报价合理并有竞争性，我们将大量订货。我们还想知道贵方对大量订货有否优惠。

请即示知为感！

Background Knowledge 背景知识

在询价时，常常查问或要求对方提供的项目有：

1. 样品方面

样品（samples）、款式（style）、花样（patterns）、质料（material）、样本（pattern-book）。

2. 型录或目录方面

商品目录（catalogue）、最新商品目录（latest catalogue）、带有说明书的目录（illustrated catalogue）、货单（list）、展览卡（display cards）。

3. 价格方面

价格(price)、出口价(export price)、最好、最低价格(best price)、竞争价格（competitive price）、价格单(price list)、估价单(quotations)、估价(estimate)、形式发票(proforma invoice)、最低报价（lowest quotation）、参考价格（indication price）。

4. 交货方面

交货日期（date of delivery）、预计交货日期（estimated delivery date）、最早交货日期（earliest delivery date）。

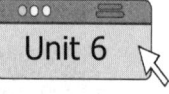

Unit 6　Quotation 报价

Dear Sirs,

We are very much pleased to have received your letter of inquiry dated June 10, 2023. We are equally pleased to know that our product "men's jackets" is in high demand at your market. In reply to your inquiry of June 10, 2023, we would like to quote as follows:

Men's Jackets USD 80.00/DZ

The above price is CIF Basra.

Package: three dozens to a carton.

We are willing to allow 5 % discount for all orders over 2,000 dozens.

You can rely on us to give your order immediate attention.

Yours sincerely.

尊敬的先生：

贵方 2023 年 6 月 10 日询函欣悉。得知我方产品"男夹克衫"在贵方市场需量很大，不胜欣慰。兹复贵公司 2023 年 6 月 10 日询价函，我们报价如下：

男夹克衫 USD80.00/DZ

上述报价均为巴士拉到岸价。

包装：纸箱，每箱 3 打。

我们对任何超过 2000 打的订货都给予 5%的折扣。请相信，我们对贵公司的订货将迅速办理。

Unit 7　Offer 虚盘

Offer 虚盘

Gentlemen,

We acknowledge receipt of your letter dated June 25.

We take pleasure in making, as per your request, the following offer:

Article number: Men's Shirt　USD 48.00/DZ

CIF. Basra

Quantity: 500 dozens

Shipment: One month after receipt of L/C

Packing: 3 DZ to a Carton

Payment: 100% by irrevocable letter of credit drawn at sight

The above offer is subject to our final confirmation.

Our stock is limited and the demand to great. Therefore your early decision is necessary.

Faithfully yours.

先生：

你方 6 月 25 日函悉。兹欣然按你方要求报盘如下：

货号：男衬衣 USD 48.00/DZ。

巴士拉到岸价。

数量：500 打。

装运：收到信用证后一个月内。

包装：纸箱，每箱 3 打。

付款：凭不可撤销信用证百分之百见单付款。

上述报盘以我方最后确认为准。我方库存不多而需求量大，盼贵方早日决定。

197

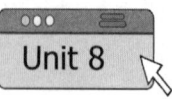 **Firm Offer 实盘**

Gentlemen,

Firm offer 实盘

Re: T-Shirts

We acknowledge receipt of your letter dated the 25th June, from which we note that you wish to have an offer from us... T-Shirts for shipment to Basra.

We are now making you, subject to our acceptance reaching us by July 6, our time, the following offer:

"...T-shirts USD 22.40/DZ CIFC 2% Basra per steamer during July/August. Other terms and conditions are the same as usual, with the exception of insurance which will cover All Risks and War Risks for 110% of the total invoice value."

We look forward to your early reply.

Yours truly.

先生：

事由：T 恤衫

接你方 6 月 25 日函，得知你方要求我们报 "T 恤衫"，货运巴士拉，我们报盘如下，以我方时间 7 月 6 日前接到复函有效。

"T 恤衫，USD22.40/DZ，巴士拉到岸价，包括 2%的佣金。7、8 月发运，按发票总额 110%投保一切险和战争险。其他条件如故。"

盼早复！

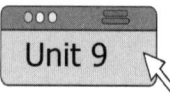 **Counter Offer 还盘**

Counter offer 还盘

Dear Sirs,

Re: Watered Poplin 4040 width 100 inch

We have acknowledgement of your letter of July 2 offering us... meters of Watered Poplin 4040 width 100 inch at USD... per m. on the usual terms.

In reply, we regret to inform you that we cannot accept your price. Information indicates that the price of your products is 10 percent higher that of the Pakistan origin.

We know clearly that the quality of Chinese products is a bit higher but the difference in price should not be so high.

To step up trade, we, on behalf of our buyers, counter offer as follows, subject to your confirmation reaching here on July 9 this month:

"... Meters of watered Poplin 4040 width 100 incite at USD…per m, CIFC2% Baras, other terms as per your letter of June 30."

As the market is declining, we recommend your immediate acceptance.

Yours truly.

尊敬的先生：

事由：幅宽 100 英寸 4040 波纹府绸

接到贵方 7 月 2 日函，按惯常条款报盘我方×××米波纹府绸，幅宽 100 英寸，每米×××元。

兹复，很遗憾，我方不能接受你方报价，有消息表明，你方产品价格比巴基斯坦的同样产品高出 10%。当然，我们清楚地了解到，贵方产品质量较高，但价格之差异不应如此之大。

为了促进我们的贸易往来，我们代表我方客户还盘如下，以当地时间 7 月 9 日前你方确认为准。

"×××米 4040 波纹府绸、幅宽 100 英寸，巴士拉到岸价，每米×××美元，包括 2%佣金在内。其他条款按你方 6 月 30 日函办理。"

因行市渐衰，建议你方速接受为盼！

 Refusal of the Offer 拒绝还盘

Refusal of the offer 拒绝还盘

Gentlemen,

Re: 100% wool gabardine

We've got your letter of July 7, 2023. While we thank you for your prompt reply, we much regret that we could not entertain any price lower than USD 6.40/YD CIFC 2 % Basra. We have to point out that your bid is obviously not in line with the price ruling in the present market. As per our information, the market is strengthening, and there is no possibility of the goods remaining unsold once this particular offer has lapsed.

In view of the above, we would suggest in your interest that you accept our price of USD 6.40/YD without any delay.

Yours faithfully.

先生：

事由：纯毛华达呢

你方 2023 年 7 月 7 日函悉。对你方迅速复信，我们表示感谢！不过，我们非常遗憾，我们不能接受低于每码 6.40 美元含佣金 2%的巴士拉到岸价。我们必须指出，你方递价与现行市价明显不符，我们获悉，现行市场坚挺，一旦此报盘失效，该货便不可能长期保存。

鉴于上述情况，为你方利益着想，我们建议你方尽快接受我方每码 6.40 美元的价格。

 Order 订货

Order 订货

Dear Sirs,

We have received your letter of July 15 and regret that you have turned down our counter offer.

As your product "bed sheets" is very much appreciated by our local customers and there is a high demand at our market, we are very anxious to finalize this order with you, for the purpose of strengthening our friendship and cooperation, we agree to accept your offer:

Bed Sheets USD 3.05/PC CIF KARACHI: with an order of 500 dozens.

We are very much pleased to have been able to finalize this order with you after exchange of business letters in the past two months and we are now anxiously looking forward your sales confirmation for this order, on receipt of which we shall immediately open relevant letter of credit by cable.

As your make is comparatively famous here, the sales will be somewhat quicker. If this first order is excited satisfactorily, we shall be glad to place further orders with you in the future.

Yours sincerely,

尊敬的先生：

你方 7 月 15 日函悉，十分遗憾，你方没有接受我们的还盘。

由于我方客户对贵方的"床单"非常欣赏，并且市场需求很大，为了增进我们之间的友谊和合作，而且我方渴望与你方做成这笔生意，我们同意你们的报盘，"床单 USD3.05/PC，卡拉奇到岸价，数量 500 打"。

我们很高兴，经过两个多月来的函件往来，我们终于与你们做成了这笔生意。我们渴望收到你们的销售确认书，收到确认书后，我们即电开有关信用证。

由于你方产品在这儿名气很大，销售也一定很快，若第一次订货合同能够满意地得到执行，我们将高兴与贵公司进一步开展交易。

Unit 12　Request to Cancel the Order 要求撤销订货

Dear Sirs,

Re: 200 Sets of Shuttle Less Looms

If you refer to our order No. 4627 of Oct. 25, you will find that we stressed the importance of delivery by Dec. 20 at the very latest.

We have already written to you twice urging dispatch and as you have failed to deliver these goods on the date asked, we are obliged very regretfully to cancel this order. We have informed our client of the action we have taken and should be glad if you would kindly acknowledge the cancellation.

Yours sincerely.

尊敬的先生：

事由：关于 200 台无梭织布机

我方 10 月 25 日第 4627 订单曾强调最后交货期限为 12 月 20 日，倘若贵方就此查阅，顿会明了。

我方曾两次去函催促发货，然贵公司未能于要求的日期内装运。我们只得非常遗憾地撤销此订单。

我们已把这一决定通知我方客户，如贵方面同意将该单撤销，将不胜欣慰。

 **Refuse to Accept the Cancellation 拒绝撤销订货**

Dear Sirs,

　　Your letter dated July 28, 2023 has been duly received, we are very much regretful to say that we could not accept your cancellation of the order as the business has been done through our repeated correspondence. We are now fully prepared to dispatch the looms upon receiving your L/C and the shipping space has been booked. If you cancel the order, we would miss a good chance because our looms sell well on foreign market and it is for friendship and long standing cooperation that we have accepted your order of 200 sets of shuttleless looms. We advise that you consider this carefully and seriously and open the L/C so that we could dispatch the machines as scheduled.

　　Best regards.

Refuse to accept the cancellation 拒绝撤销订货

尊敬的先生：

　　贵方 2023 年 7 月 28 日函悉。我们非常遗憾地通知贵方，我们不能接受你方撤销订货的要求，因为这笔生意是经过双方多次协商才成交的。我们已经做了一切准备，一旦贵方开具了有关信用证，就立即发货，并且舱位已经订妥，贵方若撤销订货，我们将丧失良好的销售机会，因为我方布机畅销国外市场，供不应求。出于我们的友谊和长期合作，我们才答应卖给贵方 200 台无梭织机，我建议贵方认真、仔细考虑此事，尽快开具信用证，以便我们按预定的时间发货。

　　谢谢！顺致问候！

 **Remind 催货**

Remind 催货

Dear Sir,

　　Through the business letters between us in the past two months, we have ordered 200 sets of open—end spinning machines from your company. The mutual agreed dispatch time is during June—July, but we are sorry to say that it is July 16, 2023 now and we still have not yet received your shipping document, not to say machines. Therefore we would like to urge you to dispatch the ordered machines as quickly as possible. Otherwise our client will waste much time in awaiting your machines to transform their spanning mill. We look forward to your prompt response.

　　With best regards.

201

尊敬的先生：

通过你我双方前两个月的信件往来，我方订购了贵公司生产的气流纺纱 200 台，双方确定的发货期是 6～7 月。如今已是 7 月 16 日了，我们遗憾地指出，至今尚未接到装运单据，更不要说机器了，因此，我们敦促贵方尽快发运我们订购的机器，否则，我方客户将丧失他们纱厂更新的良机，我们期待着贵方立即发货。

顺致问候！

 **Asking for Opening a L/C 催开信用证**

Dear Mr. Park,

We are very pleased to have signed the S/C No. CT4825 with you. But we have not received your L/C. We address this letter to you to the terms about arriving date of the L/C. We hope you will abide by the agreed articles and make the L/C reach us before Oct.10, 2023. On receiving the L/C, we will make shipment immediately.

Yours truly.

Asking open LC
要求开信用证

帕克先生：

我们非常高兴和您签订了 CT4825 合约。但是我们没有收到贵方开立的信用证，故特致此函提请您注意合约上有关信用证到达我方时间的约定。我们希望您能够按双方约定的条款将信用证于 2023 年 10 月 10 日之前开到我方。收到信用证后，我方将立即装运。

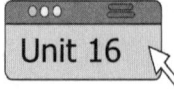 **Asking for Amendment of a L/C 要求修改信用证**

Dear Mr. Pierce,

We have received your L/C No. STB-8386, but we are sorry to tell you that there are some discrepancies between the L/C and S/C. They are as follows:

Amendment L/C
改证

L/C	S/C
1. Transshipment not allowed	Transhipment allowed
2. Equal partial shipment in June and in July	Shipment not later than July 1st
3. No more or less clause	5% more or less allowed

Please make necessary amendment. We will effect shipment after receiving your amended L/C.

Thank you for your cooperation.

Sincerely yours.

202

皮尔斯先生：

我们收到了您的信用证 STB-8386 号，但是发现信用证与合同不符，差别如下：

信用证   合同

1. 不许转船   允许转船

2. 6、7月等量装运   不迟于7月11日装运

3. 无溢短装条款   允许5%的溢短装

请做必要的修改，我们接到您的修改后才能发运。谢谢合作。

 Shipping Advice 装船通知

Shipping advice
装船通知

Gentlemen,

<u>Re: L/C No. 6254, S/C No. 2387:</u>
<u>Covering 50 tons of washed wool</u>

We are very pleased to advise you that the above mentioned goods you ordered have been prepared according to the L/C and will be dispatched to you per S/S Kennedy tomorrow morning.

Now we enclose a duplicate copy of shipping documents so that you may get prepared to take delivery of the goods:

Commercial invoice No. 88XL572 in duplicate

Non-negotiable B/L No. XBL578

Insurance policy No. IC572

We are sure that the above shipment will reach you intact and we expect to receive your further orders before long.

Thank you for having secured the business for us and hope we can establish pleasant and lasting business relations with you.

Truly yours.

先生：

<u>事由：第 6254 号信用证和第 2387 号</u>
<u>合约项下 50 吨洗净毛</u>

我们高兴地通知您，贵方所订的上述的货物已按信用证要求备好，将于明晨由肯尼迪号货船运。现附货运单据副本一套，以便您做好提货准备：

商业发票第 88XL572 号一式两份；

XBL578 号不可转让提单副本一份；

IC572 保险单一份。

我们相信上述货物将完好到达您方，并希望不久后收到您新的订单。

谢谢您为我们招揽了这笔生意，我们希望能够和您建立起愉快持久的业务关系。

 **Claim 索赔**

Claim 索赔

Dear sirs,

We would like to refer to the shipment of Nitric Fiber arriving at Qingdao Port on June 18, 2023.

We regret to inform you that after checking the ship's draft by the Qingdao Commodity Inspection Bureau, it was found that there is a short weight of 74.25 metric tons, as the actual weight after deduction comes to…metric tons only as against your final invoice weight of…metric tons after deducting 1.5% allowance and moisture. Therefore we lodge a claim against you for short weight of 74.25 metric tons as follows:

FOB Value	US$…
Freight	US$…
Insurance Premium	US$…
Inspection	US$…
Total	US$…

We are sending you herewith original Inspection Certificate No. 03/1625 issued by the Qingdao Commodity Inspection Bureau and one copy of survey record on weight by draft. Please give our claim your favorable consideration, and should it be acceptable to you, please send us your remittance to cover the shortage in due course.

Yours truly.

先生：

兹谈及 2023 年 6 月 18 日运至青岛港的"奈特里尔纤维"（Nytril Fiber）。

现遗憾地通知你方，青岛商品检验局人员检查货轮吃水尺寸时发现短重 74.25 公吨，因扣除应扣除数后的实际重量仅为……公吨。而你方最后发票所载重量扣除 1.5%的补贴和水分后仅为……公吨，为此我们向你方提出短重 74.25 公吨的索赔。

计开如下：

离岸价	……美元
运费	……美元
保险费	……美元
检验费	……美元
合计	……美元

随函附寄青岛商检局开具的第 03/1625 号检验证明书正本一份及水分鉴定重量检查记录一份，请对我们的索赔予以很好的考虑。如你方认为可以接受，请即汇款以了结此事。

Relevant Terms about Claim 相关术语

survey report 公证报告	certificate of inspection 检验报告
mate's receipt 大副收据	invoice 发票
bill of lading 提单	insurance policy 保险单

weight certificate 重量证明单
short-landed certificate 短卸证明单
weight note 磅码单

packing list 装箱单
damage report 破损证明
tally list 理货单

Unit 19　Business Mails for Home Textile 家纺贸易往来函电(实例)

Business mails for home textile trade
家纺贸易往来函电

March 15, 2023.
Mr. Daniel Stopka is interested in these products:
Subject: What is the MOQ on your Hotel Towel?
Dear Ms. Amy,
　　I am interested in hotel towels of different types in white color (main features: 100% cotton, 550gram/sq.m, washing in 95 ℃ dgr., chlorine resistant, possible to bleach, dimensions: 70x140cm). What is your MOQ for the first order and your delivery time? Do you offer also bath mats（浴垫）and bathrobes? Do you provide a quantity discounts? Please kindly send me your price offer for the above. I am also interested in hotel slippers. Do you have this product in your offer?

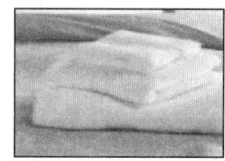

　　To send back your answer, please use my e-mail address: ×××
　　I look forward to hearing from you as soon as possible.
　　Best regards,
　　Daniel Stopka.
事由：您酒店毛巾的最低起订量是多少？
尊敬的艾米女士：
　　我对不同类型的白色酒店毛巾感兴趣（主要特点：100%棉，550克/平方米，在95摄氏度下洗涤，耐氯，可漂白，尺寸：70×140厘米）。第一个订单的最小起订量是多少？交货时间是多少？你们也提供浴垫吗？还有浴袍？你们提供数量折扣吗？请将上述产品的报价发给我。我也对酒店拖鞋感兴趣。你的报价中有这种产品吗？
　　要发回您的答案，请使用我的电子邮件地址：×××
　　我期待着尽快收到你的来信。
　　顺致敬意，
　　丹尼尔·斯托普卡

Subject：Quotation for our hotel slippers
Dear Daniel,
　　Thanks for your inquiry dated on Mar. 15th, 2010.
　　I have enclosed the price list in the attachment, Pls find it, thx!
　　We are a manufacture in China, and we mainly make products for hotel, such as bath mat, bathrobe（浴衣）, hotel slippers, hotel bedding sets and so on, we produce this for the famous hotel Sheraton（喜来登）, Hilton（希尔顿）and so on, and they have good evaluation of our quality!
　　We have a good production capacity and can provide you the sample! If you are interested in our other products, don't hesitate to contact me, I will try my best to you!
　　You early reply will be highly appreciated!
　　Best Regards!
　　Amy

205

事由：我们酒店拖鞋的报价

亲爱的丹尼尔，

感谢您2010年3月15日的询价。

我已经在附件中附上了价目表，请查收！

我们是一家中国制造商，主要为酒店生产产品，如浴垫、浴袍、酒店拖鞋、酒店床上用品等，我们为著名的喜来登酒店、希尔顿等酒店生产，他们对我们产品的品质有很好的评价！

我们有很好的生产能力，可以为您提供样品！如果你对我们的其他产品感兴趣，不要犹豫联系我，我会尽力为你服务的！

您早日回复将不胜感激！

顺致敬意，

艾米

Task 3

Business Contract（Practical Example）商业合同（实例）

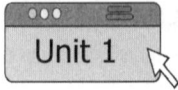 Contract（Example）合同（案例）

No. 85MK-40-I90CT

Date Issued: Dec. 20, 2003

Place of Issue: Beijing

1-8款

The Buyer: CHINA TEXTILE MACHINERY AND TECHNOLOGY IMPORT & EXPORT CORPORATION, BEIJING BRANCH

190 Chaoyang Street, Beijing, People's Republic of China

The Seller: Adolph Saucer LTD   FAX :

CH—9320 Nantes, France   TEL:

This contract is made by and between the Buyer and the Seller: where by the Buyer agrees to buy and the Seller agrees to sell the under mentioned commodity according to the terms and conditions stipulated below.

本合同在买方和卖方之间签订。双方在下列条款及条件下同意买卖以下货物。

1. Commodity 品名, **Specifications** 规格: One SAURER RAPIER Weaving Machine model S400, detail as per attachment   SAURER（苏拉）剑杆织机，S400型，详细如下：

Unit 单位

Quantity 数量

Unit Price 单价

Total Amount 总额 US$.89462.00

Total Value: US$ Eighty nine thousand four hundred and sixty two only

2. COUNTRY OF ORIGIN AND MANUFACTURERS: 原产地别和制造厂

Saucer Ltd, France 苏拉有限公司，法国

3. PACKING 包装: To be packed in strong wooden case (s) or in carton (s), suitable for long distance ocean parcel post air freight transportation and to change of climate, well protected against moisture and shocks.

装在适于长途海运、邮寄、空运的坚固木箱或纸箱内，能适应气候变化，防潮、抗震。

The Seller shall be liable for any damage of the commodity and expenses incurred on account of improper packing and for any rust attributable to inadequate or improper protective measures taken by the Seller in regard to the packing.

卖方负责由于包装不良以及因卖方在包装方面采取了不当或不良的保护措施而造成的锈蚀或货物损伤，并负担所招致的费用。

4. SHIPPING MARK 唛头: The Seller shall mark on each package with fadeless paint the package number, gross weight, net weight, measurement and the wordings **"KEEP AWAY FROM MOISTURE", "HANDLE WITH CARE", "THIS SIDE UP"** etc. and the shipping mark.

卖方须以不褪色的油漆在每件货物箱上刷上包装号、毛重、净重、尺寸及"勿使受潮""小心轻放""此端向上"等字样及唛头。

5. TIME OF SHIPMENT 交货时间: April 2023 (One shipment only 一次装运）.

6. PORT OF SHIPMENT 装货口岸: PORT NANTES, FRANCE. 法国南特港。

7. PORT OF DESTINATION 到货口岸: XIN PORT, TIANJIN, CHINA. 中国天津新港。

8. INSURANCE 保险: To be covered by the Buyer after shipment. 装运后由买方负责。

9. PAYMENT 付款条件: Under（A）(B)(C) BELOW: 选看下面（A）、(B)、(C)条。

（A）In case by L/C 使用信用证： upon receipt from the Seller of the advice specified in Clause 11 hereof, the Buyer shall open an irrevocable Letter of Credit with the Bank of China, City Branch, Beijing, 30 days prior to the date of delivery, in favor of the Seller, for an amount equivalent to the total value of the shipment. The Letter of Credit shall be payable against the presentation of the draft drawn on the opening bank and the shipping documents specified in Clause 10 hereof. The Letter of Credit remains valid until the 15th day after the shipment is effected.

9 款

买方收到卖方按本合同第 11 款所出具的装运通知后，必须在装运日之前 30 天内为卖方在中国银行北京分行开出与装运货物的总金额相等的不可撤销信用证。此信用证议付时需提供开户银行的汇票和本合同第 10 条所规定的货运单据。本信用证有效期至装运后 15 天。

（B）In case by Collection 托收： After delivery is made, the Seller shall send the shipping documents specified in Clause 10 hereof from the Seller's Bank, through the Bank of China, to the Buyer for collection.

货物装运后，卖方应根据本合同第 10 条，由卖方银行通过中国银行把货运单据寄给买方。

（C）In case by M/T or T/T 信汇或电汇： Payment shall be effected not later than 7 days after receipt of the shipping documents specified under Clause 10 of this Contract.

买方必须在收到卖方以本合同第 10 条所出具的货运单据后 7 天内支付货款。

10. SHIPPING DOCUMENTS 装运单据

（1）The Seller shall present the following documents to the paying bank for negotiation:

卖方应提交下列单据向银行议付：

10 款

（a）A complete set of clean on board ocean bills of lading marked "**FREIGHT TO COLLECT**" and made out to order, blank endorsed, and notifying the China National Foreign Trade Transportation Corporation at the port of destination.

一套注明有"运费到付"的清洁海运提单和空白抬头空白背书，并通知目的港的中国外运公司。

（b）Invoice in quintuplicate indicating contract number and shipping mark.

注明合同号码及唛头的发票一式 5 份。

（c）Packing List in quintuplicate indicating shipping weight, number and date of corresponding invoice.

装箱单一式 5 份，注明装运重量、号码及相应发票的日期。

（d）Certificate of Quantity and Quality in duplicate issued by THC manufacturer as specified in Clause 14.

根据本合同第 14 条，由制造厂出具的质量及数量证书一式两份。

（e）A copy of the Email or telex to the Buyer, advising the shipment immediately when it is effected.

货物装运通知电子邮件或电传一份。

（2）The Seller shall send together with the shipment one copy each of he above-mentioned documents, with the exception of item (e) of this Clause, to the China National Foreign Trade Transportation Corporation at the port of destination.

卖方还应将上面提到的单据（e 条除外）连同装运单一起寄给中国外运公司。

11. TERMS OF SHIPMENT 装运条款

（1）The Seller shall, 60 days before the date of shipment stipulated in the Contract, advise the buyer by cable or telex of the Contract number, description of goods, quantity, invoice value, number of cases, gross weight, dimensions and date of readiness at the port of shipment for the Buyer to book shipping space. Should any case reach or exceed 20 metric tons in weight, 10 meters in length, 3.4 meters in width and 3 meters in height, the Seller shall provide the Buyer with 5 copies of the packing drawing indicating the detailed dimensions and weight, 50 days before dispatch of the, goods so as to enable the Buyer to make shipping arrangements.

11 款

卖方将在合同规定的装运日期之前 60 天通过电报或电传通知买方合同号、货名、数量、发票金额、装运箱数、毛重、尺寸以及装船的日期，以便买方预订舱位。如果某些装运箱达到或超过 20 吨重，10 米长，3.4 米宽，3 米高，卖方就应在交货之前 50 天通知买方，并给买方提供 5 份上面写有详细尺寸及重量的装运单，以便买方做好装船准备。

（2）Booking of shipping space shall be attended to by the Buyer's shipping agent, the China National Chartering Corporation, Beijing, China.

预订舱位将由买方的装运代理者，中国船舶公司北京分公司承担。

（3）The Buyer shall, 10 days before the estimated date of arrival of the vessel at the port of shipment, notify the Seller of the name of vessel, estimated date of loading and Contract number for the Seller to arrange the shipment. The Seller is requested to get in close contact with the Buyer's shipping agent. Should it be necessary to change the vessel or should the arrival date of the vessel be either advanced or postponed, the Buyer or the shipping agent shall advise the Seller in due time. Should the vessel fail to arrive at the port of shipment within 30 days after the arrival date advised by the Buyer, the Buyer shall bear the storage and insurance expenses incurred from the 31st day.

买方应在预计货船到达装运港口日期之前 10 天，通知卖方船名、顶计装运日期和合同号，以便卖方做好装船准备。卖方应和买方的装运代理人取得密切联系。若要改船或船的到达日期提前或推后，买方或买方的装运代理人应在适当时间内通知卖方。如果船没有在买方通知的到达日期之后 30 天内到达，买方将负责从第 31 天起的储存费用和保险费用。

（4）Should the Seller fail to have the goods ready for loading when the vessel arrives at the port of shipment on time, the Seller shall be liable for any dead freight or demurrage.

船准时到达装运港，而卖方没有把货物准备好时，卖方将负责空舱费和滞期费。

（5）The Seller shall bear all expenses and risks of the goods before they pass over the rail of the vessels and are released from the tackle. After the goods have passed over the rail of the vessel and have been released from the tackle, all expenses of the goods shall be for the Buyer's account.

卖方在交货以前负责一切费用，承担一切风险。货物交接后，由买方负责一切费用。

12. SHIPPING ADVICE 装船通知

Upon completion of the loading of the goods, the Seller shall immediately notify the Buyer by cable or telex of the Contract number, description of goods, quantity, gross weight, invoice value, name of vessel and date of sailing. In the event cases exceed 9 metric tons in weight, 3.4 meters in width, or 2.35 meters in height on both sides, the Seller shall advise the Buyer of the weight and dimensions of such cases. Should the Seller's failure to cable or telex in time the information specified in this Clause prevent the Buyer from making timely arrangements for the insurance, all losses thus incurred shall be borne by the Seller.

12-14 款

货物装船完毕卖方应立即用电报或电传通知买方合同号、货物种类、数量、毛重、发票金额、货轮名称和起航日期。如果某些货箱超过 9 吨重，3.4 米宽或两边超过 2.35 米高，卖方就应通知买方其重量及尺寸。如果卖方没能及时电告买方本条款所列的信息，致使买方未能及时作投保安排，由此引起的所有损失由卖方负责。

13. TECHNICAL DOCUMENTS 技术资料

（1）Complete sets of the following technical documents in the English language shall be packed and dispatched with each consignment. 每件货物必须配备如下英文资料。

a. Foundation drawings. 基础图。

b. Writing instructions, diagrams of electrical connections. 带有文字说明的电路图。

c. Instructions and manufacturing drawings of easily worn parts. 易损零件说明及加工用图纸。

d. Spare parts catalogues. 备用零件目录。

e. Quality certificate as stipulated in Clause 15 (1). 依据本合同第 15 条 (1) 所出具的质量证书。

f. Instruction manuals for erection, operation and maintenance. 安装，操作及维修说明书。

（2）The Seller shall send to the Consignee by 3 sets of the technical documents as stipulated in Item a, b, d, e and f of Clause 13 (1) within two months after is signing this Contract.

卖方将在本合同签订后两个月内把本合同第 13 条 (1) a、b、d、e 和 f 项所列的技术资料给收货人寄上 3 套。

14. GUARANTEE OF QUALITY 质量保证

The Seller shall guarantee: that the goods are made of the best materials and of first class workmanship, brand new and comply in all respects with the quality specification and performance as stipulated in this Contract. The Seller shall guarantee that the goods, when correctly mounted and properly operated and maintained, shall give satisfactory performance for a period of 12 months from the date of its commissioning or for 15 months after delivery.

卖方将保证这些货物出自一流的加工，且是用最好材料制成的新产品，并符合本合同所规定的质量和性能要求。卖方将担保本产品在正确的安装、合理的操作和维护下，能够正常地工作 12 个月或从交货后起 15 个月。

15. INSPECTION 检验

（1）Prior to delivery, the manufacturer(s) shall make a precise and comprehensive inspection of the goods as regards the quality, specifications, performance and quantity/weight and issue certificates certifying that the goods are in conformity with the stipulations of this Contract. The certificate shall form an integral part of the documents to be presented to the paying bank for negotiation of payment but shall not be considered as final in respect of quality, specifications, performance and quantity/weight. Particulars and results of the test carried out by the manufacture(s) must be shown in a statement which has to be attached to the Quality Certificate.

在发货之前，生产厂家必须对货物的质量、规格、性能及数量和重量进行全面、详细的检查，并开出这些货物和本合同要求相符的证明书。本证书是本合同的一个组成部分，银行议付时要出具此证，但不作为质量、规格、性能、数量的最后保证。生产厂家所进行的检验的详细情况及结果必须附在质量证书上。

（2）After arrival of the goods at the port of destination, the Buyer shall apply to the China Commodity Inspection Bureau (CCIB) for a preliminary inspection in respect of the quality, specifications and quantity/weight of the goods and a Survey Report shall he issued by CCIB. If discrepancies are found by CC1B regarding specifications, and/or the quantity, except when the responsibilities lie with the insurance company or shipping company, the Buyer shall, within 120 days after arrival of the goods at the port of destination, have the right to reject the goods or to lodge a claim against the Seller.

货到目的港后，买方将委托中国商检局对货物的质量、规格、数量及重量进行初步检查，并出具一个检查报告。如果商检局发现产品规格或数量不符合规定，那么，买方在货到后120天内，有权拒绝接收货物或有权对卖方提出索赔，但是应由保险部门或装运公司负责的除外。

（3）Should the quality and specifications of the goods not be in conformity with the Contract, or should the goods prove defective within the guarantee period stipulated in Clause 14 for any reason, including latent defects or the use of unsuitable materials, the Buyer shall arrange for a survey to be carried out by CCIB and shall have the right to lodge a claim against the Seller on the strength of the Survey Report.

在第14条规定的保证期内，若发现货物的质量、规格与本合同不符，或发现货物有缺陷，无论是什么原因引起的，包括潜伏的缺陷或使用不合格的原料造成的缺陷，买方将安排中国商检进行一次检查，买方以商检报告为依据有权对卖方提出索赔。

16. CLAIMS 索赔

16 款

（1）In case the Seller is liable for the discrepancies and a claim is lodged by the Buyer within the time limit of inspection and quality guarantee period as stipulated in Clauses 14 and 15 of this Contract, the Seller shall settle the claim upon the agreement of the Buyer in one or a combination of the following ways.

如果由于货物不符，买方在本合同第14条和第15条所规定的检验期或质量保险期内对卖方提出索赔，而卖方对此负有责任，那么，卖方须按下列办法之一或全部与买方达成协议解决索赔问题。

（a）Agree to the rejection of the goods and refund to the Buyer the value of the goods so rejected in the same currency as contracted herein, and to bear all direct losses and expenses in connection therewith including interest accrued, banking charges, freight, insurance premium, inspection charges, storage, stevedore charges and all other necessary expenses required for the custody and protection of the rejected goods.

同意买方退回货物，并把所退货物的全部金额按合同规定的货币付给对方，而且必须承担所有的直接损失费和各种开支，其中包括自然增长的利息、银行手续费、运费、保险金、检验费、保管费、装卸费以及所退货物的其他一切保管和保护费用。

（b）Devalue the goods according to the degree of inferiority extent of damage and amount of losses suffered by the Buyer.

211

根据货物次劣程度、受损坏程度和买方所受损失的金额对货物进行降价。

(c) Replace new parts which conform to the specifications, quality and performance as stipulated in this Contract and bear all the expenses and direct losses sustained by the Buyer. The Seller shall at the same time, guarantee the quality of the replaced parts for a further period according to Clause 14 of this Contract.

更换新零件以达到本合同对其规格和性能的要求，并承担买方的直接损失和一切费用。同时，卖方将按本合同第 14 条所规定的延续时间继续保证所换零件的质量。

(2) The claims mentioned above shall be regarded as being accepted if the Seller fails to reply within 30 days after the Seller receives the Buyer' claim.

如果卖方在收到上述索赔要求以后 30 天内不作答复，就将被认为是接受了索赔条件。

17. FORCE MAJEURE 不可抗力

17-18 款

The Seller shall not be responsible for the delay in shipment or non-delivery of the goods due to a case of Force Majeure, which might occur during the process of manufacturing or in the course of loading or transit. The Seller shall advise the Buyer immediately of the occurrence of the event giving rise to Force Majeure and within 14 days thereafter, the Seller shall send by airmail to the Buyer for his acceptance a confirmation of the case of Force Majored issued by the competent Government Authorities where the Force Majors occurs as evidence thereof. Under such circumstances, the Seller, however, is still under the obligation to take all necessary measures to hasten the delivery of the goods. If the circumstances of Force Majored exceed 10 weeks, the Buyer shall have the right to terminate the Contract by registered letter without any other formality.

如果在生产过程或装运过程中，因不可抗力而致使卖方推迟生产，不能装运或推迟装运，卖方均不负责任。如果发生这种不可抗力事件，卖方应立即通知买方，并必须在出事后 14 天内把出事地点及主管政府部门对此所出的证书航空邮寄给买方。然而，卖方还是应采取一切必要措施，加快该项货物的发运。如果此不可抗力事件超过了 10 周，买方将有权用挂号信终止此合同，而不需任何别的方式。

18. LATE DELIVERY AND PENALTY 迟运和罚金

In case of nonobservance of the contractual delivery terms due to reasons imputable to the Seller, the Buyer may agree to postpone delivery on the condition that the Seller agrees to pay a penalty which shall be deducted by the paying bank from the payment under negotiation. The penalty, however, shall not exceed 5% of the total value the goods delivered with delay. Penalty shall be charged at a rate of 0.5% for every 7 days, odd days less than 7 days should be counted as 7 days. In case the Seller fails to make delivery 10 weeks later than the time of shipment stipulated in the Contract, the Buyer shall have the right to cancel the Contract and the Seller, in spite of the cancellation, shall still pay the foresaid penalty to the Buyer without delay.

由于卖方没有遵守合同规定的装运条款，如卖方同意支付罚金，由支付行议付的总金额里扣去这笔款，买方可同意延迟运货。但是，罚金不能超过迟运货物总金额的 5%。此罚金每 7 天按 0.5%的利率收费，不够 7 天也按 7 天算。如果卖方在本合同所规定的装运日期以后 10 周还未交货，买方将有权撤销本合同，而卖方仍需立即向买方支付罚金。

19. ARBITRATION 仲裁

19-20 款

All disputes arising in connection with this Contract or in the execution thereof shall be settled through friendly negotiations. In the event an amicable settlement cannot be achieved the disputes shall be submitted to arbitration. If the Seller is the plaintiff, the arbitration shall take place in Paris. Each party shall appoint an arbitrator within 30 days after receipt of notification from the opposite party and the two arbitrators thus appointed shall jointly nominate a third person as umpire to form an Arbitration Committee. The said umpire shall be confined to the citizens of French nationality. If the Buyer is the plaintiff, the arbitration will take place in Beijing and shall be conducted by the Arbitration Communities of the China Council for the Promotion of the International Trade in accordance with the Provisional Rules of Procedure promulgated by the said Arbitration Committee. The decisions of the Arbitration Committee shall be accepted as final and binding upon both parties and neither party shall seek recourse to a law count or other authorities to appeal for a revision of the decision. Arbitration expenses shall be borne by the losing party.

凡因执行本合同或有关本合同所发生的一切争执，双方应友好地协商解决，如果不能友好解决，将提交仲裁机关进行裁决。若卖方是原告，仲裁将在巴黎进行，每方在收到对方的通知后 30 天内，指定一个仲裁人，这两位仲裁人将共同指定一位第三者作公断人，组成一个仲裁委员会。但是这位公断人必须是法国公民；如果买方是原告，仲裁将在北京进行，并由中国国际贸易促进委员会根据上述仲裁委员会所公布的仲裁程序暂行条例进行仲裁。仲裁委员会的裁决为终局裁决，对双方均有约束力，任何一方都不能继续向法院或别的部门上诉要求重裁。仲裁费用由败诉方承担。

20. BANKING CHARGES 银行费用

All the banking charges incurred in China shall be borne the Buyer, while all the banking charges incurred outside China shall be borne by the Seller.

This Contract is made in two originals, one original for each Party in witness thereof.

China Textile Machinery & Technology

Import & Export Corp.　　　　　　　　　Adolph Sauer LTD.

The Buyer　　　　　　　　　　　　　　The Seller

在中国的所有银行费用由买方负担，在中国以外的银行费用由卖方负担。

本合同正本两份，双方各持一份。此证。

买方：中国纺织品与技术进出口公司　　卖方：Adolph Saucer 有限公司

Task 4

Certificate & Documents for International Trade 外贸单证

Unit 1 Sales Confirmation 销售确认书（实例）

To Messrs:

你方函电
Your Reference :

我方函电
Our Reference:

经启者兹确认于 2014 年 6 月 20 日售予你方下列货品，其成交条款如下：
We hereby confirm having sold to you on Jun. 20, 2014, the following goods on terms and conditions as set forth hereunder:

品名及规格 COMMODITY AND SPECIFICATIONS	数　量 QUANTITY	单价及价格条款 UNIT PRICE & TERMS	金　额 AMOUNT
（全白毛巾 100% COTTON WHITE FACE TOWEL）			

总　　值（大写）
TOTAL　VALUE

总 金 额（小写）
TOTAL AMOUNT

装运期限
SHIPMENT：

目的地
DESTINATION

付款方式　百分之百的不可撤销信用证
PAYMENT　即期付款
　　　　　　BY　100% CONFIRMED
　　　　　　IRREVOCABLE
　　　　　　L/C AT SIGHT

保险　由买方负责
INSURANCE:TO BE COVERED
　　　　　BY
　　　　　THE BUYER

特约条款
SPECIAL CLAUSE

备注
REMARKS

一般条款
GENERAL TERMS & CONDITIONS

注意：开立信用证时，请在证内注明本售货确认书号码。

IMPORTANT When establishing L/C, please indicate the Number of this Sales Confirmation in the L/C.

买方（The Buyers） 卖方（The Sellers）

请在本合同签字后寄回一份存档
Please sign and return one copy for our file

Sales confirmation 销售确认书

GENERAL TERMS AND CONDITIONS 一般条款和条件

The sale specified in this confirmation shall be subject to the following terms and conditions unless otherwise agreed upon between the Buyers and the Sellers. In case of any inconsistency of the terms and conditions between this Confirmation and any form of confirmation or order or indent sent by the Buyers to the Sellers (irrespective of its date), the provisions of this Confirmation shall prevail. If the Buyers resell the goods to, or conclude the transaction as representative of a third party, the Buyers shall still be responsible for the complete performance of all the obligation stipulated in this Confirmation.

本确认书有关内容，除双方另有协议或经卖方同意接受者外，应适用下例条款。买方任何其他合约或订单与本确认书内容如有不符，应以本确认书规定为准。买方如转售或代理第三者时，仍应对本确认书负完全履行责任。

Quantity 数量：

1. A usual trade margin of 5 plus or minus of quantities confirmed shall be allowed.

本确认书所确定的数量，卖方可有 5%的增减。

2. Where shipment is spread over two or more periods, the above mentioned trade margin of plus or minus 5% shall, when necessary, be applicable to the quantity designated by the Buyers to be shipped each period.

分批出运者，必要时卖方对每批装运数量亦得在买方规定范围内增减 5%。

Specification:

3. The counts of yarn and the numbers of ends and picks indicated are those which were in loom-state.

商品的纱支数及经纬密度，系指未经加工整理时织机状态纱支数及经纬密度。

Tolerance of measurements and weight 尺码及重量公差：

4. Reasonable tolerance of: ±3%~5% for measurement and/or weight is permissible.

有关商品等均可有合理的上下尺码公差及重量公差 3%～5%。

Design, Styles, Sizes, Colorways & Color Shades 花样、款式、尺寸及颜色：

5. With the exception of specifications for goods specially ordered, details of Designs, Styles, Sizes, Colorways and Color Shades designated or chosen by the Buyers from the Sellers' samples must reach or be made known to the Sellers at least 45 days (unless otherwise specified)

before the month of shipment stipulated in this Confirmation, subject to final acceptance by the mills, otherwise the Sellers will have the option either to cancel the transaction or to postpone the time of shipment which the Buyers should not refuse to accept on any excuse, and the Buyers shall be held responsible for compensation of whatever losses thus incurred to the Sellers.

除特定品种规格外，有关花样、式样、尺寸及颜色，如系按买方指定者或在卖方样品中选定者，均应在确认书规定装运月份前 45 天（除另有规定外）寄达或通知卖方，并应经厂方最后同意为准，否则卖方或是取消交易或是推迟装船，买方不得以任何借口不同意，因此对卖方造成的一切损失应由买方负责赔偿。

6. Acting upon the request of the mills, the Sellers shall have the right to make minor alterations to the design designated or chosen by the Buyers. For dyed, printed and yarn-dyed goods, reasonable tolerance in colors shades must be allowed.

买方所指定或选定之花色样，卖方有权根据厂方意见稍予修改，并应容许染色，印花及色织品有合理的色差。

7. If designs designated by the Buyers should be involved in infringemeant of patent right, the Buyers shall be fully responsible for the consequences and settlement.

买方指定的花样如牵涉版权问题，一切后果概由买方负责。

Folding, Labels, Packing and Marks 折法、标签、包装及商标：

8. Unless otherwise agreed upon by both parties, Sellers' trademark, labels, stamping, mode of folding and packing will be accepted by the Buyers. In case the Buyers desire to have their own trade mark, labels, stamping, mode of folding and packing, they should first obtain the consent (or they should obtain the prior consent) from the Sellers before conclusion of the business and send the detailed instructions relative to folding, packing, trade mark, labels and stamping to reach the Sellers at least 45 clays (unless otherwise specified) before the month of shipment stipulated in this confirmation. The detailed instructions being subject to final acceptance by the mills, otherwise the Sellers will have the option either to cancel the transaction or to postpone the time of shipment which the Buyers should not refuse to accept on any excuse. In case of any damage thus incurred, the Sellers shall reserve the right to claim against the Buyers.

除双方另有约定者外，买方应接受卖方之商标、标签、盖印、包装及折法，买方如须指定折法、包装、标签、商标及盖印，应在成交前经卖方同意。有关折法、包装、标签、商标及盖印之详细说明，最迟应在确认书规定装运月份前 45 天（除另有规定外）寄达卖方。有关详细说明须经厂方最后接受为推，否则卖方有权取消交易或延迟交货，买方不得借故不同意。如因此造成损失，卖方并得保留索赔权利。

9. The Buyers shall be fully responsible for all consequences in case disputes should arise from the use of the trade mark, stamping and or labeling designated by the Buyers.

如因使用买方指定之商标、印戳及标签等而引起纠纷，概由买方负完全责任。

10. The detailed instructions relative to shipping marks should be indicated in the order

sheet or in whatever form legible and sent by the Buyers to reach the Sellers 30 days before the month of shipment stipulated, otherwise the Sellers shall decide the marks at their discretion.

有关船唛之详细说明，买方应在订单上或以其他方式列明的，且必须在确认书规定的装运月份前 30 天寄达卖方，否则卖方可自行决定船唛。

Letter of Credit（付款）信用证：

11. Unless otherwise agreed to by the Sellers, payment is to be made against sight draft drawn under a Confirmed, Irrevocable, Divisible & Transferable Letter of Credit, Without Recourse, for the full amount, established through a first class bank acceptable to the Sellers.

除另有规定者外，买方应通过为卖方所接受的第一流银行开具即期保兑、可分割、可转让、不可撤回、无追索权的信用证。

12. The Letter of Credit in due form must reach the Sellers at least 15 days (unless otherwise specified) before the month of shipment stipulated in this Confirmation, failing which the Sellers shall not be responsible for shipment as stipulated; in case the Buyers' credit still fails to reach the Sellers after the expiry of the shipping period, the Sellers shall have the right to cancel this Confirmation and claim for damage against the Buyers.

买方应保证最迟在装运月前 15 天（除另有规定外）将信用证送达卖方，否则若因此不能按期装运，卖方不负责任。如超过装运期信用证仍不能到达卖方手中，卖方有权取消确认书并对因此造成的损失向买方提出索赔。

13. In general Buyers are requested to refrain from SPECIFYING ANY PARTICULAR SHIPPING LINE, NAME OF STEAMER or INSURANCE COMPANY in the Letter of Credit.

信用证内，一般要求买方不要指定航线、船名及承保保险公司名称。

14. To facilitate negotiation of the credit by the Sellers, the validity of the Letter of Credit shall be so stipulated as to remain valid for at least 10 days (expiring in China) after the last day of shipment and the amount of the credit and quantity shall allow plus or minus 5%.

信用证有效期应规定在最后装运日期后至少 10 天（在中国期间到期），信用证金额和数量应允许增减 5%，以便卖方收汇。

15. The Buyers are requested always to stipulate in the Letter of Credit that TRANSHIPMENT AND PARTIAL SHIPMENTS ARE ALLOWED, but port of Transhipment should not be stipulated.

请在信用证内规定允许转船及分批装运，但请勿指定转船口岸。

16. In the credit opened by the Buyers, no terms & conditions should be added or altered without the Sellers' previous consent.

买方所开的信用证内不得加注和变更未经卖方同意的任何条款。

17. The Buyers are requested always to state the NUMBER OF THIS CONFIRMATION and order number, if any, in the Letter of Credit.

买方应在信用证内注明本确认书号码，如有订单者，请将订单号码一并注明。

Shipment 装运：

18. Shipment may be made from any Chinese port. The date of Bill of Lading shall be taken as the date of shipment.

商品可在中国任何口岸装船，提单日期将作为装运日期。

19. Any change of destination should be agreed to by the Sellers beforehand. Extra freight and/or insurance premium thus incurred are be borne by the Buyers.

如需变更目的地，应事先经卖方同意，因此增加的运输保险费，应由买方负担。

Insurance:

20. Unless specially agreed, the Sellers are to cover insurance at invoice value plus 10% thereof of the goods sold on CIF basis. If the Letter of Credit stipulates that the goods after arrival at the port of destination are to be transported to an inland city or some other ports, and/or that coverage of insurance exceeds 110% of the invoice value, the Sellers will cover insurance on the Buyers' behalf up to that city or port and/or to the percentage required, and the Buyers are to be responsible for payment of the additional premium, which should be included in the Letter of Credit.

除另有规定者外，"到岸交货"概由卖方按发票金额的110%的投保。如信用证规定货物需转运内陆或其他口岸，或超过发票金额的110%时，卖方人为投保或代保到内陆或其他港口，但此项额外保险费应由买方负担，并需在信用证内注明。

Claim 索赔:

Claims for damage should be filed by the Buyers with the Sellers within 30 days after arrival of the goods at destination and supported by sufficient evidence for Sellers' reference; otherwise the Sellers shall refuse to consider. Claims in respect of matters within responsibility of insurance company and/or shipping company will not be considered or entertained by the Sellers.

由买方向卖方提出的索赔应在货到目的地后30天内提出，买方并须提出充分证明供卖方参考，否则卖方不予考虑。索赔属于保险公司或轮船公司责任范围以内者，卖方亦不予理睬。

Arbitration 仲裁:

22. All disputes in connection with this Sales Confirmation or the execution thereof, shall be Settled by negotiation. In case no settlement can be reached, the case under dispute shall then be submitted for arbitration to the Foreign Trade Arbitration Commission of the China Council for the Promotion of International Trade, Beijing in accordance with the "Provisional Rules of Procedure of the Foreign Trade Arbitration Commission of the China Council for the Promotion of International Trade". The decision by the Commission shall be accepted as final and binding upon both parties.

凡因执行本确认书或有关本确认书所发生的一切争执，双方应协商解决。如果协商不能获得解决，应提交北京中国国际贸易促进委员会对外贸仲裁委员会，根据中国国际贸易促进委员会对外贸易仲裁委员会的仲裁程序暂行规定，进行仲裁，对双方都有约束力。

Force Majeure 人力不可抗拒事故：

23. In the event of force majored or any other contingencies beyond the Sellers' control, the Sellers shall not be held responsible for late delivery or non-delivery of the goods.

The Buyers are requested to sign and return one original copy to Sellers for file immediately upon receipt of this Confirmation. Should the Buyers fail to do so within 10 days after arrival of this Confirmation at the Buyers' end, it shall be considered that the Buyers have accepted all the terms and conditions set forth in this Confirmation.

如因人力不可抗拒的事故而致延期交货或无法交货时，卖方不负任何责任。

买方在收到本确认书后应即行签署并寄还卖方正本一份以备存查。如本确认书到达买方后10天内买方尚未签回，则视买方已接受本确认书所规定之全部条款。

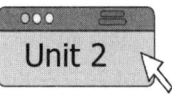

Unit 2　Import & Export Declaration 进出口报关

Import and export declarations are used primarily for the purpose of compiling periodic customs statistics. In China, import and export declarations must be lodged before cargoes can be released but in some countries or regions, these may be submitted within a prescribed period after shipment (for example, in Hong Kong export declaration must be submitted within 14 days after date of shipment). The typical types of information required including identity of the exporter/importer, description of the goods (including Harmonized System commodity Code), CIF (for import) or FOB (for export) Value, mode of transport, etc.

Import & export declaration
进出口报关

进出口报关单主要用于编制定期海关统计数据。在中国，进出口报关单必须在货物放行前提交，但在某些国家或地区，可以在装运后的规定期限内提交（例如，在香港，出口报关单必须于装运日期后14天内提交）。所需的典型信息包括出口商/进口商的身份、货物描述（包括协调制度商品代码）、CIF（进口）或FOB（出口）价值、运输方式等。

In China, import declaration consists of three basic steps:

在中国，进口报关包括三个基本步骤：

（1）Filling out the declaration form;

填写申报表；

（2）Inspection of the goods and the accompanying documents by customs officials；

海关官员对货物及其随附文件的检查

（3）Release/clearance from customs after payment of the necessary duties or taxes. The usual types of accompanying documents required for import clearance include import license (if required), import cargo declaration form (Chinese Customs), export cargo inspection form (Chinese inspection and Quarantine), commercial invoice, bill of lading or air waybill packing list, declaration of non-wood packaging, and documents on the basis of which tax reduction or

219

waiver of inspection is claimed.

在缴纳必要的关税或税款后放行/清关。进口清关所需的通常类型的随附文件包括进口许可证（如需要）、进口货物报关单（中国海关）、出口货物检验单（中国检验检疫）、商业发票、提单或航空货运单装箱单、非木质包装，以及要求减税或免除检查的文件。

The usual types of documents required for export clearance are shipping order, bill of lading or air waybill, export Cargo declaration (Chinese Customs), export cargo inspection form (Chinese Inspection and Quarantine), commercial invoice packing list, for exchange settlement certificate (for tax refund) and certificate of origin.

出口清关所需通常类型的文件包括货运单、提单或航空货运、出口货物报关单（中国海关）、出口货物检验单（中国检验检疫）、商业发票装箱单、结汇证明（退税）和原产地证明。

On the basis of the information provided by the importer/exporter, the customs authorities will compile the trade statistics for the period that show, for example, the types and total value of traded goods and services to and from a foreign country. Combining information gathered through other sources, the government then determines the balance of trade (e.g. whether the country has a trade surplus or a trade deficit) with another country during a specific time period. This type of information can be used for various purposes, for example, for trade negotiations with foreign countries. Given the importance of these official documents, strict compliance is expected from all exporters and importers in order to avoid penalties.

根据进口商/出口商提供的信息，海关当局将汇编该时期的贸易统计数据，例如，进出外国的贸易商品和服务的类型和总价值。政府结合通过其他来源收集的信息，确定特定时期内与另一个国家的贸易平衡（例如，该国是否有贸易顺差或贸易逆差）。这类信息可用于各种目的，例如，与外国的贸易谈判。鉴于这些官方文件的重要性，所有出口商和进口商都应严格遵守，以避免受到处罚。

Fig. 8.1 and Fig. 8.2 show a sample import cargo declaration form and an export cargo declaration form, respectively.

图 8.1 和图 8.2 分别显示了进口货物报关单和出口货物报关单的样本。

中华人民共和国海关进口货物报关单

预录入编号： 　　　　　　　海关编号：

进口口岸	备案号	进口日期	申报日期
经营单位	运输方式	运输工具名称	提运单号
收货单位	货易方式	征免性质	征税比例
许可证号	起运国（地区）	装货港	境内目的地
批准文号	成交方式	运费	保费	杂费
合同协议号	件数	包装种类	毛重（公斤）	净重（公斤）

集装箱号	随附单据	用途
标记喷码及备注			

项号　商品编号　商品名称、规格型号　　数量及单位　原产国（地区）单价　总价　币制　征免

税费征收情况	
录入员　录入单位　兹声明以上申报无讹并承担法律责任	海关审单批注及放行日期（签章） 审单　　　　　审价
报关员 　　　　　　　　申报单位（签章）	征税　　　　　统计
单位地址 　　邮编　　　电话　　　填制日期	查验　　　　　放行

Fig. 8.1　**Import cargo declaration** 进口货物报关单

中华人民共和国海关出口货物报关单

预录入编号：　　　　　　　　　　　　　　海关编号：

出口口岸	备案号	出口日期	申报日期
经营单位	运输方式	运输工具名称	提运单号
发货单位	货易方式	征免性质	结汇方式
许可证号	运抵国（地区）	装运港	境内货源地
批准文号	成交方式	运费　　　保费	杂费
合同协议号	件数	包装种类　毛重（公斤）	净重（公斤）
集装箱号	随附单据	用途	
标记喷码及备注			

项号　商品编号　商品名称、规格型号　　数量及单位　最终目的国（地区）　单价　总价
　　　　　　　　　　　　　　　币制　　　征免

税费征收情况	
录入员　录入单位　兹声明以上申报无讹并承担法律责任	海关审单批注及放行日期（签章） 审单　　　　　审价
报关员 　　　　　　　　申报单位（签章）	征税　　　　　统计
单位地址 　　邮编　　　电话　　　填制日期	查验　　　　　放行

Fig. 8.2　**Export cargo declaration** 出口货物报关单

New Words and Expressions

import and export declarations 进出口报关　　statistics 统计
release 放行，通关　　cargo inspection form 货物检验单
commercial invoice 商业发票　　bill of lading 提货单
tax refund 退税　　certificate of origin 原产地证书
surplus 盈余　　deficit 赤字
balance of trade 贸易平衡　　penalties 罚金

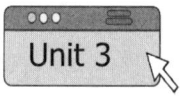

Unit 3　　Import & Export License 进出口许可证

Whereas import/export declarations are used for compiling customs statistic, import/export license are used for controlling or restricting the trading of certain types of goods their quantity. These goods must be of strategic importance to the country, such as arms and hi-tech product. Or they may be items of culture heritage that need to be preserved and protected. Examples of this are rare and precious antiques. In addition, trading of endangered specifies of animals is also prohibited. In some command economies, import licenses are also required for the importing of some goods that are either in high demand or need to be controlled for whatever purposes. The list of goods that are subject to import/export licensing is normally made public, and the administering of the licensing is put under the authority of some government agencies.Even though China is moving fast to relax its import and export licensing controls in line with requirements of the WTO, today import/export license are still required for many commodities.

Import& export license
进出口许可证

进口/出口申报用于编制海关统计数据，进出口许可证用于控制或限制某些类型货物的贸易和其数量。这些货物必须对国家具有战略重要性，如武器和高科技产品。或者它们可能是需要保存和保护的文化遗产。例如稀有和珍贵的古董。此外，濒危动物的交易也被禁止。在一些主导经济体，进口一些需求量大或出于任何目的需要控制的货物也需要进口许可证。需要进口/出口许可证的货物清单通常是公开的，尽管中国正在按照世贸组织的要求迅速放松进出口许可证管制，但今天许多商品仍然需要进出口许可。

Fig. 8.3 and Fig. 8.4 show a sample import license and a sample export license, respectively.

图 8.3 和图 8.4 分别显示了进口许可证样本和出口许可证样本。

中华人民共和国进口许可证

IMPORT LICENSE OF THE PEOPLE'S REPUBLIC OF CHINA　　No.

1. 进口商： Importer				3. 进口许可证号： Import license No.		
2. 收货人： Consignee				4. 进口许可证有效截止日期： Import license expiry date		
5. 贸易方式： Terms of trade				8. 出口国（地区）： Country/Region of exportation		
6. 外汇来源： Terms of foreign exchange				9. 原产地国（地区）： Country/Region of origin		
7. 报关口岸： Place of clearance				10. 商品用途： Use of goods		
11. 商品名称： Description of goods				商品编码： Code of goods		
12. 规格、型号 Specification	13. 单位 Unit	14. 数量 Quantity	15. 单价 Unit price	16. 总值 Amount	17. 总值折美元 Amount in USD	
18. 总计 Total						
19. 备注 Supplementary details				20. 发证机关签章 Issuing authority's stamp & signature 21. 发证日期 License date		

　　　　　　Fig. 8.3　Import License 进口许可证

中华人民共和国出口许可证

EXPORT LICENSE OF THE PEOPLE'S REPUBLIC OF CHINA　　No.

1. 出口商： Exporter				3. 出口许可证号： Export license No.		
2. 收货人 Consignee				4. 出口许可证有效截止日期： Export license expiry date		
5. 贸易方式： Terms of trade				8. 进口国（地区）： Country/Region of exportation		
6. 合同号 Contract No.				9. 支付方式： Payment conditions		
7. 报关口岸： Place of clearance				10. 运输方式： Mode of transport		
11. 商品名称： Description of goods				商品编码： Code of goods		
12. 规格、型号 Specification	13. 单位 Unit	14. 数量 Quantity	15. 单价 Unit price	16. 总值 Amount	17. 总值折美元 Amount in USD	
18. 总计 Total						
19. 备注 Supplementary details				20. 发证机关签章 Issuing authority's stamp & signature 21. 发证日期 License date		

　　　　　　Fig. 8.4　Export License 出口许可证

New Words and Expressions

import/export license 进出口许可证
culture heritage 文化遗产
endangered specifies 濒危物种
agency 机构、代理
sample 样品

strategic 战略
precious antiques 珍贵的文物
prohibit 禁止
commodity 商品

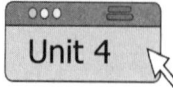

Unit 4 Commodities Quality Inspection 商品检验

A distinctive feature of trade documentation in China is the fact that export goods must go through an official inspection process conducted by the specified government agencies or other authorized agents. The China Inspection and Quarantine (CIQ) Bureau is the government agency whose mandate is to conduct sanitary and health, quarantine and quality inspections on behalf of the Chinese Government, China Quality Inspection Bureau,

Commodities quality inspection 商品检验

which is currently the country's highest-ranking administration under the State Council in charge of quality assurance and quarantine. Apart from this government agency, the China National Import and Export Commodities Inspection Corporation (CCIC) is an approved non-governmental, third party company to conduct the relevant inspections.The CCIC is similar to Society General De Surveillance (SGS) of Switzerland, and Japan overseas Merchandise Inspection Company (OMIC) of Japan.

中国贸易单证的一个显著特点是，出口货物必须经过指定政府机构或其他授权代理人进行的官方检验。中国检验检疫局是一个政府机构，其任务是代表中国政府进行卫生健康、检疫和质量检验，中国质量检验局，这是目前国务院负责质量保证和检疫的最高级别管理机构，中国进出口商品检验总公司（CCIC）是一家经批准的非政府第三方公司，负责进行相关检验。CCIC 类似于瑞士的 SGS 和日本的日本海外商品检验公司（OMIC）。

Even when official inspections are not required, the parties to a contract may still wish to have an inspection conducted before the shipment or after the shipment. The former aims to protect the interest of the importer (e.g. ensure the right goods are shipped at the right time), whereas the latter enables claims to be made for short shipment or for damages to cargoes when they arrive at destination.

即使不需要正式检查，合同各方仍可能希望在装运前或装运后进行检查。前者旨在保护进口商的利益（例如，确保在正确的时间装运正确的货物），而后者使货物能够在到达目的地时就短装或货物损坏提出索赔。

Fig. 8.5 shows a sample certificate of a quality inspection for an export cargo, which is conducted by the Chinese official agency.

图 8.5 显示了由中国官方机构进行的出口货物质量检验的样品证书。

中华人民共和国出和境检验检疫

ENTRY – EXIT INSPECTION AND QUARANTINE OF THE PEOPLE'S REPUBLIC OF CHINA 编号：No

正本

ORIGINAL

品 质 证 书

QUALITY CERTIFICATE

发货人　　　×××进出口有限公司
Consignor　×××IMPORT & EXPORT　COMPANY　LTD

收货人
Consignee＿＿＿＿＿＿＿＿＿＿＿＿＿＿＿＿＿＿＿＿＿

品名　　　　　100%棉染织物 44" 108×58/21×2　　　标记及号码
Description of Goods　　100%Cotton dyed fabric　　　Mark & No.

报检数量/重量　　　　-1200-码
Quantity/Weight Declared　　-1200-yds　　　　　　　C/No.1-120

包装种类及数量　　全幅卷筒，每卷用聚乙稀袋装
Number and Type of Packages FULL WTDTH　ROLLED ON TUBE, EACH ROLL IN IN POLY BAG

运输工具　　　　　货车
Means of Conveyance　BY TRUCK

检验结果

Fig 8.5　Quality Certificate 质检证书 (issued by CIQ)

RESULTS OF INSPECTION：
从全批货物中，按×××标准抽取样品并按×××标准规定进行检验，结果如下：
From the whole lot of goods, samples were drawn according to Standard ××× and inspected according to the stipulation of Standard ××× with the results as follows:

幅宽（英寸）
Width (inch): 44

经纬密度（根/英寸）：
Density of warp & weft (per inch): 11.6×56.6

经纬断裂强力（牛顿/5 厘米）：

Breaking strength of warp & weft (N/5cm): 1210 × 908

水洗尺寸变化（%）：

Dimensional change after washing (%): 0.8 × 0.1

耐洗色牢度（等级）：

Color fastness to washing (grade): cc: 3
cs: 4

耐磨擦色牢度（等级）：

Color fastness to rubbing (grade) （干摩）dry: 4-5
（湿摩）Wet: 4

原料成分：100%棉

Composition (%):100% cotton

外观：A 等级

Appearance: Grade A

结论：上述检验结果符合×××标准对 A 级产品的要求。

Conclusion: The above results of inspection are in conformity with the requirements of Standard ××× for grade A products.

本证书印刷号：A

印章　签证地点 Place of Issue GUANGZHOU　签证日期 Date of issue 05 APR, 2023
Official Stamp

授权签字人 Authorized Officer ZHANG XIAOSHAN 签名 Signature

New Words and Expressions

distinctive 区分的　　　　　　　quarantine 保证
sanitary 卫生　　　　　　　　　inspection 检验
commodity 商品　　　　　　　　merge 合并
rank 等级　　　　　　　　　　　State Council 国务院

Unit 5　Customs Invoice and Consular Invoice 海关和领事发票

A customs invoice is sometimes required for imports into a country. This is usually done by filling out a standardized form provided by the customs authorities at the port of entry and is used as the basis for levy of duties and/or for the purpose of compiling trade statistics. For example, shipments to Canada normally require a Canadian Customs

Customs invoice and consular invoice
海关与领事发票

226

Invoice, apart from the usual commercial invoice.

进口到一个国家有时需要海关发票。这通常是通过填写入境口岸海关当局提供的标准化表格来完成的，并用作征收关税的依据和/或用于编制贸易统计数据。例如，运往加拿大的货物通常需要加拿大海关发票，而不是通常的商业发票。

A consular invoice is required by exports to some countries in South America, mainly for customs purposes. The forms can be obtained from the embassy or consulates (located in the exporter's country) of the importer's country, or a commercial invoice may be used but it must be legalized by the consulate. This is fulfilled when the consulate signs and returns the invoice to the exporter. A fee is usually charged for this service. The consular invoice performs two main purposes:

出口到南美洲一些国家需要领事发票，主要用于海关目的。这些表格可以从进口国的大使馆或领事馆（位于出口国）获得，或者可以使用商业发票，但必须由领事馆验证。领事馆签署并将发票退还给出口商时，即可实现这一点。这项服务通常会收取费用。领事发票有两个主要用途。

First, before legalizing the invoice, the consulate of the importing country checks and makes sure that the goods are not being sold to its country at an artificially low price (e.g. below cost; this is know as dumping). The second function of the consular invoice is to provide information that forms the basis of the import duty to be paid on the goods.

首先，在使发票合法化之前，进口国领事馆会检查并确保货物不会以人为的低价（例如低于成本；这被称为倾销）出售给其国家。领事发票的第二个功能是提供信息，作为支付货物进口税的基础。

New Words and Expressions

invoice 发票　　　　　　　　　　　levy 征收
embassy 大使馆　　　　　　　　　　consulate 领事馆
fee 费用　　　　　　　　　　　　　legalize 合法化
artificially 人工的　　　　　　　　dump 倾销

Background knowledge 背景知识

海关发票是某些国家的海关（如非洲、美洲和大洋洲等）制定的一种固定格式的发票，由出口商填制以供进口商报关纳税的一种特殊发票。

海关发票的主要作用是作为进口国海关的估价定税、核定货物原产地、按照差别税率政策征收不同税率的关税依据。此外，进口国海关将其作为统计依据，并审核是否低价倾销。

海关发票的主要内容：（1）证明商品的价值；（2）证明商品的产地。所以海关发票为"产地和价值联合证明"（Combined Certificate of Value and Origin）。

Unit 5.1 CUSTOMS INVOICE 海关发票

1. SELLER 卖方	2. DOCUMENT 文件 No.	3. INVOICE 发票 No.
	4. REFERENCES 参考信息	
5. CONSIGNEE 收货人	6. BUYER 买方 No.	7. ORIGIN OF GOODS 货物原产地
8. NOTIFY PARTY 通知方	9. TERMS OF SALE.PAYMENT AND DISCOUNT 销售条件，付款和折扣	
10. ADDITIONAL TRANSPORTATION INFORMATION 附加运输信息	11. CURRENCY IN USD 货币单位：美元	12. EXCH-RATE 汇率	13. DATE ORDER ACCEPTED 认可的日期指令

14. MARKS 标记	15. NUMBER OF PACKACES 包装的数量	16. FULL DESCRIPTION OF GOODS 货物完整描述	17. QUANTITY 数量	UNIT PRICE 单价		20. INVOICE TOTALS 发票总额
				18. HOME MARKET 国内市场	19. INVOICE 发票	

If the production of these goods involved famishing goods to the seller. 如果这些货物的生产涉及将货物卖给卖方。 21. And the value is not included in the invoice price, check box (21) explain below. 并且该值不包括在发票价格中，复选框（21）将在下面进行解释。		22. PACKING COSTS 包装成本
27. DECLARATION OF SELLER/SHIPPER (OR AGENT) 卖方/托运人（或代理人）声明		23. OCEAN OF INTERNATIONAL FREIGHT 国际海运
I declare: If there are rebels, drawbacks or (A)☐Bounties allowed upon the exportation of goods, I have checked box (A) and itemized separately below. I further declare that there is no invoice differing from this one (unless otherwise describe below) and that all statements contained in this invoice and declaration are true and correct. 本人声明： 如果有背离、缺点或 （A）☐货物出口时允许的赏金，我勾选了（A）框，并在下面单独列出。 我进一步声明，没有与本发票不同的发票（除非下文另有说明），并且本发票和声明中包含的所有声明都是真实和正确的	If the goods were not sold or agreed (B) to be sold, I have checked box (B) and have indicated in column 19 the price I would be willing to receive. 如果货物未售出或未达成一致（B）☐要出售，我已经勾选了（B）框，并在第19栏中表明了我愿意接受的价格。 (C)SIGNATURE OF SELLER/SHIPPER (OR AGENT): 卖方/发货人签名 （或代理人）	24. DOMESTIC FREIGHT CHARGES 国内运费收费
		25. INSURANCE COSTS 保险成本
		26. OTHER COSTS (Specify Below) 其他费用（以下具体说明）

Unit 5.2　CONSULAR INVOICE 领事发票

Shipper 托运人 (name/address/phone)_____　　Date_____
Consignee 收货人 (name/address)_____　　Invoice No._____
Shipment 装运 per_经_____　　Order/Contract (a)_____
(Aircraft 空运 or vessel 船运）
Date_____　　Payment terms 付款条件 (b)_____
Port of Shipment 装运港_____
Destination 目的地_____
Partial Shipment 分批装运_____　　License 许可证 No._____
　　　　(Yes/NO)

MARKS & NO.	DESCRIPTION OF MERCHANDISE 商品说明	QUANTTTY	UNTT PRICE	VALUE
	TOTAL			

Merchandise 商品 Origin 原产地_____
Manufactured 制造商 by_____
Transshipped/Re-exported at 转运/再出口地点_____
The undersigned swear that the contents and value of this invoice are true and correct in every respect. 以下签字人保证本发票的内容和价值在各个方面都是真实和正确的

Signature & chop of shipper SIGNATURE 发货人签名和盖章，签名

For Consul General 总领事

New Words and Expressions

consignee 收货人　　　　　　　　　　partial 部分的
destination 目的地　　　　　　　　　　transship 转船
Signature &chop 签名盖章　　　　　　Consul General 总领事

229

Unit 6　Commercial Invoice 商业发票

发票号码
Invoice No. _____

青岛，日期
Qingdao, Date_____

To-- ---

装船口岸　　　　　　　　　　目的港
From_____　　　　　　to_____

开证银行　　　　　　　　　　信用证号码
Drawn Under_____　　　L/C No._____

唛头及号码 Marks & Numbers	数量与货品名称 Quantity & Descriptions	金额 Amount

Unit 7　Bill of Exchange 商业汇票

凭
Drawn under_____

　　　　　　　　　　年　　月　　日

日期　　　　　　　　　　　　　　信用证号
Dated _ _ _ _ _ _ _ _ _ _ 　　　L/C No. _ _ _ _ _ _ _

按息付款
Payable with interest @_____% per annum

号码　　　汇票金额　　　　中国青岛　　　年　　月　　日
No._____ **Exchange** for　　Qingdao. China_____19_____

见票　　　　　　　　　　　日后（本汇票之副本示附）付
A:_____ sight of this **FIRST** of Exchange (second of exchange being unpaid)

Pay to the order of_____或其指定人

金　　　额
The sum of

此致
To_____

Unit 8　Insurance 保险

Maine Insurance 海运险

Maine insurance
海运险

The international trade is subject to many risks. Ships may sink or consignments may be damaged in transit, exchange rates may alter, buyers default or governments suddenly impose an embargo. Therefore, exporter and importer have to insure themselves against many of these risks.

国际贸易面临许多风险。船舶可能会沉没或货物在运输过程中受损，汇率可能会改变，买家违约或政府突然实施禁运。因此，出口者和进口者必须为自己投保这些风险。

When an exporter under a CIF contract or an importer under an FOB contract wants to take out, insurance the first step he should take is to contact an insurance company whose agent, known as the "insurance man" or insurance broker, will bring along a printed proposal form. With spaces for names and amounts to be filled by the exporter or importer, also of agreeable to both parties, an agreement called a policy is signed by the party who is being insured and the representative of the insurance company (the insurer). The policy records the premiums (that is, regular payments) which the insured party promises to pay, and the compensation for a stated misfortune which the insurer promises to pay.

当 CIF 合同下的出口商或 FOB 合同下的进口商想要投保时，他应该采取的第一步是联系一家保险公司，该公司的代理人，即"保险人"或保险经纪人，将带来一份打印的投保单。出口商或进口商填写姓名和金额的空白表，双方也同意，被保险人和保险公司（保险人）的代表签署了一份称为保单的协议。保单记录了被保险人承诺支付的保费（即定期付款），以及保险人承诺为所述不幸事件支付的赔偿金。

The recommended minimum amount is the total CIF value plus 10% for other fees and normal margin of profit on the importer's part. A higher additional percentage of value can also be insured provided that an extra premium is paid.

建议的最低金额是 CIF 总价值加上 10%的其他费用和进口商的正常利润率。如果支付了额外的保险费，也可以投保更高的额外价值百分比。

In the insurance business, loss is referred to in most cases as the special term "average" which actually has nothing to do with its normal meaning. It all goes back to the situation where a ship is in danger, and for the safety of the ship and most of the cargo it and somebody's cargo has to be jettisoned (thrown overboard into the sea). Whose cargo should it be? It is the Captain who has to make a decision, the concept of general average was introduced. The idea is to spread the losses suffered by the shipper in time of peril in the voyage so that all interested parties assume their share. It means that whichever shipper loses all or part or part of his cargo, all the others will club together to recompense him for his loss. In such cases it is well established that whose property was saved must contribute proportionally to cover the losses of the one whose property was voluntarily sacrificed. Nowadays all the marine policies taken out automatically include General Average.

在保险业中，损失在大多数情况下被称为"平均"这一特殊术语，实际上与它的正常含义无关。这一切都可以追溯到船舶处于危险中的情况，为了船舶和大部分货物的安全，它和某人的货物必须被抛弃（从船外扔到海里）。这应该是谁的货物？船长必须做出决定，引入了共同海损的概念。这个概念是为了分摊托运人在航行中遇到危险时所遭受的损失，以便所有利益相关方承担他们的份额。这意味着，无论哪一托运人损失了全部或部分货物，所有其他人都会联合起来赔偿他的损失。在这种情况下，众所周知，谁的财产被保存下来，就必须按比例分摊，以弥补自愿牺牲财产的人的损失。如今，所有投保的海事保险单都自动包括共同海损。

Average in marine insurance simply means loss. General Average is a voluntary and deliberate loss and refers to sea hazards that affect all the cargo on a ship, though only one shipper, perhaps, actually suffers, while Particular Average is an involuntary and accidental loss. A partial loss which is suffered by the one whose goods are partly lost or damaged, but not voluntarily incurred, such as by jettisoning, which are covered by General Average. When there is a particular average loss, other interests in the voyage do not contribute to the partial recovery of the one suffering the loss. The cargo owner whose goods were damaged has to look to his insurance company for parent, provided his policy covers the specific type of loss suffered.

海上保险中的平均损失只是指损失。共同海损是一种自愿和故意的损失，指的是影响船上所有货物的海上危险，尽管可能只有一个托运人实际遭受了损失，而特别海损则是一种非自愿和意外的损失，例如通过抛弃，这是共同海损所涵盖的。当发生特定的平均损失时，航程中的其他利益不会对遭受损失的人的部分赔偿做出贡献。货物受损的货主必须向他的保险公司寻求母公司，前提是他的保单涵盖所遭受的特定类型的损失。

The most serious loss in marine insurance is a total loss of the entire shipment resulting from the sea such as beaching, grounding, stranding, collision, natural calamities, fire, etc. Total Loss falls into two kinds: actual total loss "where the thing insured is completely lost or is so badly damaged that it is not worth repairing" and "constructive total loss" where a ship or her cargo is so badly damaged that the cost of repair would be greater than the market value, they are treated as totally lost, and the insurers are bound to pay the total sum for which the damaged ship or cargo was insured.

海上保险中最严重的损失是由于海上原因造成的整个货物的全部损失，如搁浅、碰撞、自然灾害、火灾等。总损失分为两种：实际总损失，即被保险物完全丢失或严重损坏，不值得修理，以及"推定全损"，即船舶或其货物严重受损，维修成本将高于市场价值，则视为全损，保险公司必须支付受损船舶或货物的保险总额。

Exporters or importers arrange insurance cover for their shipments assorting to the type of goods and circumstances. There is a wide range of standard types of coverage, the three basic ones being as follows:

出口商或进口商根据货物类型和情况为其货物安排保险。保险范围有多种标准类型，三种基本类型如下：

Free of Particular Average (FPA) 平安险

This is an insurance term meaning that goods are covered only against hazards to which all the consignments on the same vessel (or other means of transport) are subject, and not against hazards affecting only the insured's consignment. FPA is the minimum and most restrictive coverage and partial loss is not covered. In other words, the insured must therefore assume the risk for any and all partial loss.

这是一个保险术语，意味着货物只承保同一船舶（或其他运输工具）上所有货物所受的危险，而不承保仅影响被保险货物的危险。FPA 是最低和最严格的保险范围，不承保部分损失。换句话说，因此，被保险人必须承担任何和所有部分损失的风险。

With Particular Average (WPA) or With Average (WA) 水渍险（又称单独海损险——编者注）

This insurance term is more comprehensive than both General Average and FPA. It means that in addition to General Average and total loss, goods are covered against partial loss due to major perils, but not due to minor perils.

这个保险条款比共同海损和平安险都要全面。这意味着，除了共同海损和全损外，货物还包括因重大危险造成的部分损失，但不包括因轻微危险造成的损失。

All Risks 一切险

This is the most coverage of the three. Under this cover, the insurer is responsible for all total or partial loss of, or damage to, the insured goods arising from natural elements or from sea perils, including all losses caused by accidents to the carrying vessel or craft or any external causes. But it is not what the name suggests. Businessmen must not be misled by the terminology of all risks. In reality, it gives the fullest possible cover, but only against those risks actually stated in the policy.

这是三种保险中承保最多的一种。根据该保险，保险人对因自然因素或海上危险导致的被保险货物的全部或部分损失或损坏负责，包括因运输船舶或航行器事故或任何外部原因造成的所有损失。但这并不是名称所暗示的。商人决不能被所有风险的术语所误导。事实上，它提供了尽可能充分的保险，但只针对保单中实际说明的风险。

Whether the additional risks, which All Risks policy does not cover, are necessary depends on a number of factors. For instance, delicate goods, such as breakable crockery, cotton piece goods or perishable foodstuffs, obviously have to be covered against more risks than sturdy articles like steel girders and iron ores. General additional risks usually are: theft, pilferage, and non-delivery (TPNI), fresh water or rain water damage, short weight, intermixture and contamination, eakage, breakage, hook damage, rust, sweating and heating, etc. It must be noted that, in China, all these general additional risks are included in "all risks".

综合险保单不承保的额外风险是否必要取决于许多因素。例如，易碎陶器、棉制品或易腐食品等易碎物品显然比钢梁和铁矿石等坚固物品要承担更多的风险。一般的额外风险通常是：盗窃、盗窃和未交货（TPNI）、淡水或雨水损坏、重量短、混合和污染、破损、吊钩损坏、锈蚀等。必须注意的是，在中国，所有这些一般额外风险都包括在"所有风险"中。

Special additional risks that are not included in All Risks and have to be taken separately are mainly: Failure to Delivery Risk, War Risk, and Strikes, Riots and Civil Commotions.

不包括在综合险中且必须单独承担的特殊附加风险主要有：交货失败风险、战争风险以及罢工、暴乱和内乱。

Whenever an actual loss occurs it is import for party having an interest in the goods to get a fair, efficient, and road adjustment of his claims. The right to lodge a claim usually belongs to whoever has the actual position of the policy. The one who files claim should get the survey report conducted by the expert, together with a copy of the bill of lading, the commercial invoice, the insurance policy, a covering letter requesting payment, and send them to the insurance company for processing. Settling a claim is not so easy, and it needs patience, evidence and knowledge.

无论何时发生实际损失，对对货物有利害关系的一方来说，对其索赔进行公平、有效和合理的调整是至关重要的。提出索赔的权利通常属于对保单有实际立场的人。提出索赔的人应获得专家的调查报告，以及提单副本、商业发票、保险单、要求付款的附信，并将其发送给保险公司进行处理。解决索赔并不那么容易，它需要耐心、证据和知识。

New Words and Expressions

alter 改变，变动	default 不履行，拖欠，未到庭
impose 加（惩，罚，税收）于	embargo 禁运令，贸易禁令
merchant （尤指国际贸易批发）商人	safeguard 保护，保卫，防护
pirate 海盗	underwriter 保险公司，保险商
accredited 认可的，合格的	initial 草签
proposal form 投保单	premium 保险费
compensation 赔偿，补偿	jettison 投弃
General Average 共同海损	peril 危险
club together 募集资金，捐款	recompense 赔偿，补偿
contribute 投资，捐助	voluntarily 自愿地
deliberate 故意的，存心的	hazard 危险
Particular Average 单独海损	partial loss 部分损失
provided (that) 如果，假若	policy （保险）单
beaching 冲上岸滩	stranding 搁浅，触礁

collision 碰撞	calamity 不幸，灾害，灾难
Actual Total Loss 实际全部损失	coverage 保险险别
Free of Particular Average (FPA) 平安险	comprehensive 综合的，全面的
With Particular Average (WPA) 水渍险	All Risks 一切险，综合险，全险
terminology 术语，专门名词	delicate 易损的，易碎的
sturdy 结实的，牢固的	girder 大梁，梁
general additional risks 一般附加（险）	short weight 短重（险）
theft，pilferage，and non-delivery (TPND) 偷盗，提货不着（险）	
fresh water or rain water 淡水雨淋（险）	intermixture and contamination 玷污（险）
leakage 渗漏（险）	breakage 破碎（险）
hook damage 钩损（险）	rust risk 生锈（险）
risk of sweating and heating 受潮热（险）	special additional risks 特殊附加（险）
failure to delivery risk 交货不到（险）	war risk 战争（险）
Strikes，Riots and Civil Commotion (SR & CC) 罢工，暴动，民变（险）	
floating policy 流动保险	open cover 预约保险
adjustment 理赔	covering letter 附函，说明信
survey 感观，检查，调查	insurance policy 保险单

Unit 8.1　中国人民保险公司

THE PEOPLE'S　INSURANCE COMPANY OF CHINA
保　险　单（实例）
INSURANCE　POLICY　　　号次

This Insurance Policy Witnesses that The People's Insurance Company of China (hereinafter called "the Company") 根据 <u>China National Textiles Imp. & Exp. Corp.</u>
　　At the request of　　　　<u>Shanghai Branch</u>

（以下简称被保险人）的要求，由被保险人向本公司缴付约定的保险费按照本保险单承保险　别和背面所载条款与下列特款承保下述货物运输保险，特立本保险单。

(Hereinafter called "the Insured") and in consideration of the agreed premium paid to the Company by the Insured, undertakes to insure the under-mentioned goods in transportation subject to the conditions of this policy as per the Clause printed overleaf and other special clauses attached hereon.

标记 Marks & No.	包装及数量 Quantity	保险货物项目 Description of Goods	保险金额 Amount Insured
As per Invoice	103 bales 包	Cotton Piece Goods 布匹	US$36,492

总保险金额：U.S. DOLLARS THIRTY - SIX THOUSAND FORTY HUNDRED & NINETY TWO ONLY

Total Amount Insured_____

保 费　　　　　费 率　　　　　装载运输工具
Premium as arranged　Rate as arranged　Per conveyance S. S. NEWHAILEE

开行日期　　　　自　　　　　　至
Slg. on or abt. as per B/L　From SHANGHAL　to HONGKONG

承保险别：
Conditions

　　　　Covering All Risks And War Risks as per 投保一切险和战争险
　　　　Ocean Marine Cargo Clauses and War Risks 海运货物条款和战争险
　　　　Clauses (1/1/1981) of The People's Insurance 人保条款（1/1/1981）
　　　　Company of China　(Abbreviated as C. I. C. All Risks & War Risks)
中国公司（简称 C.I.C）一切险和战争险
　　　　(Warehouse to Warehouse clause included 包括仓库到仓库条款)

保险货物，如遇出险，本公司凭本保险单及其他有关证件给付赔偿。
Claim, if any, payable on surrender of this Policy together with other relevant documents.

所保货物，如发生保险单项下负责赔偿的损失或事故，
In the event of accident whereby loss or damage may result in a claim under this Policy, immediate notice

应立即通知本公司下述代理人查勘。
Applying for survey must be given to the Company's Agent as mentioned hereunder:

The Ming An Insurance Co. (H. K.) Ltd.
International Building 14th Floor
141 × × × Road, Central.
Hong Kong.

赔款偿付地点
Claim payable at HONGKONG IN US$

中国人民保险公司上海分公司
THE PEOPLE'S INSURANCE CO. OF CHINA
SHANGHAI BRANCH

日期　　　　　　上海
Date　　Dec.16, 2004　　Shanghai

地址：中国上海中山东一路 23 号
Address: 23 Zhongshan Dong Yi Lu, Shanghai, China.
Postcord: 42001 Shanghai
Telex: 33123　PICCS CN

General Manager

Unit 9 Shipping Order 装货单（实例）

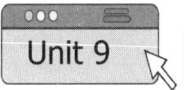

中国外轮代理公司
CHINA OCEAN SHIPPING AGENCY
装货单 SHIPPING ORDER

装单号码　　　　　日期　　　　　　　　海关编号
S/O#_____　Date_____　Customs Ves.#_____
船名　　　　　　　航次　　　　　　　　装往地点
S/S_____　　Voy_____　Destination_____
托运人
Shipper_____
受货人
Consignee_____
通知
Notify_____

| 标记及号码
Marks & Numbers | 件数
Quantity | 货名
Description of Goods | 重量 Weight | | 尺码
Measurement |
			净 Net	毛 Gross	

合计　　　　　　　　　　　　　共重
Total:　　　　　　　　　　　　Total:
合计
Say

请将上开完好之状况货物，予以装船，并希签署收货单为荷。
Please receive on board the above mentioned goods in good order and condition and sign the accompanying Receipt for same.

装入何舱
Stowed_____
实收
Received_____
理货员签名　　　　　　　　　　　　　　　　　　代理人
Tallied By _____　　　As Agents_____
注：收货单（Mate' Receipt）与上述格式完全相同，落款为 大副 Chief Officer

Unit 10　Letter of Credit 信用证

简单地说，信用证 (Letter of Credit，L/C) 是银行依照进口人的要求和指示或代表其自身，开给出口人（受益人）的在单证相符的条件下承诺支付或承兑汇票或发票金额的文件。它的确切含义为：Documentary credits mean any arrangement, however named or described, whereby a band (the Issuing Bank) acting at the request and on the instructions of a customer (the Applicant) or on its own behalf, is to make a payment to a third party (the Beneficiary), or is to accept and pay bills of exchange (Draft(s)) drawn by the Beneficiary, against stipulated documents, provided that the terms and conditions of the credit are complied with.

Letter of credit
信用证

跟单信用证是指任何安排，无论名称或描述如何，根据客户（申请人）的要求和指示或代表其自身行事的银行（开证行）将向第三方（受益人）付款，或接受和支付受益人根据规定文件开具的汇票，前提是信用证的条款和条件得到遵守。

It relates the following terms which perform various duties and responsibilities respectively:
它涉及以下分别履行各种职责的术语：

1. 受益人 (Beneficiary/In favour of…)
2. 开证行 (Issuing Bank/Opening Bank)
3. 通知行 (Advising Bank/Notifying Bank/Advised through…)
4. 议付行 (Negotiating Bank)
5. 付款行 (Paying Bank)或称代付行
6. 保兑行 (Confirming Bank)
7. 偿付行 (Reimbursing Bank)

信用证的种类

1. 可撤销和不可撤销信用证 (Revocable & Irrevocable Credits)
2. 即期和远期信用证 (Sight & Usance Credit)
（1）银行承兑信用证 (Banker's Acceptance Credit)
（2）延期付款信用证 (Deferred Payment Credit)

Chapter 9

Cross-Border E-Commerce 跨境电子商务

- The Brief Introduction to Cross-Border E-Commerce
  跨境电商主要内容简介
- Cross-Border E-Commerce Operation Mode
  跨境电子商务营运方式
- An Overview of Third-Party Cross-Border E-commerce Platform
  第三方跨境电子商务平台概述

Task 1

To Introduce Cross-Border E-Commerce 跨境电子商务

Cross-border e-commerce is developed based on the network. The network space is a new space, relatively speaking, to the physical space, and is a virtual reality of net address and password. Cyberspace's unique values and behavior patterns profoundly affect cross-border e-commerce, making it different from the traditional way of trade and showing its own characteristics.

Introduction
序言

跨境电子商务是基于网络发展起来的，网络空间相对于物理空间来说是一个新空间，是一个由网址和密码组成的虚拟但客观存在的世界。网络空间独特的价值标准和行为模式深刻地影响着跨境电子商务，使其不同于传统的交易方式，并呈现出自己的特点。

Cross-border e-commerce is a new-type mode of trade. It is to digitalize and electronize the exhibition, negotiation and conclusion of a business of the traditional trade by Chinese production and trade enterprises through e-commerce, means to finally realizing the import and export of products. At the same time, it is also an effective way to broaden overseas marketing channel, promote China's brand competitiveness and realize the transformation and upgrading of China's foreign trade.

239

跨境电子商务是我国生产和贸易企业通过电子商务手段将传统贸易中的展示、洽谈和成交环节数字化、电子化，最终实现产品进出口的新型贸易方式；同时，也是扩大海外营销渠道，提升我国品牌竞争力，实现我国外贸转型升级的有效途径。

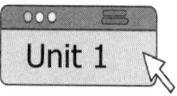 **Features of Cross-Border E-Commerce 跨境电子商务的特征**

1. Global Forum 全球性

Network is a medium body with no boundary, sharing the characteristics of globalization and decentralization. Cross-border e-commerce, attached to the network, also has the characteristics of the globalization and decentralization. E-commerce, compared with the traditional way of trade, boasts its important feature: a borderless trade, losing the geographical factors brought by the traditional exchanges. Internet users do convey products, especially high value-added products, and services to the market without crossing borders. The positive effect brought by features of network is the greatest sharing degree of information, whilst its negative impact is that the users confront risks due to different cultural, political and legal factors. Anyone, who has a certain technical means, can make information into the network, connecting with each other, at any time and in any place.

Global Forum
全球性论坛

网络是一个没有边界的媒介体，具有全球性和非中心化的特征。依附于网络发生的跨境电子商务也因此具有了全球性和非中心化的特性。电子商务与传统的交易方式相比，一个重要特点在于电子商务是一种无边界交易，没有传统交易所具有的地理因素。互联网用户不需要跨越国界就可以把产品，尤其是高附加值产品和服务提交到市场。网络的全球性特征带来的积极影响是信息的最大程度的共享，消极影响是用户必须面临因文化、政治和法律的不同而产生的风险。任何人只要具备了一定的技术手段，在任何时候、任何地方都可以让信息进入网络，与其他人建立相互联系并进行交易。

2. Intangibility 无形性

The development of the network promotes the transmission of digital products and services. And digital transmission is done through different types of media, such as data, voices and images in the global focus of the network environment. Since the media in the network are in the form of computer data code, they are invisible. Digital products and services on the basis of the characteristics of digital transmission activities also have feature of intangibility, although traditional trade in kind is given priority to the physical objects, in the electronic commerce, intangible products can replace physical objects.

Intangibility
无形性

网络的发展使数字化产品和服务的传输盛行。而数字化传输是通过不同类型的媒介（如数据、声音和图像）在全球化网络环境中集中而进行的，这些媒介在网络中是以计算机数据代码的形式出现的，因而是无形的。数字化产品和服务基于数字传输活动的特性也必然具有无形性，传统交易以实物交易为主，而在电子商务中，无形产品却可以替代实物成为交易的对象。

3. Anonymity 匿名性

Due to the decentralization of cross-border e-commerce and global features, it is difficult to identify the e-commerce user's identity and its geographical location. Online transactions of consumers often do not show their real identities and their geographical location, but the important thing is that this doesn't affect trade. Network anonymity also allows consumers to do so. In the virtual society, the convenience of concealing the identity quickly leads to asymmetric freedom and responsibility. People here can enjoy the greatest freedom，but only bear the smallest responsibility, or even simply evade responsibility.

Anonymity
匿名性

由于跨境电子商务的非中心化和全球性的特性，很难识别电子商务用户的身份和其所处的地理位置。在线交易的消费者往往不显示自己的真实身份和所处的地理位置，重要的是丝毫不影响交易的进行，网络的匿名性也允许消费者这样做。在虚拟社会里，隐匿身份的便利迅捷导致自由与责任的不对称。人们在这里可以享受最大的自由，却只承担最小的责任，甚至干脆逃避责任。

4. Real-time 即时性

For network, the transmission speed is irrelevant to geographical distance. Information communication means of traditional trade, such as letter, telegraph, fax, etc., are with a length indifferent time between the sending and receiving of information. With regard to the information exchange in the e-commerce, regardless of the actual distance of time and space, one party sends a message to the other party who receives that information almost at the same time, just like talking face to face in life. Some digital products (such as audio and video products, software, etc.), can also get instant settlement, ordering, payment, delivery done in a flash.

Real-time
即时性

对于网络而言，传输的速度和地理距离无关。传统交易模式中的信息交流方式，如信函、电报、传真等，在信息的发送与接收间，存在着长短不同的时间差。而电子商务中的信息交流，无论实际时空距离远近，一方发送信息与另一方接收信息几乎是同时的，就如同生活中的面对面交谈。某些数字化产品（如音像制品、软件等）的交易，还可以即时结算、订货、付款、交货。

5. Paperlessness 无纸化

Electronic commerce mainly takes the way of the paperless operation, which serves as the main characteristic of trade in the form of electronic commerce. In e-commerce, electronic computer communication records files

Paperlessness
无纸化

241

instead of a series of paper trading. Users send or receive electronic information. Now that the electronic information exists in the form of bits and transmission, the whole process is realized by the paperless information. Paperlessness brings positive effects in terms of making information transferred without the limitation of paper. However, many specifications of the traditional law are with the standard "paper trades" as the starting point, therefore, paperlessness brings chaos in the law, to a certain extent.

电子商务主要采取无纸化操作的方式，这是以电子商务形式进行交易的主要特征。在电子商务中，计算机通信记录取代了一系列的纸面交易文件。用户发送或接收电子信息时，由于电子信息以比特的形式存在和传送，整个信息发送和接收过程实现了无纸化。无纸化带来的积极影响是使信息传递摆脱了纸张的限制，但由于传统法律的许多规范是以标准的"有纸交易"为出发点的，因此，无纸化在法律层面带来了一定程度上的混乱。

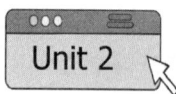

Unit 2　Classification 跨境电商分类

1. Classification by the Participants in the Transaction 依据交易中参与者分类

(1) E-commerce between enterprises and consumers (Business to Customer, B2C). 企业与消费者之间的电子商务

B2C is a business organization's e-commerce to consumers. This is the consumer use the Internet direct participation in the form of economic activities, similar to the commercial electronic retail business. With the advent of the Internet, online sales patterns are rapidly spreading. This form of E-commerce is generally based on the network retail industry, mainly carrying out online sales activities through the Internet.

B2C

B2C 即表示商业机构对消费者的电子商务。这是消费者利用互联网直接参与经济活动的形式，类同于商业电子化的零售商务。随着互联网的出现，网上销售模式迅速普及。这种形式的电子商务一般以网络零售业为主，主要借助于互联网开展在线销售活动。

The B2C model involves a wide variety of products. There is a customer evaluation mechanism to constrain the seller and provide the seller with information that can be used for reference. It is the first choice for shopping. However, due to the large number of merchants and certain difficulties in management, the existence of black-hearted businesses cannot be avoided.

B2C 模式涉及的商品种类繁多，有客户评价机制来约束卖家同时给卖家提供可以借鉴的信息，是购物的首选。但由于商家繁多，管理也存在一定的困难，避免不了黑心商家的存在。

(2) E-commerce between enterprise and enterprise (Business to Business, B2B). 企业间的电子商务

Business-to-business (B2B) is the enterprise on the Internet transactions.

B2B

Business-to-business mode is the most e-commerce applications and most of the attention of a form, enterprises can use the Internet or other networks to find the best partner for each transaction, complete from the order to settle all the transaction behavior.

B2B 是企业在互联网上进行交易，它是电子商务应用最多和最注重的一种形式。企业可利用互联网或其他网络为每笔交易寻找最佳合作伙伴，完成从订单到结算所有交易行为。

B2B contains the following three elements.

① Buying and selling: B2B website or mobile platform provides consumers with high-quality and low-price products, attracting consumers to purchase and prompting more merchants to settle in. ② Cooperation: Establishing a cooperative relationship with the logistics company to provide the ultimate guarantee for the consumer's purchase behavior, which is one of the hard conditions of the B2B platform. ③ Service: Logistics is mainly to provide consumers with purchasing services to achieve another transaction.

B2B 含有以下三要素。

① 买卖：B2B 网站或移动平台为消费者提供质优价廉的商品，吸引消费者购买的同时促使更多商家的入驻。② 合作：与物流公司建立合作关系，为消费者的购买行为提供最终保障，这是 B2B 平台硬性条件之一。③ 服务：物流主要是为消费者提供购买服务，从而实现再一次的交易。

(3) E-commerce between consumers and consumers (Consumer to Consumer, C2C). 消费者与消费者之间的电子商务

C2C business platform provides an online trading platform for both buyers and sellers, so that the seller can voluntarily provide goods for online auction and the buyer can choose the products to bid. However, in the general category of e-commerce, C2C is generally an initial strategy but hardly the mainstream, and eventually will be transformed into a B2C model.

C2C

C2C 商务平台为买卖双方提供一个在线交易平台，使卖方可以主动提供商品上网拍卖，而买方可以自行选择商品进行竞价。不过在电子商务的大范畴下，一般来说 C2C 只是一种初期的策略，难以成为主流，最终将转变成 B2C 模式。

(4) C2B is the consumer to the enterprise (Customer to Business, C2B). 消费者对企业

First popular in the United States, the core of the C2B model is to form a powerful purchasing group by aggregating a large number of users, in order to change the weak position of consumers in the one-to-one bid in the B2C model, so that a consumer can buy a single item with the price of a large wholesaler. At the same time, consumers usually customize products and prices according to their own needs, oractively participate in product design, production and pricing. Products, prices and other characteristics highlight the individual needs of consumers, and manufacturers produce customized products accordingly. At present, few domestic manufacturers really adopt this model completely.

C2B

最先流行于美国，C2B 模式的核心是通过聚合数量庞大的用户形成一个强大的采购集团，以此来改变 B2C 模式中用户一对一出价的弱势地位，使之享受到以大批发商的价格买单件商品的利益。与此同时，消费者通常根据自身需求定制产品和价格，或主动参与产品设计、生产和定价，产品、价格等特征均彰显消费者的个性化需求，生产企业据此进行定制化生产。目前中国很少厂家真正完全采用这种模式。

2. Classification by Technology Adopted 依据采用的技术分类

(1) Peer-to-peer E-commerce.

Peer-to-Peer (P2P), using peer-to-peer networking technology, allows users to share files and computer resources directly without having to go through a central web server. This approach does not require the involvement of the virtual market creator. Simply put, P2P connects people directly, allowing people to interact directly through the Internet. This makes communication on the network easier, more directly shared and interactive, and virtually eliminates intermediaries. Another important feature of P2P is to change the current Internet-centric status of the Internet, return to "decentralization", and return power to users.

P2P

（1）对等电子商务。

对等电子商务使用对等网络技术，用户不需要通过中央网络服务器，可以直接共享文件和计算机资源。这种方式不需要虚拟市场创建者的介入。简单来说，P2P 就是直接将人们联系起来，让人们能够通过互联网直接交互，这使得网络上的沟通变得容易、更直接地共享和互动，真正地消除中间商。P2P 另一个重要特点是改变互联网现在以大网站为中心的状态、重返"非中心化"，并把权力交还给用户。

(2) Mobile e-commerce.

Mobile commerce (M-commerce), which uses the mobile Internet to make online transactions by mobile devices (mobile phones, PDAs, etc.). The development potential of this model is huge and should be given full attention. Of course, this is also inseparable from the rapid development of technology and the security of users.

Mobile e-commerce
移动电商

（2）移动电子商务。

移动电子商务利用移动互联网，使用移动设备（手机、掌上电脑等）进行网上交易。该模式发展潜力巨大，应给予充分重视。当然，这同时也离不开技术的快速发展以及用户安全性的保障。

3. Classification by Related Goods 依据产品分类

(1) Direct e-commerce.

Direct e-commerce, including the provision of soft goods (also known as intangible goods) and various services to customers, such as computer software, research and advisory reports, flights, group travel and entertainment content ordering, payment redemption and Bank-related transactions in

Direct e-commerce
直接电商

business, securities and futures, and information services on a global scale, all of which can be transmitted directly through the network to ensure safe arrival at customers. The outstanding benefits of direct e-commerce are fast, easy and cheap, and the operating costs of enterprises are significantly reduced, which is very popular among customers. The limitation is that only goods and services suitable for transmission over the Internet can be operated.

（1）直接电子商务。

直接电子商务，包括向客户提供软体商品（又称无形商品）和各种服务，如计算机软件、研究性及咨询性的报告、航班、参团出游及娱乐内容的订购、支付、兑汇及银行有关业务、证券及期货的有关交易、全球规模的信息服务等，都可以通过网络直接传送，保证安全抵达客户。直接电子商务突出的好处是快速简便及十分便宜，企业的运作成本显著降低，深受客户欢迎。受限之处是只能经营适合在网上传输的商品和服务。

(2) Indirect e-commerce.

Indirect e-commerce, including the provision of physical goods (also known as tangible commodities) and related services for clients. Because a large number of traded goods and related services in the society are required to be delivered with in a wide geographical range and strict time limit, the distribution is generally completed by modern logistics distribution companies and professional service agencies. The modern logistics distribution companies and professional service organizations mentioned here are far from the warehousing and freight transport institutions and simple service departments of the traditional commerce. They are a kind of modem enterprise with a large scale and strong transportation capacity, using automated means, especially the full use of Internet information management. In this model, the use of the Internet has enabled both parties to improve their time and financial efficiency to more efficiently obtain the goods they need and to expand the source of the merchant's customers.

Indirect e-commerce 间接电商

（2）间接电子商务。

间接电子商务包括向客户提供实体商品（又称有形商品）及有关服务。显然这是社会中大量交易的商品和有关服务。由于要求做到在很广的地域范围和严格的时限内送达，一般均交由现代物流配送公司和专业服务机构完成配送工作。这里所说的现代物流配送公司和专业服务机构远非过去传统商业的仓储货运机构和简单的服务部门，而是一种具有相当规模，拥有很强运输能力，采用自动化手段，特别是充分运用互联网信息管理的现代企业。在这种模式下，互联网的使用促使交易双方提高了时间和财务效率，能够更有效地获取到自己需要的商品，也扩大了商家的客户源。

New Words and Expressions

based on 基于
traditional way to trade 传统贸易模式
profoundly affect 深远影响
a new-type mode of trade 新型贸易模式

at the same time 在同一时间
realize the transformation 实现转型
share the characteristics of 共享（分享）……的特征
digital products and services 数字化产品和服务
physical objects 实物
due to 由于……
in terms of 以……形式
...attract great attention from... 引起……高度重视
be mainly divided into... 主要划分为……

brand competitiveness 品牌竞争力
upgrade the level of foreign trade 外贸升级
be given priority to 以……为主
bring positive effect 带来积极的影响
trading body 贸易主体

Task 2

Cross-Border E-Commerce Operation Mode 跨境电子商务营运方式

Cross-border (foreign trade) e-commerce is, essentially, the latest innovation and practice of e-commerce in the field of international trade. E-commerce is a new type of commerce and trade mode based on Internet technology and infrastructure, taking both parties to the transaction as the main body, using electronic payment and electronic settlement as its means; it relies on the support of modem logistics industry as well.

Operation mode
营运方式

跨境（外贸）电子商务从本质上讲，是电子商务在国际贸易领域一种最新的创新运用与实践。电子商务是一种以互联网技术和基础设施为基础，以交易双方为主体，以电子支付和电子结算为手段，同时依靠现代物流业支撑的一种新型商务贸易模式。

From this perspective, this book defines cross-border e-commerce as an international business transaction in which the subjects of transactions belong to different countries or different regions. The subjects of transactions reach or facilitate international transactions, make payment and settlement through the e-commerce platform, followed by effecting the relevant cross-country or regional logistics support for the delivery of goods.

从这个角度看，本书对跨境电子商务的定义，是指分属不同国家或区域的交易主体通过电子商务平台达成或促成国际交易，进行支付与结算，并通过跨越国家或区域的物流支持商品送达，最终完成交易的一种国际商务活动。

Based on the direction of import and export, cross-border e-commerce can be divided into two categories: "export-oriented" cross-border e-commerce and "import-type" cross-border e-commerce. Based on transaction patterns, cross-border e-commerce can also be divided into two main categories: B2B cross-border e-commerce and B2C cross-border e-commerce.

跨境电子商务基于进出口的方向可以划分为两类："出口型"跨境电子商务和"进口型"跨境电子商务。跨境电子商务基于交易，模式可以划分为两大类：B2B 跨境电子商务和 B2C 跨境电子商务。

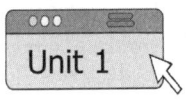 **Platform Trade Mode of Cross-Border E-Commerce 跨境电子商务平台交易模式**

1. Background 背景

Background 背景

Since entering into the 21st century, more and more domestic and overseas foreign trade enterprises hope to tap customers and conduct business with more diversified and more efficient methods as well as channels, due to the fact that the traditional marketing mode is far from satisfying with the new development of international trade trend. With the rise of "Internet" in recent years, e-commerce has been gradually emerging. The advantages of e-commerce versus traditional business models are increasingly apparent: e-commerce has made transactions more transparent by breaking the traditional trade-time constraints; e-commerce can save manpower, material and financial resources; its advantages are also supported and advocate by more and more foreign trade enterprises of all kinds. To a large extent, e-commerce has satisfied the demand of many foreign trade enterprises for the expansion of import and export business, especially the demand and expansion in overseas markets. Therefore, many traditional foreign trade companies are initiating their acts to attach importance to this latest change in the international market and gradually embark on the cross-border e-commerce path. Foreign trade companies, aiming to promote business through cross-border e-commerce, will mainly adopt two modes of operation. Namely, one is to build their own independent foreign trade business web site; the other is mainly based on third-party e-commerce platform.

进入 21 世纪以来，越来越多的国内外外贸企业希望用更多样化、更高效的方法和渠道来挖掘客户、开展业务，因为传统的营销模式已经远远无法满足新的国际贸易发展趋势。近年来电子商务伴随着互联网的崛起而逐渐兴起，与传统商务模式相比，电子商务的优点日益显现：电子商务通过打破传统的贸易时空限制，使得交易行为变得更加透明化、简单化；电子商务能够大力节省人力、物力以及财力，其优点也越来越受到外贸企业的青睐和推崇。电子商务在很大程度上满足了许多外贸企业进出口业务拓展的需求，尤其是海外市场需求和拓展，因此，不少传统外贸公司开始重视国际市场的这种最新变化，逐渐走上跨境电子商务之路。外贸公司通过跨境电子商务拉动业务，主要会采用两种模式和运营方式，一是搭建属于自己的独立的外贸商务网站；二是主要依靠第三方电子商务平台。

2. Cross-Border E-commerce Platform Trading Mode 跨境电子商务平台交易模式

Figure 9.1 illustrates the cross-border e-commerce platform transaction mode process. First of all, domestic suppliers can publish relevant product information and quest the global market demand information on cross-border e-commerce platform; international buyers can also publish their product demand information and query the global

Platform trading mode
平台培训模式

market product information on cross-border e-commerce platform; if domestic suppliers and international buyers meet the same demand with each other, they may conduct initial cross-border e-commerce cooperation intention negotiation through sending business relations invitation or direct inquiry (inquiry). If they fail to reach an agreement, they shall continue to find their own cross-border partners. After the initial negotiation on the intent of cross-border e-commerce cooperation is reached, both parties will continue their detailed negotiation and in-depth consultation on the contract so as to conclude the contract ultimately. After signing the contract, they eventually enter the actual transaction mode, that is, logistics delivery, settlement and payment procedures, until the completion of the transaction is done.

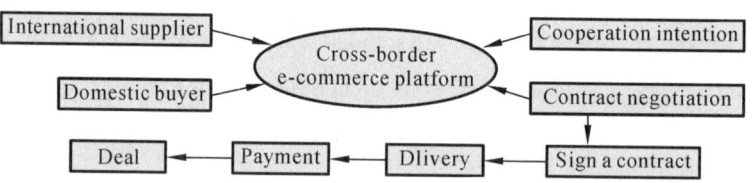

Figure 9.1　Cross Border E-commerce Platform Transaction Mode

图 9.1 体现了跨境电子商务平台交易模式流程。首先，国内供应商可以在跨境电子商务平台发布相关的产品信息并查询全球市场的需求信息；国际采购商也可以在跨境电子商务平台发布其相关的产品需求信息并查询全球市场的产品信息。基于这个平台，如果有国内供应商和国际采购商相互需求一致，则可以通过建立业务关系或直接的询盘（询价）进行初步跨境电子商务合作意向磋商，如未能达成一致，将继续寻找各自的跨境合作伙伴。初步跨境电子商务合作意向磋商达成一致后，双方将继续进行针对合同的详细洽谈和深入磋商，最后签订合同。签订合同后，便进入实际交易模式，即进行物流发货、结算支付等程序，直至完成交易。

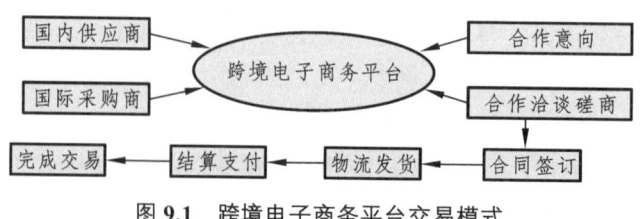

图 9.1　跨境电子商务平台交易模式

248

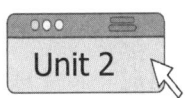 **Advantages of Cross-Border E-Commerce Operation Mode**
跨境电子商务运营模式的优势

1. Boosting the Welfare of International Trade 增进国际贸易福利

The innovation of the cross-border e-commerce operation mode has led to the change of the traditional business process, together with the realization of the electronicization and digitization of international trade. On the one hand, through the cross-border e-commerce operation mode, international trade flows, instead of international trade logistics, can drastically reduce the manpower, material and financial resources consumption in the field of international trade and cut the transaction costs of international trade. On the other hand, cross-border e-commerce operation mode has broken through the time and space constraints in international trade, making it possible for international trade activities to be truly and efficiently carried out at any time and any place, thereby greatly increasing the efficiency of international trade and boosting the welfare of international trade.

Boosting Welfare
增进福祉

跨境电子商务运营模式的创新促使传统的商务流程发生了变化，实现了国际贸易电子化、数字化。一方面，通过跨境电子商务运营模式，国际贸易电子流代替了国际贸易实物流，可以大量减少国际贸易领域的人力、物力和财力消耗，降低了国际贸易交易成本；另一方面，跨境电子商务运营模式突破了国际贸易时间和空间上的限制，使得国际贸易活动可以真正实现在任何时间、任何地点的高效进行，从而大大提高了国际贸易效率，增进了国际贸易福利。

2. Information Symmetry 信息对称

The open and global duality of cross-border e-commerce operation has created a large number of trading opportunities for cross-border e-commerce enterprises. At the same time, the cross-border e-commerce mode allows cross-border e-commerce enterprises to enter the global e-commerce trade market with similar transaction costs. The cross-border e-commerce operation mode has broken the barriers of time and space on the one hand and provided abundant and symmetrical information resources on the other hand. Moreover, this mode provides more possibilities for the reorganization and allocation of various economic resources as well as social elements, directly or indirectly affecting the layout of the global trade economy and the regional industrial structure. As a result, cross-border e-commerce SMEs are able to, just like any large enterprises, acquire the same amount of information resources and achieve "information symmetry", so as to enhance the international competitiveness of cross-border e-commerce SMEs.

Information Symmetry
信息对称

跨境电子商务运营模式具有开放性和全球性双重特点，这为跨境电子商务企业创造了大量的贸易机会。同时，跨境电子商务模式使跨境电子商务企业可以通过相近的交易成本进入全球电子商务贸易市场之中。跨境电子商务运营模式一方面破除了交易时间和空间上的壁垒，另一方面，也提供了丰富对称的信息资源，为各种经济资源和社会要素的重新组合与配置提供了更多的可能，直接或间接地影响了全球贸易经济布局和区域产业结构。因此，跨境电子商务中小企业和大企业一样可以获得等量的信息资源，实现"信息对称"，从而提高跨境电子商务中小企业的国际竞争能力。

3. Interactivity 互动性

Cross-border e-commerce business mode has redefined and subverted the traditional mode of circulation. Cross-border e-commerce business mode bears a strong interaction, that is, through the Internet, cross-border business can be exchanged directly between the negotiations and the signing of the contract. The interaction is also reflected by the fact that consumers can reflect their own real feedback suggestions on websites of cross-border businesses or businesses, and cross-border businesses or businesses can timely investigate cross-border product categories and cross-habitat quality of service, contributing to benign interaction. Cross-border e-commerce has made it possible for direct trade between producers and consumers at both ends of the cross-border e-commerce platform by virtue of reducing the intermediate links in trade, so as to largely change and subvert the way the entire world trade economy is operating.

Interactivity
互动性

跨境电子商务运营模式重新定义并颠覆了传统的流通模式。跨境电子商务运营模式具有很强的互动性，即通过互联网，跨境商家之间可以直接进行交流、谈判、合同签订。互动性还体现在消费者可以把自己的实际反馈建议反映到跨境企业或商家的网站之上，而跨境企业或者商家则可以根据消费者的反馈，及时地调查跨境产品种类及跨境服务的品质，做到良性互动。跨境电子商务通过减少贸易的中间环节，使得跨境电子商务平台两端的生产者和消费者的直接贸易成为一种现实可能，从而在很大程度上改变并颠覆了整个世界贸易经济运行的方式。

 **Current Drawbacks and Limitations of Cross-Border E-Commerce Operation Mode**
当前跨境电子商务运行模式的缺陷与局限性

1. Limitations of Network of Cross-Border E-Commerce 跨境电子商务运作网络的局限性

The network of cross-border e-commerce mode of operation has its own limitations. Mainly reflected by the large gap between the goods shown online and the real goods received offline; consumers are often unable to get all the information concerning cross-border goods or services from the Internet, in particular, they are

Limitations
局限

unable to get the most vivid and most direct impression of cross-border goods in the most rapid manner; In addition, web search function is not perfect, and there are some limitations on this aspect. One of the big questions that consumers face when shopping online across borders is how to seek cross-border goods that they really desire on numerous cross-border platform websites and buy them at the lowest price.

跨境电子商务运作模式网络本身有一定的局限性，主要体现为：网上的商品与实物的差距较大，消费者往往无法从网上得到跨境商品或服务的全部信息，尤其是无法以最快的速度获取对跨境商品最鲜明、最直观的印象；另外，网络搜索功能不够完善，有一定的局限性。当消费者在跨境网上购物时，他们面临的一个很大的问题就是如何在众多的跨境平台网站上寻找到自己真正想要的跨境商品，并以最低的价格买到。

2. Security of Cross-Border E-Commerce 跨境电子商务的安全性

Security of cross-border e-commerce mode is not decently guaranteed and this is mainly reflected in: how to deal with cross-border transactions in an open internet network, how to ensure the safety of data transmission, which has always been one of the most important factors affecting and restricting the development of cross-border e-commerce mode of operation. In addition, the current management of cross-border e-commerce is far from standardization. The concept of management actually covers many aspects, such as business management of cross-border e-commerce operations, cross-border technology management and cross-border service management. In particular, the consistency of the front-end and back-end of the business operation mode platform is also very crucial and important.

Security
安全性

跨境电子商务运作模式交易的安全性得不到适当的保障，主要体现为：在开放的互联网网络上处理跨境交易，如何保证传输数据的安全一直以来都是影响和制约跨境电子商务运作模式发展的最重要因素之一。另外，目前对跨境电子商务的管理还远远不够规范。这个管理的概念实际上涵盖了跨境电子商务运作商务管理、跨境技术管理、跨境服务管理等方面，特别是跨境电子商务运作模式平台前后端的一致性也是非常关键和重要的。

3. Standardization of Cross-Border E-Commerce 跨境电子商务标准化问题

Cross-border e-commerce supplier mode of operation is also facing the issue of standardization. Due to the different national conditions and cultures of diverse countries or regions across borders, there are bound to exist many differences and "heterogeneities" in the forms and means of cross-border e-commerce transactions. In the face of borderless and global cross-border trade activities, e-commerce operators shall establish a relevant mode of operation which entails a unified international standard, aiming to achieve a standardized cross-border e-commerce operation. At the same time, both cross-border logistics and distribution also confront the issue of standardization. Online consumers often encounter delayed

Standardization
标准化

delivery, and due to the relatively high costs of international logistics and distribution, it is imperative to form a standardized and efficient cross-border e-commerce distribution management system.

跨境电子商务供应商运作模式也面临标准化的问题。由于不同国家或区域的国情和文化不同，跨境电子商务的交易方式和手段相应必然存在许多差异和"异质性"，面对无国界、全球性的跨境贸易活动，跨境电子商务经营者亟须建立一种有意义的、目的明确的国际标准操作模式，实现标准化跨境电子商务运作。同时，跨境物流配送也面临标准化的问题。网上的消费者经常会遇到交货延迟的现象，而且由于国际物流配送的费用相对较高，亟须形成一套标准化的、高效的、完备的跨境电子商务配送管理系统。

4. Legalization of Cross-Border E-Commerce 跨境电子商务法制化问题

Cross-border e-commerce mode of operation is also facing the issue of legalization. Mainly reflected in the following aspects: the legal issues of electronic contracts. On the one hand, the existence of electronic contracts are easily tampered with, fabricated and so difficult to prove their authenticity and effectiveness of the problem; on the other hand, the digital seal of electronic contracts and the legal validity of signatures also urgently cry out for the existing laws to effectively regulate. Because of the existence of digital information on the computer network, the issue of intellectual property rights has become prominent in the field of intellectual property (patents, trademarks, copyrights, trade secrets, etc.).

Legalization
法制化

跨境电子商务运作模式还面临法制化的问题，主要体现为以下方面。电子合同的法律问题：一方面，电子合同存在容易被篡改、编造等难以证明其真实性和有效性的问题；另一方面，电子合同的数字化印章和签名的法律效力还亟须现有的法律有效地对其进行规范。除此之外，由于计算机网络上所承载的是以数字化形式存在的信息，因而，在知识产权领域（专利、商标、版权和商业秘密等），版权保护的问题就显得十分突出。

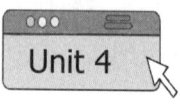

Unit 4　Current Representative Operation Mode of Cross-Border E-Commerce 目前跨境电子商务具有代表性的营运模式

1. Overseas Purchasing Cross-Border E-Commerce Mode 海外代购跨境电子商务模式

Overseas purchasing cross-border e-commerce mode is referred to as "Hai-Dai" in Chinese, this model is just after the "Hai-Tao" model, which is well-known and recognized by domestic consumers as a cross-border online shopping concept. The overseas purchasing cross-border e-commerce mode is defined, by this present book, as a mode in which a certain business overseas purchases goods for domestic consumers and further effect cross-border logistics and distribution, so as to enable the domestic consumer get the delivered goods.

Overseas purchasing
海外代购

海外代购跨境电子商务模式简称"海代",这种模式是继"海淘"之后第二个被国内消费者所熟知的跨境网购概念。本书对海外代购跨境电子商务模式的定义,就是一种为国内消费者购买商品,并进一步通过跨境物流配送,将国内消费者所购商品送达的商业模式。

2. Drop-Ship Platform Cross-Border E-Commerce 直发平台跨境电子商务模式

Drop-ship platform cross-border e-commerce mode can be referred to as drop-shipping mode. This book defines drop-ship platform cross-border e-commerce mode as a cross-border e-commerce platform that sends customer order information received to wholesalers or vendors, while wholesale merchants send consumers retail based on order information for related goods and services. In this drop-shipping mode, because the supplier is often a brand seller, a wholesaler or a manufacturer, in effect, the drop-shipping platform is a typical e-commerce B2C mode. It can also be understood as a third-party B2C model, such as Tmall in China.

Platform ship
平台直发

直发平台模式可以称为直运模式。本书对直发平台模式的定义是:通过一种跨境电子商务平台,将接收到的消费者订单信息发给批发商或厂商,而批发商或厂商则根据订单信息以零售的形式对消费者发送相关货物和服务的模式。在这种直发模式下,因为供货商往往就是品牌商、批发商或厂商,所以,实际上直发平台跨境电子商务模式是一种典型的电子商务 B2C 模式。也可以将其理解为一种第三方 B2C 模式,如国内的天猫商城。

3. Self-Run B2C Cross-Border E-Commerce Mode 自营 B2C 跨境电子商务模式

In the self-run B2C model, most cross-border e-commerce products require cross-border e-commerce platforms to fulfill their own stocking. Therefore, self-run B2C mode is the most important category in all modes. Self-run B2C model can be subdivided into two categories: self-vertical and integrated self-employed. Vertical self-supporting cross-border B2C platform refers to cross-border platform whose choice of self-cross-border category tends to focus on a particular area, such as focusing on foods, luxury items, cosmetics or clothing. The self-run cross-border category of the integrated self-run cross-border B2C platform is not limited to a specific category. Currently, representatives of the comprehensive self-run cross-border B2C platform are Amazon and No. 1 stores.

Self-run
自营 B2C

在自营的 B2C 模式下,大多数跨境电子商务商品都需要跨境电子商务平台自己备货。因此,自营的 B2C 模式是所有模式里最重要的一类。自营 B2C 模式可以细分为两大类:垂直型自营和综合型自营。垂直型自营跨境 B2C 平台是指,跨境平台在选择自营跨境品类时会集中于某个特定的范畴,如集中于食品、奢侈品、化妆品或服饰等。综合型自营跨境 B2C 平台的自营跨境品类不限于特定的范畴,目前综合型自营跨境 B2C 平台的代表是亚马逊和 1 号店。

4. Shopping Guide/Rebate Cross-Border E-Commerce Platform Mode 导购/返利跨境电子商务平台模式

Shopping guide/rebate cross-border e-commerce mode is a more "straightforward" e-commerce model. This model includes two steps: drainage step and commodity trading step. Drainage step refers to the flow of information going through the shopping guide information, commodity parity, shopping community forums, shopping blogs and user rebates, aiming to attract user traffic; the step of merchandising means that the customer submits an order to an overseas B2C e-commerce service provider or overseas purchasing service provider via an intra-site link of cross-border shopping.

导购/返利跨境电子商务模式是一种更加"简单"的电商模式，这种模式包括两个步骤：引流步骤和商品交易步骤。引流步骤是指，通过导购资讯、商品比价、海购社区论坛、海购博客以及用户返利来吸引用户流量；商品交易步骤是指，消费者通过站内链接向海外 B2C 电商或者海外代购者提交订单，实现跨境购物。

5. Overseas Flash-Purchase Cross-Border E-Commerce Mode 海外商品闪购跨境电子商务模式

In addition to the above four types of imported retail cross-border e-commerce modes, overseas flash-purchase cross-border e-commerce mode is a relatively unique approach, and here treats it separately as a separated cross-border e-commerce mode. As the supply chain environment for cross-border flash-purchase is more complicated than that in the domestic area, the platforms involved in cross-border flash-sale operations have only been in the pilot phase for a long time to come.

除了以上四种进口零售跨境电子商务模式之外，海外商品闪购是一种相对独特的做法，所以本书将其单独列为一种跨境电子商务模式。由于跨境闪购所面临的供应链环境比起境内更为复杂，所以，在很长一段时间里，涉足跨境闪购的平台都只是处于小规模试水阶段。

New Words and Expressions

from this perspective 从这个角度看
followed by 紧跟着……
due to the fact that 由于……
to a large extent 很大程度上……
it is illustrated 它说明了……

belong to 属于……
be divided into 被分为……
far from 远远不够……
embark on 踏上……
on the intent of 对……的意图

have led to 已经导致了……
reflected by 由……反映
deal with 处理
tamper with 篡改

a large number of 大量的
in addition 另外
at the same time 与此同时

Task 3

An Overview of Third-Party Cross-Border E-Commerce Platform
第三方跨境电子商务平台概述

Third-party cross-border e-commerce platforms generally refer to a kind of cross-border e-commerce operation mode in which services are rendered to those providers and demanders that are independent of cross-border products or cross-border services, mainly through network service platforms and in accordance with specific e-commerce transaction and e-commerce service standards.

第三方跨境电子商务平台，一般泛指独立于跨境产品或跨境服务的提供者和需求者，主要通过网络服务平台，并按照特定的电子商务交易与电子商务服务规范，为跨境贸易的买卖双方提供服务的一种跨境电子商务运营模式。

The service content of the third-party cross-border e-commerce platform may include, but not limited to, "publishing and searching of supply and demand information, establishment of transactions, payment, and logistics". At present, the representative third-party cross-border e-commerce platforms in China are: Alibaba's AliExpress, Dunhuang Network, China Manufacturing Network and so on.

第三方跨境电子商务平台的服务内容可以包括但不限于供求信息发布与搜索、交易的确立、支付、物流。目前国内有代表性的第三方跨境电子商务平台有阿里巴巴速卖通、敦煌网、中国制造网等。

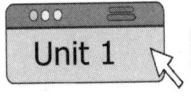

Unit 1 Features of Third-Party Cross-Border E-Commerce Platform
第三方跨境电子商务平台的特点

1. Independence 独立性

The third-party cross-border e-commerce platform is neither a trade buyer nor a trade seller, but rather, exists as a platform for cross-border e-commerce transactions. Like the trading market in physical trading, it is actually an intermediary trading market in the online world.

Features 特征

255

第三方跨境电子商务平台既不是贸易买家，也不是贸易卖家，而是作为跨境电子商务交易的一个平台存在，如同实体买卖中的交易市场一样，它实际上是网络世界的中介交易市场。

2. Relying on the Network 依托网络

With the development of e-commerce business and international trade, third-party cross-border e-commerce platform has emerged; like traditional e-commerce, it relies on the network to play its intermediary trading market role.

第三方跨境电子商务平台是随着电子商务和国际贸易的发展而出现的，和传统的电子商务一样，它必须依托于网络才能发挥其中介交易市场的作用。

3. Specialization 专业化

As a service platform for trading markets, third-party cross-border e-commerce platforms require more professional business support technologies, including order management, payment security and logistics management, so as to achieve the objective of providing safe and convenient services for both cross-border e-commerce buyers and sellers.

作为交易市场服务平台，第三方跨境电子商务平台需要更加专业的商务贸易支撑技术，包括对订单管理、支付安全和物流管理等技术支撑，实现其为跨境电子商务买卖双方提供安全便捷服务的宗旨。

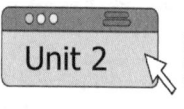

Unit 2　Profit Mode of Third-Party Cross-Border E-Commerce Platform 第三方跨境电子商务平台的盈利模式

1. Membership Fee Profit Mode 会员费盈利模式

In the form of receiving membership fee or registering as a member, third-party cross-border e-commerce platforms achieve profit through the online store rental, cross-border company certification, and cross-border product information recommendation.

Profit mode
盈利模式

第三方跨境电子商务平台以收取会员费或注册成为会员的形式，通过网上店铺出租、跨境公司认证、跨境产品信息推荐等方式实现盈利。

2. Advertising Fee Profit Model 广告费盈利模式

Third-party cross-border e-commerce platforms make money through various types of advertising fees, including text ads, such as keywords, or embedding different-color text in text-linked information articles, image ads and dynamic advertising flash. At the same time, ad networks that share ads on well-known cross-border e-commerce sites are also an important channel for profitable advertising. Mail shot and commercial survey delivery are also commonly used tools.

第三方跨境电子商务平台通过各类广告费实现盈利，其中包括文字广告，如关键字，或者是在文字链接资讯文章中嵌入不同颜色的文字、图片广告和动态广告等。同时，广告联盟分享投放知名跨境电子商务网站上的广告，也是一个重要的广告费实现盈利渠道。邮件广告和商业调查投放也是常用的手段。

3. Search/PPC Profit Mode 搜索/竞价排名盈利模式

Third-party cross-border e-commerce platform makes its margins through a variety of keywords PPC rankings for profitability. In fact, keywords PPC rankings refer to the key words rankings by customers search. In addition, the hot words link the cross-border shops or a cross-border business site is also a commonly used search/bid ranking means.

第三方跨境电子商务平台通过各类关键词竞价排名进行收费盈利，关键词竞价排名即客户通过搜索关键词得到的排名。另外，热点词汇直达跨境商铺或跨境企业网站也是常用的搜索/竞价排名手段。

4. Value-Added Service Profit Mode 增值服务盈利模式

Third-party cross-border e-commerce platforms also make margins and profits by offering various value-added services, including corporate certification, independent domain names, search engine optimization and engine downloads. The platform also provides a variety of information and reporting services, such as industry data analysis reports, industry development reports, customer messages, cutting-edge messaging services and mail services, web site data analysis reports, as well as experts online information.

第三方跨境电子商务平台还通过提供各种增值服务来盈利，包括企业认证、独立域名、搜索引擎优化和电子杂志下载等。平台还提供各种信息和报告服务，如行业数据分析报告、行业发展报告、客户留言、前沿资讯短信服务和邮件服务、网站数据分析报告以及专家在线咨询等。

5. Offline Service Profit Mode 线下服务盈利模式

Third-party cross-border e-commerce platforms also make money by offering a variety of offline physical services, including cross-border e-commerce network marketing planning training, cross-border e-commerce product exhibitions, cross-border e-commerce industry associations, cross-border e-commerce seminars and summit forums, etc. In addition, some periodicals are embedded with ads or industry information to achieve profitability.

第三方跨境电子商务平台还通过提供各种线下实体服务来盈利，包括跨境电子商务网络营销策划培训、跨境电子商务产品展会、跨境电子商务行业商会、跨境电子商务研讨会和高峰论坛等。另外，还在某些期刊内通过行业资讯、植入广告等来实现盈利。

6. Business Cooperation Profit Mode 商务合作盈利模式

Third-party cross-border e-commerce platforms also make money by cooperating with governments, industry associations, businesses and the media in cross-border countries or regions. In addition, third-party cross-border e-commerce platform can also cooperate with other websites, such as advertising networks (Baidu Union, Google Alliance).

第三方跨境电子商务平台还通过与跨境国家或区域的政府、行业协会、企业和媒体等合作实现盈利。另外，第三方跨境电子商务平台还可以与其他的网站进行合作，如广告联盟（百度联盟、谷歌联盟）等。

7. Trading Profit Charging Mode 交易环节收费盈利模式

Third-party cross-border e-commerce platforms also make profits through various trading links such as online brokerage, transaction commissions, payment services, online auctions and cross-border logistics services, etc.

第三方跨境电子商务平台还通过各种交易环节进行收费盈利，如网上业务中介、交易佣金、支付服务、网上拍卖以及跨境物流服务等。

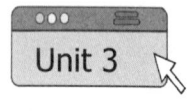

Unit 3　Classification and Brief Introduction to Third-Party Cross-Border E-Commerce Platforms 跨境电子商务平台分类与简介

1. B2B Cross-Border E-Commerce Platform　B2B 跨境电子商务平台

B2B (Business-to-Business) is carried out between cross-border businesses and enterprises. It is mainly based on general information dissemination and transaction matching, serving as the business bridge for the establishment of cross-border trade. At present, cross-border e-commerce mainstream platform mode is B-B-C rather than B2C. That is, cross-border e-commerce = cross-border commerce (B2B) + localized e-commerce (B2C, B2B), traditional enterprises are increasingly turning to conduct small orders after they switch to cross-border e-commerce. Small orders at present are with three kinds of solutions: online wholesale + overseas warehouse mode; online supply distribution mode; operation agent.

B2B platform
平台

B2B 是在跨境企业与企业之间进行的，一般以信息发布与交易撮合为主，主要是建立跨境商家之间贸易的桥梁。跨境电子商务主流平台模式不是 B2C，而是 B-B-C，即跨境电子商务=跨境贸易（B2B）+本地化电商（B2C、B2B），传统企业转向跨境电商后，越来越趋向做小订单。小订单现有三种解决方案：在线批发+海外仓模式；在线货源分销模式；代运营。

In essence, B2B cross-border e-commerce is a commerce platform for the dissemination and management of cross-border e-commerce information. With this cross-border platform, cross-border product information and cross-border company information can be rapidly released globally. Therefore, B2B cross-border e-commerce platform is ideal for small and medium enterprises to do online promotion. In addition to e-commerce platforms such as China Manufacturing Network, Alibaba, Global Sources and other cross-border commercial activities

258

conducted through third-party cross-border e-commerce website platforms, there are also e-commerce B2B platforms directly operated by enterprises such as Dunhuang Network.

B2B 跨境电子商务本质上是一个跨境电子贸易信息发布与管理的商务平台，借助这样的跨境平台可以快速将跨境商品信息和跨境公司信息发布到全球。因此，B2B 跨境电子商务平台非常适合中小企业做网上推广。除了如中国制造网、阿里巴巴、环球资源等通过第三方跨境电子商务网站平台进行跨境商业活动的电商平台外，也有企业之间直接进行商业活动的电子商务 B2B 平台，如敦煌网等。

2. B2C Cross-Border E-Commerce Platform　B2C 跨境电子商务平台

B2C (Business-to-Customer) refers to e-commerce transactions between cross-border merchants and customers. Cross-border consumers purchase cross-border goods and services frequently, and in small quantities, from cross-border vendors through the Internet. This mode, also known as online retailing, treats itself as an electronic retail because it resembles the actual sales process. This platforms offer everything ranging from flowers and books to computers and cars to consumer goods and services. For example: Dangdang, Amazon online bookstore.

B2C platform
平台

B2C（Business-to-Customer）指的是跨境商家与顾客之间的电子商务交易，跨境消费者通过网络向跨境厂商小批量、频繁地购买跨境商品或服务。这种模式又称为网上零售，因为它类似于实际中的销售过程，所以通常被看作是一种电子化的零售形式，如提供从鲜花、书籍到计算机、汽车等各种消费商品和服务。例如当当网、亚马逊网上书城。

Cross-border businesses provide cross-border consumers with a new cross-border shopping environment via the Internet cross-border online stores where consumers experience cross-border online shopping and cross-border payment. This mode saves customers and businesses a great deal of time and space, greatly improving the transaction efficiency. Major B2C cross-border e-commerce platforms are: Lightinthebox, DinoDirect, DX (DealeXtreme), Milan (Mlbuy), Focalprice, etc.

跨境企业通过互联网为跨境消费者提供了一个新型的跨境购物环境——跨境网上商店，消费者通过网络实现跨境购物、跨境支付。这种模式节省了客户和企业的时间和空间，大大提高了交易效率。目前主要的 B2C 跨境电子商务平台有兰亭集势(Lightinthebox)、大龙网(DinoDirect)、DX(DealeXtreme)、米兰网(Mlbuy)、Focalprice 等。

3. Profile of main Commerce Platforms 主要跨境电子商务平台简介

Lightinthebox was on the line in year 2007, and in its early period, it focused on the electronic products, mainly with B2B small wholesale trade. In early 2009, Lightinthebox set off on the line wedding product series, with the sales of that year hit nearly 30 million US dollars. Lightinthebox attaches great importance to the operation of social marketing tools such as SNS and BBS. It is

Main commerce platforms
主要跨境电子商务平台

based on leading online marketing technologies such as Google Marketing, Facebook, Twitter, Linkedin and other social networking communities marketing.

兰亭集势于 2007 年上线，早期主营电子产品，以 B2B 小额外贸批发为主。2009 年初，兰亭集势上线婚纱产品线，当年销售近 3 千万美元。兰亭集势非常重视 SNS、BBS 等社会化营销工具的运营，立足领先精准的网络营销技术，如谷歌营销、Facebook、Twitter、Linkedin 等社会化网络社区营销。

Established in 2006, DX (dealextreme.com)'s main business scope is the main electronic products and 3C gadgets, such as U disk, cell phone case. DX enjoys a very well-known brand image in South America. From 2008 to 2009, with soar of the small foreign trade market brought by the financial crisis, DX has witnessed a high growth. With the explosive growth of DX, it became the largest foreign trade B2C and the leader in 3C electronic products.

DX(dealextrme.com)于 2006 年成立，主营电子产品和 3C 小配件，如 U 盘、手机壳等，在南美有非常知名的品牌形象。2008 至 2009 年，金融危机带来小额外贸市场高增长，DX 借势爆发，一跃成为最大的 B2C 跨境电子商务平台，是 3C 电子产品领域的龙头老大。

Mlbuy is a first-class domestic apparel trade B2C operator and it was officially launched in2008. DinoDirect's main trading items are "colorful fast-moving consumer goods closely related to family life", including communications-related electronic technology products, small household appliances, accessories, clothing, auto parts electronics, outdoor products and handicrafts.

米兰网是国内一流的服饰外贸 B2C 运营商，于 2008 年正式上线运营。大龙网 (DinoDirect)的主要贸易对象为跟家庭生活息息相关的多姿多彩的快速消费品，具体包括通信类电子科技产品、小家电类、饰品、服装、汽车配件电子产品、户外用品、手工艺品。

In addition to C2C, eBay's B2C and B2B transactions are also qulte active. There is a wholesale zone for each category, with access to 26 countries through the global navigation at the bottom of its homepage. eBay does not provide warehousing and logistics services; it just recommended the sellers third-party cross-border logistics services. eBay began as an auction site and more as a social e-commerce website. The advantage of eBay is with PayPal, a global one-stop payment, is very attractive to small and medium-sized sellers. Therefore, eBay boasts its wider global buyer coverage.

除 C2C 外，eBay 的 B2C 和 B2B 交易也相当活跃，每一个分类都有一个批发专区，通过首页底部的全球站导航，可以进入 26 个国家发布批发信息。eBay 不提供仓储物流服务，仅为卖家推荐第三方跨境物流服务。eBay 以拍卖网站起家，更多的是一种社交型电子商务网站，eBay 的优势在于 PayPal（全球最大的在线支付平台），这种全球性的一站式支付对中小卖家具有很大的吸引力，所以 eBay 的全球买家覆盖面较广。

Started with B2C, Amazon is specialized in supply chain management and cost control, especially its global system of warehouse logistics system. Amazon is more popular in the United States market.

Amazon 以 B2C 起家，擅长供应链管理和成本控制，尤其是其全球化的系统仓储物流体系在美国市场比较受欢迎。

　　AliExpress is the global trading platform created by Alibaba group, and thus the majority of sellers calls it the "international Edition Taobao". Launched in April 2010, after rapid development in recent years, AliExpress has now covered overseas buyers in more than 220 countries and regions, the daily flow of overseas buyers has reached more than 50 million, with the highest peak reached 100 million; AliExpress has become the world's largest cross-border trading platform.

　　速卖通是阿里巴巴旗下面向全球市场打造的在线交易平台，被广大卖家称为"国际版淘宝"。速卖通于 2010 年 4 月上线，经过近几年的迅猛发展，目前已经覆盖 220 多个国家和地区的海外买家，每天海外买家的流量已经超过 5000 万，最高峰值达到 1 亿。速卖通已经成为全球最大的跨境交易平台。

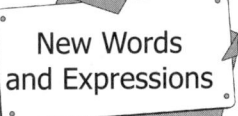
New Words and Expressions

be rendered to 被呈现　　　　　　　　　in accordance with 与……一致
include, but not limited to 包括但不限于……　rely on 依靠……
in the form of 以……形式　　　　　　　various types of 各式各样
be carried out 被执行　　　　　　　　　in essence 本质上
ranging from 从……到……　　　　　　established in 创建于……
bring by 由……导致　　　　　　　　　be officially launched 正式发布
recommend sb. sth. 向……推荐……　　global buyer coverage 全球买家覆盖面
the majority of 大部分

Chapter 10

Terminology & Oral Communication for Foreign Trade of Textiles 外贸术语与纺织外贸口语实践

- To be familiar with relevant terms of foreign trade.
  熟悉外贸相关术语。
- To do oral practice & training for foreign trade communication of textiles.
  纺织外贸口语实践训练。

Task 1

Terms of Foreign Trade 外贸术语

 Declaration 报关

报关 declaration (at the customs) /apply to the customs/declare at the customs
报关单 bill of entry/application to pass goods through customs
报关费 customs clearing fee
报关行 customs broker/customs house broker
报关经纪人 customs agent
报关港口 port of entry
报关文件 entry file

 Price Terms 价格术语

运费 freight   单价 unit price

码头费 wharf age
总值 total value
净价 net price
折扣 discount/allowance
印花税 stamp duty
现货价格 spot price
现行价格（时价）current price
卸货港 port of discharge
批发价 wholesale price
进口许可证 import licence
离岸价（船上交货价）FOB-free on board
成本加运费价（离岸加运费价）C&F-cost and freight
到岸价（成本加运费、保险费价）CIF-cost, insurance and freight
国际市场价格 world (International) market price

卸货费 landing charges
金额 amount
含佣价 price including commission
港口税 port dues
关税 customs duty
期货价格 forward price
装运港 port of shipment
目的港 port of destination
零售价 retail price
出口许可证 export licence

Unit 3 Terms of Delivery 交货条件

轮船 steamship（缩写 S.S）
租船 charter
装运期限 time of shipment
托运人（一般指出口商）shipper, consignor
班轮 regular shipping line
舱位 shipping space
报关 clearance of goods
提货 to take delivery of goods
正本提单 original B/L

装运、装船 shipment
定程租船 voyage charter
定期租船 time charter
收货人 consignee
驳船 lighter
油轮 tanker
陆运收据 cargo receipt
空运提单 airway bill
选择港（任意港）optional port

选港费由买方负担 optional charges to be borne by the Buyers
一月底装船 shipment not later than Jan. 31st./shipment on or before Jan. 31st.
在……（时间）平均分两批装船 shipment during...in two equal lots
分三个月，每月平均装运 in three equal monthly shipments
立即装运 immediate shipments
即期装运 prompt shipments
收到信用证后 30 天内装运 shipments within 30 days after receipt of L/C
不允许分批装船 partial shipment not allowed (unacceptable, permitted)

Unit 4　Claim 索赔

补偿 compensate

提出索赔 to make a (one's) claim/to register a (one's) claim/to file a (one's) claim/to raise a (one's) claim

向某方提出索赔 to make a claim with (against) sb.

Unit 5　Sale 销售

畅销的 salable

畅销 good market

有销路的 popular

试销 trial sale, test sale, test market

畅销货 salable goods

快货 popular goods

热门货 the best selling line (the best seller)

很有销路 to have a strong footing in a market/selling

畅销货 goods that sell well/sell like wild fire

滞销 poor (no) market

推销及管理费用 selling and administrative expense

销售费用 selling expense

代销人；销售代理商 sales agent

廉价出售 sell at a bargain, sell at a profit

高价出售 sell goods at a high figure

卖方市场 seller's market

买方市场 buyer's market

销售综合方法，销售策略 marketing mix

销售策略 marketing strategies

销售企业，销售公司 marketing establishment

（口语）女售货员 saleslady, salesgirl, saleswoman

男售货员（美国口语）sales clerk

销售实验 market test

倾销 dumping

偶尔，非持久性倾销 sporadic dumping

掠夺性倾销 predatory dumping

国际反倾销法 International Dumping Code
促销 sales promotion
市场分割 market segmentation

Unit 6 Commission 佣金

两笔或几笔佣金 two or several items of commission
佣金率 rate of commission or scale of commission
付佣金的交易 commission transaction
代理商；代办人 commission agent
追加佣金 overriding commission

Unit 7 Insurance 保险

保险商（指专保水险的保险商）保险承运人 underwriters
保险公司 insurance company
保险经纪人 insurance broker
保险人 insurer
被保险人，受保人 insurant, the insured
保险承保人 insurance underwriter
投保人 insurance applicant
投保 to cover (effect, arrange, take out) insurance
保险范围 insurance coverage; risks covered
保险金额 insured amount
海洋运输货物保险条款 ocean marine cargo insurance clauses
陆上运输保险 overland transportation insurance, land transit insurance
航空运输保险 insurance against air risk, air transportation insurance
邮包运输保险 parcel post insurance
水险（海运货物保险）ocean marine cargo insurance, marine insurance
一切险 All Risks
海损 average
海损 Marine Losses
单独海损 Particular Average (P.A)
共同海损 General Average (G.A)
部分损失 partial loss

265

Unit 8　Quality 品质

品质条款 quality clause
品质证明书 quality certificate
进出口商品质量 quality of export and import commodities
全销质量 good merchantable quality
与……一致 to be in conformity with
转让者 transferer
受让者 transferee

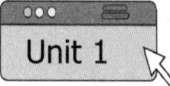

Task 2

Communication and Conversation for International Trade
外贸交流与对话

Unit 1　Foreign Trade Policy 外贸政策

Communication and conversation for international trade
外贸交流与对话

1. We stick to a consistent policy in our foreign trade.
我们的外贸政策是一贯的。

2. We have adopted a flexible policy in our foreign trade work.
我们在外贸工作中采取了一些灵活政策。

3. Our principle is to introduce advanced technology with foreign capital on the basis of self-reliance.
我们的方针是在自力更生的基础上，利用外资引进先进技术。

4. It is said that you have adopted some new practices in your foreign trade. Is that true?
听说贵国的对外贸易有一些调整，是这样吗？

5. I was told that there has been a great change in China's foreign trade policy compared with that of several years ago. Could you tell me something about it?
我听说贵国外贸政策与几年前相比已有了很大变化。您能跟我介绍一下吗？

6. These are all traditional methods used in international trade. For example, we've started accepting orders according to buyers' designs and materials, compensations trade, joint ventures, partnership, payment by installments, deferred payment, etc. But we still need time for their practice and perfection.
这都是些国际贸易中常用的习惯做法。举例说吧，我们已经采纳的有加工贸易、补偿贸易、合作生产、合资经营、分期付款、延期付款等，但这些都还有待于实践和完善。

7. We are following international practices. For instance, we'd welcome the establishment of representative offices by foreign companies, and we are also thinking of opening up offices abroad.

我们正在采取国际惯常用法，例如，欢迎外国公司建立代表处，同样我们也打算在国外设立办公室。

8. To be frank, you see, we are trying to do away with over rigid ways, and to go along with the usual international trade practices.

坦率地说，我们正设法消除过分僵硬的做法，并采纳通常的国际贸易惯例。

9. We readjust our prices according to the international market.

我们是根据世界市场的行情来调整价格的。

10. If these principles are abided by, I'm certain that mutually beneficial business will result.

如果遵守这些原则，我想互惠业务一定能实现。

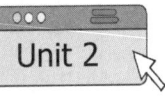

Unit 2　Establishment of Business Relation 建立贸易联系

1. They mainly trade with Japanese firms.
他们主要和日本商行进行贸易。

2. For the past five years, we have done a lot of trade with your company.
在过去的五年中，我们与贵国进行了大量的贸易。

3. Our trade is conducted on the basis of equality.
我们是在平等的基础上进行贸易。

4. There has been a slowdown in the wool trade with you.
和你们的羊毛贸易已有所减少。

5. Our foreign trade is continuously expanding.
我们的对外贸易在不断扩展。

6. They are well-known in trade circles.
他们在贸易界很有名望。

7. We trade with people in all countries on the basis of equality and mutual benefit.
我们在平等互利的基础上和各国人民进行贸易。

8. Our purpose is to explore the possibilities of developing trade with you.
我们的目的是和你们探讨一下发展贸易的可能性。

9. Is it still a direct barter trade?
这还算是一种直接的易货贸易吗？

267

10. If you agree to our proposal of a barter trade, we'll give you textiles in exchange for your timber.

如果你方同意我们进行易货贸易的建议，我们将用纺织品与你们交换木材。

Unit 3　Inquiries 询价

1. May I know what particular items you are interested in this time?

你们这次来主要想谈哪方面的生意？

2. I'm interested in your corduroy, gabardine and wool serge. I've seen the exhibits and studied your catalogues, and I think they will find a ready market in Japan.

我对你们的灯芯绒、华达呢和毛哔叽有兴趣。在看了展品和商品目录后，我觉得这些商品在日本会很有销路。

3. Could you give us an indication of price?

请你提出一个估计价格好吗？

4. Could you give us some idea about your prices?

请你介绍一下你方的价格好吗？

5. Our prices compare favorably with what you might get elsewhere.

我们的价格和你们能从别处得到的价格相比是较为优惠的。

6. OK! We'll come back to discuss it to some details tomorrow.

好吧，明天我们再具体地讨论这件事。

7. Can I have a look of your catalogue?

我能看一看你们的样本吗？

8. If your prices are favorable, I can place the order right away.

如果你们的价格优惠，我可以马上订货。

9. How long does it usually take you to make delivery?

你方通常需要多长时间交货？

10. However, it takes a longer time for special orders. But it'll never take longer than 6 months.

不过特殊订货的交货时间要长些，但绝不会超过6个月。

Unit 4　Offer 报价

1. 这是我们的最新价格单，请您看一下。

Here are our latest price sheets. Would you like to have a look?

2. 请您介绍一个你们的价格。我们要订的数量很大程度上取决于你方的价格。

Would you please let us know about your prices? The amount of our offer depends largely on your prices.

3. 价格这么高，我方很难销售。

That's a high price! It will be difficult for us to make any sales.

4. 这是我方的最低价格，不可能再让了。

This is our rock-bottom price. We can't make any further concessions.

5. 我们双方都坚持自己的价格是不明智的，能不能双方都让让步，生意就可成交。

It's unwise for either of us to stick to one's own price. How about meeting each other half way, and in that way business can be concluded.

6. 好吧，你真有办法，把我说服了。顺便告诉你，我们的报价三天内有效。

All right. You really have a way of talking me into it. That's settled. By the way, our offer remains open for 3 days.

7. 你一定会注意到我们的价格比目前市场价格低。

You'll notice our quotation is much lower than the current price.

8. 如果你方接受我方的数量，我们就接受你方的价格。

We accept your price if you take the quantity we offer.

9. 我们恐怕不可能接受你们的还盘，因为我们的价格与你方还盘之间的差距太大。

I'm afraid that it's impossible for us to accept your count offer because the difference between our price and your offer is too wide.

10. 您知道，丝绸的价格从去年以来一直上涨，所以我们的价格相对来说还是较为优惠的。

You know the price of silk has gone up since last year. Our price is relatively favorable.

11. 但您必须考虑到质量问题，同行中人人皆知中国丝绸质地优于其他国家（的供货）。

But you must take the quality into consideration. Everyone in the trade knows that China's silk is of superior quality to that from other countries.

12. 这些花色都是目前国际市场上比较流行的。这些产品也都是畅销货。你们大概要定多少？

These patterns are quite popular in the international market, and the products are also our best selling lines. Will you please give us an approximate quantity you require?

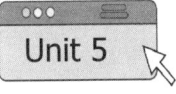

Unit 5 Disagreement on Price 价格争议

1. 看了你们的价目单后，我要说你们的价格太高了。

I can tell you that your prices are much too high after I have a glance of your sheet.

2. 如果把各种因素都加以考虑的话，你们会发现我们的价格比别处的要便宜。

If you have taken everything into consideration, you'll find our prices compare favorably with the quotations you can get elsewhere.

269

3. 如果你们订货数目大，我们可以考虑减价 2%。

If your order is large enough, we will consider reducing our prices by 2 percent.

4. 我们要订多少在很大程度上取决于价格，就让我们解决价格的问题吧。

The amount of our order depends largely on the prices. Let's settle that matter first.

5. 你能不能说一个大概的数字？

Can you give me a rough idea?

6. 我认为大约给 10%的折扣才行。

I should say a reduction of 10 percent at least.

7. 你们的价格今年又涨了。

Your prices have gone up again this year.

8. 这种精纺梳毛机尽管价格很高，但仍很畅销。

The worsted carding machine is selling well in spite of the high price.

9. 好吧，根据你们要订的数量多少，我们对价格也做点相应的调整。

Well, according to the quantity you wish to order from us, we may adjust our prices accordingly.

10. 你们必须首先考虑质量问题。

You should take quality into consideration first.

11. 如果按这个价格买进，我方实在难以推销。

It would be very difficult for us to push any sales if we buy it at such a price.

12. 我们只能降价 2%，不能再多了。

We can't do more than a 2% reduction.

13. 为了我们长期的友好关系，我们愿意以这个价格报实盘。

We are willing to make you a firm offer at this price for our long-standing good relationship.

14. 在谈判价格之前，我们希望你方报出船上交货的价格。

Before coming to the discussion of price, we would like to have you quote us on an FOB basis.

15. 尽管毛毯成本上涨，我们保证价格不变。

We'll keep our prices despite the rising cost of the blanket.

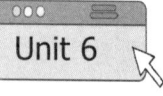

Unit 6　Order 订货

1. 我想订你们的服装。

I'd like to place an order for your garments.

2. 我们订 30 万码的涤/棉混纺织物。

We'll place an order for three hundred thousand (300,000) yards of polyester cotton blended fabric.

3. 我们想增加衬衫的订货。

We'd like to increase the order for shirts.

4. 最少得订多少？

What's the minimum quantity of an order?

5. 你们最多能提供多少？

How much can you supply at most?

6. 你知道这只是试订。

This is only a trial order, you know.

7. 抱歉，我们得取消订货。

Sorry, but we'll have to cancel our order.

8. 我希望将订货减少20万码。

I wish to cut down the order by 200,000 yards.

9. 请告诉我你们对哪些货物感兴趣。

Please tell me what you are interested in.

10. 我们只能提供那么多了。

I'm afraid we cannot supply you with any more than that.

11. 我们只能提供30万码供即期装运。

We have only 300,000 yards available for prompt shipment.

12. 真抱歉，我们目前无法满足你们的要求。

I am sorry, we cannot meet your requirement at present.

13. 我们工厂订货已满，不能再接受今年的订货了。

Our factory has been fully committed, so we cannot take any more orders for this year.

14. 如果前一半货能在两月内到达，我想订两千。

We wish to order 2,000 provided the first half will reach us within two months.

15. 谢谢订货，我们等候你方确认。

Thanks for placing an order. We will be looking forward to your confirmation.

Unit 7　Discount 折扣

1. 这种商品在你方市场很畅销，所以我们不考虑折扣。

This commodity sells very well in your market, so we won't consider any discount.

2. 折扣要按你方订货量决定。

The discount is given according to the quantity you order.

3. 如果你坚持不给折扣，我们就无法达成一致。

I don't think we can possibly reach an agreement if you insist on giving no discount.

4. 通常我们每增订一万码，增加1%的折扣。

We usually allow 1 percent discount for each extra ten thousand yards.

5. 订这么大量的货你看能打几折？

How much discount you think is possible for such a large order?

6. 我坚持至少要3%的折扣。

I insist 3 percent should be the minimum.

7. 棉布我们最多九九折。

For cotton cloth we can allow no more than 1 percent discount.

8. 你们订货加倍，否则我们就不同意九七折。

We will allow 3 percent discount only if you double your order.

9. 你不觉得九六折太多吗？

Don't you think 4 percent discount is a bit too much?

10. 我们谈妥的价格是最优惠的，所以不可能再多打折扣了。

The price we agreed on is the most favorable therefore any further discount is impossible.

Unit 8 Commission 佣金

1. 我们很关心佣金问题。

We are very much concerned about the question of commission.

2. 如果你们不给佣金，就会失去不少的顾客。

You will lose a lot of customers if you don't allow commission.

3. 我们的顾客不熟悉你方产品，推销的花费会很大。

Your product is not familiar to our customers. It will cost a lot to push sales.

4. 如果你们订货量大，我们就考虑给佣金。

We'll consider the question of commission if you place a large order.

5. 我们通常得到3%的佣金。

We usually get a commission of three percent.

6. 我们报的是最低价，所以不能给佣金。

We have quoted the lowest possible price, so we can't offer any commission.

7. 考虑到你们订货量大，我们给3%的佣金。

Considering the quantity of your order, we will allow you 3 percent commission.

8. 从欧洲出口商那里订同样数额的货，我们通常能得5%的佣金。

From European sellers we usually get 5 percent commission for the transaction of the same amount.

9. 你们提出的佣金的确太低了。

The commission you have offered is really too little.

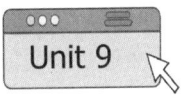

Unit 9 Signing a Contract 签订合同

1. 这个合同是从 2023 年 1 月 1 日到 12 月 31 日的一年内有效。

This contract is valid for a period of one year from Jan. 1, 2023 to Dec. 31, 2023.

2. 我们双方均应信守合同中的条款和条件。

Both of us should abide by the terms and conditions of this contract.

3. 这个合同有两份原稿，每份均用英、汉两种文字打出，两份同样有效，双方各持一份。

This Contract is made out in two originals, each in Chinese and English languages, both being equally effective, each party holds one original.

4. 我们对所有条款都没有什么意见了。何时我们能拿到合同？

We have no questions about the terms. When can we have the contract?

5. 明天下午我们就把合同准备好，并立即送您签字。

We'll have the contract ready tomorrow afternoon and immediately send it to you for your signature.

6. 请您在仔细检查一下合同的条款，看看还有什么不清楚的地方。

Please carefully check all the terms written in the contract and see if there is anything unclear.

7. 我看在这儿最好加上这样一句："如果一方未按本合同条款执行，另一方有权中止本合同"。

I think we'd better add one sentence here: "If one side fails to honor the contract, the other side has the right to cancel it."

8. 你看合同是否把我们谈判的内容基本上都写进去了？

Do you think that the contract contains basically all we have agreed on during our negotiation?

9. 我觉得合同中的付款条款也是很重要的，您觉得呢？

I think that payment terms in the contract are important too, don't you think so?

10. 关键是无论做零售还是批发，要求交货后立即付款。

The point is, whether in the retail or whole, we trade you should get immediate payment against delivery.

11. 包装、唛头、装船日期和索赔的条款你有没有意见？

Have you any questions about the packing, shipping marks, date of shipment and claims?

12. 许多合同中都有一条，就是假如供货商延误交货期，则被罚款。

In many contracts there's a clause stating that the supplier will be charged a penalty if there's a delay in delivery.

273

13. 是的，这很重要，延误越久，罚款越多；不仅如此，买主还常常有权干脆撤销合同。

Yes, that's very important. The longer the delay, the higher the penalty, and in addition, the buyer often has the option of canceling the contract altogether.

14. 我们双方对各项条款都达成了协议，那么现在就请你在这儿签字吧！

We both have reached an agreement on all the terms. Then please sign your name here.

 **Unit 10   Terms of Payment 付款方式**

1. 我们一般付款条件是保兑的、不可撤销的信用证，凭装运单据见票即付。

Our usual terms of payment are by confirmed, irrevocable L/C payable by sight draft against presentation of shipping documents.

2. 我们一定要 L/C 付款。

We insist on payment by L/C.

3. 我们出口一直是要求信用证的。

We always require a letter of credit for our exports.

4. 我们想前一半用 L/C，后一半用 D/P。

We are thinking of the first half by L/C and the second half by D/P.

5. 你必须在发货前三周开出信用证。

You must open the L/C three weeks before delivery.

6. 用人民币付货款行吗？

Can we pay for the goods in Renminbi?

7. 你们同意分期付款吗？

Do you accept payment by installments?

8. 信用证要在发运的那个月之前 15 天寄达我方。

The L/C should reach us 15 days before the month of shipment.

9. 你方是否同意 D/P 见票现付？

Could you agree to payment by D/P at sight?

10. 因为要付押金，开信用证会增加我的费用。

A letter of credit will increase my cost, since I will have to pay a deposit.

 **Unit 11   Packing 包装**

1. 由于上次有些纸箱损坏了，我希望你们能更加注意包装质量。

As several cartons were damaged last time, I would like you to be more careful about packing.

2. 你们能否改进一下包装？

Will you make some improvements in packing?

3. 我们希望包装的色彩更鲜艳一些。

We hope the packing will be of a brighter colour.

4. 荷花的图案在我们国家销不动的。

The lotus design will not sell in our country.

5. 你断定这种包装能经得起海运吗？

Are you sure that this kind of packing is strong enough for transport by sea?

6. （包装的）尺寸怎样？

What are the dimensions?

7. 外包装怎样？

How about the outer packing?

8. 它们装在纸板箱里，每箱 6 个。

They are packed in cardboard boxes of half a dozen each.

9. 每盒毛重是 0.5 公斤。

The gross weight of each box is 0.5 kilograms.

10. 由于盒子比以前厚，皮重为 1.5 公斤。

The tare is 1.5 kilograms, as the box is thicker than before.

11. 我们用塑料包装带。

We use plastic strappings.

12. 他们曾建议用铁皮包装带，不过这没有必要。

They suggested using iron straps instead, but this is not necessary.

13. 纸箱长 50 厘米，宽 40 厘米，高 30 厘米。

The cartons are 50 cm long, 40 cm wide and 30cm high.

14. 纤维含量标签得由我们订到衣服上。

The fiber content label should be sewn to the suits by ourselves.

15. 标签要放在塑料包装袋上。

We want the label to be fixed on the polythene wrapper.

Unit 12 Terms of Shipping 装运条件

1. 你们何时能装运这批货？

When can you ship the goods?

2. 我们希望这批货能立即付运。

We hope to have this batch for prompt shipment.

3. 装运文件尚未办完。

The shipping documents have not been made out.

4. 这些都是季节性货物，希望能早点装运。

We'd rather have an earlier shipment since they are all seasonal goods.

5. 你们能否提前装运。

Can you advance your shipment in any way?

6. 这些货分三批装运。

We will ship the goods in three batches.

7. 我方要求你们允许转船。

We request that you accept transshipment.

8. 我以为直运可避免纺织机器受损。

I suppose a direct shipment will prevent the textile machines from damage.

9. 我们订了9月和11月的舱位。

We have booked shipping space for September and November.

10. 买方负责租船。

The buyers will be responsible for chartering a ship.

11. 我们在上海装船。

We'll make Shanghai the port of loading.

12. 收到你方信用证后两周内装船。

The shipment will be effected within two weeks of receipt of your L/C.

13. 我想改变先前的货运安排。

I'd like to modify our previous arrangement for shipment.

14. 轮船公司已通知我们在一月底以前没有舱位了。

The shipping company has informed us that there will be no more shipping space available till the end of January.

15. 我们无法答应提前发货，因为没有船直达你们港口。

We cannot promise an earlier delivery because there is no direct sailing to you port.

Unit 13 Quality 品质

1. If the quality of your products is satisfactory, we may place regular orders.
如果你们产品的质量使我们满意，我们将不断订货。

2. If the quality of your initial shipment is found satisfactory, large repeats will follow.
如果贵方第一批运来的货令人满意，随后将有大批续订。

3. There is no marked qualitative difference between the two.
两者在质量上无显著差异。

4. We sincerely hope the quality are in conformity with the contract stipulations.
我们真诚希望质量与合同规定相符。

5. As long as the quality is good, it hardly matters if the price is a little bit higher.
只要能保证质量，售价高点都无所谓。

6. Prices are fixed according to their quality, aren't they?
价格按质量的好坏而定，对吗？

7. The transferee must see to it that the quality of the product is maintained.
接受转让一方要负责保持产品的质量。

8. Our Certificate of Quality is made valid by means of the official seal.
我们的质量证明书盖公章方为有效。

9. We'll improve the quality of our products and production efficiency.
我们将改进产品质量，提高生产率。

10. They are fully qualified to pass opinions on the quality of this merchandise.
他们完全有资格对这种产品的质量发表意见。

 Unit 14　　Commodity Inspection 商检

1. Shall we take up the question of inspection today?
今天我们讨论商品检验问题吧？

2. The inspection of commodity is no easy job.
商检工作不是那么简单。

3. As an integral part of the contract, the inspection of goods has its special importance.
作为合同里的一个组成部分，商品检验具有特殊的重要性。

4. The exporters have the right to inspect the export goods before delivery to the shipping line.
出口商在向船运公司托运前有权检验商品。

5. The inspection should be completed within a month after the arrival of the goods.
商品检验工作在到货后一个月内完成。

6. The importers have the right to re-inspect the goods after their arrival.
进口商在货到后有权复验商品。

7. It's very complicated to have the goods re-inspected and tested.
这批货测试和复验起来比较复杂。

8. What if the results from the inspection and the re-inspection do not coincide with each other?
如果检验和复验的结果有出入该怎么办呢？

Unit 15　Claim 索赔

1. 我们要求对这批质量低劣的毛织品起先索赔。

We are lodging a claim for the woolen fabrics in inferior quality.

2. 这批针织品没有达到我们要求的标准。

This shipment of hosiery is not up to the standard we request.

3. 这批丝绸女衫由于包装不善而油污了，你们负责赔偿全部损失。

The silk blouses were greased because of bad wrapping. You should be liable for the total loss.

4. 这些织布机的损坏是在运输途中造成的。

The damage of these looms was caused during transit.

5. 我敢肯定织布机损坏不是发生在途中，而是在码头搬动装船时操作不当造成的。

I'm quite sure that the damage did not occur on the way, but was caused by rough handling when the looms were being loaded on board ship at the dock.

6. 很遗憾，我们不能受理你们的索赔，因为它和我方毫无关系。

We regret that we can't entertain your claim as it has nothing to do with us.

7. 如果你们投保了这个险的话，你们可向保险公司提出索赔。

Your claim should be referred to the insurance company, if you have covered this risk in your insurance.

8. 假如你们的索赔是合理的，对你们提出的索赔，我们将全部予以解决。

If your claim is reasonable, we'll effect a full settlement of your claim.

9. 看来我们只好放弃索赔了。

It seems we'll have to waive the claim.

10. 感谢你在解决这起不幸事中进行的合作，希望我们之间的友好业务关系得到进一步发展。

We appreciate your cooperation in settling this unfortunate affair and look forward to a further extension of pleasant business relations between us.

11. 我们打开包装的时候，看到木箱是干的，但是里面的细纱机却严重生锈了。

When we unpacked the goods we found the wooden cases dry, yet the spinning frame inside were terribly rusty.

12. 很明显，细纱机在装箱以前就生锈了。

It is obvious that the spinning frame was rusty before it was packed into the wooden case.

13. 确实如此，我同意调换有毛病的纺织机器。

That's true indeed. I agree to replace the defective textile machines.

14. 你们没有严格遵照我们合同中规定的加工要求去做。

You didn't strictly observe the processing requirements as stipulated in our contract.

15. 我很高兴你们准备给予赔偿。
I'm very glad that you are prepared to meet our claim.

Unit 16　Situational Dialogue 情景对话

进口商（B）为寻求符合本身利益的保险，就保险的险别、期限以及日后万一出事应如何申请索赔等问题特别请教一家保险公司的经理（A）。

A: What kind of insurance policy would you like? I'm sure we can help you in any way you need.
你想投保哪一种险？我们肯定可以提供您所需要的任何服务。

B: We'll have a shipment from the United States. We want to find out your marine insurance.
我们有一批从美国装运的货物，我想了解一下你们的海上保险。

A: Well, since you told me the goods are very important, I think insurance against All Risks would be best.
嗯，既然您说这批货很重要，我想保一切险是最好的。

B: I know All Risks is the broadest kind of standard coverage. But I don't think there is any chance that our goods will be stolen, for example, so I think we don't need a policy that is so expensive.
我知道一切险是保险范围最广的险别。但是，比如说我想我们的货不可能被偷，所以我认为我们不需要这么贵的保险。

A: May I suggest a Free from Particular Average Policy? That will cover you if the ship sinks or burns, or gets stuck.
那平安险如何？如果船沉了、烧毁了或搁浅了，您都可以得到赔偿的。

B: That's better, but I think we need to cover more kinds of things, like damage by seawater, for example.
这个好些，不过我想我们需要多一点保险，例如水渍损害之类。

A: How about With Particular Average? It covers more risks than the FPA. It covers you against partial loss in all cases.
水渍险如何？它比平安险所负的责任范围要宽。它为您在任何情况下的部分损失保险。

B: That's a good idea. I have one more question here. How long is the period from the commencement to termination of insurance?
好主意。我还有一个问题，保险责任的期限是多久？

A: The cover shall be limited to sixty days upon discharge of the insured goods from the seagoing vessel at the final port of discharge.
被保险的货物在目的港卸离海轮后，保险责任以六十天为限。

279

B: By the way, in the event of loss or damage to my goods, what is the procedure for filing a claim?

随便问一句，如果货物丢失或受损，该如何提出索赔呢？

A: If any loss or damage occurs, you may lodge a claim with their agent at your port. The claim is to be supported by a survey report and put in within sixty days after the arrival of the consignment. In the light of the actual findings, they'll compensate you for the loss according to the provisions of the insurance policy.

如果发生任何丢失或损坏，您可在你方港口向其代理商提出索赔。索赔得由检验报告证实，并在货物抵达后六十天内提出。根据实际调查结果，他们会按保险条款对你方进行赔偿。

B: Thank you very much. You've answered so many questions about insurance for me.

谢谢您。您已回答了我许多有关保险的问题。

A: You're welcome. Come back if you have any questions, OK?

别客气。如有问题再来，好吗？

B: OK. See you.

好的，再见。

A: See you.

再见。

背景知识：关于保险

1. Insurance Coverage: 险别，即保险合同所列的承保各种不同风险的范围。如在国际贸易中，海洋货物运输保险的基本险别有平安险、水渍险、一切险等。

2. With Particular Average: 水渍险 (WPA)，海洋货物运输保险的一种主要险别。英文原意是"负单独海损责任"。投保这类险的货物在海运中因遇到自然灾害所遭受的一切损失，保险公司应予赔偿，即除平安险责任范围内应予赔偿的损失外，还对自然灾害所引起的单独海损负责赔偿。在国际保险条款中，它与平安险统称为"基本险"。

3. Free from Particular Average: 平安险 (FPA)，海洋货物运输保险的一种险别。英文原意为"单独海损不赔偿"。指船舶在航行中没有发生搁浅、触礁、沉没、焚船等意外事故的情况下，对自然灾害所造成的单独海损不予赔偿。

4. All Risks: 一切险，又称"综合险"，是海洋货物运输保险的一种主要险别。货物在海上运输途中，除自然灾害和海上意外事故外，还会遇到其他各种事故，如偷窃、钩损、短量、破碎、渗漏等。投保一切险，除平安险和水渍险的各项责任外，还负责被保险货物在运输途中因上述外来原因所造成的全部或部分损失。

Bibliography 参考文献

［1］陈林堂. 外贸英语应用文写作手册[M]. 北京：中国纺织出版社，1996.

［2］佟昀. 纺织应用英语[M]. 北京：中国纺织出版社，2004.

［3］白世贞. 报关英语[M]. 北京：中国物资出版社，2006.

［4］王正元，马静波，等. 外企工作英语口语[M]. 大连：大连理工大学出版社，2002.

［5］黄故. 纺织英语[M]. 北京：中国纺织出版社，2008.

［6］佟昀. 实用机织面料设计与创新[M]. 北京：中国纺织出版社，2018.

［7］徐凡. 跨境电子商务基础与实务（中英双语版）[M]. 北京：中国铁道出版社，2019.

［8］易露霞，尤彧聪. 跨境电子商务双语教程[M]. 北京：清华大学出版社，2019.